Strategic Human Resource Man.

The Open University Business School

The Open University Business School offers a three-tier ladder of opportunity for managers at different stages of their careers: the Professional Certificate in Management; the Professional Diploma in Management; and the Master of Business Administration.

This Reader is the prescribed MBA Course Reader for the Managing Human Resource Module (B824) at The Open University Business School. Opinions expressed in this Reader are not necessarily those of the Course Team or of The Open University. If you are interested in studying this course or related courses, please write to the Course Reservation and Sales Centre, PO Box 724, Milton Keynes MK7 6ZS, UK, or visit The Open University Business School website at http://oubs.open.ac.uk for more information.

Strategic Human Resource Management

A Reader

edited by
Christopher Mabey, Graeme Salaman and John Storey

The Open University Business School

SAGE Publications
London • Thousand Oaks • New Delhi

in association with

SAGE Publications Ltd
6 Bonhill Street
London EC2A 4PU

SAGE Publications Inc.
2455 Teller Road
Thousand Oaks, California 91320

SAGE Publications India Pvt Ltd
32, M-Block Market
Greater Kailash – I
New Delhi 110 048

British Library Cataloguing in Publication data

A catalogue record for this book is available from the British Library

ISBN 0 7619 6032 5
ISBN 0 7619 6033 3 (pbk)

Library of Congress catalog card number 98–061093

Typeset by Mayhew Typesetting, Rhayader, Powys
Printed in Great Britain by The Cromwell Press Ltd,
Trowbridge, Wiltshire

Contents

Why should they give SHRM?
see Ch 18

Acknowledgements

The editors and publishers wish to thank the following for permission to use copyright material: Blackwell Publishers for material from Frank Mueller, 'Human resources as strategic assets: an evolutionary resource-based theory', *Journal of Management Studies*, 33: 6 (1996), pp. 757–85; Paul du Gay and Graeme Salaman, 'The cult[ure] of the customer', *Journal of Management Studies*, 29: 5 (1997); and E. Ferlie and A. Pettigrew, 'Managing through networks', *British Journal of Management*, 7, special issue, (1996), pp. 581–97; Cambridge University Press for material from P. Rosenthal, S. Hill and R. Peccei, 'Checking out service: evaluation excellence, HRM and TQM in retailing', *Work, Employment and Society*, 11: 3 (1997), pp. 481–99; Eclipse Group Ltd for material from Paul Miller, 'Strategy and the ethical management of human resources', *Human Resource Management Journal*, 6: 1 (1996), pp. 5–18; Charles Noble, 'International comparisons of training policies', *Human Resource Management Journal*, 7: 1 (1997), pp. 5–18; Tim Newton and Patricia Findlay, 'Playing God? The performance of appraisal', *Human Resource Management Journal*, 6: 3 (1996), pp. 42–56; and Ken Kamoche, 'A critique and a proposed reformulation of strategic human resource management', *Human Resource Management Journal*, 4: 4 (1994), pp. 29–41; Harvard Business School Press for material from Thomas Kochan and Paul Osterman, *The Mutual Gains Enterprise*, (1994), pp. 45–66, 71–6. Copyright © 1994 by the President and Fellows of Harvard College; International Thomson Publishing Books for material from Nils Brunsson and Johan P. Olsen, *The Reforming Organization*, (1993), pp. 33–47; and David E. Guest, 'Human resource management, trade unions and industrial relations', in *HRM: A Critical Text*, ed. J. Storey, (1995), pp. 110–38; The Open University Press for material from John Storey and Keith Sisson, *Managing Human Resources and Industrial Relations*, (1993), pp. 138–48; Oxford University Press, Inc. for Ikujiro Nonaka and Hirotaka Takeuchi, *The Knowledge-creating Company: How Japanese Companies Create the Dynamics of Innovation*, (1995), pp. 8–11. Copyright © 1995 by Oxford University Press, Inc.; Routledge for material from Nicolas Bacon, Peter Ackers, John Storey and David Coates, 'It's a small world: managing human resources in small businesses', *The International Journal of Human Resource Management*, 7: 1 (1996), pp. 82–98; and Peter Miller and Nikolas Rose, 'Governing economic life', *Economy and Society*, 19: 1 (1990), pp. 71–102; Sage Publications for material from Karen Legge, 'The morality of HRM', in *Experiencing Human Resource Management*, eds. C.

Mabey, D. Skinner and T.A.R. Clark (1998); and R. Jacques, *Manufacturing the Employee*, (1996); The Regents of the University of California for material from Homa Bahrami, 'The emerging flexible organization: perspectives from Silicon Valley', *California Management Review*, 34: 4 (1992), pp. 33–48. Copyright © by The Regents of the University of California; John Wiley & Sons, Inc. for material from Paul R. Sparrow and Jean-Marie Hiltrop, 'Redefining the field of European human resource management: a battle between national mindsets and forces of business transition?', *Human Resource Management*, 36: 2 (1997), pp. 201–19. Copyright © BSA Publications, reproduced with permission from Cambridge University Press for P. Rosenthal, S. Hill and R. Peccei, 'Checking out service: evaluating excellence, HRM and TQM in retailing', *Work, Employment & Society*, 11: 3 (1997), pp. 481–503.

Every effort has been made to trace the copyright holders but if any have been inadvertently overlooked the publishers will be pleased to make the necessary arrangement at the first opportunity.

Strategic Human Resource Management: The Theory of Practice and the Practice of Theory

Christopher Mabey, Graeme Salaman and John Storey

First and Second Waves of SHRM Theory and Practice

It is now a couple of decades since the idea of Human Resource Management as a distinctive approach to people and organization management established itself as a significant presence in the USA (Beer et al., 1985). The phenomenon struck a chord also in Britain and in many other countries (Hendry and Pettigrew, 1986; Storey, 1987, 1992, 1995). While the dual usage of the term has, perhaps somewhat surprisingly, been sustained (denoting, in the weak sense, the whole field of people management and, in the stronger sense, of one rather unique approach to employment management) the controversy which it has provoked has hardly abated.

The idea of HRM in the distinctive sense of the term was, and is, based around the notion that people management can be a key source of sustained competitive advantage. This contention or belief is, in turn, based on four main precepts: first, that people can 'make the difference' because in the final analysis it is human *capability and commitment* which distinguish successful organizations from the rest, accordingly they need to be treated as assets and not costs; secondly, that, in consequence, managing the human resource is a matter of no little consequence – indeed it is a matter of truly *strategic importance*; thirdly, that managing human resources is therefore too important to be left entirely to personnel specialists – it has to be an activity which is owned by all managers; fourthly, that the key levers must be internally *integrated* with each other and externally integrated with the business strategy. In this full-blown sense the term HRM can be regarded as synonymous with strategic human resource management (SHRM). In order to emphasize this strategic connotation and to conform with the usage in the accompanying textbook (Mabey et al., 1998) we here refer to SHRM as standing for these far-reaching ideas.

These sorts of central tenets, while elaborated and analysed in some considerable detail, have rarely been subject to any major revision. There have been critiques a plenty who have suggested that there is a massive gap between rhetoric and the reality of employment practice; others have suggested that there are many internal contradictions; and the ambiguous character of the model attracted much comment – most often as a source of critique but sometimes to emphasize that the very ambiguity is part of the power of the idea (Blyton and Turnbull, 1992; Keenoy, 1990; Storey, 1995). These sorts of comments might be regarded as 'first wave' critiques. The 'second wave' is represented by the collection gathered together in this volume. Herein we can observe four distinct new strands of significant analysis and debate. Each of these four strands is allocated a separate section in this volume.

The first strand of the new agenda is alert to the significance of the social and economic context in shaping and reshaping the contours of SHRM. Attention to these wider aspects brings into focus discussions of the range of stakeholders and the question of whose interests are actually served or affected by this sort of agenda. This same terrain of discourse therefore tends to bring ethical issues and questions into play. In addition, the variations wrought by different national economic systems have become a major theme and this too is reflected in this collection. Finally, in terms of the economic and social context, there has in the second wave been more attention to the wider ideological issues which underpin some of the assumptions of SHRM, as reflected, for example, in the work of du Gay and Salaman.

The second strand of the second-wave agenda has been the massive attention paid in the late 1990s to a searching examination of the outcomes associated with SHRM. In particular, scholars have begun to scrutinize large data sets for the bottom-line business performance measures. This has been witnessed in the USA in the influential work of Huselid (1995), Becker and Huselid (1997), MacDuffie (1995) and Ulrich (1997), and echoed in the UK. For example, researchers at the Institute of Work Psychology, University of Sheffield, have reported on an extensive ten-year longitudinal study (1991–2001) involving over a hundred manu-facturing companies. This has revealed that among the many factors affecting company performance (including investment in R&D, different competitive strategies, technology and a focus on quality) the most significant variable associated with performance was the set of human resource management practices (Patterson et al., 1997). The link between SHRM and business performance was also the subject of a special series of seminars funded by the Economic and Social Research Council (ESRC) and organized by Shaun Tyson, David Guest, John Purcell and John Storey between 1996 and 1997 (Tyson et al., 1997). The papers delivered at these conferences revealed a whole series of issues com-plicating the apparently simple link between SHRM and business per-formance. A central theme turns on the identification of which, if any, set or bundle of HRM practices can be shown to link with superior business performance. Is it simply a question of paying greater regard to people management of any sort or does the precise composition and combination of practices have an effect? This strand of the second-wave SHRM debate is still very active and seems likely to remain so for some time to come.

The third strand of what we have identified as second-wave SHRM discussion is concerned with an interesting re-focusing of attention from what might be considered as mainstream human resource management practices (for example, the traditional attention to recruitment and selection, performance management and reward systems). In this strand attention is directed to attempts to restructure organizational forms and organizational relationships. Traditionally, organizational structuring was regarded as very distinctive from managing relationships. However, given the emergence of new organizational forms (some of these forms are so loose as to render the term 'structure' barely appropriate), the nature of the resultant relationships have also radically altered. For example, in the various types of network or virtual organizations, relations based on employment contracts are largely replaced by relations based on commercial or quasi-commercial contracts. Even where work takes place on the 'employer's' premises, the bases of the relationship may well be a contract-for-service rather than a conventional contract of employment. In the selection of chapters included in Part III of this volume these and other themes are explored.

The fourth and final strand of the second-wave SHRM discourse in recent years has been the massive attention paid to a host of interconnected ideas concerning knowledge and capability. At the beginning of the 1990s influential works in the USA focused attention on the strategic importance of the internal resources of the firm (rather than the traditional concern with portfolio management, market positioning and niche markets for products). The so-called resourced-based view (or theory) of the firm derived from the work of institutional economists (e.g. Barney, 1991). It melded neatly into the work of the new corporate strategy writers and consultants such as Hamel and Prahalad (1994) who stressed the critical importance of 'core competencies'. Similarly, the highly influential work of Senge (1990) on 'the learning organization' formed part of the same set of ideas. Indeed, the work of Stalk et al. (1993), extolling the idea of 'competing on capabilities' can be seen as providing a bridge between these literatures.

In the later 1990s the fundamental ideas of learning, competencies and resources have been given a further boost by the extensive attention given to the importance of 'knowledge' in organizations. Corporate memory, knowledge sharing, securing, utilizing and storing knowledge for future use have become key themes in managerial discourse. Despite the mushrooming literature on knowledge management and intellectual capital, the work by Nonaka and Takeuchi remains as one of the most significant contributions to date and we feature this in Chapter 20. This whole collection of interconnected ideas we group under the heading of 'Building

Organizational Capability' – the title we give to our fourth and final section. With the selection of chapters in this section it can be seen that in many ways the second-wave texts have picked-up and amplified some of the basic tenets of the original SHRM agenda. The idea of the crucial importance of human commitment and capability are once again highlighted, emphasized and clarified. As is the case for each of the sections in this volume, the message is however far from uniform. We have purposely selected contributions which reveal a diversity of perspectives and viewpoints and here, as in the other sections, we feature critics of the ideas (see, for example, the chapter by Kamoche) as well as the exponents (for example, Nonaka and Takeuchi).

Although we have identified what we regard as the important contours of the developing SHRM agenda, it is necessary for us to emphasize that we do not regard our selections as neutral or theory-free. There can be no 'innocent' mapping of the field and it is to the considerations underlying this point that we now turn.

The Myth of Innocence

One does not have to be very familiar with the world(s) of SHRM before coming to the realization that this is an area of activity and discussion where there are a number of fundamental distinctions and differences, and where contributions are stratified – that is occur at different levels of analysis. The differences are of definition, approach and even of objectives – some write to suggest what should be done, others describe what is being done and yet others criticize the suggestions people make. This volume inevitably reflects these differences. The stratification is essentially a difference of perspective and objective. At one level, practitioners – managers, heroic executives, management gurus, consultants and occasional academics (for example, in *Harvard Business Review*) – offer advice and prescription. They tell managers how to improve corporate capability. At another level, academics of various types and persuasions comment on these writings and on the relationship between these writings and organizational realities. This volume mainly consists of writings from this latter category. However, these processes of commentary, which are informed by the academics' disciplinary background and theoretical persuasion, do more than simply comment; they also re-create and re-constitute the field of SHRM. Academic critique of this nature highlights some contributions (for example, the so-called 'excellence' school) but ignores others. It asks certain sorts of questions and not others. It identifies certain sorts of key issues (for example, rhetoric versus reality or hard versus soft conceptions of human resource strategy) and not others. There are reasons for this.

For some, these differences are an unnecessary source of irritation, causing confusion and disagreement, and blocking progress in discussions which should lead to practical progress. Our view is different. We see these differences and disagreements not as the result of arbitrary, incidental and unnecessary differences of definition or perspective, nor as a result of a failure to agree terms, but as a systemic consequence of the way contributors to the field of SHRM carry out their analyses, conduct their research, and execute their assessments and critiques. These differences in choice of topic, in approach to the topic, in definition of SHRM itself, reflect basic theoretical predispositions among the contributors. The arena of SHRM is irrevocably and inevitably theorized, but these theories, which produce many of these differences, are rarely made explicit.

Contributors to SHRM debates, whether academics, critics, consultants or management gurus, structure and direct their contributions to the field in terms of the way they – often implicitly – theorize the issue or process in question. Frequently SHRM writers, especially consultants and gurus, will insist on the common-sense quality of their suggestions and ideas, stressing their innate practicality, their relevance to the down-to-earth values and objectives of the manager. They will claim therefore to have moved beyond theory, to be theory-free. Similarly, some (but by no means all) academic commentators may also claim – by implication – that the grounds for their assessments and analyses of SHRM ideas and practices are similarly neutral and obvious, having nothing to do with their theoretical preferences or commitments.

But the reality is different. Inevitably, the various differences in definition, approach, perspectives and objectives, are heavily influenced by the theoretical position and preferences of the authors. Understanding this enables us to understand the origins and manifestations of some of the differences apparent in the literature. For example, most of those who contribute to the practitioner literature (although this category is itself internally differentiated) identify whole-heartedly with a managerialist perspective. They do this not only in the sense that they are committed to management's values and objectives (performance, output, efficiency) as opposed to the objectives of other 'stakeholders', but also in the sense that the theory of organization they implicitly espouse is one that sees the organization itself and its working from a management point of view. For example, they tend to assume a consensus on organizational goals. This approach stresses a rational, instrumental view of organizations. It assumes that by identifying objectives, appropriate organizational forms can be identified which would be most functional and effective for these objectives. It assumes that the development of the organization must be a result of control, rationality, leadership and authority, and it further assumes that all parties within the organization, and without, will not only share this view but will also defer to the figures and processes of authority and their consequences.

This view has such dominance in recent thinking that it may seem unproblematic, as simply the ways things are. But it is not the way things are: it is the way things are commonly seen and defined, which is very different. We must not confuse the frame through which we look for the object we are looking at. There is another view to the rational-legal view which is equally valid (and lucidly articulated in the reading by Brunsson and Olsen in this volume). This view sees organizations as arenas of conflict where decisions are coloured by irrationality and politics, where organizational change programmes are driven by social and political agendas and logics which determine, for example, what will be seen as rational and appropriate principles and directions of change. While the first perspective sees organizations as rational, the alternative perspective sees them as structures of (competing) beliefs and meaning systems. Needless to say, contributions using these two perspectives will not only approach the world of SHRM differently, they will also define what is meant by such basic concepts as organization and human resource strategy itself in different ways.

If approaches to the study of SHRM are in some degree theory-driven, then this has significant implications for volumes such as this which, in varying degrees, map the field of SHRM. Now we have already noted that *our* selection does not claim to be representative or to resolve differences of approach or perspective. This volume is certainly about SHRM, but like all such collections, this volume and the chapters collected here represent a variety of theoretically informed positions which significantly structure the style of approach and selected subject-matter. In other words, if this book is seen as an attempt to 'map' the field of SHRM, then we have to recognize that this map defines and constitutes the terrain to which it refers and does not simply describe it. So what we find here is an illustration of the ways in which writings about SHRM simultaneously address human resource issues and constitute or define these issues, and of course they do this in very different ways. This is why it is so hard (in fact impossible) to obtain agreement on what SHRM really is; and this is why we find such a strange confusion and medley of different sorts of writings with different sorts of approaches and agendas.

Some illustration of this can be gained from Part I of this collection. The chapters included in this section differ in approach and focus, and in so doing they set up different key problematics and issues. We hope this adds greatly to the interest of the volume as a whole. For example, Karen Legge's approach explicitly seeks to move beyond a simplistic managerialist perspective. Her first concern is not efficiency. She does not position herself alongside managers' values, nor does she agree with or even accept management statements. Not only does she wish to widen the stakeholder basis on which strategic human resource practices could be evaluated, she also points to the role of management ideologies in influencing certain sorts of research findings on the impact of SHRM. Furthermore, she confronts the cosy complacency of much practitioner SHRM writings – as represented for example in the Ford mission statement – remarking dryly that if human resource practices are ethically informed, then employees will respond positively, but that this situation is 'highly unlikely'. Miller, too, takes an ethical standpoint, suggesting that *unless* human resource policies are ethical they can hardly be considered strategic.

Miller and Rose, and du Gay and Salaman approach SHRM in a way which is similar to Legge's in its unwillingness to accept management objectives or management values as the only conceivable or proper approach, but differ in that their concerns are more focused on drawing connections between the power and appeal of current management logics and arguments. This sort of analysis could not be more different from that of practitioners, for whereas practitioners seek to offer or to echo current theories of how to improve organizational efficiency, these authors go behind these ideas to assess not their efficiency but the grounds for their effective claims to assist efficiency. In other words, they try to draw attention to the grounds on which current SHRM ideas and knowledge make human resource programmes of change appear feasible and sensible. One major such ground, discussed by du Gay and Salaman, is the appeal and reference to the notions of enterprise and the market – ideas of course that owe their appeal to extra-organizational, socio-political projects. In terms of the earlier discussion of the role of the rational-instrumental view of organizations that underlies much HRS (human resource strategy) writing, noted earlier, these authors are exploring the qualities and processes that allow bodies of thought and forms of analysis to appear as rational.

The chapter by Sparrow and Hiltrop is also 'critical' not in the sense that it espouses a cause to foreground ethics, or a variety of stakeholders' interests, or to identify the forms of knowledge (and interests) that structure HRS thinking, but in another sense: that it applies rigorous empirical analysis in an attempt to identify and explore the possible relationships between four major sets of factors. In this it is not identified with any set of stakeholder's values and objectives; its only commitment is to rigorous empirically based analysis. The same could be said for Storey and Sisson's extract on performance-related pay. It is the fact that the introduction of PRP is being poorly managed which prompts them to search for the conditions, the motivations, the reasons as to why this should be the case; and, although they locate their analysis in the wider context of individualism-collectivism debates, their primary concern appears to be to explain an empirical gap between the claims and the cool reality of a particular facet of SHRM.

The Persistence of Preferred Treatments

Let us look at this lack of innocence in a different way by taking one common and central jewel in the SHRM crown: that of linking individual performance in some way to organizational performance. Given this fairly non-controversial, shared starting point, it is instructive to note how various theorists and commentators go about treating this issue, and the very different conclusions they draw. Newton and Findlay (Chapter 8), for example, come to the heart of this topic by examining the HR episode of performance appraisal. They are critical of previous research, which they claim to be acontextual and too focused on techniques with insufficient attention to outcomes and employee concerns. This seems to clear the way for a fresh empirical analysis to redress these shortcomings – some field-work research that will tell a fuller story. Instead, the authors consign the current discourse on appraising performance to 'neo-human relations' thinking with all its unitarist inadequacies, and enlist the help of first labour process theory and then Foucauldian analysis to show how appraisals are yet one more example of how employees are subject to managerial moni-toring, surveillance and control. They call for more research on the subjec-tive experience on those being appraised, but provide little themselves. Rather, their declared starting (and ending point) is that 'appraisal remains inextricably linked to the contested terrain of control . . .', and the device used to support their view is judicious reference to existing theories, since they provide 'a framework by which to explore the control metaphor'. This, then, represents a particular approach in SHRM writing whereby a par-ticular 'jewel' is held up for scrutiny against the searchlight of prior theory, and found wanting. Such a viewpoint even gives the writers the privilege of recasting existing data to support their underlying critique.

The linking of individual and corporate productivity is also the central concern of the chapter by Kamoche (Chapter 18). He is deeply suspicious of such attempts to 'match' and 'integrate' because they all too conveniently mask the contradiction of applying solely economic criteria to efforts to humanize work. However, unlike Newton and Findlay who find the neo-human relations school unpalatable, Kamoche appears to be arguing for its rescue from the clutches of the so-called organizational imperative, a bottom-line logic which evaluates activities and performance solely on the basis of criteria that are underpinned by market considerations. This conjures the image of HR managers standing on the touchline as innocent spectators, bystanders minding their own 'business'; suddenly they are asked to change into some 'kit' and are whisked on to the field of play among excited shouts that their contribution is now vital for the team's success. After initial bemusement at this new-found attention they begin to revel in their senior team status and before long are constructing credible cases as to why their contribution is indeed invaluable. Unfortunately, most fail to notice, or choose to ignore, that the rules and objectives of the game they have joined conflict fundamentally with those they have trained for. They are playing on the wrong pitch. Part of Kamoche's rescue package is to turn to researchers of the resource-based view for help. Their notion of the firm as a collection of rare and difficult-to-emulate resources and capabilities, provides a way for SHRM to make a strategic contribution by building on rather than selling out on its humanizing principles.

Mueller (Chapter 10) is equally optimistic that this can be achieved and elaborates on a number of conditions under which human resources can be grown as strategic assets, again borrowing heavily from the insights of strategic management writers. The recognition that strategic assets evolve incrementally over time (and therefore the need to resist expectations of a quick fix through SHRM), the sustained cultivation of certain attitudes and the nurturing of tacit knowledge, the valuing of problem-centred, informal and incidental learning in the workplace, together with a willingness to challenge corporate habits of non-learning are among the conditions he explores. However, by specifying 'how these assets in interdependence with other assets sustain the company's resource position and competitive performance', it would seem that the organizational imperative is, once again, becoming the dominant logic.

For others in this volume this is precisely the case. Indeed, their explicit purpose is to demonstrate that SHRM has finally come of age by assembling an armoury of economic evidence which is designed to confound all but the most hardened sceptics. Nonaka and Takeuchi, for example, single out knowledge-creation as the key to commercial success, and parade the contrasting fortunes of Western and Japanese companies to make their point. The recipe is breathtakingly simple: 'It is a highly individual process of personal and organizational self-renewal. The personal commitment of the employees and their identity with the company and its mission become indispensable. . . . The essence of innovation is to recreate the world according to a particular ideal or vision.' No conflict of interests here. And middle managers, far from being disenfranchised and/or disempowered laggards in the change process, are cast by these authors as 'knowledge engineers', playing a crucial, facilitative role in the creation and dissemination of knowledge in their organizations. For his part, Huselid (Chapter 7) employs all the apparatus of quantitative research to make his point: hypothetically driven data-gathering and regression analysis, leading to some impressive statistical connections between investment in strategic HR practices and corporate financial performance, as well as other 'hard' measures as labour turnover and productivity. Leaving aside the veracity and generalizability of these conclusions, the notable feature of this study is that it represents a concerted and growing literature that seeks to substantiate the strategic credentials of SHRM. The language alone of this stream of writing is indicative of its intent: phrases like 'balanced scorecard', 'strategic fit', 'leveraging resources' litter their papers, and titles like 'Reorienting human resource measurement to drive business performance' and 'Measuring human resources: an overview of practice and prescription for results' leave us in no doubt as to the underlying motivation of this literature. All this could indicate a growing ebullience concerning strategic approaches to the management of human resources. Alternatively, as with earnest attempts to monitor, measure and demonstrate impact in other arenas, it could also be construed as a major crisis of confidence.

Obviously, a collection of writings as disparate and varied as that contained in this volume will represent a variety of theoretical positions, but nevertheless it is possible to see some general patterns in this collection –

and probably in all HRS writings. First, there are a number of contributions – Legge, Miller, du Gay and Salaman, Miller and Rose, Brunsson and Olsen, Jacques, Guest – who adopt various forms of humanist critical perspective. This consists of a refusal to accept the pervasive commitment to managerial values and objectives, and a commitment to analysing the nature, origins and implications (particularly power) of management (and HRS) knowledge. This echoes Berger and Luckmann's insistence that 'sociological enquiry must concern itself with everything that passes for "knowledge" in society' (Berger and Luckmann, 1967: 26).

It also involves an interest in the implications of this knowledge – and associated practices – for the well-being and experiences of all members of the organization. Such a concern falls within a proud tradition within the social sciences: that is, a concern not to accept prevailing practices or values but to confront and challenge them. This is a tradition that has been well articulated by Wright Mills as the 'sociological imagination' which

> enables its possessor to understand the larger historical scene in terms of its meaning for the inner life and the external career of a variety of individuals. . . . The sociological imagination enables us to grasp history and biography and the relations between the two. That is its task and its promise. (Wright Mills, 1959: 5–6)

Another central social science tradition that is represented here could be called sceptical empiricism – the refusal to accept received wisdom, but instead to assess the value and implications of pervasive practices and beliefs. This is evident in the writings of Sparrow and Hiltrop, and Storey and Sisson.

Even this brief reflection on the way different authors approach a common and central theme of SHRM reveals some stunningly different points of departure and destination. To be fair, most, if not all, declare their colours at the outset. Having done this, each appears content to work within their chosen paradigm and to engage the sympathy of their chosen audience, with little attempt to proselytize. Much of this follows from the predisposition of their disciplines, and, more particularly, their customary ways of handling data. Some assemble qualitative data (sweeping international comparisons as in Noble, and Nonaka and Takeuchi), some quantitative (precise statistical analyses, as in Huselid), some using primary sources (Bacon et al.; Ferlie and Pettigrew), most secondary (for instance, Legge, Storey and Sisson, and Guest), sometimes taking these sources at face value, but sometimes reinterpreting them (for instance, Newton and Findlay, du Gay and Salaman). Nothing surprising here perhaps. It might, in consequence, be concluded that the field of SHRM is unhelpfully confused and chaotic. But one is left wondering about the ever more fragmentary nature of a field of study where writers appear unable to communicate with and influence each other, to say nothing of those practitioners busy crafting HR in twenty-first century organizations.

It has been noted that this area is a complex mixture of descriptive and prescriptive readings with influential prescriptive texts basing their advice on insubstantial research grounds but having considerable influence because of the virtuosity of the presentation or the appeal of its latent values or its promises. As well as description (the heroic accounts of transformative executives, the over-hyped case studies) and prescription there is also the popular genre of academic critique – those writers who point out the empirical, conceptual, theoretical, even ethical limitations of the practitioner literature. And we have seen that these critiques are often informed by the theoretical affinities of the critics as much as by the qualities of the objects under critical analysis. And furthermore, we are aware that the SHRM literature is further bedevilled by a series of basic distinctions or fractures: open and closed models, hard and soft approaches, market-based and resource-based approaches, rhetoric versus realities, and so on. It would be easy to see this situation as a problem – as an untidiness that required clarification, mapping, tidying up.

It would be easy to see these overlaps and differences as a result of a failure of the SHRM debate as a whole to reach or enforce agreement on terminology or objectives, definitions or research strategies. But this is not how we in this volume see it. For us, these differences in definition and approach, these problems of conceptualization or critique, are normal and healthy in two major ways, both of which are celebrated in this volume.

First, they are a witness to the vitality and variety of debates about what is and what should be happening in the development of the modern corporation. Although in many areas of life standardization and uniformity are becoming the norm as large corporations enforce a dominant technology or a standardized shape or product, in the area of SHRM a wonderful and stimulating variety thrives. There is no one agenda and the sheer cussedness of everyone involved in thinking and writing about SHRM will probably ensure that discussions of what is or should be SHRM structures and systems are not hijacked by single sets of interests or by particular points of view. This variety is certainly messy but it is also stimulating and creative. And this volume is dedicated to these qualities.

Secondly, the complexity and variety of the SHRM debates ensures that no one single voice or stakeholder has become dominant. Obviously the managerialist perspective is powerful in this area, but it is not dominant and it is not alone. Again we value this. Just as we do not subscribe to the unitarist perspective within organizations, so we do not support an unitarist perspective on organizations. And much of the variety of perspective in writings on SHRM derives ultimately from differences in theoretical perspective or in stakeholder perspective, which we welcome and which, again, this volume is intended to reflect.

Finally, the complexity and confusions of SHRM could be seen as unhelpful to the achievement of progress in thinking about new organizational forms – as a barrier. Again we reject this. We hope that this volume will demonstrate a very different possibility: that diversity and difference in

SHRM writings encourages a wealth of perspectives and analyses which ensures that a whole range of highly important and relevant matters are energetically pursued and researched from a wide variety of competing perspectives, and it is precisely this variety and competition that will ensure that thinking about the modern organization, like the modern organization itself, does not fall into the rather glib and uncritical thinking that passes for analysis in some of the more accessible SHRM writings. The value of SHRM debates and the scope and richness of work in this area is well demonstrated by the chapters in this volume.

References

Barney, B. (1991) 'Firm resources and sustained competitive advantage', *Journal of Management*, 17 (1): 99–120.

Becker, B.E. and Huselid, M. (1997) 'HR as a source of shareholder value: research and recommendations', *Human Resource Management*, 31 (1): 1–27.

Beer, M., Spector, B., Lawrence, P., Mills, D. and Walton, R. (1985) *Human Resources Management: A General Manager's Perspective*. New York: The Free Press.

Berger, P. and Luckmann, T. (1967) *The Social Construction of Reality*. London: Allen Lane.

Blyton, P. and Turnbull, P. (ed.) (1992) *Reassessing Human Resource Management*. London: Sage.

Hamel, G. and Prahalad, C.K. (1994) *Competing for the Future*. Boston, MA: Harvard Business School Press.

Hendry, C. and Pettigrew, A. (1986) 'The practice of strategic human resource management', *Personnel Review*, 15 (3): 3–8.

Huselid, M. (1995) 'The impact of human resource management practices on turnover, productivity and corporate financial performance', *Academy of Management Journal*, 38 (3): 635–72.

Keenoy, T. (1990) 'HRM: a wolf in sheep's clothing', *Personnel Review*, 19 (2): 3–9.

Mabey, C., Salaman, G. and Storey, J. (1998) *Human Resource Management: a Strategic Introduction*. Oxford: Blackwell.

MacDuffie, J.P. (1995) 'Human resource bundles and manufacturing performance: organizational logic and flexible production systems in the world auto industry', *Industrial and Labor Relations Review*, 48 (2): 197–221.

Patterson, M.G., West, M.A., Lawthom, R. and Nickell, S. (1997) *Impact of People Management Practices on Business Performance*. London: Institute of Personnel and Development.

Senge, P. (1990) *The Fifth Discipline: The Art and Practice of the Learning Organization*. London: Century Business.

Stalk, G., Evans, P. and Shulman, L.E. (1993) 'Competing on capabilities: the new rules of corporate strategy', in R. Howard (ed.), *The Learning Imperative: Managing People for Continuous Innovation*. Cambridge, MA: Harvard University Press.

Storey, J. (1987) 'Developments in the management of human resources: an interim report'. *Warwick Papers in Industrial Relations* (No. 17). Coventry: University of Warwick.

Storey, J. (1992) *Developments in the Management of Human Resources*. Oxford: Blackwell.

Storey, J. (ed.) (1995) *Human Resource Management: A Critical Text*. London: Thompson International.

Tyson, S., Guest, D., Purcell, J. and Storey, J. (1997) Report to ESRC on *The Link Between HRM and Business Performance*. Cranfield: Cranfield School of Management.

Ulrich, D. (1997) 'Measuring human resources: an overview of practice and a prescription for results', *Human Resource Management*, 36 (3): 303–20.

Wright Mills, C. (1959) *The Sociological Imagination*. Oxford: Oxford University Press.

Part I

HUMAN RESOURCE MANAGEMENT IN ECONOMIC AND SOCIAL CONTEXT

This section consists of contributions which in different but significant ways seek to raise some key questions about SHRM. Some address issues of ethics and human resource management (a curiously underdeveloped area of analysis); others look at what passes for management and SHRM theory or knowledge, or address the implications for (and fairness of) employees' experience of human resource strategies. Finally, two look at variations in patterns of SHRM across different country contexts: Noble contrasts national training systems, while Sparrow and Hiltrop compare how different European countries have developed strategic HR approaches.

In one sense this is a diverse mixture of contributions; in another sense, a cross-section of some of the best representatives of current critical analyses of SHRM. What does it mean to be critical in this sense? It certainly does not mean simply to be anti-SHRM. None of these contributions assume a basically negative position. And some of them – for example Legge – explicitly spell out what in their view would be necessary to ensure the success of SHRM. Legge notes that this may require organizations to demonstrate genuine commitment to practices and principles which may run counter to current management priorities. But all these contributions ask questions which may reveal that there is more to SHRM than is usually admitted or even recognized by its advocates and practitioners.

There are various grounds on which these chapters critique or question SHRM. Karen Legge, as noted, explores the stratification of SHRM – the ways in which many accounts of SHRM draw upon management views rather than those of employees in general, and probably overestimate not only the incidence of strategic approaches to the management of people, but also their effects or performance. But her concerns go wider than this: she is not interested simply in whether or not SHRM 'works'. She is interested in the far bigger and less frequently considered question: what do we mean by 'works'? To answer this in her view one must have recourse to some ethical criteria, and must relate these to the reality of SHRM theory and practice. This leads her to some significant conclusions, as you will see, for she does not entirely reject the possibility of a positive relationship between an effective human resource strategy and an ethical human resource strategy. But the achievement of this in practice is of course another matter.

An interest in ethics is essential to any concern for SHRM matters. Even the most hard-nosed manager, who would reject any consideration of ethical questions when considering SHRM options, is actually in the grip of a set of ethical beliefs and commitments, usually implicit. Often this means a commitment to the 'market' or to shareholder value as moral and undeniable forces. Often, as Paul Miller points out, these forces mean causing harm to some people in order to avoid harm, or bring advantage, to others. Miller's chapter is useful not only because it assists us to think a little more clearly about these matters, but also because he explores the ways in which an ethical approach to the management of human resources is possible. Interestingly, then, both Miller and Legge, who could be seen to adopt an unusual and non-practical approach to SHRM, actually conclude that it is possible and ultimately effective to pursue an ethical human resource strategy (indeed, for Miller, this is a defining feature of SHRM). But it is also unusual and at odds with much current management thinking.

Management thinking – comprising knowledge, theories, formula and the like – is addressed by Peter Miller and Nick Rose, and Paul du Gay and Graeme Salaman. These two chapters explore the nature, origins, appeal and implications of currently pervasive systems of management (human resource) thinking. Miller and Rose draw attention to the ways in which systems of knowing about organizations and employees, and how they interact and how organizations and employees 'work', are ultimately mechanisms that link ideas to broadly 'political' objectives. By 'political' they mean issues connected with the location and play of power and with the interests and priorities of the powerful within organizations. One particularly telling example of this is their discussion of the ways in which expert knowledge (for example of HR practitioners and consultants) is used to encourage employees to regulate themselves in terms of the frameworks and objectives of the dominant coalitions in organizations. One thinks of appraisal, 360-degree feedback, management competences, career counselling, and the like.

The piece by du Gay and Salaman explores a very similar theme but their focus is less on the internal world of the organization and the employee and more on the relationship between the ideas which underpin management and SHRM knowledge (for example, the current emphasis on the market as a principle not only of ethical resolution but also of organizational restructuring) and external socio-political forces. They examine the notion of enterprise and the widely prevalent idea that internal organizational structures and relationships should be organized in terms of market forces and relationships. It is precisely this connection between an organization's HR priorities and the broader institutional and cultural environment in which it operates that is the subject of Charles Noble's chapter. In his discussion of the relative merits and demerits of the national training systems in Australia, Britain, France and Germany, he warns against the folly of indiscriminately transplanting one country's training institutions and policies to another. Three themes consistently feature in his cross-country review as important, yet unquestioned: first, training activity is linked to and justified by market forces; secondly, the success of training effort is judged solely in terms of organizational and national productivity; thirdly, those involved in defining the content and provision of training vary from country to country (government agencies, chambers of commerce, trade unions, TECs) but rarely include trainees themselves.

A key point of the chapters in this section is that they seek to demystify management and SHRM ideas and principles which are all too often taken at face value. Certainly, Paul Sparrow and Jean Hiltrop do not take anything at face value. Their focus is also the diversity of national human resource practices across Europe – itself a finding of some interest to those who have unwittingly adopted an ethnocentric perspective. If the strategic management of human resources can be undertaken differently, who is to say which approach is correct? By offering a comparative analysis Sparrow and Hiltrop in effect raise doubts about the nature and value of any particular set of SHRM ideas. But they go further, and this is one of the strengths of their piece. Like other contributors to this section, they are concerned with the origins and implications of SHRM ideas. They note how these can vary with national factors, they raise questions about the validity of any particular set of ideas and, like other contributors, they seek to understand the appeal of these ideas. They, too, demystify and contextualize SHRM theories and knowledge.

1   The Morality of HRM

Karen Legge

When reading accounts of HRM practice in the UK and North America, it is noticeable the extent to which the data are (literally) the voices of management. To take a few examples. John Storey's classic research study of mainstream UK organizations involved interviews with 'a vertical slice of mainly line managers . . . drawn from corporate level, through MDs of various businesses, works managers and so on down through the operational structure to first line management' (1992: 19). Similarly, the Warwick Company Level survey 2 (Marginson et al., 1993: 2–3) involved a questionnaire administered via interviews with a senior executive responsible for personnel and industrial relations matters, and one responsible for finance at 812 UK corporate offices. Again, Wood (1995, 1996) and Wood and Albanese's (1995) recent research on high commitment management in manufacturing plants chose as respondents 'a senior member of the personnel department or, where one did not exist . . . the senior person in the plant responsible for personnel who was normally a production manager', even though the avowed intention was to gain 'information on production workers, respondents being told that we were interested in direct or indirect, skilled or unskilled, workers, "groups, which in the past, have been called hourly paid or manual workers"' (Wood and Albanese, 1995: 58). Guest and Peccei's postal questionnaires to NHS provider trusts were sent to 'the most senior personnel specialist and the deputy general manager/deputy chief executive in each unit' (1994: 225). Not surprisingly, given the positivistic, quantitative research preferences of most North American academics, postal questionnaires to senior management are generally the order of the day. Huselid (1995), for example, directed his postal questionnaires at the senior HR professional in each firm. Even WIRS 3 (Millward et al., 1992: 3) which *did* administer its questionnaires via interview to worker representatives as well as management (again 'the senior person at the establishment dealing with industrial relations and personnel matters and a financial manager') has a preponderance of management responses (2,550 as opposed to 1,466 from worker representatives).

Originally published in Christopher Mabey (ed.) (1997) *Experiencing Human Resource Management*. London: Sage (abridged).

[. . .]

While the management accounts of HRM initiatives range from the messianic to the equivocal, not to say, sceptical, the shopfloor accounts are generally even more guarded. This is not to say that the voice of non-managerial employees has been entirely muted. Case study research from the avowedly Marxist to the pluralist in orientation has surfaced the shopfloor experience, though the usual problems of generalisation remain (e.g., Garrahan and Stewart, 1992; Sewell and Wilkinson, 1992a, 1992b; Geary, 1992). At best they appear to reflect disappointed expectations (e.g., Wilkinson et al., 1992) and, at worst, a realisation of labour intensification (e.g., Garrahan and Stewart, 1992).

[. . .]

John Storey (1992) and Ken Starkey and Alan McKinlay (1993) have written of the changes at Ford, notably the employee involvement programme. The change package, entitled 'Mission Values and Guiding Principles' contains such statements as:

- *Customers are the focus of everything we do* – Our work must be done with our customers in mind, providing better products and services than our competition.
- *Employee involvement is our way of life* – We are a team. We must treat each other with trust and respect.
- *Integrity is never compromised* – The conduct of our Company world wide must be pursued in a manner that is socially responsible and commands respect for its integrity and for its positive contribution to society. Our doors are open to men and women alike without discrimination and without regard to ethnic origin or personal beliefs. (cited in Storey, 1992: 57)

All this is good 'soft' model HRM stuff. Hence, how do we account for the embarrassing incident in February 1996, when Ford admitted to an 'error' involving their advertising agency whereby five black/Asian workers appeared in promotional material as white people. Following an unofficial three-hour stoppage (reportedly costing £2.8 million), Ford apologised and paid the four remaining employees (one had left since the original 1991 promotional material had been drawn up) £1,500 each.

There are various ways of looking at this incident. At first sight this is reassuringly familiar. Ford has not changed, standardisation still rules, but its 'any colour as long as they're not black' (*The Times*, 19 February 1996). At second sight it clearly contravenes 'new' Ford's aspirations to treat employees with respect and violates assertions of mutual trust. It completely contradicts Ford's proclamation of treating people 'without regard to ethnic origin'. Further, it is clear that the employees involved found this a hurtful and humiliating experience. As one of them said: 'They wanted me in the picture when they wanted to show the mix of ethnic groups in Ford's workplace, but suddenly I wasn't good enough' (*The Guardian*, 19 February 1996). The employee, Douglas Sinclair, with Ford for 30 years, did not appreciate being transformed from being black, bearded and with perfect eyesight into a clean-shaven white man with glasses, nor being called 'two face' by 'humorous' workmates. Patricia Marquis, aged 30, was not keen on suddenly ageing 20 years and turning white: 'I felt humiliated and angry. I wanted an explanation.'

And, of course, there is an explanation. The advertising agency had altered the photograph for use in marketing promotions in Poland, where it was believed black faces would not be as acceptable as white ones. Hence, while the action taken by the advertising agency condones a market's perceived racial prejudice (and hence contradicts 'integrity is never compromised'), paradoxically it supports 'customers are the focus of everything we do'. Again, the familiar contradiction between HRM's 'external' and 'internal' fit surfaces again. Nevertheless, it could be argued that Ford's efforts in retrieving the situation (public apology, compensation payments, public assertion of equal opportunities policy) are either a reassertion of 'soft' model HRM's mutuality principles or it is a pragmatic attempt to avert an all-out strike – or that there are elements of both positions.

[. . .]

Evaluating the Experience of HRM

The perspective I wish to bring to the experience of HRM is one derived from business ethics. In very general terms I would suggest that the experience of HRM is more likely (but not necessarily) to be viewed positively if its underlying principles are ethical. This sounds like a statement of the obvious. It is less obvious if we consider that, depending on the ethical position adopted, a given set of HRM policies and practices may be viewed in very different lights.

Business ethics is about reflection on the nature and place of morality in business (for some general discussions of business ethics, see Beauchamp and Bowie, 1988; Donaldson, 1989; Donaldson and Werhane, 1993; de George, 1990). As this seems to limit the focus to profit-seeking organisations, I prefer to think in terms of organisational ethics. Key concepts when we think in terms of organisational ethics might include right, obligation, justice, fairness, good, virtue, responsibility, trust, and so on. Such concepts are implicit in any evaluation of our socio-economic order. Just as capitalism highlights such 'goods' as freedom, autonomy, efficiency and sees 'justice' in terms of equality of opportunity, so the Marxist critique would point to the injustice of exploitation, alienation and the protection of the interests of the few at the expense of social justice for the many. Capitalism rests on the premise that a transaction is fair if both parties engage without coercion and with adequate and appropriate knowledge of relevant aspects of the transaction. Marxism would question this assumed lack of coercion and equality of knowledge in a social system of structural inequalities. All organisation rests on an assumption of some level of trust, but we sometimes forget the extent to which our assumptions about the management of employment relationships have ethical foundations. The concepts that I have mentioned are embedded in three normative ethical theories in terms of which we can evaluate HRM policies and practices. These are deontological, utilitarian and stakeholder theories. So, first, let us briefly outline their respective basic tenets.

Deontological theories maintain that the concept of duty is, in some respects, independent of the concept of good and that some actions are right or wrong for reasons other than their consequences. Kantian ethics fall into this category. Kant argues that what makes an action right or wrong is not the sum of its consequences but the fact that it conforms to moral law. Moral laws of duty demand that people act not only in accordance with duty but for the sake of duty. It is not good enough to perform a morally correct action, because this could stem from self-interested motives that have nothing to do with morality. Rather, an action is moral if it conforms to moral law that is based not in intuition, conscience or utility, but in pure reason. We can determine moral law by analysing the nature of reason itself and what it means to be a rational being. Reason has three major characteristics: consistency (hence moral actions must not contradict one another); universality (because reason is the same for all, what is rational for me is rational for everyone else); and a priori derivation (it is not based on experience – hence the morality of an action does not depend on its consequences). A person acts morally if the sole motive for an action is the recognition of moral duty based on a valid rule.

In sharp contrast to a deontological position is *utilitarianism*. Utilitarianism claims that the morality of actions is to be judged by their consequences. An action is moral if, when compared to any alternative action, it produces the greatest amount of good (or the least possible balance of bad consequences) for the greatest number of people directly or indirectly affected by that action. The 'good' may be variously conceptualised as 'pleasure', 'happiness' or 'intrinsic value'. The maximisation of the good calls for efficiency. It also allows that people might be treated as a means to an end, if the end is the maximisation of the good (or minimisation of the bad) for the greatest number.

Finally, we have the *stakeholder* theories of justice. These have a rather different emphasis than the deontological and utilitarian theories, in that the emphasis is less on the 'good' than on the 'right' (i.e., the just distribution of the 'good'). Popular versions of stakeholder theory (e.g., Evan and Freeman, 1988) assert that organisations have stakeholders, that is, groups and individuals who potentially benefit from, or are harmed by, an organisation's actions. Stakeholders of an organisation might comprise, for example, not just shareholders (owners), but management, other employees, customers, suppliers and the local community. The stakes of each group are reciprocal, since each can affect the others in terms of harms and benefits as well as rights and duties. This principle of reciprocity leads to two further principles:

- The organisation should be managed for the benefit of its stakeholders: its customers, suppliers, owners, employees and local communities. The rights of these groups must be ensured and, further, the groups must participate, in some sense, in decisions that substantially affect their welfare.
- Management bears a fiduciary relationship to stakeholders and to the organisation as an abstract entity. It must act in the interests of the stakeholders as their agent, and it must act in the interests of the organisation to ensure the survival of the firm, safeguarding the long-term stakes of each group.

'Participating in decisions that substantially affect their welfare' has resonances of Rawls's egalitarian theory of justice. Rawls (1971) argues that we should look for a conception of justice that nullifies the accidents of natural endowment and the contingencies of social circumstances as counters in the quest for political and economic advantage. His approach is, in a sense, Kantian in that he attempts to derive principles of distributive justice that should be acceptable to all rational people and, hence, universal. In order to find such principles, Rawls suggests we perform a thought experiment. Suppose all people are behind a 'veil of ignorance', where we know we are rational beings and that we value our own good, but we do not know if we are male or female, rich or poor, talented or untalented, able bodied or suffering disability, white or black, and so on. What principles would we call just or fair if we did not know what place we would have in society (read 'organisation'). In such circumstances, Rawls argues, people would agree two principles of justice. First, each person is to have an equal right to the most extensive basic liberty compatible with similar liberty for others. Secondly, social and economic inequalities are to be arranged so that they are both (a) reasonably expected to be to everyone's advantage and (b) attached to positions and offices open to all. Now obviously there are some difficulties with all these theories. It is often said that deontologists covertly appeal to utilitarian consequences in order to demonstrate the rightness of actions, particularly when there is a clash of moral rules. Utilitarianism has to cope with the problem of lack of knowledge of all consequences, of weighing together different kinds of good and evil and of the issue of unjust consequences. Stakeholder analysis has the problem of short- versus long-term justice and the dangers of pseudo-participation. Rawls's second principle can be attacked as being too strong (as long as equal opportunities exist, why should rewards have to take account of producing benefit for the least advantaged groups in society?) or too weak (in that it would allow the very, very rich to get very much richer as long as the very, very poor got only a little less poor). But, leaving these on one side, I want to take the central tenets of each theory and evaluate HRM policies and practices in their light. For the purposes of this chapter, I see the central tenets, very much simplified, as follows:

- *Deontology*: treat people with respect and as ends in their own right, not solely as means to other's ends. Any moral rule (such as 'A fair day's work for a fair day's pay') must be capable of being consistently universalised, must respect the dignity of persons, and must be acceptable to rational beings. Any action performed out of self-interest is not moral.
- *Utilitarianism*: the greatest good to the greatest number allows people to be treated as means to ends, if it is to the advantage of the majority. Actions should be judged in terms of their consequences.
- *Stakeholder/Rawlsian Theory*: the good must be distributed with mutual consultation and so that no organisational stakeholders are complete losers while others are clear winners. Management must place a priority on the long-term interests of stakeholders and the survival of the organisation.

The Ethics of HRM Policy and Practice

How ethical is HRM? This very much depends on the theory of ethics you adopt.

The deontological position at first sight resonates with the values embedded in 'soft' model HRM. For a start, it is consistent with HRM's emphasis on individualism and responsible autonomy. Take Walton's (1985) classic statement of mutuality in HRM: 'The new HRM model is composed of policies that promote mutuality – mutual goals, mutual influence, mutual respect, mutual rewards, mutual responsibility.' This also asserts respect for human beings and is consistent with the idea of responsible autonomy for rational beings. In theory, I guess, it could be universalised. However, there is a potential problem. Walton (1985) goes on to say: 'The theory is that policies of mutuality with elicit commitment, which in turn will yield both better economic performance and greater human development.' Even in this most 'utopian' model (Purcell, 1996: 130), treating people with respect is justified in terms of 'better economic performance' and hence, in part, people are being used as means to an end, contradicting a basic principle of Kantian ethics. However, it might be argued that all is not lost. According to some commentators (Beauchamp and Bowie, 1988: 38), Kant does not prohibit the use of persons categorically and without qualification. He argues only that we must not treat another person exclusively as a means to our own ends. What must be avoided is to disregard someone's personhood by exploiting or otherwise using him or her without regard to his or her own interests, needs and conscientious concerns. If 'soft' model HRM genuinely promotes 'greater human development' for *all* employees, it could be argued that, if so implemented, it would pass muster in terms of the deontologists.

The problem is, how often does this occur? If we follow the core/periphery ideas about organisational design and the employment contract, for example, can we be sure that employees on non-standard contracts are being treated with equal regard as those in the core? Possibly, when terms and conditions are equalised pro-rata and the non-standard contract is freely chosen.[1] However, much anecdotal evidence would suggest this is not the case. On the day I was writing this paragraph, there was a report in *The Independent* (5 March 1996: 6), 'School-leavers' pay down 20%'. Reporting a study by the Low Pay Unit on data from the careers service and Job Centres in Greater Manchester, it was claimed that nearly half the 16-years-olds who leave school are paid less than £1.50 per hour and that their average wage has dropped in real terms by one-fifth in five years. However, the anecdote that caught my eye was the story of a 16-year-old who was paid £30 for a 40-hour week in a garage. When he inquired about compensation for losing the top of a finger at work, apparently he was told that he was a 'subcontractor'. Obviously, this is an example of what Guest (1995: 125) calls a 'black hole' firm, rather than an adherent to 'soft' model HRM, but note the HRM-type language of the flexible firm. The author of the report, Gabrielle Cox, is reported as saying: 'It is bad enough for adult workers to face exploitation, but a society which allows its young people to be treated in this way must question its sense of values' (*The Independent*, 5 March 1996: 6).

But, another difficulty remains. For an action to be moral it must be consistently universalised. But what happens if there is a clash between the actions that two second-order moral rules command? What if 'I must respect the interests of my employees' clashes with 'I must respect the interests of my shareholders'. Either we must allow for an exception to resolve the conflicting interests, or we must decide which course of action takes priority in terms of prima-facie obligations. The problem with the latter, as hinted earlier, is that in prioritising prima-facie obligations, we tend to resort to evaluating consequences (if in terms of respect for people) and hence are incorporating utilitarian reasoning.

The deontologist's notion that for a rule (and consequent action) to be moral it must be capable of being consistently universalised, may be acceptable if a 'best practice' (Purcell, 1996) model of HRM is adopted.[2] However, if integration with business strategy points to a contingent rather than absolutist approach (Legge, 1989; Purcell, 1996), the universalisation of any moral rule (e.g., respect for the employee, from which might derive injunctions about employee development and training, job security, fair rewards and so on) becomes suspect both in theory and practice. The contradictions embedded in HRM are illustrative of the Kantian dilemma that second-order moral rules can clash and that resolution can often only be achieved by a back-door admission of utilitarianism.

So, in terms of deontological ethics there is a question mark over HRM. There is no problem if respect for the individual is universally and consistently applied as a moral good irrespective of consequences; not so, if otherwise. By these injunctions empowerment, for example, must genuinely be about increasing employees' autonomy, choices and development as a good in itself, not, as Sisson has it: 'making someone else take the risk and responsibility' (1994: 15). While 'soft' model HRM, on the most generous interpretation, may just qualify as ethical from the deontologist standpoint, 'hard' model HRM, which treats the human resource as something to be used like any other factor in production (or, in Marxist terms to be 'exploited') is definitely immoral.

Happily, utilitarianism sends a far more reassuring message. Irrespective about what downsizing and labour intensification implies for respect for individuals as ends in themselves, utilitarianism is the route to justifying such activities. It is perfectly ethical to use people as means to an end, if this is for the greatest good of the majority. Leaving aside the practical difficulty of quantifying different forms of goodness (and evil), here is the moral justification for choosing whatever strategies would appear to deliver competitive advantage. The argument would be that competitive advantage ensures organisational survival and organisational survival protects employees' jobs, quite apart from maintaining employment in suppliers, satisfying consumer needs and so on. Hence, using people to achieve competitive advantage is quite acceptable as long as it does deliver positive consequences to the majority of – dare I say it – stakeholders. So 'tough love' in all its forms is morally justifiable: employees may be compelled to work harder and more flexibly for 'their own good', or they may be made redundant for the greater good. Injustices, in terms of prima-facie obligations (e.g., to 'do as you would be done by'), are justified if the consequences of such actions are to the benefit of the majority. And it could well be argued that such a logic has prevailed in the years of the enterprise culture and the advent of HRM in all its forms. The standard of living of the majority in employment has increased markedly over the last 16 years. Even in the depths of recession in manufacturing industry in the early 1980s, with high levels of inflation and inexorably rising unemployment, real earnings for the majority in work rose steadily. With falling unemployment in the mid-late 1980s, combined with rising house prices but otherwise fairly low inflation, the experience of the majority was of 'feeling good' with 'loadsamoney'. This diminished in the 1990s because not only did the real standard of living of those in employment remain static or marginally decline (pay increases below the rate of inflation, negative equity), but employees who had been and always saw themselves as part of the benefiting majority (white-collar and managerial employees in large bureaucracies) now became victims of downsizing, delayering, labour intensification and other manifestations of 'tough love'. But such actions, as far as utilitarianism is concerned, are perfectly ethical if the balance of good consequences outweigh the negative. The problems technically of making such an assessment, as already suggested, are enormous. But, very loosely speaking, if, as a result of such actions, the majority remains in employment, and this employment is more secure and capable of generating enhanced benefit to its recipients (than if the action had not been taken), and if only a minority suffer and their suffering does not outweigh the benefits to the majority, then the action is ethical.

But what of this minority? If a deontologist would not accept their fate, those engaging in stakeholder analysis would also raise critical questions. Stakeholder analysis, asserting the Kantian principle that stakeholders should be treated with respect and not just as means to an end, would be concerned that some employees might lose out in order that the interests of other stakeholders are protected. Thus, if you accept Garrahan and Stewart's (1992) and Delbridge and Turnbull's (1992) critical accounts of JIT [just-in-time] and TQM [Total Quality Management], employees are called upon to experience a measure of labour intensification in the interests of customers (enhanced quality and customer responsiveness) and share-holders (greater competitive advantage leading ultimately to capital growth and/or profit). However, by this logic, shareholders themselves may be required to forego the maximum amount of dividend payment, in the interests of investment in job-creating new plant and in long-term devel-opment activities such as training. In practice, though, management are provided with a loophole, through their obligation to act to ensure the survival of the organisation, safeguarding the long-term stakes of each group. Almost any action (redundancy, wage-cutting, freezing of recruit-ment and training expenditure, seeking cheaper suppliers, cutting dividends) could be justified in terms of the short-term survival of the organisation, irrespective of the damage to the present incumbents of the stakeholder position. All that is required for the action to be moral is that the groups involved must participate in decisions that affect their welfare. And here we are back to the Marxist criticism of capitalist 'free' transactions, that structural inequalities do not allow an equal participation in such decision-making. How meaningful is employee consent to decisions that adversely affect them, if they perceive little choice or if, via HRM-type cultural management, their awareness of their real interests is obscured (see Lukes, 1974)? Further, stakeholder analysis, in its very commitment to safe-guarding 'the long-term stakes of each group' affords little protection to individual members of each group in the face of present (possibly adverse) action in the interests of organisational survival. As a shareholder, I might have to forego dividends in order that the organisation can invest for future survival and profitability, for the good of future shareholders. Hence shareholders as a *group* are not damaged, even if I as an individual share-holder (who might walk under a bus tomorrow) have lost out.

Rawls's ethical stance might be seen as pointing to the golden means of 'do as you would be done by' – certainly such a maxim would seem consistent with the implications of the 'veil of ignorance' and the idea that inequalities should only be tolerated if reasonably expected to be to everyone's (including those who are least advantaged) benefit. Is the core-periphery distinction, or performance-related pay, or any other form of differentiation to which differential benefits are attached, clearly to everyone's advantage? Certainly a case can be made that all organisation rests on differentiation. Concepts of fairness may accord too with differential benefits for differentiated work. The importance of fairness in relation to satisfaction and motivation and, hence, contribution may be argued. The problem is the quantitative issue. How much extra should be given to scarce skills, high levels of contribution, even if it is recognised that such differentiation benefits all? Certainly, Cedric Brown's vast salary increase at British Gas, at a time when showroom staff were confronting, at best, real pay cuts and, at worse, redundancy, could hardly be said to be ethical in terms of Rawlsian principles (particularly given the declining levels of performance of British Gas *vis-à-vis* its range of stakeholders, on virtually every performance measure you would care to take). Is it ethical to justify high levels of pay and job security for core staff on the grounds that they are crucial to the achievement of competitive advantage and organisational survival, when paying very low wages to staff in the periphery? And to do this by arguing that the core staff in the long term are guaranteeing the jobs of the staff in the periphery, therefore someone must subsidise core-staff wages in the long term interests of all?

Conclusions

I have raised the issue of ethics in employment relationships as I think that people's experience of HRM policies and practices is likely to be both directly and indirectly influenced by the sorts of ethical concerns outlined here. Directly, in the sense that, if ethical values are embodied in HR policies, at least some recipients are likely to have a positive experience of employment. Indirectly, in that, if the experience is not positive, but informed by values that intend to deliver goods to a majority, at least some justification may be offered for unpalatable actions, which may (or may not) make negative outcomes easier to swallow.

If deontological ethics inform HRM, there is a good chance of Walton's mutuality model of HRM seeing the light of day and, if so, of employees experiencing HRM positively. This is highly unlikely. At best, in my view, such a model may be implemented by organisations in knowledge-based industries seeking high-value added contribution, but even here the motive is likely to reflect self-interest, regarding employees as a means to an end. This, of course, is perfectly acceptable in terms of utilitarianism. The majority of employees can enjoy the benefits of soft-ish HRM at the core and in the first periphery, and a quite reasonable justification can be given for the rightness of actions that result in unfortunate consequences for the minority. This is fine as long as such consequences only touch a minority. When most of us are on non-standard, temporary, fixed-term contracts, facing high employment insecurity and ever-increasing labour intensification, the fact that a minority have salaries like telephone numbers becomes unacceptable. Utilitarianism obviously only provides a moral justification if actions taken in its name *do* produce benefits for the majority that outweigh the costs to the minority. As already discussed, the ethics of stakeholder analysis, while looking persuasive at first sight, contain potential escape clauses that can render them little more than well-meaning rhetoric in practice. (Hence, no doubt, the appeal to well-meaning politicians.) The recognition of the customer's stake is certainly in tune with the ideas of flexibility and responsiveness that underlie most models of HRM. Perhaps it is helpful too in according employees a dual identity. 'You may not like what is happening to you as an employee, but you'll appreciate the outcomes as a customer.' Finally, Rawlsian ethics, though formally Kantian in their attempt to derive a priori principles of distributive justice that are acceptable to all rational persons, in practice, comes over as a form of utilitarianism. In a world of scarce resources this is likely to mean that, as employees are used as a means to an end, there will be some that lose out. For these people 'soft' model HRM may be an irrelevancy, while 'hard' model HRM is likely to be an uncomfortable experience.

Notes

1 This has been referred to as 'supply side' factors in terms of employment choice as, for example, when people actually seek part-time in preference to full-time work (Hunter et al., 1993).

2 Such as 'High Performance Work Practices' or 'High Commitment Management'. Indeed, Wood (1995: 57) explicitly states: 'The implication of this research is that high commitment management is universally applicable'.

References

Beauchamp, T.L. and Bowie, N.E. (1988) *Ethical Theory and Business* (3rd edn). Englewood Cliffs, NJ: Prentice-Hall.
de George, R.T. (1990) *Business Ethics* (3rd edn). New York: Macmillan.
Delbridge, R. and Turnbull, P. (1992) 'Human resource maximization: the management of labour under just-in-time manufacturing systems', in P. Blyton and P. Turnbull (eds), *Reassessing Human Resource Management*. London: Sage. pp. 56–73.
Donaldson, J. (1989) *Key Issues in Business Ethics*. London: Academic Press.
Donaldson, T. and Werhane, P.H. (eds) (1993) *Ethical Issues in Business: A Philosophical Approach* (4th edn). Englewood Cliffs, NJ: Prentice-Hall.
Evan, W.M. and Freeman, R.E. (1988) 'A stakeholder theory of the modern corporation: Kantian capitalism', in T. Beauchamp and N. Bowie (eds), *Ethical Theory and Business* (3rd edn). Englewood Cliffs, NJ: Prentice-Hall. pp. 97–106.

Garrahan, P. and Stewart, P. (1992) *The Nissan Enigma: Flexibility at Work in a Local Economy*. London: Mansell.

Geary, J. (1992) 'Employment flexibility and human resource management', *Work, Employment and Society*, 6 (2): 251–70.

Guest, D.E. (1995) 'Human resource management, industrial relations and trade unions', in J. Storey (ed.), *Human Resource Management: A Critical Text*. London: Routledge.

Guest, D.E. and Peccei, R. (1994) 'The nature and cause of effective human resource management', *British Journal of Industrial Relations*, 32 (2): 219–42.

Hunter, L., McGregor, A., MacInnes, J. and Sproull, A. (1993) 'The "flexible firm": strategy and segmentation', *British Journal of Industrial Relations*, 31 (3): 383–407.

Huselid, M. (1995) 'The impact of human resource management practices on turnover, productivity and corporate financial performance', *Academy of Management Journal*, 38 (3): 635–72.

Legge, K. (1989) 'Human resource management: a critical analysis', in J. Storey (ed.), *New Perspectives in Human Resource Management*. London: Routledge. pp. 19–40.

Lukes, S. (1974) *Power – A Radical View*. London: Macmillan.

Marginson, P., Armstrong, P., Edwards, P. and Purcell, J. with Hubbard, N. (1993) 'The control of industrial relations in large companies: an initial analysis of the second company level industrial relations survey'. *Warwick Papers in Industrial Relations* (No. 45) IRRU, School of Industrial and Business Studies, University of Warwick, December.

Millward, N., Stevens, M., Smart, D. and Hawes, W.R. (1992) *Workplace Industrial Relations in Transition*. The ED/ESRC/PSI/ACAS Surveys. Aldershot: Dartmouth.

Purcell, J. (1996) 'Human resource bundles of best practice: a utopian cul-de-sac?'. Paper presented to the ESRC Seminar Series. 'Contribution of HR Strategy to Business Performance', Cranfield, 1 February.

Rawls, J. (1971) *A Theory of Justice*. Cambridge, MA: Harvard University Press.

Sewell, G. and Wilkinson, B. (1992a) 'Empowerment or emasculation? Shopfloor surveillance in a total quality organization', in P. Blyton and P. Turnbull (eds), *Reassessing Human Resource Management*. London: Sage. pp. 97–115.

Sewell, G. and Wilkinson, B. (1992b) '"Someone to watch over me": surveillance, discipline and the just-in-time labour process', *Sociology*, 26 (2): 271–89.

Sisson, K. (1994) 'Personnel management: paradigms, practice and prospects', in K. Sisson (ed.), *Personnel Management* (2nd edn). Oxford: Blackwell. pp. 3–50.

Starkey, K. and McKinlay, A. (1993) *Strategy and the Human Resource*. Oxford: Blackwell.

Storey, J. (1992) *Developments in the Management of Human Resources*. Oxford: Blackwell.

Walton, R.E. (1985) 'Toward a strategy of eliciting employee commitment based on policies of mutuality', in R.E. Walton and P.R. Lawrence (eds), *Human Resource Management: Trends and Challenges*. Boston, MA: Harvard Business School Press. pp. 35–65.

Wilkinson, A., Marchington, M., Goodman, J. and Ackers, P. (1992) 'Total quality management and employee involvement', *Human Resource Management Journal*, 2 (4): 1–20.

Wood, S. (1995) 'The four pillars of HRM: are they connected?', *Human Resource Management Journal*, 5 (5): 48–58.

Wood, S. (1996) 'High commitment management and payment systems', *Journal of Management Studies*, 33 (1): 53–78.

Wood, S. and Albanese, M.T. (1995) 'Can we speak of high commitment management on the shop floor?', *Journal of Management Studies*, 32 (2): 215–47.

2 Strategy and the Ethical Management of Human Resources

Paul Miller

There is a hotel not too far from where I work; it is a member of a group, itself a subsidiary of a much larger, publicly quoted, corporation. In that hotel the waiters are paid approximately £3.00 per hour until midnight. Of course, not too many people eat after midnight, but some do, in which case the waiters have to serve them and, once the last diners have left, they clear away and set the tables for breakfast. For hours that are worked after midnight, waiters are paid nothing. This needs clarifying. The job of 'waiting' in this hotel involves being in attendance until the last diner has left, clearing away and setting breakfast. Management assumes that these tasks will be complete by midnight, if they are not, the duties of a waiter are performed free of charge. Furthermore, if public transport is not available (which it is not after midnight), waiters are expected to get home at their own expense and return by 7.00 am to serve breakfast.

This hotel has a human resource manager. She reports to another at group level.

This chapter is about the ethics of human resource management (HRM). It is embedded in the literature on strategic human resource management because issues associated with the behaviour of corporations are clearly strategic ones. My purpose is to place a range of relatively well-known HRM developments and issues in an ethical context. The reasons for this are simply stated. The first is that the ethical issues surrounding business are becoming of increasing interest to most sections of the community – fuelled by a range of high-profile cases in the United Kingdom. The second is that the employment of people gives rise to unique and important ethical considerations which have been largely ignored, while those attaching, for example, to the environment have been well discussed, if not addressed. A glance at the indices of a range of current texts in HRM will testify to the absence of considerations of 'ethics', 'morals', 'standards' and so on. And reference to material on 'policies' and 'procedure' are similarly bereft of

Originally published in *Human Resource Management Journal*, 6 (1), 1996: 5–18 (abridged).

ethical content (see, for example, Armstrong, 1992; Hendry, 1995; Sisson, 1994; Storey, 1995).

Systems, Procedures and Outcomes

What is wrong with the employment situation 'enjoyed' by the waiter described above? In order to identify the concerning factors, we must separate three issues. We call these 'system', 'procedure' and 'outcome' issues (Sheppard et al., 1992). A discussion of each will illuminate the broad reasons why many will feel concerned at the waiter's plight and relieved (if employed) that his or her own employment conditions are rather better.

System Justice

This set of issues is concerned with 'fairness'. It is the issue on which all others hinge, so I propose to consider it in some detail. The notion of fairness at work has a long history and an evolving one. What used to be considered 'fair' no longer is. However, that is not to say that judgments about fairness are difficult to make. They are extremely easy and this must be so because we make them all the time and very often. When we do, we are applying two broad principles. The first principle requires some notion of balance – the comparison of an action with some other action. The most common example is the rule of law and the scales of justice – the punishment must fit the crime.

   In the example, the application of this principle suggests a comparison between the waiter's conditions of employment and those of other people. There are at least three things that tip the scales. The first is that the waiter is getting no reward at all for effort after midnight. There is no balance in other words. The second is that we have become used to a situation in which the majority of those working after a certain hour should in fact get more pay and not less; and the third feature that appears to tip the scales is that the employer makes no provision for the employee to get home, if the latter, at the insistence of the former, has to work after public transport has closed. Again, this conflicts with our understanding of what happens in other employment situations. Or does it?

   As I have argued, the notion of balance requires a comparative judgment. This judgment changes over time and we have become used to the standards we apply becoming ever higher. We do not, for example, expect a horsethief to be hanged any longer; we do not expect an employee to be fined a week's wages for not saluting the boss. However, it is possible that the standards to which I referred earlier are no longer becoming higher in the context of employment and may indeed be lowering.

The second principle which we apply to help us reach a conclusion as to the fairness of something is that of 'correctness'. Whether an action is 'correct' encompasses aspects of consistency, clarity, procedural thoroughness and compatability with the morals and values of the times. The first three features are, of course, meat and drink to the human resource manager; the last is perhaps a little more unusual. 'Moral problems are concerned with the harms caused or brought to others, and particularly with (those that) are outside their own control' (Hosmer, 1994).

Moral problems in management are often complex because harm to some groups is often accompanied by benefits to others; for instance, the decision to transfer production from a high wage economy to a low wage one. In the case of our waiter, our judgment as to the 'correctness' of his conditions of employment returns us to the question of whether the (employment) morals and values of our times are somehow eroding. Thus, the debate for our waiter might revolve around the choice between employment and unemployment; for the company, it might be said to revolve around the nature of the competitive environment. In other words, the dialogue in a modern economy has evolved in the last decade so that the boundaries of 'right' and 'wrong' in an employment context have been changed in ways that appear to do harm to employees. For example, the 'market' has been used often to justify drastic reductions in salaries – a phenomenon almost unheard of a decade ago and yet now so commonplace, it makes the news only when the directors of the same company award themselves significant increases at the same time!

Procedural Justice

This is the second of the three issues, an understanding of which informs our decision as to the rightness or wrongness of the employment conditions faced by our waiter.

The issue in the definition of procedural justice is the presence of checks and balances against biased decisions and the unintended consequences of decision processes. Traditionally, the presence of strong, representative trade unions ensured a measure of procedural justice, but as has been well recorded (Clark and Winchester, 1994), this role has substantially eroded. Without other appropriate substitutes, there is little prospect of procedural justice in the employment relationship. This suggests that other ways must be found in the search for procedural justice.

As in 'system' justice, the search for procedural justice requires correctness as well as balance. In traditional systems for the management of employees, organisations relied substantially on the procedural 'balance' conferred by trade unions. In a trade union-free environment, those concerned to display procedural justice must rely much more on the search for correctness. In our example, it is unlikely that the waiter is represented by a trade union (or at least one strong enough to have influence) and this means that the employer must use alternative ways to show procedural fairness. He does this by emphasising the correctness of decisions. How is this done?

There are three standards of procedural correctness – neutrality, trust and standing (Lind and Tyler, 1988). Neutrality suggests a thorough information search which focuses on securing accurate data and permits monitoring and review. Trustworthiness suggests a procedure which is followed consistently and, finally, standing suggests that individuals are treated in a manner consistent with their status. There is some limited empirical evidence for these principles (Sheppard et al., 1992) and for the related principle of 'correctability' in which the capacity to appeal a decision causes a related procedure to be perceived as more fair (Sheppard, 1985).

An obvious example of these principles is the system for the determination of teachers' pay in the UK. Here is a situation in which trade unions were barred from the pay determination process (denying procedural balance) and in which the government tried to replace it with procedural correctness. However, the system for procedural correctness does not meet the three criteria of neutrality, trust and standing. The party most affected (the teachers) are suspicious of the process and doubt its neutrality. The teachers do not trust the process, partly because they do not believe it to be neutral (their representatives are absent from it), partly because they do not believe it is consistently applied (for example to others in the public sector) and finally because the teachers do not believe it recognises their status.

However, it is not difficult to imagine how a procedure that meets the needs of procedural correctness might be introduced. In a single organisation, it is possible to imagine the human resource manager being pivotal in its design and instrumental in its maintenance. None of this is to deny the fact that systems for procedural balance are no longer important; it is merely to recognise the reality of the declining influence of collective representation for employees – whatever the reason might be. I will return to this HRM role.

Outcome Justice

The notion of 'outcome justice' will perhaps be most familiar to HRM practitioners. Traditionally, judgments about outcomes (and by this we mean reward, punishment and allocation) are based on comparisons with those of others. Our choice of 'other' is based on:

1 Similarity – we tend to compare ourselves with others who have similar jobs, backgrounds, education and so on.
2 Proximity – we compare ourselves with neighbours, people we work with and so on.
3 Salience – we compare ourselves with people who come to mind quickly, either because we know them personally or they are notable.

Festinger (1954) suggested that the need to compare ourselves with others is especially important in the absence of an absolute standard for making judgments, such as a yardstick for measuring length or a clock for measuring time.

It is perhaps not a surprising thing to say to an audience of HRM professionals that there is no such absolute standard in the determination of outcome justice. However, we should recognise that others have made the attempt. Here we delve into the debate on 'distributive justice'. Because the HRM professional is concerned (perhaps above all) with the distribution of the organisation's product, it is important to disentangle the elements of this organisational justice.

The Core Elements of Distributive Justice

There are some things on which we can all agree when considering issues of distributive justice. For example, race, sex, IQ and rank are not grounds for just difference in the distribution of wealth and income. Part of the reason many of us agree about this is that people, by their own voluntary choices, cannot determine their own sex, IQ and so on. 'Properties can be the grounds for just discrimination between people, only if they have had a *fair opportunity* to acquire or avoid them' (Feinberg, 1973, italics in the original). This leaves us with five possible reasons for justifying difference in the distribution of the organisation's added value. These five are:

- the principle of perfect equality;
- the principle of need;
- the principle of merit and achievement;
- the principle of contribution; and
- the principle of effort.

The first two principles are fundamentally similar and different from the last three. The former are concerned with 'need', the latter are concerned with 'desert'. The argument here is that, on the assumption that basic needs are met by the organisation, the human resource manager should be concerned only with the distribution of added value based on contribution and effort.

Although I do not intend to argue it here, the principle of perfect equality is a difficult one to sustain beyond the fact that most of us would agree that all human beings have certain basic rights (to food, shelter and so on). Although there is no way to refute the principle, those who argue it usually base their argument on need or desert. The problem with basing an argument for equality on need is that, beyond the satisfaction of the basics, need is extremely elastic. It follows that the HRM manager would do well to avoid discussion of distribution based on need and concentrate on issues of 'desert'. It follows that for most organisations, a minimum wage (an appropriate one) would mean the avoidance of discussion of distribution based on need.

Distribution of added value based on merit focuses not on what a person has done, but rather on what kind of person he or she is. This being so, we should recognise that the possession of native skill is ruled out as a basis for distributing reward because it is an inherited characteristic, like race and IQ. It should not be rewarded, therefore, any more than the racial characteristics of someone should be penalised. Of course, people may enhance the characteristics they inherit, but we should be clear that what we reward here is effort. This principle can be seen at work in the considerable rewards that accrue to world-class performers in sport or music. We know that behind the success of these men and women lies determined practice to enhance (possibly) inherited characteristics. It is the effort which produces the results and the attendant rewards.

The principle of reward to contribution is a well established one. It is stated in the form – A's share of X is to B's share of X as A's contribution to X is to B's contribution to X. This appears to be a very strong and plausible principle of distributive justice, but the difficulties of measuring contribution are severe; for instance, separating out luck, the contribution of demographics, of people now dead and so on.

The principle of effort is perhaps the one that meets most of our criteria most easily. Although we do not escape entirely the fact that people may be endowed with effort-type characteristics, effort is something that is susceptible to measurement in individuals. Of course, the application of this principle does suggest that the gas showroom salesperson should get the same as the chief executive for the expenditure of the same effort. The fact that he or she does not has nothing, however, to do with the application of the principle of distributive justice.

If we return to the case of our waiter, it is now clear why the example appears so offensive. Because the reward of effort is the one principle of distributive justice which we recognise (admittedly intuitively) to have a sound basis, then clearly when it is broken so thoroughly (the waiter gets nothing for working after midnight) we react severely.

When we combine our (workable) principles of distributive justice with the factors that we use to determine comparative fairness, we see that what happens is that another balance is necessary. To pursue the example from the gas industry, we cannot argue that people believe it right that the chief executive should earn more than the salesperson. All we can say is that the salesperson and the majority of us do not compare our situation with that of the chief executive. However, what the board of British Gas has asked us to do is make a new comparison – after the chief executive salary has gone *up* and the salesperson's has gone *down*. Having made the comparison, we implicity recognise the issues to do with distributive justice – namely that differences logically can only be based on effort differences and (if anything) the efforts of the salesperson are rather more transparent than the chief executive's!

It is, furthermore, interesting that the salary issue in this company has not been justified by resort to relative contribution (because it is both difficult to sustain and insulting to the salesperson) but by resort to system justice issues. Thus, the justification put before the public has been that salaries of the magnitude paid to the British Gas chief executive are necessary in order to attract and retain high-calibre people. However, as we have seen, this argument cannot be sustained for two reasons. It fails as an argument based on system justice, because we cannot judge the 'balance' between the chief executive's reward and the effort he puts into the job. The difficulty is compounded by the fact that most of us recognise that the company is a virtual monopoly and we recognise that conventional measures of success are inappropriate. The argument fails also because we are not convinced it is 'correct'. I argued earlier that for the system to be thought just, it must be thought 'correct' – the argument must display 'consistency, clarity, procedural thoroughness and compatability with the morals and values of the times'.

The argument that the salary of the chief executive must be high to retain him cannot easily be shown to be any of these things. It is an argument that is not applied to other occupations, it has not been demonstrated to be correct (and most of us recognise that it would be quite easy empirically to demonstrate the argument with examples) and it is not (yet) consistent with the morals and values of the time.

Unsurprisingly, in the absence of system justice in this area, the government has had to resort to procedural justice. It has endorsed the committee established under the chairmanship of Sir Richard Greenbury to consider ways to police the salaries of directors. However, this mechanism fails both of the tests for the display of procedural justice. I argued that for procedural justice to prevail there must be checks and balances against biased decisions and the unintended consequences of decision processes. The Greenbury Committee contains no such checks and balances.

Similarly, to ensure procedural correctness the system must be neutral, trustworthy and have standing (Lind and Tyler, 1988). The Greenbury Committee will be unable to convince its audience of any of these things. It is also the case that the power vested in shareholders to correct unreasonable decisions of company boards is recognised to be very limited.

[. . .]

Ethical Analysis and HRM

Human resource managers have two roles to play in the context of the ethical management of organisations. They bring together what we might call the traditional role (to do with systems, procedures and so on) and a role to do with how people *should* be managed in an ethical organisation.

The Traditional Role

It is not difficult to see the role of the human resource manager in the organisation that wishes to establish procedures for the ethical treatment of its employees. The procedures would display 'balance' and they would be considered to produce outcomes seen to be 'correct'. A first question that it is not possible to duck, therefore, is the role of trade unions.

It was not too long ago that survey after survey showed the then personnel manager in favour of trade unions and the structures they brought to the organisation – the 'closed shop' is an heroic example. There will have been many reasons for the encouragement of these systems and processes, not least of them was the recognition that they brought legitimacy to much management decision making, through the presumption of procedural balance. In a review of recent trade union history, the conclusion is disappointing: 'trade unions have been a phenomenon of the twentieth century, displaced in the twenty first' (Guest, 1995). A strategy for the trade unions in these circumstances is difficult to determine and it may be that, in the face of apparently terminal structural decline, it is possible only to advise them to 'take an active role in the more positive aspects of human resource management' (Guest, 1995). However, it is important to note that the decline is primarily in their role of ensuring procedural balance in the employment relationship. The trade unions have not traditionally played a role in ensuring procedural correctness and it is worth thinking about what that role might be and its potential relationship with HRM.

The traditional roles of the personnel manager and the trade union official have mirrored one another. Within each occupational grouping, the negotiating role has been the high-status sub-occupation. The transition from 'personnel management' to 'human resource management' has altered significantly this traditional 'sub-hierarchy' within the profession. Clearly, the human resource manager has embraced this change more readily. For the trade union movement, embracing the change means involvement with the systems and processes associated with ensuring procedural correctness and abandoning its traditional role associated with ensuring balance. What would this mean?

It would mean bringing 'the back office' to the front. In other words, the research role, which has traditionally supported the bargaining role with information to 'correct' that which flows from management, would play the lead. There is some evidence that trade unions are assuming (albeit reluctantly) elements of this – for example in seeking representation on TQM councils (Storey, 1992). For the human resource manager, there are potential benefits to such a change in the trade union role, similar to those he [*sic*] has traditionally enjoyed. In other words, trade union involvement in the ensuring of procedural correctness would confer legitimacy – this time on the data, systems and so on that inform managerial behaviour, if not the behaviour itself.

The Ethical Management of Organisations

Is human resource management an ethical occupation? Those who have been working as human resource managers for some time may reflect on the changing nature of the role. In particular, the metamorphosis of the 'welfare officer' into the 'human resource manager' (passing through as 'personnel manager' on the way). A moment's reflection will reveal how profound this transformation has been.

About thirty years ago, the professional literature on the role of the personnel manager indicates concern about the changes being made to it. Debate raged on whether or not the 'welfare officer' was actually a member of the organisation's management or whether she (it was often a woman) was actually there in some sense to represent the views of the employees. Women were attracted to the profession because it was often seen as social work in an industrial context – a view presumably shared by those that recruited women to the role. We can argue about the reality of the view, but the perception was a real one. Indeed, that perception was buttressed by the then Institute of Personnel Management which talked of the personnel role as being about employee care and so on.

The change in the role through the 1980s was cataclysmic. There is no question of the role of human resource manager being a management one and, indeed, he or she is often the instrument of the kind of exploitation of which the case referred to at the opening of this chapter is an example. The story of this transition is not one with which I am concerned here but the extent to which the manager of human resources has been integrated into the organisational machine is indeed interesting. In the following, Morgan (1986) may well be describing the role of the modern human resource manager:

> While we have advanced a long way from the naked exploitation found in slavery and in the developing years of the industrial revolution, the same pattern of exploitation continues today in a more subtle form. . . . Striking evidence of this (is found) in the way organisations structure job opportunities to produce and reproduce the class structure of modern societies; in the way organisations approach the problem of hazardous work situations, industrial accidents and occupational disease; and in the way organisations perpetuate structures and practices that promote workaholism and associated forms of social and mental stress.

For some this transformation has been profoundly 'amoral' (Hart, 1993) and fundamentally different from the traditions which informed the practice of 'personnel management'. However, it is important to recognise that not everyone believes the transformation to be that great. Karen Legge (1995), in particular, has argued consistently that HRM is little more than 'old wine in new bottles'. If so, and the argument is persuasive, then the amorality which Hart sees now, has been around for quite a while.

And yet, mission statement after mission statement makes reference to the enlightened treatment of employees:

'we have trust and respect for individuals' (i.e., employees) – *Hewlett Packard*
'human and ethical values play a pivotal role in the way FI Group conducts itself' – *FI Group*
'BICC strives to provide an open, challenging and involving environment for all' – *BICC*
'. . . practising always a concern for our staff' – *Portsmouth and Sunderland Newspapers*

It is also true to say that concerns about the ethical management of organisations are not new. In his famous treatise on the functions of the executive, Chester Barnard concluded by saying that the executive process 'is not intellectual; it is aesthetic and moral involving a sense of fitness, of appropriateness, of responsibility' (Barnard, 1938).

The role of the human resource manager in this is viewed by many practitioners as pivotal and benign both for the organisation and its employees. The full mission statements, of which the examples above are extracts, reveal that organisations believe that realising the potential of employees will be of benefit both to them and the organisation. Clearly the practical implementation of HRM policies may be unethical (in other words, the gap between what the company says it does and how it actually behaves is large). Alternatively, the theoretical pursuit of HRM policies is, by definition, unethical. I should like to illuminate these issues by arguing a number of propositions.

Proposition 1: It is possible *objectively* to identify unethical employment practices. I have set out earlier the reasons for our discomfiture with the employment conditions enjoyed by the waiter. They are to do with 'offences' against well-established principles of system, procedural and outcome justice. Furthermore, it is possible to imagine mechanisms which may be established to display procedural correctness in employment situations.

Proposition 2: 'Management' (human resource, financial, marketing, production or strategic) is recognisably good and recognisably bad. The evidence for this proposition is all around us in the failure of organisations, or products, in the acquisition of poorly performing companies, in the 'downsizing' or 'rightsizing' of companies, in the alienation that many people feel at work and which is evidenced in well-established ways such as sickness rates and turnover rates. On the other side of the equation, the evidence is there in the ability of companies to bring new products to the marketplace very rapidly, of others to win major contracts, of some to provide stable and enduring employment over considerable periods of time.

Nor are these sets of statements wholly to do with failures of, or fundamental discontinuities in, the capitalist mode of production. 'Management' (of which HRM is but one facet) is necessary in all types of organisation (universities, charities, public utilities and private ones) and in all socio-political systems (democratic, theocratic, autocratic). And in each of these organisations and societies there is management which is 'good' and management which is palpably awful.

In other words, the 'balance sheet' I describe is not restricted to private sector corporations. Organisational failure has been attributed to the United Nations as well as BICC and made manifest at War on Want as well as Barings. At the same time as Greenpeace celebrated success against Shell over the Brent Spa, it lost two ships in the South Pacific and the local campaigns manager.

The effects of good and bad management are many, but there is one thing that we can say with reasonable confidence and that is that they are visited on the employees of the managed organisation. Thus, the employees of a well-managed organisation (perhaps innovative, perhaps proactive, perhaps just appropriately strategic) enjoy stable employment and a reasonable standard of living (I use the term 'enjoy' advisedly). Conversely, the employees of a badly managed organisation are unlikely to enjoy decent wages and are likely, in the long run, to be out of a job altogether. It is also worth bearing in mind just who we mean when we speak of 'employees'. We are not usually talking about the board of directors which suffers the consequences of its own lousy management – the generals are rarely shot.

The notion of HRM and, in particular, strategic HRM should therefore be thought of as associated with the 'good' management of organisations. This sounds a cliché, but it appears to have been overlooked in the debate about what HRM and strategic HRM is or is not. So what is 'good' in this context?

Good Management

Management is about 'deliverables'. It is about delivering dividends to shareholders, products to customers, harmless by-products into the environment, a water treatment plant in a third world country, food, heat and light where it is wanted. However, given that we are concerned primarily with employment, I should like to suggest that the following four elements would be the deliverables that most of us (as employees) have the right to expect from an employer:

- employment for as long as we want it;
- terms and conditions of employment that do not deteriorate from those that we were originally engaged on;
- a just distribution of added value; and
- a reasonable level of enjoyment of the working day.

I suggest that these factors recognise two fundamental criteria associated with the ethical management of organisations. The first is that the ethical management of organisations is relative. In other words, the factors will change over time. The second is that the factors are indivisible. I argued earlier that, in the UK, we appear to have tolerated a diminution in our expectations of an employment contract. This will have an impact on one or two of the factors above, but a lowering across all four dimensions is not possible.

I should also emphasise my use of the term 'deliverables'. I use this term to distinguish it from 'outcomes'. A good 'outcome' might just be a 'job' and it is certainly true that many 'successful' businesses use lousy employment practices to remit healthy returns to some stakeholders (the hotel which employs our waiter is a 'successful' one).

My argument here is that it is possible for the human resource manager to think ethically about what he or she must deliver to employees. I see nothing different here to either marketing or production managers thinking ethically about their constituencies. It is also worth emphasising that it is possible to identify tools and techniques to assess the delivery of the 'goods'. I have suggested some earlier, but the armoury of opinion and attitude surveys is available.

Proposition 3: In order for good employment conditions to be delivered to employees, the organisation must pursue a 'good' strategy. 'Good' HRM and 'bad' HRM are by-products of the management systems of which they are a sub-set.

It is not possible for employees to enjoy the benefits of 'good' HRM unless the organisation's strategy works. It has been argued elsewhere that strategic HRM is a 'downstream' function dependent on the organisation's (market-driven) strategy (Miller, 1987). There has been much debate about what exactly this might mean (Boxall, 1991) and a large degree of scepticism that a linkage or fit between HRM and strategy exists or indeed is possible (see Purcell and Ahlstrad, 1994: 36–7 for a summary of the problems).

Fit Revisited

What is fit? One way of thinking about it (Miller, 1989) has been described as 'arguably the most extreme' (Sisson, 1994). It is, broadly, that HRM initiatives are *strategic* HRM initiatives only if they are congruent with the organisation's market-oriented strategy. Although 'extreme', this is not a million miles away from most people's understanding: 'all definitions of HRM agree on one point: that there must be a link between a firm's strategy and the deployment and utilisation of its human resource' (Purcell, 1995). Purcell goes on to say, however (and this is often the nub of the theoretical criticism of the 'fit' argument), that

it is relatively easy, but ultimately highly deceptive, to generate normative statements of what ought to happen and the way in which policies towards people at
work should be constructed to maximise productivity, performance and
ultimately profit.[1]

He goes on to say, 'there are no obvious roles for a corporate personnel
department'.

This strikes me as a counsel of despair and I am not convinced that
Purcell himself thinks it to be true because a little further on he does indeed
identify three roles for a corporate personnel department. These include
involvement with first-order decisions and the determination of budgets.
The fundamental difference between these 'normative statements of what
ought to happen (sic)' and the statements of what we might call the 'fit
school' of HRM is that the former are prescriptions that are held to be
strategic solely by virtue of their location in the organisation's hierarchy.
For HRM to be strategic, this is not good enough. This argument has been
put before (Miller, 1987) but it is worth restating.

An example will illustrate the issue. IBM is a company that many
recognise to be a shadow of its former self. As a result of some fundamental
strategic errors, it has found itself in the position of having to 'downsize'
substantially. It is certain that these decisions were taken corporately and it
is possible that a personnel voice was party to them. These are 'first-order'
decisions with 'budgetary' implications (Purcell, 1995). But, they are actions
taken downstream of poor strategic decisions and visited on a large number
of employees to their profound detriment. I do not see anything skilfull,
praiseworthy, strategic or ethical in a human resource manager implementing downsizing policies or wage reduction initiatives. Similarly, the
drawing of distinctions between personnel management, on the one hand,
and HRM on the other is useful only in so far as it helps to tease out good
management from bad.

To illustrate this, consider the elements in Table 2.1 – a selection from
27 points of difference between personnel and HRM (Storey, 1992). Good
management is not about positioning an organisation down the right or
middle column, it is about determining, for example, pay, communication
flow, decision making and so on, in a way that is congruent with the needs
of the business.

Consider a famous exemplar like Hewlett Packard (HP). Here is a
company whose business strategy appears to include bringing to market an
innovative product every nine months or so. We know also, from work that
has lengthy antecedent in industrial sociology (Burns and Stalker, 1961),
that particular organisational forms are suited to this kind of environment.
If HP had many job categories and restricted information flows it would
not get innovations to the marketplace. On the other hand, it is a high-
technology business and it is unlikely to succeed with a top-down, unitarist
management style. Is HP an ethical company? To the extent that it meets
the standards set earlier, then yet it is. Is IBM? No, it is not. Could HP be

TABLE 2.1 *Personnel versus HRM*

Dimension	Personnel/IR	HRM
Nature of relations	Pluralist	Unitarist
Speed of decision	Slow	Fast
Key managers	Personnel	General/line
Pay	Job evaluation	Performance related
Job categories	Many	Few
Communication	Restricted	Increased

an ethical company in HRM terms if it does not establish a fit between its business strategy and its HRM strategy? The answer is 'no' – not in the long term.

The Long Term versus the Short Term

The distinction between the short and long term is often mentioned but rarely considered. For organisations and individuals the difference has profound implications for behaviour. For example, consider a company whose manufacturing process expels a range of harmful chemicals into the atmosphere – the accumulation of which will deplete the ozone layer. In the short term, the company says it cannot do anything because it cannot afford it, or its competitors do the same, or the market would not sustain the cost – or whatever. In the long term, however, there may not be a company because the depleted ozone layer will destroy it (along with the rest of us).

A similar argument may be deployed for the short-term treatment of employees. John Towers, chief executive of Rover, in commenting about the company's no redundancy policy, explained that it was not possible to introduce major organisational change if employees were concerned about job security.[2] In the long term, the ethical treatment of employees has profound strategic implications; considered in the short term, employees are as expendable as the ozone layer.

It will be clear from my argument that an organisation which establishes an appropriate fit between strategy and HRM *can* be described as practising strategic HRM. If the strategy is a good one, it is likely to be the case that the organisation's HRM will be ethical. In other words, it is likely to be 'delivering' to its employees. A 'good' strategy is also likely to be an ethical one, although the argument for this is not one I can pursue here (see Hosmer, 1994).

Catastrophe and HRM

It should follow from the preceding paragraphs that strategic HRM should not be about the management of surprise. In the world I am describing, organisational catastrophe does not happen. It cannot happen because an organisation whose strategy is appropriately matched to its environment, anticipates it. This is perhaps a revolutionary thought but it is one that several writers are beginning to address, most notably in work on organisational knowledge and learning (Senge, 1990) and the relationship of these characteristics to the resources available to the organisation (Krogh et al., 1994). The challenge for HRM is to find a role for itself in these developments. It is unlikely to do so without theoretical flights of fancy to generate a range of normative prescriptions of what the relationship might be between the management of human resources and, for example, the creation and preservation of those knowledge-based resources vital to the organisation.

Conclusion

In this chapter, I have argued the case for an ethical approach to the management of human resources. The proposition has been put that it is both possible and desirable to establish procedures and mechanisms for the creation of procedural justice at work and that the ethical management of human resources is conditional on an appropriate fit between it and the organisation's strategy. Human resource management cannot be ethical unless it is strategic. //

recent M+S job reductions in France deemed as illegal? 04/01

Notes

1. It is equally deceptive to say that organisations are about maximisation and profit. Some are, some are not. Surely more productive is to address the issue of 'management' rather than the 'firm'.

2. Quoted in 'High Interest – The Car Wars', a Channel 4 production broadcast in March 1994.

References

Armstrong, M. (1992) *Human Resource Management: Strategy and Action*. London: Kogan Page.

Barnard, C.I. (1938) *The Functions of the Executive*. Cambridge, MA: Harvard University Press.

Boxall, P.F. (1991) 'Strategic human resource management: beginning of a new theoretical sophistication', *Human Resource Management Journal*, 2 (3).

Burns, T. and Stalker, G.M. (1961) *The Management of Innovation*. London: Tavistock Publications.

Clark, J. and Winchester, D. (1994) 'Management and trade unions', in K. Sisson (ed.), *Personnel Management*. Oxford: Blackwell.

Feinberg, J. (1973) *Social Philosophy*. Englewood Cliffs, NJ: Prentice-Hall.

Festinger, L. (1954) 'A theory of social comparison processes', *Human Relations*, 7.

Guest, D. (1995) 'Trade unions and industrial relations', in J. Storey (ed.), *Human Resource Management*. London: Routledge.

Hart, T.J. (1993) 'Human resource management: time to exercise the militant tendency', *Employee Relations*, 15 (3).

Hendry, C. (1995) *Human Resource Management: A Strategic Approach to Employment*. London: Butterworth.

Hosmer, L.T. (1994) 'Strategic planning as if ethics mattered', *Strategic Management Journal*, 15 (Summer).

Krogh, G., von Roos, J. and Slocum, K. (1994) 'An essay on corporate epistemology', *Strategic Management Journal*, 15 (Summer).

Legge, K. (1995) 'HRM: rhetoric, reality and hidden agendas', in J. Storey (ed.), *Human Resource Management: A Critical Text*. London: Routledge.

Lind, E.A. and Tyler, T.R. (1988) *The Social Psychology of Procedural Justice*. New York: Plenum Press.

Miller, P. (1987) 'Strategic human resource management – distinction, definition, recognition', *Journal of Management Studies*, 24 (4).

Miller, P. (1989) 'Strategic human resource management: what it is and what it isn't', *Personnel Management*, February.

Morgan, G. (1986) *Images of Organisation*. London: Sage.

Purcell, J. (1995) 'Corporate strategy and its link with human resource management strategy', in J. Storey (ed.), *Human Resource Management: A Critical Text*. London: Routledge.

Purcell, J. and Ahlstrad, B. (1994) *Human Resource Management in the Multi Divisional Company*. Oxford: Oxford University Press.

Senge, P. (1990) *The Fifth Discipline*. New York: Doubleday Currency.

Sheppard, B.H. (1985) 'Justice is no simple matter', *Journal of Personality and Social Psychology*, 49.

Sheppard, B.H., Lewicki, R.J. and Minton, J.W. (1992) *Organizational Justice*. New York: Lexington.

Sisson, K. (1994) *Personnel Management*. Oxford: Blackwell.

Storey, J. (1992) *Developments in the Management of Human Resources*. Oxford: Blackwell.

Storey, J. (ed.) (1995) *Human Resource Management: A Critical Text*. London: Routledge.

3   Governing Economic Life

Peter Miller and Nikolas Rose

In advanced liberal democracies, political power has come to embrace many facets of economic, social and personal existence. Political power is exercised today through a multitude of agencies and techniques, some of which are only loosely associated with the executives and bureaucracies of the formal organs of state. In this chapter we suggest that Michel Foucault's concept of 'government' provides a potentially fruitful way of analysing the shifting ambitions and concerns of all those social authorities that have sought to administer the lives of individuals and associations, focusing our attention on the diverse mechanisms through which the actions and judgements of persons and organizations have been linked to political objectives (e.g., Foucault, 1979). We argue that an analysis of modern 'government' needs to pay particular attention to the role accorded to 'indirect' mechanisms for aligning economic, social and personal conduct with socio-political objectives. We draw upon some recent work in the sociology of science and technology in analysing these mechanisms, borrowing and adapting Bruno Latour's notion of 'action at a distance' (cf. Latour, 1987). We argue that such action at a distance mechanisms have come to rely in crucial respects upon 'expertise': the social authority ascribed to particular agents and forms of judgement on the basis of their claims to possess specialized truths and rare powers. And we contend that the self-regulating capacities of subjects, shaped and normalized in large part through the powers of expertise, have become key resources for modern forms of government and have established some crucial conditions for governing in a liberal democratic way.

We begin with a general discussion which sets out and seeks to develop the concept of 'governmentality'. In the remainder of the chapter we seek to exemplify the mechanisms and processes discussed through a consideration of attempts to transform the calculative procedures of economic actors.

First, let us consider the notion of government. Michel Foucault argued that a certain *mentality*, that he termed 'governmentality', had become the

---

From Peter Miller and Nikolas Rose (1993) *Governing Economic Life*. London: Routledge. pp. 75–105 (abridged).

common ground of all modern forms of political thought and action. Governmentality, he argued, was an 'ensemble formed by the institutions, procedures, analyses and reflections, the calculations and tactics, that allow the exercise of this very specific albeit complex form of power' (Foucault, 1979: 20). And, he claimed, since the eighteenth century *population* had appeared as the terrain *par excellence* of government. Authorities have addressed themselves to the regulation of the processes proper to the population, the laws that modulate its wealth, health, longevity, its capacity to wage war and to engage in labour and so forth. Thus, he implies, societies like our own are characterized by a particular way of *thinking* about the kinds of problems that can and should be addressed by various authorities. They operate within a kind of political a priori that allows the tasks of such authorities to be seen in terms of the calculated supervision, administration and maximization of the forces of each and all.

This way of investigating the exercise of political rule has a number of advantages. Rather than 'the State' giving rise to government, the state becomes a particular form that government has taken, and one that does not exhaust the field of calculations and interventions that constitute it.

It is to the analysis of these aspirations and attempts that the notion of government directs us. It draws attention to the fundamental role that knowledges play in rendering aspects of existence thinkable and calculable, and amenable to deliberated and planful initiatives: a complex *intellectual* labour involving not only the invention of new forms of thought, but also the invention of novel procedures of documentation, computation and evaluation. It suggests that we need to consider under what ethical conditions it became possible for different authorities to consider it legitimate, feasible and even necessary to conduct such interventions. It suggests that the concerns that have occasioned and animated policy are not self-evident. The emergence of unemployment, crime, disease and poverty as 'problems' that can be identified and construed as in need of amelioration is itself something to be explained. It points to the diversity of the groupings that have problematized such aspects of existence in relation to social and political concerns, and that have developed and sought to implement policies. These are not just 'political' authorities, in the traditional sense, but also those whose basis is intellectual, spiritual, and so forth.

Hence the notion of government highlights the diversity of powers and knowledges entailed in rendering fields practicable and amenable to intervention. It suggests that the analysis of 'policy' cannot be confined to the study of different administrative agencies, their interests, funding, administrative organization and the like. A complex and heterogeneous assemblage of conditions thus makes it possible for objects of policy to be problematized, and rendered amenable to administration.

Of course, these dimensions can be studied, and have been studied, without drawing upon the notion of government. But the approach suggested by these writings of Michel Foucault has two further features that we consider important. Policy studies tend to be concerned with evaluating policies, uncovering the factors that led to their success in achieving their objectives or, more usually, deciphering the simplifications, misunderstandings, miscalculations and strategic errors that led to their failure. We, on the other hand, are not concerned with evaluations of this type, with making judgements as to whether and why this or that policy succeeded or failed, or with devising remedies for alleged deficiences. Rather, we are struck by the fact that this very form of thinking is a characteristic of 'governmentality': policies always appear to be surrounded by more or less systematized attempts to adjudicate on their vices or virtues, and are confronted with other policies promising to achieve the same ends by improved means, or advocating something completely different. Evaluation, that is to say, is something internal to the phenomena we wish to investigate. For us, this imperative to evaluate needs to be viewed as itself a key component of the forms of political thought under discussion: how authorities and administrators make judgements, the conclusions that they draw from them, the rectifications they propose and the impetus that 'failure' provides for the propagation of new programmes of government.

'Evaluation' of policy, in a whole variety of forms, is thus integral to what we term the *programmatic* character of governmentality. Governmentality is programmatic not simply in that one can see the proliferation of more or less explicit programmes for reforming reality. It is also programmatic in that it is characterized by an eternal optimism that a domain or a society could be administered better or more effectively, that reality is, in some way or other, programmable. Hence the 'failure' of one policy or set of policies is always linked to attempts to devise or propose programmes that would work better, that would deliver economic growth, productivity, low inflation, full employment or the like. While the identification of failure is thus a central element in governmentality, an analysis of governmentality is not itself a tool for social programmers. To analyse what one might term 'the will to govern' is not to enthusiastically participate in it.

[. . .]

The Technologies of Government

'Government', of course, is not only a matter of representation. It is also a matter of intervention. The specificity of governmentality, as it has taken shape in 'the West' over the last two centuries, lies in this complex interweaving of procedures for representing and intervening (cf. Hacking, 1983). We suggest that these attempts to instrumentalize government and make it operable also have a kind of 'technological' form (cf. Foucault, 1986: 225–6). If political rationalities render reality into the domain of thought, these *'technologies of government'* seek to translate thought into the domain of reality, and to establish 'in the world of persons and things' spaces and devices for acting upon those entities of which they dream and scheme.

We use the term 'technologies' to suggest a particular approach to the analysis of the activity of ruling, one which pays great attention to the actual mechanisms through which authorities of various sorts have sought to shape, normalize and instrumentalize the conduct, thought, decisions and aspirations of others in order to achieve the objectives they consider desirable. To understand modern forms of rule, we suggest, requires an investigation not merely of grand political schema, or economic ambitions, nor even of general slogans such as 'state control', nationalization, the free market and the like, but of apparently humble and mundane mechanisms which appear to make it possible to govern: techniques of notation, computation and calculation; procedures of examination and assessment; the invention of devices such as surveys and presentational forms such as tables; the standardization of systems for training and the inculcation of habits; the inauguration of professional specialisms and vocabularies; building design and architectural forms – the list is heterogeneous and is, in principle, unlimited.

[. . .]

It is for these reasons that we have suggested the need for the analysis of the 'indirect' mechanisms of rule that are of such importance in liberal democratic societies: those that have enabled, or have sought to enable *government at a distance*. In conceptualizing such indirect mechanisms by which rule is brought about, we adapt for our own ends Bruno Latour's notion of 'action at a distance' (Latour, 1987: 219ff.). He develops this notion in answering the question 'how is it possible to act on events, places and people that are unfamiliar and a long way away?'

Our notion of 'government at a distance' links this idea to a related approach developed in the work of Latour and that of Michel Callon (Callon and Latour, 1981; Callon, 1986; Latour, 1986). In the context of analysing the establishment and generalization of scientific and technical innovations, Callon and Latour have examined the complex mechanisms through which it becomes possible to link calculations at one place with action at another, not through the direct imposition of a form of conduct by force, but through a delicate affiliation of a loose assemblage of agents and agencies into a functioning network. This involves alliances formed not only because one agent is dependent upon another for funds, legitimacy or some other resource which can be used for persuasion or compulsion, but also because one actor comes to convince another that their problems or goals are intrinsically linked, that their interests are consonant, that each can solve their difficulties or achieve their ends by joining forces or working along the same lines. This is not so much a process of appealing to mutual interests as of what Callon and Latour term *'interessement'* – the

construction of allied interests through persuasion, intrigue, calculation or rhetoric. In the process occurs what Callon and Latour refer to as 'translation', in which one actor or force is able to require or count upon a particular way of thinking and acting from another, hence assembling them together into a network not because of legal or institutional ties or dependencies, but because they have come to construe their problems in allied ways and their fate as in some way bound up with one another. Hence persons, organizations, entities and locales which remain differentiated by space, time and formal boundaries can be brought into a loose and approximate, and always mobile and indeterminate alignment.

Language, again, plays a key role in establishing these loosely aligned networks, and in enabling rule to be brought about in an indirect manner. It is, in part, through adopting shared vocabularies, theories and explanations, that loose and flexible associations may be established between agents across time and space – Departments of State, pressure groups, academics, managers, teachers, employees, parents – while each remains, to a greater or lesser extent, constitutionally distinct and formally independent. Each of these diverse forces can be enrolled in a governmental network to the extent that it can translate the objectives and values of others into its own terms, to the extent that the arguments of another become consonant with and provide norms for its own ambitions and actions. The language of expertise plays a key role here, its norms and values seeming compelling because of their claim to a disinterested truth, and the promise they offer of achieving desired results. Hence expertise can appeal, in one direction, to the ambitions of politicians, administrators, educators and others seeking to achieve particular objectives in the most efficacious manner, and, on the other, to those who have come to feel the need for expert guidance for their conduct in the firm, the office, the airline, the hospital or the home.

Such networks are, of course, not the simple aggregate of rationally planned technologies for shaping decisions and conduct in calculated ways (Thompson, 1982). 'Governmentality' is embodied in innumerable deliberate attempts to invent, promote, install and operate mechanisms of rule that will shape the investment decisions of managers or the child care decisions of parents in accordance with programmatic aspirations. But such attempts are rarely implanted unscathed, and are seldom adjudged to have achieved what they set out to do. While 'governmentality' is eternally optimistic, 'government' is a congenitally failing operation. The world of programmes is heterogeneous and rivalrous, and the solutions for one programme tend to be the problems for another. 'Reality' always escapes the theories that inform programmes and the ambitions that underpin them; it is too unruly to be captured by any perfect knowledge. Technologies produce unexpected problems, are utilized for their own ends by those who are supposed to merely operate them, are hampered by underfunding, professional rivalries, and the impossibility of producing the technical conditions that would make them work – reliable statistics, efficient communication systems, clear lines of command, properly designed buildings, well-framed regulations or

whatever. Unplanned outcomes emerge from the intersection of one technology with another, or from the unexpected consequences of putting a technique to work. Contrariwise, techniques invented for one purpose may find their governmental role for another, and the unplanned conjunction of techniques and conditions arising from very different aspirations may allow something to work without or despite its explicit rationale. The 'will to govern' needs to be understood less in terms of its success than in terms of the difficulties of operationalizing it.

In the remainder of this chapter, we wish to illustrate some of the mechanisms to which we have drawn attention.

[. . .]

Governing the Psychological World of the Enterprise

Governing involves not just the ordering of activities and processes. Governing operates through subjects. The individual manager who comes to think of investments in terms of the discounting of future cash flows is a resource for a strategy of government oriented toward economic growth. Government to that extent is a 'personal' matter, and many programmes have sought the key to their effectiveness in enrolling individuals as allies in the pursuit of political, economic and social objectives. To the extent that authoritative norms, calculative technologies and forms of evaluation can be translated into the values, decisions and judgements of citizens in their professional and personal capacities, they can function as part of the 'self-steering' mechanisms of individuals. Hence 'free' individuals and 'private' spaces can be 'ruled' without breaching their formal autonomy.

Experts have played a key role here. They have elaborated the arguments that the personal capacities of individuals can be managed in order to achieve socially desirable goals – health, adjustment, profitability and the like. They have latched on to existing political concerns, suggesting that they have the capacity to ameliorate problems and achieve benefits. They have allied themselves with other powerful social authorities, in particular businessmen [*sic*], translating their 'lay' problems into expert languages and suggesting that rational knowledges and planned techniques hold the key to success. They have problematized new aspects of existing and, in the very same moment, suggested that they can help overcome the problems that they have discovered. And they have acted as powerful translation devices between 'authorities' and 'individuals', shaping conduct not through compulsion but through the power of truth, the potency of rationality and the alluring promises of effectivity.

We will take our examples from economic life, focusing here upon the internal world of the enterprise and the management of the productive subject. The government of economic life across the twentieth century has entailed a range of attempts to shape and modulate the relations that individuals have with society's productive apparatus. In the process, the activities of individuals as producers have become the object of knowledge and the target of expertise, and a complex web of relays has been formed through which the economic endeavours of politicians and businessmen [*sic*] have been translated into the personal capacities and aspirations of subjects.

The programmes of 'scientific management' that were devised in the first two decades of this century – called Taylorism after their leading proponent – are often taken as the paradigm of all 'scientific' attempts to make the worker an object of knowledge and an asset for management. Within Taylorism and associated techniques such as standard costing, the worker was depicted as a brute, the motivations of the person were viewed as purely economic, and the only tactic available to management was to issue commands derived from the imperatives of the productive process. But Taylorism was not merely a cynical attempt to increase control over the workplace and maximize the rate of exploitation of the worker. Rather, it was one of a set of programmes articulated in the language of 'efficiency', entailing an alliance between macro-political aspirations and the powers of expertise. These programmes sought to increase the national wealth and international competitiveness of states through employing scientific knowledge and rational techniques to make the most productive use of natural, mechanical and human resources. The labouring subject came into view as an object of knowledge and a target of intervention, as an individual to be assessed, evaluated and differentiated from others, to be governed in terms of individual differences.

The productive subject, for Taylorist programmes and the technologies that sought to implement them, was essentially a passive entity to be managed externally through a complex technology of the workplace. This entailed assembling and creating a range of practical and intellectual instruments to produce what Taylor termed the 'mechanism' of scientific management: standard tools, adjustable scaffolds, methods and implements of time study, books and records, desks for planners to work at, experiments leading to the establishment of formulae to replace the individual judgement of workmen [*sic*], a differentiation of work into standard tasks, written instructions and instruction cards, bonus and premium payments, the scientific selection of the working man [*sic*] and many more. Taylor here provides a perfect example of what we have termed a technology of government, an attempt to produce a stable, standard and reproducible form of relations among persons and things that purports to enable production to be predictably undertaken in the most efficient manner.

But Taylorism does not provide a diagram for all technical interventions to govern the productive subject through expertise. In Britain in the interwar years, a new vocabulary and technology for programming the employment relationship was born, associated in particular with the writings of Charles Myers and the work of the National Institute of Industrial

Psychology (cf. Myers, 1927). This new way of construing the productive subject had its own intellectual conditions of possibility, in the 'new psychology' of instincts and adjustment that had been formulated in the years following the First World War, and in the mental hygiene movement that sought the roots of a plethora of social troubles in the minor and untreated problems of mental life that prevented efficient functioning (Rose, 1985). When this new intellectual technology as applied to industry, it had three distinctive features. First, it addressed the relationship individuals have with their selves in their work. The worker came to be viewed as having a personal life that continues into his or her productive work, and that influenced the ways in which it was carried out. The worker was to be understood as an individual with a mind, with fears and anxieties. Not just monotony, fatigue, and attentiveness, but motivation and morale became a concern for various expertises of the psyche. This way of construing the psychology of the working individual was linked to a range of attempts to produce a congruence between the needs of production and the motives, fears and wants of the worker. Secondly, this new vocabulary brought into view the relationships that individuals have with other workers – colleagues, superiors and subordinates. The informal life of the enterprise emerged as a new terrain to be known through expert investigations and administered by expertise. Thirdly, this language established an interdependence between the worker as a productive machine and the worker as a person with a family and home life. Departures from specified norms in a worker's home and personal life could henceforth be seen to have possibly disruptive effects on his or her work performance. From now on, the mental hygiene of the worker would be a key concern for experts, for managers, for bosses and for politicians.

At issue in this new attentiveness to the personal dimension of the productive process is more than simply a concern to increase productivity. Doubtless this is an objective that animates the history of the capitalist enterprise. Doubtless too the new promoters of mental hygiene sought to convince the bosses that their expertise would contribute to such an end. But the novel ways of understanding the relationship of the worker to the productive apparatus in the inter-war years contributed more than this. They opened up a new domain of knowledge and possible intervention. A new conception and practice of the worker emerged. This had as its objective to ensure that the bond linking the individual to the enterprise, and also the individual to society, would henceforth not be solely economic. The wage relation and the power of the boss would be supplemented by a personal bond that would attach individuals to the lives they lived in the world of work, to their co-workers and bosses, and to society as a whole. It would be possible to conceive of administering the working environment in such a way as to ensure simultaneously the contentment and health of the worker and the profitability and efficiency of the enterprise. Macro-political programmes, the quest for profit of entrepreneurs and the personal well-being of employees could be brought into alignment through a psychological expertise that was allied with none of these parties but only with the values of truth and rationality.

Within this new set of programmes and technologies of the productive subject, the subjectivity of the worker still tended to be viewed in terms of individual capacities, and judged in the negative sense of departures from norms. The worker was still to be administered externally, by a wise and prescient management informed by a rational knowledge and a neutral expertise. Following the Second World War a further transformation occurred in conceptions of the worker which entailed the formulation of a concern with *positive* mental health in the workplace. 'Defective' individuals still had to be identified, but a more important terrain was to be opened up – one which would seek to optimize the mental health of all individuals in their relation to their work. New alliances had been forged between industrialists, psychologists, managers and politicians in the course of managing the human problems of the war: it appeared that the enlightened administration of human relationships in work and elsewhere could maximize contentment at the same time as it maximized productivity, as well as corresponding to the values of democracy with its respect for the citizen (e.g., Taylor, 1950; Brown, 1954). The responsibility for promoting the health of a society did not reside just in its medical services, but in its social practitioners – managers, politicians, teachers and others in positions of leadership. These new concerns were articulated in terms of the expert management of human relations in groups. In the new vocabulary of group relations, the intersubjective life of the enterprise could be construed as a vital mechanism upon which government should operate, not only binding the individual psychologically into the production process, but also, through work, linking the worker into the social order as a democratic citizen with rights and responsibilities.

The new technologies of the enterprise promoted by government reports, management organizations and industrial psychologists, sought to instrumentalize its relational life for economic ends (Miller and Rose, 1988). It appeared that the subjective capacities and intersubjective dynamics of employees could be shaped and utilized in such a way that would simultaneously recognize the stake of the employee in the firm and the stake of the firm in the employee. Leadership could be utilized as a resource for management, not only the leadership capacities of the top employees, but also those of crucial intermediaries such as foremen. The key to this technology was that leadership could be re-conceptualized, not as an individual quality to be obtained by careful selection procedures, but as the effectiveness of an individual in a specific role within a specific group united for a particular purpose. Hence leadership could be produced and promoted by a relational technology of the workplace, a calculated reorganization of the relations of persons and tasks.

Similarly, it was argued by industrial psychologists that industrial accidents should not be understood as the result of personal attributes. 'Accident-proneness' rather should be understood as a phenomenon of the group. Accidents were to become social as well as personal events, caused by virtue of the fact that the people concerned are members of some kind of work organization. In this and other ways, the vocabulary of the group provided here a new route for understanding and operating on the personal dimension of productive activity. Productivity and efficiency were now to be understood in terms of the attitudes of workers to their work, their feelings of control over their place of work and environment, their sense of cohesion within their small working group, and their beliefs about the concern and understanding that the bosses had for their individual worth and their personal problems.

The point here is not just that a new vocabulary emerges for speaking about the tasks of management. It is that a new importance is accorded to regulating the internal psychological world of the worker through a calculated administration of the human relations of the workplace, in order to turn the personal wishes of the employee from an obstacle into an ally of economic efficiency. This would profess to overcome the centuries-old opposition between work as a sphere of dull compulsion within which selfhood is denied or suppressed, and the home, family and leisure as spheres for the satisfaction of personal wants and the realization of the self. From this time forth, management would seek to recruit the self-regulating capacities of the worker, and the desires of the worker for personal goals, for its own ends. A neutral, rational and humane expertise was to assume the task of aligning the ethics of the worker as a psychological individual whose needs were worthy of consideration with the bosses' quest for profitability.

A range of new tasks emerged to be grasped by knowledge and managed in the factory. Rendering the intersubjective world of the factory into thought as a calculable entity required more than a new theory, it entailed the invention of new devices to chart and evaluate it. Social psychologists were to enter the workplace, using such instruments as non-directed interviews to get at the thoughts, attitudes and sentiments among workers, foremen, supervisors and so forth which gave rise to problems, dissatisfactions and conflict (Rose, 1989, 1990). Techniques of measurement and scaling could be developed and deployed in order to render intersubjectivity into tables and charts which could give management material upon which to calculate, to diagnose the problems of the factory, to evaluate the consequences of this or that initiative. And the technology of the interview was a regulatory mechanism in its own right, for in speaking and being heard, worker's subjective states were to be transformed: frustrations dispelled, anxieties reduced, contentment increased and solidarity and commitment enhanced.

In the 1950s and 1960s, the social psychological experts of industry, and the management theorists with whom they allied, did not confine their programmatic aspirations within the factory walls. The new vocabulary of the group and its attendant technologies established a series of relays that enabled connections to be made between interventions on the interior life of the enterprise and calculations concerning the economic well-being of the nation. The notion of the proper sphere of politics and appropriate modes of intervention by the State could be transformed. A variety of programmes argued for little less than a complete reorganization of industry and the economy along social-psychological lines (e.g., Taylor, 1950; Trist et al., 1963; Brown and Jaques, 1965; Emery and Thorsrud, 1969). These programmes may have remained little more than a dream in the United Kingdom, though not in Denmark, Norway, Sweden and elsewhere. The point we wish to make concerns not their implementation, or lack of it, but rather the new relations that they make possible: expertise could secure its position by finding a way of linking the values of economic productivity, political democracy and personal contentment into a single theoretico-practical matrix.

[. . .]

Conclusion

In this chapter we have suggested that Michel Foucault's concept of 'governmentality' can be usefully developed to analyse the complex and heterogeneous ways in which contemporary social authorities have sought to shape and regulate economic, social and personal activities. We have proposed an analysis of political rationalities that pays particular attention to the role of language, and the language of social science in particular. Vocabularies and theories are important not so much because of the meanings that they produce, but as intellectual technologies, ways of rendering existence thinkable and practicable, amenable to the distinctive influence of various techniques of inscription, notation and calculation.

We have sought to draw attention in particular to the programmatic character of government, and to suggest that an analysis of this programmatic field of government should not be restricted to a judgement of success or failure. We have highlighted the ways in which expert knowledges, and experts as accredited and skilled persons professing neutrality and efficacy, have mobilized, and have been mobilized within such programmes. We have argued that an analysis of modern 'governmentality' needs to free itself from a focus upon 'the State' and from a restricted conception of the kinds of mechanism through which authorities seek to regulate the activities of a differentiated assembly of social agencies and forces. Further, we have proposed that the analysis of 'governmentality' needs to be accompanied by an investigation of the 'technologies' which seek or claim to give effect to the aspirations of programmers. Our argument has been that in advanced liberal democracies such as our own, these technologies increasingly seek to act upon and instrumentalize the self-regulating propensities of individuals in order to ally them with sociopolitical objectives.

References

Brown, J.A.C. (1954) *Social Psychology of Industry*. Harmondsworth: Penguin.

Brown, W. and Jaques, E. (1965) *Glacier Project Papers*. London: Heinemann Educational Books.

Callon, M. (1986) 'Some elements of a sociology of translation', in J. Law (ed.), *Power, Action and Belief*. London: Routledge & Kegan Paul.

Callon, M. and Latour, B. (1981) 'Unscrewing the Big Leviathan: how actors macro-structure reality and how sociologists help them to do so', in A. Cicourel and K. Knorr-Cecina (eds), *Advances in Social Theory*. London.

Emery, F. and Thorsrud, E. (1969) *Form and Content in Industrial Democracy*. London: Tavistock.

Foucault, M. (1979) 'On governmentality', *I & C*, 6: 5–22.

Foucault, M. (1986) 'Space, Knowledge and Power', in P. Rabinow (ed.), *The Foucault Reader*. Harmondsworth: Penguin.

Hacking, I. (1983) *Representing and Intervening*. London: Cambridge University Press.

Latour, B. (1986) 'The powers of association', in J. Law (ed.), *Power, Action and Belief*. London: Routledge & Kegan Paul.

Latour, B. (1987) *Science in Action*. Milton Keynes: Open University Press.

Miller, P. and Rose, N. (1988) 'The Tavistock Programme: the government of subjectivity and social life', *Sociology*, 22 (2): 171–92.

Myers, C.S. (1927) *Industrial Psychology in Great Britain*. London: Cape.

Rose, N. (1985) *The Psychological Complex: Psychology, Politics and Society in England 1869–1939*. London: Routledge & Kegan Paul.

Rose, N. (1989) 'Social psychology as a science of democracy'. Paper presented at Cheiron-Europe Conference on the History of the Human Sciences, Goteborg, August.

Rose, N. (1990) *Governing the Soul: The Shaping of the Private Self*. London: Routledge.

Taylor, G.R. (1950) *Are Workers Human*. London: Falcon Press.

Thompson, G. (1982) 'The firm as a "dispersed" social agency', *Economy and Society*, 11: 233–50.

Trist, E.L., Higgins, G.W., Murray, H. and Pollock, A.B. (1963) *Organizational Choice*. London: Tavistock.

4   The Cult[ure] of the Customer

Paul du Gay and Graeme Salaman

In this chapter we explore the nature, origins and consequences of a major aspect of current managerial thinking and theorizing about the structure and direction of work organization and the employment and governance of staff. Our subject matter is the managerial attempt to reconstruct work organizations in ways which are defined as characteristically commercial – and customer-focused. A fundamental aspect of managerial attempts to achieve this reconstruction involves the re-imagination of the organization. Frequently this means the supplanting of bureaucratic principles by market relations.

The restructuring of work and work relations is supported by the discourse of enterprise (within and without the employing organization) as it is determined by environmental pressures. What we find currently is the coming together of environmental challenges, many of which are defined in terms of the imperative of fundamental organizational restructuring and the dominance of a discourse of enterprise. The most obvious location for the conjuncture of these two elements is in the 'excellence' literature.

[. . .]

Current emphasis on the customer as a means of analysing and defining work performance and work relations represents a highly significant addition to management attempts to understand and explain the nature of the enterprise. Recent emphasis on a clearly defined notion of the customer as representing the key dynamic of market relations has become a central feature of work reorganization, and critically, of attempts by managers and their advisers to delineate and intervene into the organization of paid work.

Many researchers have identified a cluster of related environmental developments which put pressure upon organizations to find new ways of enhancing their competitiveness and their market share: 'increased competition from foreign industry, a more quality-conscious consumer population, rapidly changing product markets, deregulation and new

Originally published in *Journal of Management Studies*, 29 (5), 1992: 615–33 (abridged).

technologies' (Fuller and Smith, 1991: 1). Most important of these developments is the increasing differentiation of demand.

[. . .]

The Enterprising Cult[ure] of the Customer

If bureaucratic and Taylorist forms of administration are intimately linked to the process of differentiation, then governing organizational life in an enterprising manner is intricately bound up with the process of de-differentiation: with a pronounced blurring between the spheres of 'production' and 'consumption', the 'corporate' and 'culture' (Jameson, 1990; Lash, 1988). As the language of 'the market' becomes the only valid vocabulary of moral and social calculation, 'civic culture' gradually becomes 'consumer culture', with citizens reconceptualized as enterprising 'sovereign consumers'.

In the public sector, for example, there can hardly be a school, hospital, social services department, university or college in the UK that has not in some way become permeated by the language of enterprise. Enterprise has remorselessly reconceptualized and remodelled almost everything in its path.

While this process of relabelling may appear as a totalitarian attack on diversity and difference, it is never conceived or represented as such. Rather, the enterprising customer/consumer is imagined as an empowered human being – the moral centre of the enterprising universe. Within the discourse of enterprise customers/consumers are constituted as autonomous, self-regulating and self-actualizing individual actors, seeking to maximize the worth of their existence to themselves through personalized acts of choice in a world of goods and services. [. . .] While the enterprising language of the consumer structures political debate, providing the rationale for programmes of intervention and rectification in the public domain, it is also linked to a transformation in programmes and technologies for regulating the internal world of the business enterprise.

Enterprising Enterprises

Within the discourse of enterprise, private sector corporations are not considered to be inherently enterprising. Certainly the free-market system provides the inherently virtuous model through which all forms of social relation should be structured, but in order to guarantee that maximum benefits accrue from the workings of this intrinsically virtuous system it is the moral obligation of each and every commercial organization, and each and every member of such an organization, to become obsessed with 'staying close to the customer' and thus with achieving 'continuous business improvement'. To put it simply: commercial organizations must continually struggle to become ever more enterprising. Thus the discourse of enterprise also envisages a new type of rule and imagines new ways for people to conduct themselves within the private business enterprise, as well as in public sector institutions.

The notion of 'Total Customer Responsiveness' (Peters, 1987), in this sense, appears as both symptom of, and answer to, the problems thrown up by the increasingly dislocated ground upon which globalized capitalism operates. The more dislocated the ground upon which business organizations must operate, the less they are able to rely upon a framework of stable social and political relations and the more they are forced to engage in a project of 'hegemonic construction' (Laclau, 1990: 56). In other words, the effects of dislocation require constant 'creativity' and the continuous construction of collective operational spaces that rest less and less on inherited objective forms (bureaucracy) and more frequently on cultural reconstruction. The only way to 'run a tight ship' in the inherently 'chaotic' global economy, it is argued, is through 're-enchanting' the work organization around the figure of the 'customer':

> the focus on the outside, the external perspective, the attention to the customers, is one of the tightest properties of all . . . it is perhaps the most stringent means of self-discipline. If one really is paying attention to what the customer is saying, being blown in the wind by the customer's demands, one may be sure he [*sic*] is sailing a tight ship. (Peters and Waterman, 1982: 32)

Re-imagining the corporation through the culture of the customer means encouraging organizations and their participants to become more enterprising. In this sense enterprise refers to a series of techniques for restructuring the internal world of the organization along 'market' lines in order to anticipate and satisfy the needs and desires of the enterprising sovereign consumer, and thus ensure business success. Through the medium of various technologies and practices inscribed with the presuppositions of the 'enterprising self' – techniques for reducing dependency by reorganizing management structures ('de-layering'); for cutting across internal organizational boundaries (the creation of 'special project teams', for example); for encouraging internal competitiveness through small group working; and for eliciting individual accountability and responsibility through peer-review and appraisal schemes – the internal world of the business organization is reconceptualized as one in which customers' demands and desires are satisfied, productivity enhanced, quality assured, innovation fostered, and flexibility guaranteed through the active engagement of the self-fulfilling impulses of all the organization's members.

Through the discourse of enterprise, the relations between 'production' and 'consumption', between the 'inside' and 'outside' of the corporation, and crucially between work- and non-work-based identities, and progressively blurred (Sabel, 1990). Operating with a unitary frame of reference, enterprise projects the vision of a cohesive but inherently flexible organization where an organic complementarity is established between the 'greatest possible realization of the intrinsic abilities of individuals at work' and the 'optimum productivity and profitability of the corporation'. In this vision the 'no win' scenario associated with a mechanistic, bureaucratic lack of enterprise is transformed into a permanent 'win/win' situation through the active development of a flexible, creative and organic entrepreneurialism. Enterprising corporations are those in which 'customer relations' mirror 'employee relations', where 'staying close to the customer' means gaining 'productivity through people' (Peters and Waterman, 1982: 166).

Governing the business organization in an enterprising manner is therefore said to involve 'empowering', 'responsibilizing' and 'enabling' all members of that organization to 'add value' – both to the company for which they work and to themselves. 'Total customer responsiveness' inaugurates a 'new form of control – self control born of the involvement and ownership that follows from, among other things, training people . . . to take on many traditionally supervisory roles. Being fully responsible for results will concentrate the mind more effectively than any out of touch cop' (Peters, 1987: 363).

In this way the government of the enterprising firm can be seen to operate through the 'soul' (Foucault, 1988a) of the individual employee. These firms get the most out of their employees by harnessing 'the psychological strivings of individuals for autonomy and creativity and channelling them into the search for 'total customer responsiveness', 'excellence' and success. Enterprising companies 'make meaning for people' by encouraging them to believe that they have control over their own lives; that no matter what position they may hold within an organization their contribution is vital, not only to the success of the company but to the enterprise of their own lives. Peters and Waterman (1982: 76, 81), for example, quote approvingly Nietzsche's axiom that 'he who has a why to live for can bear almost any how'. They argue that 'the fact . . . that we think we have a bit more discretion leads to much greater commitment'. The enterprising firm is therefore one that engages in control-led de-control. To govern the corporation in an enterprising fashion is to 'totalize' and 'individualize' (Foucault, 1988b) at one and the same time; or, to deploy Peters and Waterman's (1982: 318) terminology, to be 'simultaneously loose and tight' – 'organizations that live by the loose/tight principle are on the one hand rigidly controlled, yet at the same time allow, indeed, insist on, autonomy, entrepreneurship, and innovation from the rank and file'.

The key to 'loose/tight' is culture. According to Peters and Waterman, the effective management of meanings, beliefs and values (which accompanies the increasing 'capitalization' of all areas of human activity) can transform an apparent contradiction – between increasing central control while extending individual autonomy and responsibility – into 'no contradiction at all'. If an organization has an appropriate 'culture' of enterprise, if all its members adopt an enterprising relation to self, then efficiency, economy, autonomy, quality and innovation all 'become words that belong on the same side of the coin' (Peters and Waterman, 1982: 321).

At truly enterprising companies:

> cost and efficiency, over the long run, follow on from the emphasis on quality, service, innovativeness, result-sharing, participation, excitement and an external problem-solving focus that is tailored to the customer. . . . Quite simply these companies are simultaneously externally focused and internally focused – externally in that they are driven by the desire to provide service, quality and innovative problem-solving in support of their customers, internally in that quality control, for example, is put on the back of the individual line worker, not primarily in the lap of the quality control department. Service standards are likewise largely self-monitored. . . . This constitutes the crucial internal focus: the focus on people. . . . By offering meaning as well as money, they give their employees a mission as well as a sense of feeling great. Every man [sic] becomes a pioneer, an experimenter, a leader. The institution provides the guiding belief and creates a sense of excitement, a sense of being part of the best. (Peters and Waterman, 1982: 321–3)

Although the recourse to 'culture' by Peters and Waterman and other proponents of enterprise is often criticized within the social sciences for its 'remarkable vagueness' (Howard, 1985), these 'cultural intermediaries' of enterprise are quite adamant that 'the aesthetic and moral vision' driving the enterprising organization from above only finds life 'in details, not broad strokes' (Peters, 1987: 404). In other words, the 'culture' of the business enterprise is only operationalized through particular practices and technologies – through 'specific measures' (Hunter, 1987) – which are linked together in a relatively systematic way.

Rather than being some vague, incalculable 'spirit', the culture of enterprise is inscribed into a variety of mechanisms, such as application forms, recruitment 'auditions', and communication groups, through which senior management in enterprising companies seek to delineate, normalize and instrumentalize the conduct of persons in order to achieve the ends they postulate as desirable. Thus governing the business organization in an enterprising manner involves cultivating enterprising subjects – autonomous, self-regulating, productive, responsible individuals – through the development of simultaneous loose/tight 'enabling and empowering vision' articulated in the everyday practices of the organization.

The discourse of enterprise brooks no opposition between the mode of self-presentation required of managers and employees, and the ethics of the personal self. Becoming a better worker is represented as the same thing as becoming a more virtuous person, a better self. In other words, under the regime of enterprise, technologies of power – 'Which determine the conduct of individuals and submit them to certain ends or domination, an objectivizing of the subject' – and technologies of the self – 'which permit individuals to effect by their own means or with the help of others, a certain number of operations over their own bodies and souls, thoughts, conduct, and way of being, so as to transform themselves in order to attain a certain state of happiness, purity, wisdom, perfection or immortality' – are imperceptibly merged (Foucault, 1988a: 18). The values of self-realization, of personal responsibility, of 'ownership', accountability and self-management are both personally attractive and economically desirable (Hollway, 1991; Miller and Rose, 1990).

This 'autonomization' and 'responsibilization' of the self, the instilling of a reflexive self-monitoring which will afford self-knowledge and therefore self-mastery, makes paid work, no matter how ostensibly 'deskilled' or 'degraded' it may appear to social scientists, an essential element in the path to self-fulfilment, and provides the reasoning that links together work and non-work life. The employee, just as much as the sovereign consumer, is represented as an individual in search of meaning and fulfilment, looking to 'add value' in every sphere of existence. Paid work and consumption are just different playing grounds for the same activity; different terrains upon which the enterprising self seeks to master, fulfil and better itself. In making oneself a better sovereign consumer, or a better employee, one becomes a more virtuous and empowered human being.

The Discourse of 'Enterprise'

Although the discourse of enterprise, and contemporary attempts to create an 'enterprise culture' in the UK, are virtually synonymous with the politico-ethical project of 'Thatcherism', they are not reducible to this phenomenon. Rather, as Robins (1991: 25) has indicated, the development of an 'enterprise culture' must be located within the context of increasing globalization. In other words, the project of reconstruction that the notion of an 'enterprise culture' signifies and encapsulates may be seen as one that has its roots in developments outside the will and control of any one national government (Held, 1991). At the same time, this also suggests that the decline of Margaret Thatcher herself in no way heralds an end to the project of enterprise and the cult of the customer. Indeed it can be persuasively argued that the 'entrepreneurial revolution' to which Thatcherism contributed with such passionate brutality is 'still working its way through the system' (Hall, 1991: 10).

In Britain attempts to construct a culture of enterprise have proceeded through the progressive enlargement of the territory of the market – of the realm of private enterprise and economic rationality – by a series of redefinitions of its object. Thus the task of creating an 'enterprise culture' has involved the reconstruction of a wide range of institutions and activities along the lines of the commercial business organization, with attention focused, in particular, on their orientation towards the customer.

At the same time, however, the market has also come to define the sort of relation that an individual should have with him/herself and the 'habits of action' he or she should acquire and exhibit. Enterprise refers here to the 'kind of action, or project' that exhibits 'enterprising' qualities or characteristics on the part of individuals or groups. In this latter sense, an 'enterprise culture' is one in which certain enterprising qualities – such as self-reliance, personal responsibility, boldness and a willingness to take risks in the pursuit of goals – are regarded as human virtues and promoted as such. [. . .] No longer simply implying the creation of an independent business venture, enterprise now refers to the application of 'market forces' and 'entrepreneurial principles' to every sphere of human existence.

According to Gordon (1987: 300), rather than being a travesty of genuine value, the pervasive presence of the language of enterprise is indicative of a profound mutation in governmental rationality whereby 'a certain idea of the enterprise of government promotes and capitalizes on a widely disseminated conception of individuality as an enterprise, of the person as an entrepreneur of the self'.

This idea of an individual human life as an 'enterprise of the self' suggests that there is a sense in which, no matter what hand circumstance may have dealt a person, he or she remains always continuously engaged (even if technically 'unemployed', for example) in that one enterprise, and that it is 'part of the continuous business of living to make adequate provision for the preservation, reproduction and reconstruction of one's own human capital' (Gordon, 1991: 44). The power of enterprise lies in its apparent universality and in its simplicity, in its ability to offer a standard benchmark by which all of life can be judged. By living one's life as an 'enterprise of the self', modes of existence that often appear to be philosophically opposed – business success and personal growth, for example – can be brought into alignment and achieve translatability. Hence the discourse of enterprise establishes links between the 'ways we are governed by others, and the ways we should govern ourselves' (Rose, 1989: 7–8).

Here, enterprise refers to the plethora of 'rules of conduct' for everyday life mentioned earlier: energy, initiative, calculation, self-reliance and personal responsibility. This 'enterprising self' is a calculating self, a self that 'calculates about itself, and that works upon itself in order to better itself'. In other words, enterprise designates a form of rule that is intrinsically ethical – 'good government is to be grounded in the ways in which persons govern themselves' (Rose, 1989: 7–8) – and inherently economic, enterprising self-regulation accords well with Jeremy Bentham's rallying cry of 'Cheap Government!'. Thus enterprise is the contemporary 'care of the self' which government commends as the corrective to collective greed (Foucault, 1988c; Gordon, 1991).

For Miller and Rose (1990: 24), the significance of enterprise as a discourse resides in its ability to act as translation device, a cypher 'between the most general a priori of political thought', and a range of specific programmes for managing aspects of economic and social existence. Thus, enterprise can be seen to be more than a political rationality, it also takes a technological form: it is inscribed into a variety of often simple mechanisms – contemporary organizational examples could include quality circles, assessment centres, appraisal systems and personality profiling – through which various authorities seek to shape, normalize and instrumentalize the conduct of persons in order to achieve the ends they postulate as desirable. Inscribed with the presuppositions of the 'enterprising self', these technologies accord a priority to the self-steering and self-actualizing capacities of individuals.

The discourse of enterprise can be understood, therefore, in terms of the linkages it forges between the 'political', the 'technological' and the 'ethical'. Enterprise acts as a 'nodal point' connecting a powerful critique of contemporary institutional reality, a seemingly coherent design for the radical transformation of social, cultural and economic arrangements, and a 'seductive' ethics of the self (Rose, 1990).

Although the removal of Margaret Thatcher from office quickly spawned talk of a 'post-enterprise culture' and even of a return to 'business as usual', our argument is an attempt to indicate that such views severely underestimate the power and pervasiveness of the discourse of enterprise and the cult of the customer. Certainly, the political atmosphere in the UK has changed very noticably since Thatcher's departure, but this does not in any way signal the decline and fall of the whole entrepreneurial edifice. Enterprise was always bigger than Thatcherism alone, and has entered peoples' daily lives in a number of ways not directly related to the policy initiatives of successive Conservative administrations. Enterprise has operated on many fronts at the same time, changing the world by rewriting the language, redefining the relation between the public and the private, the corporate and culture. Rather than viewing this process of translation as in some sense a side-show to, or 'ideological distortion' of, the realities of restructuring, it is important to recognize that if an activity or institution is redefined, re-imagined or reconceptualized it does not maintain some 'real', 'essential' or 'originary' identity outside of its dominant discursive articulation, but assumes a new identity.

Similarly, it is useful to note that in order for an ideology/discourse to be considered hegemonic it is not necessary for it to be loved. Rather, 'it is merely necessary that it have no serious rival' (Leys, 1990: 127). Certainly the discourse of enterprise appears to have no serious rivals today. While critics of enterprise (Jessop et al., 1990) point to people's continued attachment to the welfare state, and to equality rather than 'excellence', in order to highlight their lack of conscious identification with the aims and objectives of enterprise, they tend to forget that the dominance of that discourse is not so much inscribed in people's consciousness as in the practices and technologies to which they are subjected. As Zizek (1989: 32; 1991) has argued, people 'know very well how things really are, but still they are doing it as if they did not know'. In other words, even if people do not take enterprise seriously, even if they keep a certain cynical distance from its claims, they are still reproducing it through their involvement in the everyday practices within which enterprise is inscribed.

Thus enterprise should not be viewed as a 'pure' discourse as that term is often (mis)understood – i.e., as a combination of speech and writing – but always and only as a dimension of material practices, with material conditions of emergence and effectiveness. While the success of enterprise indicates that 'articulation is constitutive of all social practice' (Laclau, 1990), it is not the case that 'just anything can be articulated with everything else'. All discourses have conditions of possibility and emergence which put 'limits or constraints on the process of articulation itself' (Hall, 1988: 10–11).

By focusing upon the context within which enterprise emerged, rather than dismissing it out of hand as 'evil', 'philistine' or 'wicked' – in other words, as part of the old capitalist conspiracy – it becomes possible to reveal its contingent nature, and thus the possibility of its transformation. It must be remembered, for example, that the current 'triumph of the entrepreneur' within the public sector is directly related to the crisis of the Keynesian state and its attempts at the social management of the economy. Enterprise may well be the colonization of the public sphere by the market but its ascendance is certainly predicated upon the visible failure of the welfare state's own utopia (Wright, 1987).

References

Foucault, M. (1988a) 'Technologies of the self', in L.H. Martin, H. Gutman and P.H. Hutton (eds), *Technologies of the Self*. London: Tavistock.
Foucault, M. (1988b) 'The political technology of individuals', in L.H. Martin, H. Gutman and P.H. Hutton (eds), *Technologies of the Self*. London: Tavistock.
Foucault, M. (1988c) *The Care of the Self: The History of Sexuality, Vol. 3*. Harmondsworth: Penguin.
Fuller, L. and Smith, V. (1991) 'Consumers' report: management by customers in a changing economy', *Work, Employment and Society*, 5: 1–16.
Gordon, C. (1987) 'The soul of the citizen: Max Weber and Michel Foucault on rationality and government', in S. Whimster and S. Lash (eds), *Max Weber: Rationality and Modernity*. London: Allen & Unwin.
Gordon, C. (1991) 'Governmental rationality: an introduction', in G. Burchell, C. Gordon and P. Miller (eds), *The Foucault Effect*. London: Harvester Wheatsheaf.
Hall, S. (1988) *The Hard Road to Renewal*. London: Verso.
Hall, S. (1991) 'And not a shot fired', *Marxism Today*, December: 10–15.
Held, D. (1991) 'Democracy, the nation-state and the global system', *Economy and Society*, 20 (2): 138–72.
Hollway, W. (1991) *Work Psychology and Organizational Behaviour*. London: Sage.
Howard, R. (1985) *Brave New Workplace*. New York: Viking Penguin.
Hunter, I. (1987) 'Setting limits to culture', *New Formations*, 4: 103–23.
Jameson, F. (1990) 'Clinging to the wreckage – a conversation with Stuart Hall', *Marxism Today*, September: 29.
Jessop, B., Bonnett, K. and Bromley, S. (1990) 'Farewell to Thatcherism? Neo-liberalism and "new times"', *New Left Review*, 179: 81–102.
Laclau, E. (1990) *New Reflections on the Revolution of Our Time*. London: Verso.

Lash, S. (1988) 'Discourse or figure? Postmodernism as a regime of signification', *Theory, Culture and Society*, 5: 311–36.

Leys, C. (1990) 'Still a question of hegemony', *New Left Review*, 180: 119–28.

Miller, P. and Rose, N. (1990) 'Governing economic life', *Economy and Society*, 19: 1–31.

Peters, T. (1987) *Thriving on Chaos*. Basingstoke: Macmillan.

Peters, T. and Waterman, R.H. (1982) *In Search of Excellence*. New York: Harper & Row.

Robins, K. (1991) 'Tradition or translation: national culture in its global context', in J. Corner and S. Harvey (eds), *Enterprise and Heritage*. London: Routledge.

Rose, N. (1989) 'Governing the enterprising self'. Paper presented to a conference on 'The Values of the Enterprise Culture', University of Lancaster, September.

Rose, N. (1990) *Governing the Soul*. London: Routledge.

Sabel, C. (1990) 'Skills without a place: the reorganization of the corporation and the experience of work'. Paper presented to the British Sociological Association Annual Conference, University of Surrey, Guildford, April.

Wright, P. (1987) 'Excellence', *London Review of Books*. May.

Zizek, S. (1989) *The Sublime Object of Ideology*. London: Verso.

Zizek, S. (1991) *For They Know Not What They Do: Enjoyment as a Political Factor*. London: Verso.

5 Redefining the Field of European Human Resource Management: A Battle between National Mindsets and Forces of Business Transition?

Paul R. Sparrow and Jean-Marie Hiltrop

The need to understand HRM from a European, as opposed to a United States (US), perspective has become a dominant theme in the international literature (Brewster, 1995; Guest, 1990; Hickson, 1993; Pieper, 1990). If European management exists, it is in terms of greater cautiousness, sophistication of methods, and pursuance of elitist reward and career systems. Compared with US (or indeed British) concepts of HRM, a European perspective needs to take the following into account.

- More restricted levels of organization autonomy in HRM decisions such as recruitment, dismissal, and training.
- A history which has produced a lower exposure of organizations to market processes.
- A greater emphasis on the role of the group over the individual.
- The increased role of social partners (trade unions and employee representatives) in the employment relationship.
- Higher levels of government intervention in the management of the business and the people within it.

Only 'HRM in Europe' should be discussed, as opposed to any European model of HRM, since there is no such thing as a single European pattern of HRM, and marked differences exist between countries in terms of their practice. Nevertheless, as a composite group European countries are sufficiently alike in their HRM to be distinguished from US patterns. Historically, the concept of HRM has not had the same élan in Europe; in part it has been socially and culturally by-passed (Lawrence, 1993). This chapter identifies the main factors that have influenced national patterns of

Originally published in *Human Resource Management*, 36 (2), 1997: 201–19 (abridged).

HRM within Europe and synthesizes the emerging body of comparative data in order to develop a 'force field framework' that may move beyond the old convergence/divergence hypothesis.

We argue that in order to understand the managerial and organizational frames of reference that are currently guiding the field, it is necessary to develop a more dynamic and change process oriented, as well as a more comparative, framework of HRM in Europe than has been suggested in recent analyses (see for example Brewster and Hegewisch, 1994; Kirkbride, 1994). The field of comparative HRM is long on description but short on analysis. In developing a force field framework, it is hoped that future in-depth comparative studies of HRM among nations may provide a deeper and improved quality of analysis of the linkages between the main factors we argue are at play. European managers and academic researchers need to appreciate four major sets of factors:

1   Cultural factors, such as national understandings of distributive justice and manager–subordinate relationship.
2   Institutional factors, including the scope of labor legislation and social security provisions and role of trade unions.
3   Differences in business structure and system, such as the degree of state ownership and fragmentation of industrial sectors.
4   Factors relating to the roles and competence of HRM professionals.

The main conclusion reached in this chapter is that researchers and practitioners have to switch from a spirited description of national differences in HRM to a deeper analysis and explanation of the impact of factors that result in distinctive national patterns of HRM. This, however, has to come hand in hand with an articulation of a series of 'uncoupling' forces that are making national patterns of HRM more receptive to change and an examination of the main processes through which convergent or divergent developments of HRM in Europe will occur. It is only when the interplay and connections between these competing dynamics are understood that the changing nature of HRM in Europe will be truly understood.

European Patterns of Human Resource Management

Differential Business Structures and Systems

The first set of factors that have led to distinctly national patterns of HRM across Europe concerns the influence of the business structure and the nature of the business system. Economic activities and resources are controlled and coordinated differently, as are market connections and the development of skills within organizations. The impact of the Single

European Market on HRM in Europe will be mediated by differing organizational strategies in the context of such national business systems, the outcome of which is still unfolding. These corporate strategies reflect a differential distribution of value added between investors and employees and create distinct corporate performance criteria across Europe.

In some countries strong competitive forces may uncouple previously stable and distinct patterns of HRM, while in other countries the existence of different national business systems and cultures may be reflected in a wider level of strategic discretion to organizations. The United Kingdom (UK), Greece and Spain are the most vulnerable, in terms of employment levels, to the dislocative effects of the transition in business systems. Other European 'business recipes', such as that found in Germany, appear to be more tightly integrated and consistent and, therefore, are likely to be more enduring of external pressures for change. Indeed, German concepts of HRM, while not in line with US models, are nevertheless in tune with the need for a highly motivated, flexible, trained workforce, and high wage levels reinforce the pressure to improve productivity through enhanced skill levels and technology. Seen in this light, HRM is neither a new nor alien concept for German organizations. Paradoxically, these are the very business recipes that are coming under considerable philosophical pressure to change as the competition between different forms of capitalism accelerates.

Powerful Public Sectors

The relative size and strength of the private and public sectors and differences in the degree of integration between public and private sector have helped create national differences in HRM practices, as have differences in the typical size of organizations. For example, public sector employment in the Price Waterhouse Cranfield Project (PWCP) study varied from 15% to 40% of total employment in the ten European countries (Brewster et al., 1991). In countries such as Denmark, Norway, the Netherlands, and Sweden, public and private sector personnel management are fairly integrated with considerable overlap in professional bodies, training courses, and educational routes. In countries such as Spain and Italy, however, there are particularly large public sectors that are institutionally separate to the private sector – leading to a formalized 'social engineering and responsibility' focus in public sector personnel management.

Small Family-owned Businesses

Organizations are also likely to have a more formalized approach to HRM if they employ over 200 employees (Sisson et al., 1991). Of the 18 million businesses in the European Union (EU) fewer than 15,000 employ more than 500 people, and the importance of small businesses increases in

European countries with less developed economies. Although the small firm sector is less significant in Britain and Sweden, in countries like Denmark, the Netherlands and Spain this definition excludes at least half of the working population from any analysis of HRM. In Italy, nearly 70% of workers in the industrial private sector are employed in businesses of fewer than 100 employees. Similarly, in Spain just over 2,000 organizations employ more than 100 people while over 300,000 employ fewer than 100 people. In countries like Greece the extremely small size of most organizations (and therefore personnel departments) and the highly fragmented range of industrial sectors are felt to constrain the role of HRM accompanied by a relatively low level of professional and functional development.

The ability to survive with low productivity, the family ownership structure of many businesses, the lack of separation between ownership and management control, and the high centralization of decision-making are all associated with a continuance of poorer management (including HRM) practices. HRM developments in France have also been strongly influenced by the small size of organizations, the late process of industrialization, and a preference for centralization (Poirson, 1993).

Institutional Context

The second 'force field framework' consists of institutional factors. The role of the state, financial sectors, national systems of education and training, and labor relations systems combine to create unique 'logics of action' in each country which guide management practice (Whitley, 1992). Despite the increasing internationalization of European organizations, many national differences in institutional systems (social, legislative, and welfare) still exist today. Some of the most pertinent institutional factors are discussed in detail in the following sections. The issue of organizational autonomy separates European HRM from American concepts in that there is less freedom and autonomy of organizations from the state in Europe. High organizational autonomy from the state is clearly reflected in a number of important areas in relation to HRM. For example, 'right of managers to manage' as opposed to rights to employee participation, antagonism toward unions, less corporate and social responsibility toward full employment, and less state intervention in either the external or internal labor markets of organizations.

The heightened importance of trade unions (along with their differential structures, strike patterns, levels of bargaining, and rights of representation) has been documented by several writers (see Brewster, 1995; Ferner and Hyman, 1992). So too have national differences in the scope of employment legislation in terms of its potential impact on recruitment and dismissal, formalization of educational certification, pay, health and safety, the working environment, hours of work, forms of employment contract, consultation, and codetermination rights (Pieper, 1990). There are, however, more subtle institutional influences on HRM in Europe, such as the extent to which taxation or employment legislation encourages corporate responsibility and discourages employers from making employees redundant. Although many countries such as Germany, France, and Spain have made moves toward a more flexible employment contract (Britain has made marked moves in this direction) by relaxing 'hiring and firing' rules and making it easier for employers to recruit staff on a part-time or temporary basis (Brewster et al., 1994), some argue that the institutional web means that most member states have only made revisions at the margin.

The relative burden of social security payments on individuals versus organizations also shapes patterns of HRM. Reflecting high levels of foreign ownership, funding for social welfare in Denmark puts a high degree of emphasis on the individual and not on the organization, making it easier for firms to make employees redundant and encouraging a high mobility culture. In Belgium the individual taxation system blunts the impact of incentives and fringe benefits, limiting the reliance of HRM managers on rewards as an integrating mechanism and lessening the impact of Anglo-Saxon-style performance management techniques.

Prevalent employment philosophies influence the shape of HRM in Europe, such that employer–employee relationships are typically collegial and participatory in Germany and paternalistic or patriarchal in Greece. These employment philosophies are reflected in national labor legislation through different biases along the continuum from employee to employer. For example, Portuguese legislation incorporates a high employee bias while in the UK the bias is strongly in favor of employers. The proliferation of generally protectionist labor legislation, high levels of state ownership, and a reliance on internal regulation are all expected to slow the progress toward a pan-European HRM, particularly in Italy, Ireland, and Spain. Similarly in Greece, historically hostile employer/employee industrial relationships militate against rapid integration of HRM practices, as does the bewildering complexity of laws and inefficiency of public administration (Sparrow and Hiltrop, 1994).

Finally, the recency with which employment legislation has been enacted impacts patterns of HRM. For example, in Greece the complex labor legislation and the recency with which it has been codified means that the HRM function spends considerable time and effort in a reactive administrative role (simply ensuring compliance with legal requirements) rather than focusing on proactive human resource development. In contrast, Denmark, with its highly structured welfare system, has for a long time exceeded the minimum standards of social and employment legislation being set by the EU.

Impact of National Culture on European HRM Systems

The third 'force field framework' moves into the familiar territory of national culture. The findings of Hofstede (1991), Trompenaars (1993), and others have made it clear that management theories and practices are constrained by national cultures. National culture shapes behavior and structures the perceptions that managers have of the world. Managers are guided by implicit theories of managing and organizing that can neither be divorced from society nor guided by universals (Hickson, 1993). HRM impacts directly on culturally specific ways of doing things and is buttressed by national institutions and value systems, so HRM researchers need considerable historical and cultural insight into local conditions to understand the processes, philosophies, and problems of national models of HRM (Hofstede, 1993a).

Reanalysing his IBM data for European subsidiaries along the four statistical dimensions of individualism, uncertainty avoidance, power distance, and masculinity, Hofstede (1993b) pursues two themes: first, culturally Europe does not exist; and secondly, Europe is becoming a cultural laboratory for the world. Although the original six EC countries had a degree of homogeneity around individualism (with only 26% of the variation seen across the worldwide samples) and power distance (with only 35% of the variance), the EC of the 12 or a broader set of 18 European countries explodes into massive diversity. Nowhere on earth does such variation exist in such a small geographical space. Eighty-six percent of worldwide variance on individualism–collectivism, and 70% of variance across power–distance are found in Europe. Europe is not becoming more similar but is, rather, learning to collaborate. Cultural accommodation, not assimilation, is the key to understanding European management practice.

European managers approach the 1990s with a number of different cultural assumptions about some of the most value-laden aspects of HRM, such as the role of collectivism, the definition of managerial skills, attitudes toward authority, need for interpersonal feedback, assumptions about reward and equity, and the social and cognitive constructs that managers use to think about organizations and their careers (Sparrow, 1995). A number of critical cross-cultural questions pervade the literature. Whether the affinities and attributes that managers perceive to be linked to national cultures have any substance in the actual skills and competencies of European managers or whether the cultural and educational traditions predispose managers from different countries to excellence in different fields of management by encouraging mindsets that are more naturally attuned to different management disciplines are unknown. It is uncertain how far organizations should go in their attempts to standardize management development programs. In attempting to answer these questions, the literature indicates that the most obvious links between national culture and HRM in Europe are to be found through the following mechanisms:

- The attitudes and definitions of what makes an effective manager and their implications for the qualities recruited, trained, and developed.

- The giving of face-to-face feedback, levels of power distance, and uncertainty avoidance and their implication for recruitment interview, communication, negotiation, and participation processes.
- Readiness to accept international assignments and expectations of what will get you promoted.
- Expectations of manager–subordinate relationships and their implications for performance management and motivation.
- Pay systems and differential concepts of distributive justice, socially healthy pay, and the individualization of reward.
- The mindsets used to think about organizational structuring or strategic dynamics.

Differential Managerial Qualities

The first point can be considered by articulating three of the cultural traditions or management models that pervade the literature: the Anglo-Saxon, the Germanic, and the French. The Anglo-Saxon notion portrays management as something separate, definable, and objective. Management ability is seen to be a general and transferable skill with strong emphasis placed on interpersonal skills. Organizations and business schools are driven by assumptions about the basic character of the individual in terms of personality and behavior, focusing on man-management, interpersonal, political, and leadership skills. Management development traditions in the German part of Europe are virtually a mirror image of Anglo-Saxon norms. German executives have difficulty with the idea that management is something that can be taken in the round, analysed and generalized across the organization (Lawrence, 1993). Traditions place great value on the entrepreneur and not the manager. German managers do not 'manage' but are instead seen to manage 'something'. German and Swiss-German managers rely more on formal authority and attach a higher value and degree of respect to technical competence and functional expertise than do managers from other European countries (Derr, 1987). Selected for their professional and expert knowledge, interorganization mobility is not viewed as bad but is expected to take place only within the same industry or sector or between contiguous technical functions.

Management in France connotes an identity, with managers with at least five years of university education at the *grande-écoles* or *polytechniques* collectively known by the term *les cadres*. It is a position from which authority, delegated by the employer, is legitimately exercised over subordinates (Bournois and Roussillon, 1992). Late completion of industrialization meant that industry was influenced by the prior development of the educational system. There was no need to combat the negative image of early industrialization prevalent in Britain. Management became an attractive career for intelligent and educated people as social élites were valued as a source of wealth and industrial activities were pursued for reasons of social prestige as opposed to profit-only motives (Naulleau and Harper, 1993). Managers were seen to have special needs within the state education system. A strong distinction developed between the skills of managers and administrators in the recent private, profit-making sector and the long-standing public sector and the other areas of society. To this day organizations, staffed by a bright 'cadre' of technical experts and managed by the application of Cartesian rationality, see management as an intellectually (rather than interpersonally) demanding task.

Distinctive Career Maps

National culture, however, also shapes the individual's definition of his/her career. It is associated with different levels of career mobility. It signals different determinants of career success in terms of the traits, attitudes, and behaviors that employees believe their employers see as valuable. European career dynamics are embedded in national culture (Derr and Laurent, 1989; Derr and Oddou, 1991). While Anglo-Saxon managers emphasize the need for interpersonal skills and job visibility, being labeled 'high potential' is the most important criterion for French managers (reflecting the élitist management development systems), and having a creative mind is the most important indicator for German managers (Laurent, 1986).

Perceptions of the Manager–Subordinate Relationship

National culture is also associated with a differential efficiency of the manager–subordinate relationship, such that managers in certain countries are less effective than others in leading and motivating their subordinates (Bournois and Chauchat, 1990). The efficiency of this relationship is at its lowest in Portugal, Spain, and Greece, making these countries clear targets for improved performance management techniques. Britain and Italy also have relatively inefficient relationships followed by France and Ireland (Saias, 1989). Cultural factors are also seen to obscure the need for improved performance management techniques in Latin countries as evidenced by the situation in France. Despite increasing widespread use of performance appraisal, there are philosophical differences in the way performance management tools are used (Rojot, 1990). Observational studies of comparative management practice using unstructured exercises reveal subtle cultural implications for the practice of performance management systems (Barsoux and Lawrence, 1990). Two dimensions of national culture identified by Hofstede (1980) are used to explain appraisal interview behavior: (1) power distance (reflected in greater differences in formal power across the hierarchy and a higher tolerance of inequalities of power) and (2) uncertainty avoidance (reflected in a greater desire to control the future through planning procedures and contingency arrangements). Uncertainty avoidance and power distance have also been associated with selection interview behavior (Shackleton and Newell, 1991).

Distributive Justice and Socially Healthy Pay

National cultural preferences are associated with different perspectives on pay and benefits, primarily through assumptions about social distance between grades (Lane, 1989), the motivating potential of nonmonetary incentives (Henzler, 1992), and views on distributive justice (Miles and Greenberg, 1992). Gomez-Mejia and Welbourne (1991) highlighted the different dominant values, corporate features, and compensation strategies associated with each of Hofstede's cultural variables. Empirical study suggests that executive pay serves different functions reflecting national culture. In French and Dutch organizations executive bonuses are small and uniform, typically ranging from 0% to 10%, while in US organizations there are sharp differences in executive pay with bonus payments often exceeding the salary by several multiples (Pennings, 1993). Whereas American managers assume there is a link between variable pay and corporate performance, most European managers need to be convinced of the connection, preferring to proceed in a direction that reflects a 'may be' and 'in certain organizations' philosophy.

Different Mindsets about Organization Structure

Finally, national culture differences in power distance and uncertainty avoidance impact decision-making about structuring the organization, coordination preferences, and organizational designs. High power distance cultures such as France, Belgium, and Turkey prefer centralized decision-making, rigidly obeyed structures, and authority-based communications; while low power distance countries such as Denmark, Sweden, Austria, and Ireland tend to decentralization. Uncertainty avoidance is related to the degree of formalization (formalization, rules, specialization, and assignment of tasks to experts). Distinctions have also been drawn between the 'individualistic' orientation of the UK and the US which emphasizes informal structure through leadership, instrumental attitudes to interpersonal relationships, relaxed arrangement of reporting relations, and flexible behaviors within the structure, and two-boss relationships or multiple matrix management; and the 'group relationship' orientation in countries such as Italy and Spain which emphasizes horizontal differentiation between groups in the structure and within-group communication (Lane and DiStefano, 1988). Such cultural differences are reflected in the metaphors managers use to explain their understanding of the purpose of organization, decisions about employee roles, patterns of communication and interaction, time spans of discretion in decision-making, and coordination-control mechanisms across the vertical and horizontal dimensions of the structure (Sparrow and Hiltrop, 1994).

Differences in Professional Allegiance, Role, and Structure of HRM *Functions*

The fourth and final set of factors that create distinctly national patterns of HRM concerns the role and structure of domestic HRM functions. There is a tendency for European HR managers of international organizations to 'reinterpret' organizational agendas at a local level. This reinterpretation results largely because of differences across a fourth set of factors, which includes:

- the role, technical training and career path, competence and credibility of different European HRM systems and specialists;
- levels of in-house specialization versus contracting out of activity;
- level of devolution of HR issues to line management;
- degree of involvement in corporate strategy.

The competence, career paths, and professional background of European HRM managers vary considerably (Tyson and Wikander, 1994). German HRM professionals with their strong legalistic background have a very different mindset when compared to their less formal Anglo-Saxon colleagues, while the financial backgrounds of many Dutch and Italian HRM professionals produce yet a different focus.

The focus of functional activity varies across Europe. For example, Dany and Torchy (1994) found four different resourcing models across Europe: (1) the German model with a recruitment system reliant on apprenticeship, low levels of subsequent organization training and reskilling, and judicious use of flexitime practices to facilitate recruitment of scarce resources; (2) the Scandinavian model characterized by advanced labor market planning, low skill shortages, high line manager involvement, high levels of advertising, and a maintenance of qualification or age standards; (3) the central European model (France, Ireland, the UK, and the Netherlands) utilizing a professionalized personnel function (supported by line managers) and agencies, low levels of apprenticeship, a wide range of recruitment techniques to accommodate skills shortages, and international resourcing; and finally (4) Spain, Portugal, and Turkey who rely heavily on the external labor market (especially for technical skills) and have adopted several flexible work methods to attract scarce labor.

Transitions in the Nature of European Organizations

Societal and institutional-level research clearly continues to demonstrate the distinctive nature of national HRM practice. A second theme that dominates the field of European HRM, however, is the concept of transition. A wide range of pressure points in the business environment has created an irresistible force for change in Europe – a remixing and recasting of national patterns of HRM. National differences in HRM seem neither as stark nor as important when European organizations consider their future in facing such major economic and social transitions. In our opinion, these pressures for change will not only shape the context for European HRM, but will increasingly determine its content. They have created two imperatives:

- a pan-European requirement to create organizational structures and HRM systems that are capable of surviving rapid and 'discontinuous' change; and
- the need to respond to these strategic pressures by reshaping national patterns of HRM.

Changing Professional Frames of Reference

Strategically minded HR specialists and senior line managers must anticipate a wide range of business trends, understand their implications, and implement new policies and practices in order to continuously improve their organizations (Hiltrop, 1993) while also maintaining sensitivity to the key differences in HRM in Europe outlined in the previous section. There is some empirical evidence to support a shift in the frames of reference and mindsets of European HRM managers and chief executives, indicating the potential for significant future convergence in practice. A survey of HRM managers by the European Association of Personnel Management suggests that attention has shifted away from the traditional and specialist areas of personnel management toward broader strategic issues as organizations attempt to change their culture, redesign their structure, and resource themselves with a more appropriate set of skills and competencies. These changes place a premium on the ability of European organizations to develop their HRM practices. Political influences, the level of leadership within European organizations, and the extent to which personnel functions can manage their credibility will all play a role in determining how successful they will be in achieving change.

Increased Competitiveness versus Social Protection and Welfare

A number of economic forces are making national models of HRM more receptive to change. Developments in organizational practice will create a number of inherent conflicts and tensions. The fierce debate about the benefits of HRM that took place in Britain in the 1980s can be anticipated within European organizations throughout the 1990s (Sparrow and Hiltrop, 1994). One major source of tension is the trade-off that is required between the need for increased competitiveness and the strong tradition of social protection and welfare provisions in most European countries. Europe (taken as a whole) is plagued by lower levels of productivity in comparison to its worldwide competitors, is an expensive location to produce goods, and has a large trade deficit (Hofheinz, 1992; Lewis and Harris, 1992). International quality, efficiency, and productivity pressures are turning attention around the world to the social costs of employment as competition between business systems grows (Thurow, 1992).

High levels of taxation, strong trade unions, a growing web of employment legislation, and high levels of social welfare provision have combined to produce perhaps the world's best standard of living and quality of life, but the removal of trade barriers and globalization of trade means that underlying quality differentials can no longer be guaranteed. Many European organizations believe a different competitive means is required as they redefine their problem of poor competitiveness. Conflicting arguments abound as to whether Europe should equalize differentials in social costs, reduce working time and share out what employment there is, or reduce entitlement in a response to this competitive pressure. All three processes will likely occur, each forcing change in HRM policies and practices.

This tension has been met in Europe by attempts to create the Single European Market and a deregulation of markets. Deregulation of markets was intended to create a supply-side shock with lowered costs and prices and therefore more competitive and higher levels of purchasing power. The Single European Market witnessed a degree of harmonization of national and pan-European legislation and rising levels of regulation on employment and labor regulations. One consequence has been declining wage disparities and a degree of wage convergence across Europe. Spanish wages rose from 29% of German wages in 1970 to 68% by 1991 while Italy's wage disparity with Germany decreased from 58% to 26%. This wage convergence conflicts with other productivity and efficiency pressures that are placing a downward pressure on wage levels and social costs. Consequently, there are fears that a process of social dumping is taking place with an export of jobs across and outside Europe. Some transnational organizations have moved facilities and jobs across the EU or to countries outside the EU on the grounds of relative labor costs, market expansion, or technological deregulation (McDermott, 1993).

State Subsidies versus the Rising Cost of Unemployment

A second source of tension results from legal and economic pressures on governments to reduce or stop the flow of state subsidies to organizations and regions in declining sectors of the economy versus the question of who bears the rising costs of unemployment, political extremism, racism, and crime across Europe. Rising unemployment has also already afforded European organizations the opportunity to break up many traditional patterns of HRM by redistributing the industrial relations role and the scope and level of collective bargaining (Ferner and Hyman, 1992). Unemployment levels have risen across Europe. While there are large differences in unemployment between industrial sectors, geographical regions, and demographic groups, concerted efforts at job creation have done little to dent the rising tide of unemployment and the increasing pressure on social costs and social unrest. Declining birth rates may ease unemployment pressures in the short term, but increase them in the longer term as skills shortages are experienced and the size and purchasing power of domestic markets are reduced (Carson, 1992).

Significant reductions in employment and number of management levels have been seen not just in the UK but across many European organizations (Kozlowski et al., 1993; Vollmann and Brazas, 1993) thus organizations are afforded the opportunity to evolve new organizational forms and structures. Despite current national differences in the shape of organizations, the process of rationalization and business process redesign is associated with the intention (if not the eventual practice) to converge around new concepts of design. Deep-rooted cultural differences accounting for many differences in organizational structure are set against changes in organizational form intended to create generic structures at middle and lower management levels. Persistent unemployment and rationalization are leading to a greater instrumentality in the employment relationship, pressure on the social contract (with a shift in power to the employer), structural imbalances in the creation of jobs across regions and sectors, and demands for more flexible employment patterns.

Higher Flexibility and Productivity versus Commitment

A third major source of tension within the European business system has been the inherent conflict between this drive for higher flexibility, speed, and productivity (with a shift toward downsizing, outsourcing, and subcontracting) and the growing need for employee commitment, training, and mobility across countries and functions. During the 1980s and 1990s there has been an extensive process of restructuring and rationalization as European organizations have responded to the growing international competitive threat (Hamill, 1992) resulting in a redistribution of assets and decision-making power over production and distribution across Europe. While the final internal economic architecture of Europe has yet to emerge, this process of asset redistribution on a pan-European scale in the years immediately preceding the launch of the Single European Market has triggered new developments in HRM, particularly within key sectors such as automobiles (Mueller and Purcell, 1992; Rehder, 1992). Many technological innovations now sweep around the world within a three-year period (Lewis and Harris, 1992), and distinctive national models of HRM have been challenged as organizations respond to more pressing industrial sector competitive dynamics (Mueller and Purcell, 1992) with new employment contracts and practices and a redistribution and redefinition of the boundaries between their internal and external labor markets.

To complicate matters, a series of social and demographic pressures including (1) high and variable social costs of employment, (2) rising levels of unemployment, (3) demographic shifts, (4) an increased participation of women in the labor force, (5) higher levels of part-time and temporary employment, (6) a shift from manufacturing to service employment and from manual to nonmanual jobs, (7) a rise in self-employment and levels of education, (8) increasing skills shortages, (9) new patterns of labor mobility, (10) concern over immigration, and (11) changing values and expectations of the labor force, have created a mosaic of influences on European HRM policies and practices (Hiltrop, 1993). The pan-European trend toward flexibility of employment is eroding historical differences in employment protection and social legislation as deregulation, attacks on employment rigidity, and the availability of new patterns of work have both attracted new entrants to the labor force and opened up internal labor markets (Treu, 1992). At a societal level this organizational flexibility may result in a pauperization, not just peripheralization, of employment and an increase in divisions between socially protected workers and those in unprotected jobs.

[. . .]

Managers are expected to have a weak loyalty to any one organization and will have to be retained through more attractive and progressive HRM policies (Bartlett, 1992). Organizations face the prospect of coping with powerful élites, fluctuating alliances, continuous groupings and regrouping of teams, and global movements of a small cadre of executives. Managers will need to be developed in ways very different from the existing national management development systems. Instead of having careers that are driven by vertical moves up the hierarchy, the focus will shift to managing lateral moves aimed at broadening and sharpening experience. The way managers are aligned to assignments and temporary projects will need to be managed more tightly, and these projects will become more cross-functional, cross-business, and cross-country. There is evidence that European multinationals are pursuing such forms of internationalization (Derr and Oddou, 1993).

The HRM implications of transnational integration, however, run much deeper than creating a mobile international cadre of managers (Barham and Berthoin Antal, 1994). European organizations will need to create strong coordinating centres – no longer wielding centralized command and control policies – but providing a vision, a purpose, and a set of principles that help create a 'binding glue'. Patterns of HRM within European organizations are being driven more and more by sector and business solutions rather than by national solutions (Hendry, 1994). Several organizations, such as Kodak, Asea Brown Boveri, and Hoescht, in reconfiguring their matrix structures have changed their European structures in ways which have taken power away from the line of country and have vested more power for HRM issues in the line of business or sector (Sparrow and Hiltrop, 1994). The logic of sector is superseding national country patterns of HRM in such instances.

New Competencies and New Patterns of HRM

The need to manage significant cultural change in the organization becomes paramount, with important implications for training. Lower down the organization (where the current technical expertise lies) the need for new skills and competencies is being created, with greater emphasis on creativity, entrepreneurial behavior and managers acting as coaches of learning. Before academics finish debating the arguments, organizations will lead the way toward new patterns of HRM in Europe, without realizing all the consequences and pressures this will create, by:

- recruiting managers of a transnational persuasion;
- developing and shaping internal management development programs;
- re-orienting matrix structures away from line of country toward line of business; and
- redirecting training and career development moves (Bartlett, 1992).

There may yet be a yawning gap between rhetoric and reality. This integrating force for HRM in Europe still sounds distant and is perhaps more speculative than the obvious impact of foreign direct investment (FDI). Certainly its final impact will be relatively slow and the implementation problems associated with it will always provide scope for localized patterns of HRM still seeped in this continuity. It will necessarily set in motion a series of generic HRM responses that will challenge national continuity. As European organizations grapple with the problems of transnationalism, foreign direct investment, and new structures to accommodate downsizing and business process redesign, inevitably the field of HRM will become a central focus.

Conclusions

The context for managing people in European organizations bears witness to competing forces of economic, social, and political integration and disintegration. The business literature paints idealistic and contrasting pictures of Europe as a prosperous, expanding, and increasingly integrated union, or a declining, protective, xenophobic, and fragmented community; while the academic literature focuses on a simple convergence–divergence thesis for key management practices such as HRM. This chapter demonstrates that such a simplistic view does not fit reality. While many US academics and practitioners have portrayed the Single European Market as a unifying force that will simplify international man-management in multi-nationals, in reality Europe faces additional HRM problems associated with the implementation of the Single European Market and added levels of complexity.

There are, at the organizational level, complex patterns of both convergence and divergence in management practice. *The first conclusion is that despite the clear link between national culture and patterns of HRM, the available 'culture bound' research findings should not be accepted without thinking and questioning.* If national culture were a primary determinant of HRM one might expect that cultural clusters would each have their own distinctive pattern of overall HRM. This is not so. For example, the Price Waterhouse Cranfield Project data reveal different cultural clusters for different HRM issues. Relying on a statistical technique akin to cluster analysis, Dany and Torchy (1994) found four different resourcing models across Europe; yet using the same technique, Bournois and his colleagues (1994) found five different clusters of European countries each with its own training and development model. The research agenda for the culture-bound view of European HRM is massive because description of variation is not enough. For HRM specialists such analysis leaves the important 'so what' questions in abeyance. The 'culture-bound' perspective runs the gauntlet between generalizability and stereotyping and fails to consider the equally pervasive impact of both individual differences and organizational choice over resource development. In terms of IIRM theory, what is now needed is a clearer targeting of research on the national culture-to-HRM link.

A second conclusion is that there is a deep problem of research focus. A process of redesign of many HRM systems is taking place in European organizations. If the sole objective of the current reappraisal of HRM in a European context is to assimilate the 'culture-bound' perspective, as appears to be the case in much of the material reviewed in the early parts of this chapter, then theory again may be created that in catching up with the current reality in Europe still looks backward and merely captures past omissions (Sparrow, 1995). The processes through which new patterns of HRM are being created at the organizational level must also be captured. As organizations develop more transnational structures they begin to recruit managers of this new persuasion, develop and shape more international development programs, re-orient their matrix structures away from line of country toward line of business, and redirect training and career moves. Foreign direct investment (seen through mergers, acquisitions, strategic alliances, and international cadres) is associated with changes in criteria for corporate performance, changes in geographic composition and scale, rationalization in employment, power imbalances, new business networks, and political legitimacy for different HRM pathways. There are changes to patterns of HRM both during the process of merger and subsequent integration. A more dynamic (i.e., change process orientated), not just comparative, framework of HRM is therefore needed that incorporates both a broader cultural understanding of existing HRM as well as an appreciation of the international competitive forces and the role of multinational corporations in engineering a degree of convergence.

References

Barham, K. and Berthoin Antal, A. (1994) 'Competences for the pan-European manager', in P. Kirkbride (ed.), *Human Resource Management in Europe*. London: Routledge.

Barsoux, J.-L. and Lawrence, P. (1990) *Management in France*. London: Cassell.

Bartlett, C. (1992) 'Christopher Bartlett on transnationals: an interview', *European Management Journal*, 10 (3): 271–6.

Bournois, F. and Chauchat, J.-H. (1990) 'Managing managers in Europe', *European Management Journal*, 8 (1): 3–18.

Bournois, F. and Roussillon, S. (1992) 'The concept of "highflier" executives in France: the weight of the national culture', *Human Resource Management Journal*, 3 (1): 37–56.

Bournois, F., Chauchat, J.H. and Roussillon, S. (1994) 'Training and management in Europe', in C. Brewster and A. Hegewisch (eds), *Policy and Practice in European HRM: The Price Waterhouse Cranfield Survey*. London: Routledge.

Brewster, C. (1995) 'Developing a "European" model of human resource management', *Journal of International Business Studies*, 21 (6): 1–21.

Brewster, C. and Hegewisch, A. (eds) (1994) *Policy and Practice in European HRM: The Price Waterhouse Cranfield Survey*. London: Routledge.

Brewster, C., Hegewisch, A. and Lockhart, J.T. (1991) 'Researching human resource management: methodology of the Price Waterhouse Cranfield Project on European trends', *Personnel Review*, 20 (6): 36–40.

Brewster, C., Hegewisch, A. and Mayne, L. (1994) 'Flexible working practices: the controversy and the evidence', in C. Brewster and A. Hegewisch (eds), *Policy and Practice in European Human Resource Management: The Price Waterhouse Cranfield Survey*. London: Routledge.

Carson, I. (1992) 'Europe's pension deficit', *International Management*, October: 80–3.

Dany, F. and Torchy, V. (1994) 'Recruitment and selection in Europe: policies, practices and methods', in C. Brewster and A. Hegewisch (eds), *Policy and Practice in European Human Resource Management: The Price Waterhouse Cranfield Survey*. London: Routledge.

Derr, C.B. (1987) 'Managing high potentials in Europe: some cross-cultural findings', *European Management Journal*, 5 (2): 72–80.

Derr, C.B. and Laurent, A. (1989) 'The internal and external career: a theoretical and cross-cultural perspective', in J. Arthur, P. Lawrence and D. Hall (eds), *Handbook of Career Theory*. Cambridge: Cambridge University Press.

Derr, C.B. and Oddou, G. (1991) 'Are US multinationals adequately preparing future American leaders for global competition?', *International Journal of Human Resource Management*, 2 (2): 227–44.

Derr, C.B. and Oddou, G. (1993) 'Internationalising managers: speeding up the process', *European Management Journal*, 11 (4): 435–42.

Ferner, A. and Hyman, R. (eds) (1992) *Industrial Relations in the New Europe*. Oxford: Basil Blackwell.

Gomez-Mejia, I.R. and Welbourne, T. (1991) 'Compensation strategies in a global context', *Human Resource Planning*, 14 (1): 29–42.

Guest, D. (1990) 'Human resource management and the American dream', *Journal of Management Studies*, 27 (4): 377–97.

Hamill, J. (1992) 'Employment effects of changing multinational strategies in Europe', *European Management Journal*, 10 (3): 334–40.

Hendry, C. (1994) 'The Single European Market and the HRM response', in P. Kirkbride (ed.), *Human Resource Management in Europe*. London: Routledge.

Henzler, H.A. (1992) 'The new era of Eurocapitalism', *Harvard Business Review*, 70 (4): 57–68.

Hickson, D.J. (ed.) (1993) *Management in Western Europe: Society, Culture and Organisation in Twelve Nations*. Berlin: de Gruyter.

Hiltrop, J.-M. (1993) 'European HRM: strategic pressures driving European HRM', *European Management Journal*, 11 (4): 424–42.

Hofheinz, P. (1992) 'Can Europe compete?', *Fortune*, 14 December: 47–54.

Hofstede, G. (1980) *Culture's Consequences: International Differences in Work-related Values*. Beverly Hills: Sage.

Hofstede, G. (1991) *Cultures and Organisations: Software of the Mind*. London: McGraw-Hill.

Hofstede, G. (1993a) 'Cultural constraints in management theories', *Academy of Management Executive*, 7 (1): 81–93.

Hofstede, G. (1993b) 'Intercultural conflict and synergy in Europe', in D.J. Hickson (ed.), *Management in Western Europe: Society, Culture and Organisation in Twelve Nations*. Berlin: de Gruyter.

Kirkbride, P. (ed.) (1994) *Human Resource Management in Europe*. London: Routledge.

Kozlowski, S.W., Chao, G.T., Smith, E.S. and Hedlund, J. (1993) 'Organisational downsizing: strategies, interventions and research implications', in C. Cooper and I. Robertson (eds), *International Review of Industrial and Organisational Psychology* Vol. 9. Chichester: John Wiley.

Lane, C. (1989) *Management and Labour in Europe*. Aldershot: Edward Elgar.

Lane, H.W. and DiStefano, J.J. (1988) *International Management Behaviour: From Policy to Practice*. Ontario: Nelson.

Laurent, A. (1986) 'The cross-cultural puzzle of international human resource management', *Human Resource Management*, 25 (1): 91–102.

Lawrence, P. (1993) 'Management development in Europe: a study in cultural contrast', *Human Resource Management Journal*, 3 (1): 11–23.

Lewis, W.W. and Harris, M. (1992) 'Why globalisation must prevail: an economic rationale for the inevitable defeat of protectionism', *McKinsey Quarterly*, (2): 114–31.

McDermott, M.C. (1993) 'Restructuring in the domestic appliances industry: implications for Maytag Corporation and its European operations', *European Management Journal*, 11 (3): 347–92.

Miles, J. and Greenberg, J. (1992) 'Cultural diversity as a challenge to achieving Distributive Justice within the European Community'. Unpublished paper.

Mueller, F. and Purcell, J. (1992) 'The Europeanisation of manufacturing and the decentralisation of bargaining: multinational management strategies in the European automobile industry', *International Journal of Human Resource Management*, 3 (1): 15–34.

Naulleau, G. and Harper, J. (1993) 'A comparison of British and French management cultures: some implications for management development practices in each country', *Management Education and Development*, 24 (1): 14–25.

Pennings, J.M. (1993) 'Executive reward systems: a cross-national comparison', *Journal of Management Studies*, 30 (2): 261–80.

Pieper, R. (ed.) (1990) *Human Resource Management: An International Comparison*. Berlin: de Gruyter.

Poirson, P. (1993) 'The characteristics and dynamics of human resource management in France', in S. Tyson, P. Lawrence, P. Poirson, L. Manzolini and C.S. Vincente (eds), *Human Resource Management in Europe: Strategic Issues and Cases*. London: Kogan Page.

Rehder, R.R. (1992) 'Sayonara, Uddevalla?', *Business Horizons*, 35 (6): 8–18.

Rojot, J. (1990) 'Human resource management in France', in R. Pieper (ed.), *Human Resource Management: An International Comparison*. Berlin: de Gruyter.

Saias, M. (1989) 'Compétitivité et stratégies des enterprises face à l'horizon 93', *Revue Française de Gestion*, May.

Shackleton, V. and Newell, S. (1991) 'Management selection: a comparative survey of methods used in top British and French companies', *Journal of Occupational Psychology*, 64 (1): 23–36.

Sisson, K., Waddington, J. and Whitston, C. (1991) 'Company size in the European Community', *Human Resource Management Journal*, 2 (1): 94–109.

Sparrow, P.R. (1995) 'Towards a dynamic and comparative model of European human resource management: an extended review', *International Journal of Human Resource Management*, 6 (3): 935–53.

Sparrow, P.R. and Hiltrop, J.-M. (1994) *European Human Resource Management in Transition*. London: Prentice-Hall.

Thurow, L. (1992) *Head to Head*. London: Nicholas Brealey.

Treu, T. (1992) 'Labour flexibility in Europe', *International Labour Review*, 131 (4): 497–512.

Trompenaars, F. (1993) *Riding the Waves of Culture*. London: The Economist Books.

Tyson, S. and Wikander, L. (1994) 'The education and training of human resource managers in Europe', in C. Brewster and A. Hegewisch (eds), *Policy and Practice in European Human Resource Management: The Price Waterhouse Cranfield Survey*. London: Routledge.

Vollmann, T. and Brazas, M. (1993) 'Downsizing', *European Management Journal*, 11 (1): 18–29.

Whitley, R.D. (ed.) (1992) *European Business Systems: Firms and Markets in their National Contexts*. London: Sage.

6   International Comparisons of Training Policies

Charles Noble

The chapter starts by examining the importance of international comparisons of industry training as an area of research. Attention is given to the nature, benefits and limitations of comparative analysis in analysing policy issues. To further evaluate the use of comparative analysis, the case for reintroducing a training levy in Britain is assessed.

The study is limited to four members of the Organisation for Economic Cooperation and Development (OECD) – Australia, Britain, France and Germany. These are market economies which attach considerable importance to training and development to accelerate economic growth. At the same time, there are important differences in their training systems and especially in the degree of their commitment to government intervention in training markets. Interviews were carried out with officials of government departments and international agencies in each of these countries – except Australia – in the second half of 1994. The aim of this fieldwork was to gather up-to-date information about policy developments, especially in relation to different forms of government intervention in training markets.

Importance of International Comparisons

Training and development has received considerable attention in recent years, both in relation to policy-making in several countries and in management research. It is part of a resurgence of interest in workforce qualifications and skills (OECD, 1991: 135) and a growing recognition of the importance of 'learning organisations'. Training and development have generated considerable debate, especially in countries experiencing economic problems, about ways in which training can improve productivity and accelerate economic growth.

Originally published in *Human Resource Management Journal*, 7 (1), 1997: 5–18 (abridged).

A related issue is the appropriate role of government in achieving a stronger commitment by industry to training. Australia and Britain have, at different times, looked to Germany, France, Sweden, the United States of America and Japan for inspiration. Because they appear to be economically successful, the factors that seem to explain the success of these countries have been the subject of several studies.

Probably more than any other country, Britain has shown an abiding interest in international comparisons of vocational education and training (VET) (Prais, 1993: 3; Sheldrake and Vickerstaff, 1987: 55). The major government-funded study *Training in Britain* drew on comparative research. It acknowledged that much more needs to be done before firm conclusions can be drawn based on comparative evidence (Department of Employment, 1989: 65), making selective comparisons of Japan, the USA, Germany and France. The National Institute of Economic and Social Research (NIESR) has developed comparative analysis by focusing on particular industries. Mason et al., 1994; Oulton, 1993; O'Mahony, 1992; Steedman et al., 1991; and Prais and Wagner, 1988 are five examples from NIESR's extensive list covering more than a decade. A good overview of research and policy developments up to the early 1990s is provided by Ryan (1991). Whitley (1992) examines European business systems and complements Ryan's book. Many comparative analyses of France and Germany are from the British perspective, including NIESR's work, Wagner (1991) and Lane (1992).

An important early step in comparative analysis is to establish the parameters of the system in which the issue under consideration is placed. In this regard Marsden and Ryan (1992: 251) identify two requirements for international comparisons:

- sufficient institutional and cultural similarity between countries to make them meaningful;
- they must consider the institutions in which particular training practices are embedded.

Benefits and Limitations

The fact that comparative analysis is used in policy-making does not mean that comparisons are always justified or desirable. It may be that policy analysts and decision makers have become attached to the comparative approach without stopping to assess the benefits and limitations. For comparison to be useful in policy development, an appropriate methodology must be developed and used.

To the extent that countries have important policy issues in common, it is reasonable to expect that there will be some solutions in common, or that it is possible to learn from the experience or research of other countries. Another benefit of comparison is, to quote Goyder (1994: 26), 'to see ourselves differently by understanding the things that we find strange and that others take for granted. It may not be applicable this morning, but it opens our minds to new ways of approaching business issues.'

Comparative analysis has many limitations. Research evidence points to the need to be critical of a blind faith in training and development and to treat international comparisons with caution. In particular, broad brush comparisons are unlikely to be effective, especially when based on short visits by bureaucrats or politicians. The OECD (1991: 135) points out that no dominant pattern is evident across countries. This reflects data quality and training definitions, and real institutional differences including educational systems and the organisation of work.

Comparisons may also founder through statistical inadequacies. Chapman (1993: 129) contends that it is possible to argue that the UK lags behind many comparable countries in terms of training and education, but it is extremely doubtful whether this conclusion is based on sufficiently reliable data. The OECD's view (1993: 8) is that the apparent convergence of views on training is 'deceptive, and consensus unravels the closer one gets to formulating public policies' that would affect practice. Taken together, these are strong warnings for the comparativist which, if not heeded, could lead to unwarranted conclusions about the transferability of international practices.

Myth may be an important constraint on the analytical contribution of comparative research (Ryan, 1991: 12–13). This is illustrated by those writers who depict British VET as a failure by comparison with the overwhelming success of the German or Japanese system. Myths such as this may contain a substantial element of truth, but oversimplify, stereotype or distort (ibid.: 13). Another danger inherent in myths is that they may encourage selectivity, focusing on parts of the system that conform to the myth, and ignoring those that do not (Raffe, 1992: 49).

Institutional differences are a further limitation. Attempts to transfer part of one VET system from country to country have no sound economic justification (Chapman, 1993: 123). Effective forms of economic organisation vary considerably across European countries and they are deeply embedded in their particular institutional contexts (Whitley, 1992: 267). NIESR studies have recently considered such differences. Mason and Wagner (1994: 61) refer to the likelihood that at least some institutions operating at the national level do influence relative innovative performance. They conclude that institutional arrangements for knowledge transfer between the science base and industry in Britain are less comprehensive and well organised than in Germany (ibid.: 69). This does not mean, of course, that the solution is to attempt to transplant institutions from one country to another, something that is readily acknowledged in another NIESR study (Mason et al., 1994: 77).

The time horizon for policy development is an important factor. In Australia, the three-year federal political cycle favours a short-term approach. Political expediency frequently dictates the use of less sophisticated tools than comparative research. Other more superficial forms of information gathering are more swiftly digestible and less likely to question the effectiveness of simple remedies (Keep, 1992: 28).

Use of Comparisons in Analysing Policy Issues

Having considered the nature of comparative analysis, the point has been reached where any further discussion will be too general to assist policy analysis. To further explore the potential of international comparisons, analysis is confined to attempts to increase employer involvement in training through training levies and other means. This is timely as, after 16 years of voluntarism in Britain, the pendulum is starting to swing towards increased government intervention. The reintroduction of a training levy is being debated, with the Liberal Democrats and the Trades Union Congress leading the debate in favour (Clough, 1994: 10; *Employee Development Bulletin*, 1995: 2).

If a government is looking at ways of increasing industry's commitment to training, a levy is clearly an option. It has the advantage of dealing with the poaching problem; that is, firms that do not train are able to recruit from firms that invest in training. Furthermore, the levy can be of considerable support to training professionals who might otherwise find it difficult to persuade senior managers of the benefits of training.

Assuming the government becomes convinced of the benefits of a levy, how may comparative analysis be used? A starting point might be to look at the experience of countries with a similar socio-economic system, such as Australia, France and Germany. Further evidence could be obtained from Singapore which has operated a skills development fund for many years, but reservations could be expected about using this country as a model because of differences in national culture and level of development. Britain's own experience must be included, as it had a levy but subsequently abolished it.

France – an Interventionist Approach

France's approach has considerable attraction to policy makers who favour centralised decision-making. The government follows a consensual route which involves negotiations between the social partners: representatives of trade unions and employers' federations (interview, Ministry of Work, Employment and Continuing Professional Education, 1994). Two important statutory requirements traceable to the Continuing Vocational Training Act of 1971 influence employers' training efforts. The first is the requirement that employers spend a certain proportion of their payroll on training, currently 1.5 per cent – this aspect is considered below. The other main statutory requirement is paid training leave for workers. In 1971 the government legislated to ensure that all employers with more than ten workers participate in the financing of continuing professional education based on a proportion of payroll (Caspar, 1992: 23).

Since the 1971 Act employers have been directly involved in formulating training policies. Within the framework of this Act, planning of continuing education takes place as a result of discussion between employees and workers at the company level (Atchoarena, 1993: 2). The system has been refined progressively and in July 1994 the social partners signed a new training agreement. The agreement made several changes, including the option for companies to pay the apprentice training levy to an apprentice training centre, upgrading qualifications awarded at the end of fixed-term training contracts, and extending the availability of other training (Incomes Data Services, 1994a: 5; 1994b: 11). In 1991 companies allocated 3.2 per cent of their payroll to in-service training and in 1992 it was estimated that 30 per cent of the active population benefited from continuing education (Atchoarena, 1993: 4). There appears to be a nationwide consensus on the importance of education and training (Gordon, 1990: 58; Caspar, 1992: 21).

France was a partial model for the training levy operating in Australia from June 1990 until its suspension for two years from July 1994. It has a system of mandatory contributions by employers to fund training. Funds levied from employers are managed either by the company which draws up its training scheme by consulting its works council, or by organisations with government authorisation to collect funds and finance educational activity (Blachere, 1992: 41; Caspar, 1992: 26). In 1991, 52 per cent of vocational training expenditure were provided by the government, compared with 42 per cent by companies (Atchoarena, 1993: 4). Employers play an important role in defining the content of training and the beneficiaries (ibid.).

The proportion of the total payroll allocated by companies to training has increased from 2.97 per cent in 1989, to 3.2 per cent in 1991 and 3.7 per cent in 1994. The amount allocated has been consistently above the legal requirement (Atchoarena, 1993: 7; Caspar, 1992: 26; interview, Ministry of Work, Employment and Professional Continuing Education, 1994). There are large disparities according to company size and category of worker. The 390 very large companies (over 2,000 employees) spend on average 4.68 per cent of their wage bill on training, while those 1,770 companies employing above 500 and below 2,000 spend 2.91 per cent (Caspar, 1992: 26). Small companies experience difficulties in formulating training policies and in allowing their workers to undertake training; for example, 37,920 companies with 20 to 49 employees spend 1.44 per cent of their payrolls on training (ibid. and Atchoarena, 1993: 7). Also, there are inequalities according to occupation, as continuing education still favours people with a high educational level (Atchoarena, 1993: 7).

In evaluating the French approach, the importance of the social partnership must be stressed. If one side of the partnership has a lesser role, as with the unions in Britain, it is hard to see the training levy system being transplanted successfully. It must also be taken into account that the system has other features (notably paid educational leave) that are integral to its functioning.

Germany's Corporatist Model

In the search for international models to emulate, Germany stands out as a success. It is cited regularly as a model in the development of national training systems. Australia and Britain have both drawn on German experience in formulating policy. Lane (1990) identifies lessons for Britain from vocational training and new production concepts in Germany. Compared with Germany, Lane (ibid.: 256) considers that 'the institutional framework of British society continues to impede the widespread adoption of sound training policy'. In a recent study Oulton (1993) set out to see whether the UK's poor performance in manufactured trade compared with Germany's can be explained by the UK's well-known and well-documented skills deficiencies. Evidence was found that the UK's skill deficiencies influence the volume, but not the quality of exports (ibid.: 27). In comparing productivity levels in British and German manufacturing industry, O'Mahony (1992: 54) acknowledges the difficulties of estimating differences in levels of physical capital and to compare qualification levels across countries.

Whereas in Australia and Britain it has been difficult to get employers to increase their commitment to training, Germany has strong employer involvement. Its VET system is regarded by many industrialised countries as a source of competitive advantage (Randlesome, 1990: 14). In the late 1980s it was estimated that the German training system produced about seven times as many formally qualified foremen as the British system (Prais and Wagner, 1988: 34). German labour costs are among the highest in Europe, emphasising the need to achieve a high level of efficiency. NIESR case studies show that German productivity is linked to strong vocational skills among the labour force (Wagner, 1991: 132).

A major advantage of the German VET system is that there is a high degree of consensus in decision-making. This is admittedly time-consuming, but all points of view are represented (interview, Chamber of Industry and Commerce, Frankfurt, 1994; interview, Chamber of Crafts, Munich, 1994). Roles are clearly defined and well established, so that there is widespread understanding of how the system operates.

In Germany there is an element of voluntarism, as no company is obliged to provide training and no young person is obliged to undergo training. Investment in training takes place, according to official rhetoric, to provide for their own need for a skilled workforce and as a means of increasing their own performance and competitiveness (BMBW, 1993: 24). This suggests reliance on the market mechanism. Adaptation of the training capacity of the dual system is largely left to the self-regulatory mechanisms of the training market (Koch and Reuling, 1994: 76). The decisions of individual companies make up both the aggregate demand for skills and the aggregate supply of trainee vacancies (Reichel, no date: 11).

Government regulation plays a strong role. The Vocational Training Act 1969 is pivotal to the operation of the system. It regulates initial vocational training, further training and vocational retraining. An important aspect is that the position of trade associations and chambers of commerce and industry, and craft is confirmed by legislation. No business can operate without being a paid-up member of the appropriate chamber. The chambers are financed by compulsory members' fees. The central government uses various instruments to influence the decisions of individual training enterprises, including the legally binding standard for major facets of training quality (Koch and Reuling, 1994: 101).

The role of the chambers is far greater than their counterparts in Australia or Britain. Their legal duty is the counselling, control and recognition of vocational education in the region – they register training contracts, set up examination boards, and decide on individual regulations to meet regional demand. Chambers supervise training and ensure that regulations are carried out and determine whether a company is competent to train and register trainers (interview, Chamber of Industry and Commerce, Munich, 1994). However, they do not undertake training – this is the responsibility of the training companies. Is this the missing institutional link for Australia and Britain?

The transplantation of the dual system requires many factors, including a legislative framework, companies being prepared to fund the main part of training, and the cooperation of trade unions (interview, 1994). In addition, the states (*Lander*) have a key role in planning and financing vocational education, corresponding to local need (Lane, 1992: 66). Even if these elements could be replicated in Britain or Australia, there would be other issues to be resolved. Leaving aside the pros and cons, Australia appears to be moving gradually to a more deregulated labour market and Britain has already gone down this path. In contrast, the German VET system requires a highly regulated labour market (Shackleton, 1992: 47). Furthermore, there is a strong tradition of industrial democracy operating through works councils (Randlesome, 1990: 14).

Germany remains an international benchmark for industry training policies and practice. Nevertheless, there are stresses and strains evident and an open acknowledgement that some reform may be necessary. As a government report expresses it, 'more and more people in Germany are warning against erroneous developments in vocational education' (BMBW, 1993: 7). There has been a shift in demand from vocational education to higher education and there are signs that the trend towards seeking academic qualifications will continue (ibid., and interview, 1994). More fundamentally, the dual system is being criticised because it is failing to respond to workplace changes. The system produces a surplus of skilled blue-collar workers, but fails to provide workers with more sophisticated computer knowledge and the flexibility to switch from one kind of work to another (*The Economist*, 1994: 26). Furthermore, there is uncertainty about whether future challenges can be met by adjustments to the vocational training system or whether structural reform will be necessary (Koch and Reuling, 1994: 121). The integration of the new federal states into the economy and the vocational training system will be a challenge for many years. It is difficult at present to assess where the system is heading and to evaluate the importance of emerging trends for other systems. If the dual system loses the confidence of employers, its appeal as a guide to other countries will be reduced.

Australia's Training Levy Experiment

Like Britain, Australia has revamped its training system in recent years. An important goal is to try to find a balance between intervention and market forces. Australia provides 'a training culture' (Beresford and Gaite, 1994). These comments were confirmed by an ABS [Australian Bureau of Statistics] study that reported an increase in the time and cost of keeping training records as a result of the TGA by more than half of the employers who were above the threshold (ABS, 1994: 18). Another submission to the Senate enquiry expressed the view that it is doubtful if the TGA is the most appropriate way of encouraging training in the longer term, concluding that 'further productivity gains from a compulsory system may be slight' (Noble, 1994: 1). At the same time, the government apparently failed to consider the factors, including opposition from the small business sector, that led Britain to abandon its training levy. An alternative approach was proposed by the government's Economic Planning Advisory Council, allowing industry organisations to levy member firms, and provide generic training to their employees. Firms would minimise the risk of losing the benefits of their training expenditure, as all members would participate and employees learn relevant and portable skills (Clare and Johnston, 1993: 75–6).

The decision to suspend the Training Guarantee Act for two years from July 1994 was taken after considerable debate. A bill amending the legislation was introduced in 1993, designed to minimise compliance costs and give greater flexibility to the scheme. A Senate standing committee on employment, education and training considered a range of comments on the bill and recommended that it be passed without amendment (Parliament of the Commonwealth of Australia, 1994: 6). Despite this endorsement, the government announced in its *Working Nation* white paper that the scheme would be suspended 'in the light of the commitment by industry to meet its training obligations over the past few years.' It further promised to abolish the training levy altogether if business showed a 'credible commitment' to increasing substantially the level of training places (Commonwealth of Australia, 1994: 103). Two years after the suspension of the TGA was announced, there is little expectation that it will be revived. There has been a call by a coalition of peak community groups for a training levy to be imposed by employers who do not offer trainee-ships to the unemployed (The *Australian*, 2 May 1995: 2), but it seems unlikely that this will be supported by the government.

It is hardly surprising that the TGA failed to become institutionalised. The government did not convince the business community of the desirability of the levy before or after its introduction. Constant criticism in the financial press and even from its own advisory body (the Economic Planning Advisory Council) meant that the levy had little chance of surviving. Had comparative evidence been explored, there is every possibility that the government would have been spared the wrath of business interests. The Australian experience does not help the case for reintroducing a training levy in Britain. To conclude, by opting to rely on reforms to the training system and incentives to employers to provide training places, the Australian government has moved closer to the British than to the French model.

Britain's Experience

Britain's experience must be considered in detail to complete the compara-tive picture. A statutory levy was introduced in 1964 and industrial training boards (ITBs) were established in the major industries and empowered to impose a levy/grant system on employers. The system involved employers paying a levy on payroll tax, the size of which varied between industries. Grants were paid to firms achieving acceptable volumes and levels of training (Keep, 1989: 187). Many smaller firms had grievances with the levy/grant system because, although paying the levy, they did not benefit from grants (Sheldrake and Vickerstaff, 1987: 37). Other criticisms related to the type of training promoted by the scheme. Some firms became preoccupied with trying to maximise their grant and engaged in training designed to meet the general standard requirements of an ITB rather than their own particular needs (Ziderman, 1978: 46).

The system was reviewed in 1973. ITBs were empowered to give exemp-tion from levy payments to employers who demonstrated that they were training for their own requirements. These arrangements continued until 1981 when the Conservative government engineered an abrupt shift to a voluntaristic training system. The levy/grant/exemption system was abolished along with all but six of the ITBs (Keep, 1989: 188).

Those in favour of a training levy argue that exhortation to train is insufficient. The TUC sees the need for a levy to address the problem that the British economy is 'trapped in a low skills equilibrium underpinned by a voluntary training system'. It proposes a national statutory minimum levy paid by companies, underpinned by collective bargaining. Some of the levy income might be pooled to help fund craft training centres, similar to the German chamber system. The TUC acknowledges that it does not want to go back to the old system administered by industry training boards, since this did not meet the needs of young women and the adult workforce, or of small and medium-sized enterprises (Clough, 1994: 10–11). A further argument in favour is that the imposition of a training levy has the effect of discouraging poaching within and across industries (Chapman, 1993: 103).

There is greater support for a training levy among the TECs than from the Industry Training Organisations and representative bodies of employers. A 1993 *Financial Times* survey of TEC directors showed that 40 per cent supported a training levy (cited by Keep and Mayhew, 1994: 17). More recently, the TUC consultation exercise found that trade unions and TECs are generally in favour of a modern training levy, while support by industry training organisations and 'key national players' including the Confederation of British Industry (CBI) is relatively low (Corney, 1995: 14). The CBI training survey conducted with its membership found that 76 per cent of respondents are opposed to the idea of a training levy, of which 61 per cent are against any form of compulsion. The introduction of a levy, or its retention where it already operates, is supported by 23 per cent (Corney, 1995: 91).

The CBI has argued in favour of a voluntary approach by which employers train in order to meet business objectives, and market mechanisms operate to balance the supply and demand for training. Government intervention is only required where there is market failure; for example, in the case of the long-term unemployed. In line with this approach, the CBI considers that it should be left to industry bodies to decide if they wish some degree of compulsion and regulation. It notes that the construction and engineering sectors have found that adequate training provision is particularly difficult to secure without a levy system (CBI, 1994: para. 168). In regard to the provision of training for part-time or casual workers ('flexible workers'), the CBI survey gave a low ranking to a training levy as an option to stimulate employer investment (ibid.: para. 167).

The TUC is a strong advocate of a modern training levy. It considers that under-investment in training is one of the weaknesses of the voluntary system. A levy system can help to ensure that organisations which do not train their workers make a fair contribution to the training of the workforce, and rewards those companies which invest in transferable skills. The TUC recommends the introduction of a levy to be collected centrally, of which part could be disbursed by a national skills fund. This would help develop and maintain national standards through sectors and national bodies, address skill shortages and support innovations. The rest of the levy funding could be remissible and paid back to companies on evidence of investment in their workforce. Exemption from the levy could be based on an enhanced Investors in People standard or other criteria to be determined.

Conclusions

What conclusions can the policy maker draw from these comparisons?

The comparative analysis shows that if one country has a lower level of training expenditure and poorer productivity than another, a training levy will not necessarily be an effective solution. A levy may not be able to target problem areas such as insufficient training for small and medium-sized enterprises or industries which invest less in training than others. Additional administrative costs may be imposed on business in meeting statutory requirements and this may impact heavily on small business.

The issue of a training levy cannot be seen in isolation from the broader question of labour market regulation. Where market failure occurs, intervention is justified; for example, there may be inadequate provision of training for part-time or casual workers if left to the market. However, even in these cases it is important to weigh the costs and benefits of different types of government intervention.

There is a big difference between learning from another country's experience and trying to copy the whole or part of an overseas system (Keep, 1992: 32). This is an obvious point, but one easily and frequently overlooked in policy formulation. Comparative analysis, if handled carefully, can be a useful means of reviewing policies, monitoring performance and identifying future trends. After all, how is a government to judge whether its industry training policies are successful unless it is prepared to look at what its competitors are doing? While it may be inappropriate to transplant another country's institutions or policies, a critical examination of training policies may be sharpened by reference to alternative systems. A parallel is provided by Britain's near obsession with Germany's economic performance that has prompted a careful analysis of that country's vocational education and training system. In general, policy development and implementation may be better informed if the similarities and differences of comparable systems are studied in detail. In conducting such studies it is essential that comparisons are exposed to critical scrutiny. It is always possible to find something to copy – effective policy formulation requires that the system being copied is transferable to a new situation without undue impediments.

If an interventionist approach is to succeed, it may be desirable for the social partners to be consulted over policy changes. The experience of France in particular points to the need to have the support of the business community in implementing a levy. Trade union support is also desirable, as with France and Germany. Acceptance of the need for consultation is far from universal and strong arguments may be advanced against it being the basis of policy formulation.

The recent experience suggests a need to look for alternatives to levies to improve the efficiency and effectiveness of training. It is more likely that a combination of programmes to support training initiatives of enterprises and institutional arrangements to facilitate employer involvement will work in the long-term. There is a case for industry-specific initiatives to tackle issues or problems experienced by particular sectors. Also, training in small and medium enterprises needs to be addressed as a separate issue.

One of the lessons of comparative analysis of training strategies is that it may be more important to aim for some stability in institutions so that users can develop some confidence that they know how to operate. For example, Germany's dual system is well established and well accepted. Institutions need to change to reflect emerging needs and issues, but the frequent restructuring of institutions may confuse the groups they are meant to help.

References

Atchoarena, D. (1993) *Profile and Trends of Continuing Education in France, with Special Reference to Company Training and Higher Education Institutions.* International Institute for Educational Planning. Paris: UNESCO.

Australian Bureau of Statistics (ABS) (1994) *Employer Training Practices: Australia, 1994.* Canberra: Australian Bureau of Statistics.

Australian, The (1995) 'Community groups set up push for training levy', 2 May: 2.

Beresford, K. and Gaite, J. (1994) 'Comment and advice to the Senate committee on the Training Guarantee (Administration) Amendment Bill 1993 with particular reference to small business'. *Report on the Training Guarantee (Administration) Amendment Bill 1993.* Canberra: Australian Parliament.

Blachere, M. (1992) 'The French system of vocational training', in D. Atchoarena (ed.), *Lifelong Education in Selected Industrialised Countries.* Paris: International Institute for Educational Planning.

BMBW (Federal Ministry of Education and Science) (1993) *Report on Vocational Education 1993.* Bonn.

Caspar, P. (1992) 'Lifelong education in France', in D. Atchoarena (ed.), *Lifelong Education in Selected Industrialised Countries.* Paris: International Institute for Educational Planning.

Chapman, P.G. (1993) *The Economics of Training.* Hemel Hempstead: Harvester Wheatsheaf.

Clare, R. and Johnston, K. (1993) *Education and Training in the 1990s.* Canberra: Economic Planning Advisory Council.

Clough, B. (1994) 'The case for a training levy', *Employee Development Bulletin*, 60: 10–11.

Commonwealth of Australia (1994) *Working Nation: Policies and Programs.* Canberra: AGPS.

Confederation of British Industry (1994) *Flexible Labour Markets. Who Pays for Training?* London: CBI.

Corney, M. (1995) *The CBI Training Survey. A New Partnership for Company Training: The TUC Consultation Exercise.* Kent: MC Consultancy.

Department of Employment (1989) *Training in Britain: A Study of Funding, Activity and Attitudes. The Main Report.* London: HMSO.

Economist, The (1994) 'Education in Germany: the next generation', 20 August: 26.

Employee Development Bulletin (1995) 'CBI rejects call for compulsory levy', February: 10.

Gordon, C. (1990) 'The business culture in France', in C. Randlesome, W. Bierley, K. Burton, C. Gordon and P. King (eds), *Business Culture in Europe.* Oxford: Heinemann.

Goyder, M. (1994) 'Review: reliving goals over a bottle of beer', *The Independent*, 10 August.

Incomes Data Services Ltd (1994a) 'Social partners amend national training agreement', *IDS European Report 392*, August.

Incomes Data Services Ltd (1994b) 'IDS country profile: France', *IDS European Report 393*, September.

Keep, E. (1989) 'A training scandal?', in K. Sisson (ed.), *Personnel Management in Britain*. Oxford: Basil Blackwell.

Keep, E. (1992) 'The grass looked greener – some thoughts on the influence of comparative vocational training research on the UK policy debate', in P. Ryan (ed.), *International Comparisons of Vocational Education and Training for Intermediate Skills*. London: Falmer Press.

Keep, E. and Mayhew, K. (1994) 'Training policy for competitiveness – time for a fresh perspective'. Paper presented to the Policy Studies Institute conference on training, December.

Koch, R. and Reuling, J. (1994) 'The responsiveness and regulation of training capacity and quality', *Vocational Training in Germany: Modernisation and Responsiveness*. Paris: OECD.

Lane, C. (1990) 'Vocational training and new production concepts in Germany: some lessons for Britain', *Industrial Relations Journal*, 2 (4): 247–59.

Lane, C. (1992) 'European business systems: Britain and Germany compared', in R. Whitely (ed.), *European Business Systems: Firms and Markets in their National Contexts*. London: Sage.

Marsden, D. and Ryan, P. (1992) 'Initial training, labour market structure and public policy: intermediate skills in British and German industry', in P. Ryan (ed.), *International Comparisons of Vocational Education and Training for Intermediate Skills*. London: Falmer Press.

Mason, G., van Ark, B. and Wagner, K. (1994) *Productivity, Product Quality and Workforce Skills: Food Processing in Four European Countries*. Discussion paper no. 34. London: NIESR.

Mason, G. and Wagner, K. (1994) 'Innovation and the skill mix: chemicals and engineering in Britain and Germany', *National Institute Economic Review*, May: 61–72.

Noble, C. (1994) 'Submission to the Senate standing committee on employment, education and training', *Report on the Training Guarantee (Administration) Amendment Bill 1993*. Canberra: Parliament of the Commonwealth of Australia.

O'Mahony, M. (1992) 'Productivity levels in British and German manufacturing industry', *National Institute Economic Review*, February: 46–58.

OECD (1991) 'Labour markets in dynamic ASEAN economies', *Employment Outlook 1991*. Paris: OECD.

OECD (1993) *Industry Training in Australia, Sweden and the United States*. Paris: OECD.

Oulton, N. (1993) *Workforce Skills and Export Competitiveness: An Anglo German Comparison*. London: NIESR.

Parliament of the Commonwealth of Australia (1994) *Report on the Training Guarantee (Administration) Bill*. Canberra: Senate standing committee on employment, education and training.

Prais, S.J. (1993) *Economic Performance and Education: The Nature of Britain's Deficiencies*. Discussion paper no. 52. London: NIESR.

Prais, S.J. and Wagner, K. (1988) 'Productivity and management: the training of foremen in Britain and Germany', *National Institute Economic Review*, February: 34–43.

Raffe, D. (1992) 'Scotland v England: the place of "home internationals" in comparative research', in P. Ryan (ed.), *International Comparisons of Vocational Education and Training for Intermediate Skills*. London: Falmer Press.

Randlesome, C. (1990) 'The business culture in West Germany', in C. Randlesome, W. Bierley, K. Burton, C. Gordon and P. King (eds), *Business Cultures in Europe*. Oxford: Heinemann.

Reichel, M. (no date) *The System of Dual Training in the FRG*. Munich: Chamber of Industry and Commerce.

Ryan, P. (ed.) (1991) *International Comparisons of Vocational Education and Training for Intermediate Skills*. London: Falmer Press.

Shackleton, J.R. (1992) *Training Too Much? A Sceptical Look at the Economics of Skill Provision in the UK (Hobart Paper 118)*. London: Institute of Economic Affairs.

Sheldrake, J. and Vickerstaff, S. (1987) *The History of Industrial Training in Britain*. Aldershot: Avebury.

Steedman, H., Mason, G. and Wagner, K. (1991) 'Intermediate skills in the workplace: deployment, standards and supply in Britain, France and Germany', *National Institute Economic Review*, May: 60–73.

Wagner, K. (1991) 'Training efforts and industrial efficiency in West Germany', in J. Stevens and R. Mackay (eds), *Training and Competitiveness*. London: Kogan Page.

Whitley, R. (1992) 'The comparative study of business systems in Europe: issues and choices', in R. Whitley (ed.), *European Business Systems: Firms and Markets in their National Contexts*. London: Sage.

Ziderman, A. (1978) *Manpower Training: Theory and Policy*. London: Macmillan.

Part II

HUMAN RESOURCE MANAGEMENT AND BUSINESS PERFORMANCE

The five chapters in this section are all concerned with the connection between the adoption of HR strategies/policies and a firm's performance. Those by Huselid and Mueller take an organizational view in seeking to explain the impact or lack of impact of organizational HR systems upon competitive performance; they typify different parts of a literature anxious to demonstrate the commercial possibilities of wisely managed human resources. The focus of the chapters by Newton and Findlay and Storey and Sisson is quite different: they explore two specific and increasingly popular HR practices aimed at improving performance, appraisal and performance-related pay respectively, in order to develop a better understanding of the theoretical and empirical issues associated with managing performance in organizations.

In many ways the chapter by Mark Huselid is not in keeping with others in this volume. It describes an hypothesis-driven piece of empirical research, reporting in detail the statistical results, their significance and their implications for HR practice. Yet it is for these reasons that we have included it here, representing as it does, an early and influential example of a genre of writing dedicated to demonstrating the strategic contribution of SHRM to organization performance. Following a decade of academics postulating the value of linking human resource and business objectives, and debates about the relative merits of best-fit and best-practice HR systems, Huselid is keen to put the various claims to the test. As his independent variable he deliberately chooses a collection of HR practices (which he terms high performance work practices) as against single HR measures, and his dependent variables include both intermediary employment outcomes (turnover and productivity) as well as the financial performance of the firms in the sample. If not the first of its kind, this study is nevertheless among the more comprehensive and ambitious in its scope. And the reported results are, if taken at face value, good news for HR directors battling in their boardrooms for resources and recognition. It has to be said that, although more sophisticated than previous attempts, some of the questionnaire items connoting high performance work practices are still highly instrumental. In other words, *the way in which* various HR policies are derived and managed is probably a more accurate gauge of their effectiveness than the fact that, for example, employment tests are used in recruitment as an indication of enlightened 'employee skills and organizational structures', or the proportion of the workforce participating in formal appraisals as a measure of 'employee motivation'.

It is this issue of process, rather than practice *per se*, that is taken up by the other writers in this section. Each comes at it from a different angle. Tim Newton and Patricia Findlay wish to 're-direct empirical investigations' on appraisals by highlighting the insights and shortcomings of the conceptual frameworks that have hitherto guided research in this area. So, drawing on labour process theory and Foucauldian perspectives, the notion that performance appraisal affords an opportunity for employer and employee to participate in performance discussions that benefit both parties is largely discredited. The authors urge that greater attention be given to the wider context of appraisal (given that appraising is a constant and multi-faceted activity) and to the neglected subjective experience of appraisal (given that individuals interpret and respond very differently to the same appraisal procedures). John Storey and Keith Sisson, in this extract from their book on human resources and industrial relations, consider the HR policy of performance-related pay. Their starting point is the 'significant gap between assumptions and reality in those many organizations which have introduced PRP'. Unlike the more theoretical analysis of Newton and Findlay, the focus here is upon the more pragmatic issues of implementing PRP. Thus, the internal contradiction of PRP where organizations are seeking to encourage teamworking, the confusion of motives for introducing PRP, the problem of differing perceptions of fairness and the time-lag between prescription and practice are all cited as impediments to the effective adoption of performance-related reward systems. It is not that the piece is atheoretical (implicit reference is made to expectancy theory, for instance), rather that it chooses primarily survey-based data to spotlight ill-judged and flawed managerial thinking.

Both chapters problematize performance management in organizations. While Newton and Findlay draw attention to conceptual inadequacies underpinning performance appraisals, Storey and Sisson assemble a range of more practical stumbling-blocks to the 'simple' management of performance via rewards. In contrast, Rosenthal et al. report enhanced performance (in terms of actions and attitudes) amongst retail staff in their study which assesses the outcomes of a quality programme, comprising a number of discrete HR policies and practices. The authors find little evidence for 'sham empowerment, work intensification and increased surveillance'. On the contrary, their study finds that a majority of the employees endorse the quality programme and a half say that they engage in the sort of behaviours required by the increased focus of customers. To them, the quality initiative made sense and they were prepared to commit themselves to it in practice. In his chapter, Frank Mueller lifts our sights back up from specific HR interventions to the overall synergistic impact of strategic human resource management (SHRM) upon the overall financial performance of the organization. However, he is less optimistic than Huselid that such a relationship automatically follows. For many of the reasons explored by Newton and Findlay and Storey and Sisson, Mueller is sceptical that enlightened HR practices will necessarily be translated into competitive superiority. If it was as simple as this, imitation of best practice and erosion of market dominance would surely swiftly follow? He specifies a number of more subtle conditions which are necessary for human resources to become 'strategic assets'. Essentially, these concern the social architecture of an organization which builds up over the long term, encompassing the less planned and intentional processes of skill formation, tacit knowledge and spontaneous cooperation. In passing, Mueller notes the 'little evidence for stating a *direct* link between SHRM on the one hand and a firm's performance on the other'. It would seem that the study by Huselid, since followed by others in the same robust ilk, to some extent answers this call for evidence. Conversely, the shortcomings of the Huselid approach noted above, particularly the emphasis on examples of HR practices, at the expense of a real understanding of the socio-political processes invested in such practices, are extensively addressed by Mueller's evolutionary approach to strategic human resources. Between them, these five chapters succeed in demonstrating more fully the potential contribution of SHRM to business performance, while pointing out the considerable (and, for some, insurmountable) difficulties in first seeking, then achieving such a link.

7   The Impact of Human Resource Management Practices on Turnover, Productivity, and Corporate Financial Performance

Mark A. Huselid

The impact of human resource management (HRM) policies and practices on firm performance is an important topic in the fields of human resource management, industrial relations, and industrial and organizational psychology (Boudreau, 1991; Jones and Wright, 1992; Kleiner, 1990). An increasing body of work contains the argument that the use of *High Performance Work Practices*, including comprehensive employee recruitment and selection procedures, incentive compensation and performance management systems, and extensive employee involvement and training, can improve the knowledge, skills, and abilities of a firm's current and potential employees, increase their motivation, reduce shirking, and enhance retention of quality employees while encouraging nonperformers to leave the firm (Jones and Wright, 1992; US Department of Labor, 1993).

Arguments made in related research are that a firm's current and potential human resources are important considerations in the development and execution of its strategic business plan. This literature, although largely conceptual, concludes that human resource management practices can help to create a source of sustained competitive advantage, especially when they are aligned with a firm's competitive strategy (Begin, 1991; Butler et al., 1991; Cappelli and Singh, 1992; Jackson and Schuler, 1995; Porter, 1985; Schuler, 1992; Wright and McMahan, 1992).

In both this largely theoretical literature and the emerging conventional wisdom among human resource professionals there is a growing consensus that organizational human resource policies can, if properly configured, provide a direct and economically significant contribution to firm performance. The presumption is that more effective *systems* of HRM practices, which simultaneously exploit the potential for complementarities or

Originally published in *Academy of Management Journal*, 38 (3), 1995: 635–72 (abridged).

synergies among such practices and help to implement a firm's competitive strategy, are sources of sustained competitive advantage. Unfortunately, very little empirical evidence supports such a belief. What empirical work does exist has largely focused on individual HRM practices to the exclusion of overall HRM systems.

This study departs from the previous human resources literature in three ways. First, the level of analysis used to estimate the firm-level impact of HRM practices is the system, and the perspective is strategic rather than functional. This approach is supported by the development and validation of an instrument that reflects the system of High Performance Work Practices adopted by each firm studied. Secondly, the analytical focus is comprehensive. The dependent variables include both intermediate employment outcomes and firm-level measures of financial performance, and the results are based on a national sample of firms drawn from a wide range of industries. Moreover, the analyses explicitly address two methodological problems confronting survey-based research on this topic: the potential for simultaneity, or reverse causality, between High Performance Work Practices and firm performance and survey response bias. Thirdly, this study also provides one of the first tests of the prediction that the impact of High Performance Work Practices on firm performance is contingent on both the degree of complementarity, or internal fit, among these practices and the degree of alignment, or external fit, between a firm's system of such practices and its competitive strategy.

Theoretical Background

Limitations of the Prior Empirical Work

Prior empirical work has consistently found that use of effective human resource management practices enhances firm performance. Specifically, extensive recruitment, selection, and training procedures; formal information sharing, attitude assessment, job design, grievance procedures, and labor-management participation programs; and performance appraisal, promotion, and incentive compensation systems that recognize and reward employee merit have all been widely linked with valued firm-level outcomes. These policies and procedures have been labeled High Performance Work Practices (US Department of Labor, 1993), a designation I adopt here.

However, if this line of research is to be advanced, several serious limitations in the prior empirical work have to be addressed. Two are methodological, and one involves both conceptual and measurement issues. The first issue concerns the potential simultaneity between High Performance Work Practices and corporate financial performance, a problem exacerbated by the prevalence of cross-sectional data in this line of research.

For example, if higher-performing firms are systematically more likely to adopt High Performance Work Practices, then contemporaneous estimates of the impact of these practices on firm performance will be overstated.

A second methodological problem is related to the widespread collection of data via questionnaire. Because survey respondents generally self-select into samples, selectivity or response bias may also affect results.

Systems of HRM *practices and the concept of fit.* The third significant limitation of prior work is its widespread conceptual focus on single High Perform-ance Work Practices, and the measurement problems inherent in broad-ening the focus to a system of such practices. A focus on individual practices presents both theoretical and methodological dilemmas, as both recent research (Arthur, 1992; MacDuffie, 1995; Osterman, 1987, 1994) and con-ventional wisdom would predict that firms adopting High Performance Work Practices in one area are more likely to use them in other areas as well. Therefore, to the extent that any single example reflects a firm's wider propensity to invest in High Performance Work Practices, any estimates of the firm-level impact of the particular practice will be upwardly biased. This likely bias presents a significant limitation for a line of research that attempts to estimate the firm-level impact of a firm's entire human resources function, as the sum of these individual estimates may dramatically over-state their contribution to firm performance.

[. . .]

In short, although a growing empirical literature focuses generally on the impact of High Performance Work Practices, prior work has been limited in terms of the range of practices evaluated, the dependent variables, and the industry context. For example, a finding that systems of work practices affect turnover or productivity does not necessarily mean that these practices have any effect on firm profits, and the discovery that systems of High Performance Work Practices affect profitability begs the important issue of the processes through which they influence firm financial perform-ance. Therefore, unlike prior work, this study included the full range of organizational human resource practices, examined those practices in terms of their impact on both immediate employment outcomes and corporate financial performance, and did so within the context of a broad range of industries and firm sizes. My initial summary hypotheses can be stated as follows:

> *Hypothesis 1a: Systems of High Performance Work Practices will diminish employee turnover and increase productivity and corporate financial performance.*

> *Hypothesis 1b: Employee turnover and productivity will mediate the relationship between systems of High Performance Work Practices and corporate financial performance.*

The second hypothesis will allow for one of the first empirical tests of a diverse theoretical literature positing the importance to firm performance of synergies and fit among human resource practices as well as between those practices and competitive strategy (Milgrom and Roberts, 1993). Baird and Meshoulam (1988) described the first of these complementarities as internal fit. Their primary proposition was that firm performance will be enhanced to the degree that firms adopt human resource management practices that complement and support each another. Thus,

> *Hypothesis 2: Complementarities or synergies among High Performance Work Practices will diminish employee turnover and increase productivity and corporate financial performance.*

A second form of complementarity, Baird and Meshoulam's (1988) external fit, occurs at the intersection of a firm's system of HRM practices and its competitive strategy. The notion that firm performance will be enhanced by alignment of HRM practices with competitive strategy has gained considerable currency in recent years and in fact underlies much of the recent scholarship in the field (Begin, 1991; Butler et al., 1991; Cappelli and Singh, 1992; Jackson and Schuler, 1995; Schuler, 1992; Wright and McMahan, 1992). Although no empirical work has suggested that firms with better external fit exhibit higher performance, the expectation that they should provides my final hypothesis:

> *Hypothesis 3: Alignment of a firm's system of High Performance Work Practices with its competitive strategy will diminish employee turnover and increase productivity and corporate financial performance.*

Fit versus 'Best Practices'

The internal fit perspective suggests that the adoption of an internally consistent system of High Performance Work Practices will be reflected in better firm performance, *ceteris paribus*: it should be possible to identify the best HRM practices, those whose adoption generally leads to valued firm-level outcomes. The external fit perspective raises the conceptual issue of whether any particular human resources policy can be described as a best practice, or whether, instead, the efficacy of any practices can only be determined in the context of a particular firm's strategic and environmental contingencies. Although prior work has yet to provide a direct test of these competing hypotheses, recent research finding strong main effects for the adoption of High Performance Work Practices lends credence to the best practices viewpoint.

The argument that firm performance will be enhanced to the degree a firm's HRM practices are matched with its competitive strategy is, however, compelling. In fact, the internal and external fit hypotheses may not be altogether inconsistent: all else being equal, the use of High Performance Work Practices and good internal fit should lead to positive outcomes for all types of firms. However, at the margin, firms that tailor their work practices to their particular strategic and environmental contingencies should be able to realize additional performance gains. For example, most firms should benefit from the use of formal selection tests, although the results of such tests could be used to select very different types of people, with those differences perhaps depending on competitive strategy. Likewise, the use of formal performance appraisal and incentive compensation systems has been widely found to enhance firm performance. However, each of these practices can be used to elicit very different types of behaviors from employees. In short, the process of linking environmental contingencies with HRM practices may vary across firms, but the tools firms use to effectively manage such links are likely to be consistent. The issue of whether internal, external, or both types of fit affect firm performance is central, and later in this chapter I provide an explicit test of these hypotheses.

Methods

Sample and Data Collection

A study of this type presents a number of data collection challenges. It requires as broad a sample as possible and at the same time requires that each data point provide comprehensive information on both organizational human resource practices and strategies and firm-level performance. Thus, my sample was drawn from Compact Disclosure, a database containing comprehensive financial information from 10-K reports[1] on nearly 12,000 publicly held US firms. Firms were included in the sample if they had more than a hundred employees and excluded if they were foreign-owned, holding companies, or publicly held divisions or business units of larger firms. These criteria yielded 3,452 firms representing all major industries.

Firm-level data on High Performance Work Practices were collected with a questionnaire mailed to the senior human resources professional in each firm.

Measurement of High Performance Work Practices

[. . .] Thirteen items broadly represent the domain of High Performance Work Practices identified in prior work (US Department of Labor, 1993). These items also represent important choice variables on which many firms differ significantly (Delaney et al., 1989). However, the substantial conceptual and empirical overlap among these items and my desire to adopt a systems perspective make determination of the independent contribution of each practice to firm performance impractical. Therefore, to uncover the underlying factor structure associated with these practices, I factor-

TABLE 7.1 *Factor structure of High Performance Work Practices*

Questionnaire Item	1	2	Alpha
Employee skills and organizational structures			.67
What is the proportion of the workforce who are included in a formal information sharing program (e.g., a newsletter)?	.54	.02	
What is the proportion of the workforce whose job has been subjected to a formal job analysis?	.53	.18	
What proportion of nonentry level jobs have been filled from within in recent years?	.52	−.36	
What is the proportion of the workforce who are administered attitude surveys on a regular basis?	.52	−.07	
What is the proportion of the workforce who participate in Quality of Work Life (QWL) programs, Quality Circles (QC), and/or labor–management participation teams?	.50	−.04	
What is the proportion of the workforce who have access to company incentive plans, profit-sharing plans, and/or gain-sharing plans?	.39	.17	
What is the average number of hours of training received by a typical employee over the last 12 months?	.37	−.07	
What is the proportion of the workforce who have access to a formal grievance procedure and/or complaint resolution system?	.36	.13	
What proportion of the workforce is administered an employment test prior to hiring?	.32	−.04	
Employee motivation			.66
What is the proportion of the workforce whose performance appraisals are used to determine their compensation?	.17	.83	
What proportion of the workforce receives formal performance appraisals?	.29	.80	
Which of the following promotion decision rules do you use most often? (a) merit or performance rating alone; (b) seniority only if merit is equal; (c) seniority among employees who meet a minimum merit requirement; (d) seniority.	−.07	.56	
For the five positions that your firm hires most frequently, how many qualified applicants do you have per position (on average)?	−.15	.27	
Eigenvalue	2.19	1.76	
Proportion of variance accounted for	16.80	13.60	

analyzed each item's standard score, using principal component extraction with varimax rotation. Two factors emerged from these analyses; and I constructed a scale for each by averaging the questions loading unambiguously at .30 or greater on a single factor. Table 7.1 shows these results and the questionnaire items.

Following Bailey (1993), I named the first factor 'employee skills and organizational structures'. This factor includes a broad range of practices intended to enhance employees' knowledge, skills, and abilities and thereafter provide a mechanism through which employees can use those attributes in performing their roles. Specifically, a formal job design program and enhanced selectivity will help ensure employee–job fit, and providing formal training will enhance the knowledge, skills, and abilities of both new and old employees. Quality of work life programs, quality circles, and labor–management teams are all forms of participation that allow employees to have direct input into the production process. Likewise, information-sharing programs, formal grievance procedures, and profit- and gain-sharing plans help to increase the probability that employee participation efforts will be effective because such programs provide a formal mechanism for employer–employee communication on work-related issues. The Cronbach's alpha for this scale was .67.

The second factor, which I named 'employee motivation' (Bailey, 1993), is composed of a more narrowly focused set of High Performance Work Practices designed to recognize and reinforce desired employee behaviors. These practices include using formal performance appraisals, linking those appraisals tightly with employee compensation, and focusing on employee merit in promotion decisions. Conceptually, core competencies among employees are developed through selection, training, and the design of work (factor 1, employee skills and organizational structures) and are subsequently reinforced through the second factor, employee motivation. The Cronbach's alpha for the employee motivation scale was .66.

[. . .]

Measurement of Internal and External Fit

Despite prior work arguing that enhanced internal and external fit will enhance firm performance, the relevant research has not specified the functional form that fit can be expected to take. In the business strategy literature, however, Venkatraman (1989) concluded that fit is most commonly measured in terms of a moderated relationship, or interaction, between two variables. For example, the relationship between a firm's competitive strategy and its performance could co-vary with the type of environment in which it operates. A second category of fit that is relevant in this context is the degree of match between two variables. Fit as matching differs from fit as moderation in that an explicit external performance criterion is lacking (Venkatraman, 1989). For example, one might argue that fit has been achieved if a firm's competitive strategy and its structure have been aligned, based on an a priori theoretical prediction, regardless of the outcome. In the following sections, I develop several alternative indexes to assess degree of internal and external High Performance Work Practices fit, using Venkatraman's categories of fit as moderation and fit as matching. Given the paucity of prior work in the area, however, these measures should be considered highly exploratory and the results interpreted with caution.

Internal fit as moderation   Internal fit among work practices could be expected to take the form of complementarity or synergy both within and between the employee skills and organizational structures and employee motivation factors. Thus, the first measure of internal fit I developed consists of the interaction between the degree of human resources policy consistency and the respective factors. Human resources policy consistency was assessed with this Likert-scale survey item: 'How would you describe the *consistency* of your *human resource policies* across any *divisions* or *business units* your firm may have?' (emphasis in original). Unfortunately, this measure is less than ideal for two reasons. First, it has restricted range, as firms that by definition do not adopt human resource policies consistently, such as holding companies, were excluded from the sample. Secondly, because the two factor scales were based on the proportions of coverage of exempt and nonexempt employees throughout a firm, a firm with a high score on these variables must have widely adopted each practice.

The second measure of internal fit as moderation I adopted consists of the interaction between these two measures. Based on the assumption that the returns from investments in employee skills and organizational structures will be higher to the extent that firms have also devoted significant resources to employee motivation, this measure provides a straightforward test of the magnitude of any such returns. This scale is superior to the first internal fit-as-moderation measure in that it does not exhibit the psychometric problems outlined above.

Internal fit as matching   The second broad category of internal fit consists of the degree of match between the two factor scales (Venkatraman, 1989). In the current context, internal fit as matching would occur if a firm were consistently low, medium, or high on both factors. As a test of the matching model of internal fit, I calculated the absolute value of the difference between a firm's scores on the employee skills and organizational structures and employee motivation scales (Venkatraman, 1989).

External fit as moderation   My first measure of external fit as moderation indicates the degree of correspondence between each firm's competitive strategy and its system of High Performance Work Practices. Porter (1985) provided the dominant typology of competitive strategies in the business policy literature; the types specified are cost leadership, differentiation, and focus. To provide an estimate of a firm's competitive strategy, each respondent indicated the proportion of its annual sales derived from each of those strategies. In view of prior work (Jackson and Schuler, 1995; Jackson et al., 1989), I assumed that a predominantly differentiation or focus strategy would require more intensive investments in High Performance Work Practices than would a cost leadership strategy. Thus, to test the external fit-as-moderation hypothesis, I interacted the proportion of sales derived from either a differentiation or focus strategy with scores on the employee skills and organizational structures and employee motivation scales, respectively.

My second measure of external fit as moderation is based on behavioral indication of the emphasis each firm placed on aligning its human resource management practices and competitive strategy. Specifically, respondents indicated whether or not they attempted to implement each of seven strategic human resource management activities for all employees (the Appendix lists these activities). I then constructed an index by adding the number of affirmative responses to each question ($\alpha = .69$). To test my expectation that the returns from investments in both factors will be greater when firms explicitly attempt to link human resources and business objectives, I interacted each firm's score on the strategic 'HRM index' with each factor score.

External fit as matching   Finally, I calculated the fit-as-matching variable by taking the absolute value of the difference between the Z score of the proportion of sales resulting from a differentiation or focus strategy and the respective factor scores (Venkatraman, 1989). This variable indicates the degree to which firms adopting differentiation or focus strategies also employ high levels of High Performance Work Practices and vice versa.

My expectation was that each fit-as-moderation interaction would be positive and significant for the financial performance dependent variables. Given that a lower score for the fit-as-matching variables indicates greater fit, I expected each of these measures to be negative and significant.

Dependent Variables

Turnover   The level of turnover within each firm was assessed with a single questionnaire item, 'What is your *average annual rate* of turnover?' (emphasis in original). This question was asked separately for exempt and nonexempt employees, and the level of turnover for each firm is therefore the weighted average across each of these categories.

[. . .]

Productivity   The logarithm of sales per employee is a widely used measure of organizational productivity and was adopted here to enhance comparability with prior work (Ichniowski, 1990; Pritchard, 1992).

[. . .]

Corporate financial performance   Prior work on the measurement of corporate financial performance is extensive. Perhaps the primary distinction to be made among the many alternative measures is between measurements of accounting and economic profits (Becker and Olson, 1987; Hirsch, 1991). Economic profits represent the net cash flows that accrue to shareholders; these are represented by capital (stock) market returns. Accounting profits can differ from economic profits as a result of timing issues, adjustments for depreciation, choice of accounting method, and measurement error. Additionally, economic profits are forward-looking and reflect the market's perception of both potential and current profitability, but accounting data reflect an historical perspective. Although there is widespread agreement in the literature that capital market measures are superior to accounting data, accounting data provide additional relevant information (Hirschey and Wichern, 1984). Moreover, accounting data are often the focus of human resource managers who must allocate scarce resources. Therefore, I used both a market-based measure (Tobin's q) and an accounting measure (gross rate of return on capital, or GRATE) of corporate financial performance. Each is the best available measure of its type (Hall et al., 1988; Hirsch, 1991; Hirschey and Wichern, 1984).[2]

[. . .]

Control Variables

The estimation models were developed to provide unbiased estimates of the impact of High Performance Work Practices on firm performance. Thus, the selection of the control variables for each dependent variable was based on a careful review of the prior empirical work (cf. Huselid, 1993), focusing on those variables likely to be related to both the dependent variables and the use of High Performance Work Practices. The controls for each dependent variable included firm size (total employment), capital intensity, firm- and industry-levels of union coverage, industry concentration, recent (five-year) growth in sales, research and development intensity, firm-specific risk (beta), industry levels of profitability, net sales, total assets, and 34 dummy variables representing 35 two-digit Standard Industrial Classification (SIC) codes. Unfortunately, there was no straightforward measure of firms' total wage bills available for inclusion in the turnover model. However, selling, general, and administrative expenses is a common income statement item that serves as a proxy for employee compensation.

Financial data were taken primarily from Compact Disclosure. I took considerable care to ensure that all data were matched to the same accounting period (1 July 1991 to 30 June 1992). Missing data were retrieved from *Moody's Industrial Manual* or the *Standard & Poor's Stock Price Guide*, where possible. Otherwise, missing data were eliminated listwise for each dependent variable. Stock price data were gathered from the *Investment Statistics Laboratory Daily Stock Price Record* for 31 December. Stock dividend and stock split data were gathered from *Standard & Poor's Stock Price Guide*. Capital intensity was calculated as the logarithm of the ratio of gross property, plant, and equipment over total employment. The five-year trend in sales growth and R&D intensity (the logarithm of the ratio of R&D expenditures to sales) and compensation levels (proxied by selling, general, and administrative expenses) were calculated directly from the accounting data. Firm-level union coverage and total employment were taken from the questionnaire, and industry-level unionization data were taken from Curme et al. (1990). Concentration ratios were calculated by dividing the sum of the largest four firms' sales within each industry by the total sales for that industry. The systematic component in the variability of a firm's stock price (systematic risk, or beta) was calculated using the Center for Research on Stock Prices (CRSP) database and a 250-day period. Initially, betas were only available for 543 firms. Using an auxiliary regression equation, I inputed data for the missing observations ($R^2 = .40$).

Results

Table 7.2 presents means, standard deviations, and correlations. The employee skills and organizational structures and employee motivation scales reflect an average of standard scores, so their means are very near zero. Turnover averaged 18.36 percent per year, and the logarithm of the productivity averaged 12.05, or annual sales of $171,099 per employee. The mean q was .46, and the average annual gross rate of return was 5.10 percent. This value for q ($e^{.46} = 1.58$) implies that the market value of the average firm was 58 percent greater than the current replacement cost of its assets. This result indicates that managements were generally working in the interest of the shareholders to increase the value of their equity. A GRATE value of 5.10 implies that each dollar invested in capital stock generates five cents in annual cash flow. Each of these values is consistent with the results of prior work (Becker and Olson, 1992; Hirsch, 1991). Average total employment was 4,413 (the logarithm of this variable was used in all subsequent analyses); firm-level unionization averaged 11.34 percent; and industry-level unionization averaged 13.97 percent. Total employment and union coverage were lower than in most prior work in this area, primarily because previous research has focused on the manufacturing sector, which is more heavily unionized. Finally, as expected, the employee skills and organizational structures scale was negatively related to turnover, while both scales were positively related to productivity and corporate financial performance.

Tables 7.3 through 7.6 present the regression analysis results for Hypotheses 1a and 1b. The first equation in each table contains the first factor scale, employee skills and organizational structures, the second equation contains the employee motivation scale, and the third equation contains both. These analyses provide some indication of the sensitivity of the findings to my specification and a very rough estimate of the degree of bias associated with a focus on individual facets of High Performance Work Practices. As a test of Hypothesis 1b, in the fourth equation in Tables 7.5 and 7.6 I added turnover and productivity to the models for Tobin's q and GRATE.

TABLE 7.2 Means, standard deviations, and correlations[a]

	Variables	Means	s.d.	1	2	3	4	5	6	7	8	9	10	11	12	13	14	15	16	17
1.	Turnover	18.36	21.87																	
2.	Productivity	12.05	0.99	-.24																
3.	Tobin's q	0.46	1.64	-.10	.07															
4.	Gross rate of return on assets	5.10	23.00	-.03	.15	.35														
5.	Employee skills and organizational structures	0.02	0.52	-.08	.06	.09	.13													
6.	Employee motivation	0.00	0.78	.04	.03	.20	.01	.15												
7.	Total employment	4,412.80	18,967.45	.13	-.22	.02	.12	.18	-.15											
8.	Capital intensity	3.96	1.32	-.29	.48	-.11	.02	.05	-.23	-.01										
9.	Firm union coverage	11.34	24.28	-.14	.05	-.09	.02	-.05	-.51	.21	.29									
10.	Industry union coverage	13.97	13.55	-.22	.11	-.11	.00	.04	-.36	.19	.40	.36								
11.	Concentration ratio	0.38	0.25	.05	-.15	-.03	-.14	-.08	-.12	.17	.02	.08	.16							
12.	Sales growth	0.61	1.08	.06	.06	.13	.01	-.03	.12	-.02	-.04	-.16	-.03	.10						
13.	R&D intensity	0.03	0.06	-.09	-.01	.10	-.11	-.01	.18	-.14	.06	-.12	-.12	.03	.04					
14.	Systematic risk	1.06	0.32	.09	-.08	.05	-.05	.00	.19	.06	-.23	-.18	-.20	.08	.09	.10				
15.	Selling, general & administrative expenses[b]	286.54	1,522.02	-.02	.31	.09	.18	.23	.00	.77	.21	.16	.13	-.01	.00	-.11	-.01			
16.	HRM policy consistency	4.54	1.10	-.10	-.04	.01	.04	.14	.23	-.12	-.06	-.12	-.07	-.08	.00	.03	-.03	-.08		
17.	Differentiation/focus	-0.01	1.02	-.03	-.10	.12	-.02	.05	.18	-.03	-.13	-.15	-.15	.00	.01	.10	.06	.01	.05	
18.	Strategic HRM index	3.36	1.98	-.02	.01	.00	.08	.33	.06	.25	-.01	.08	.01	-.04	.01	-.04	.07	.24	.05	.05

[a] N = 816. All correlations greater than or equal to .05 are significant at the .05 level; those > .07 are significant at the .01 level, and those > .10 are significant at the .001 level (one-tailed tests). Raw means are reported for total employment and selling, general, and administrative expenses to ease interpretation. The logarithms for these variables are used in all subsequent analyses.
[b] In millions of dollars.

TABLE 7.3   *Results of regression analysis for turnover*

Variables	Model 1 b	Model 1 s.e.	Model 2 b	Model 2 s.e.	Model 3 b	Model 3 s.e.
Constant	44.965***	9.418	46.363***	9.420	44.758***	9.486
Logarithm of total employment	2.656***	0.772	2.507***	0.778	2.637***	0.783
Capital intensity	−2.229***	0.659	−2.279***	0.663	−2.240***	0.663
Firm union coverage	−0.088***	0.029	−0.089***	0.032	−0.090***	0.032
Industry union coverage	−0.222***	0.080	−0.225***	0.080	−0.222***	0.080
Concentration ratio	−1.376	3.611	−1.369	3.617	−1.360	3.615
Sales growth	0.329	0.592	0.362	0.592	0.332	0.593
R&D/sales	−3.509	11.298	−3.211	11.409	−3.278	11.403
Systematic risk	1.490	2.158	1.577	2.177	1.532	2.176
Selling, general, & administrative expenses	−2.168***	0.749	−2.175***	0.763	−2.145***	0.763
Employee skills and organizational structures	−1.769*	1.245			−1.743*	1.258
Employee motivation			−0.359	1.036	−0.162	1.045
R^2	0.385***		0.383***		0.385***	
ΔR^2	0.002[a]		0.120[a]		0.002[a]	
F for ΔR^2	2.017		0.730		1.020	
N	855		855		855	

[a] These statistics reflect the incremental variance accounted for when employee skills and organizational structures and employee motivation, respectively, are added to the complete specification for each model. The impact of High Performance Work Practices on the dependent variable is underestimated by this statistic because the assumptions that the independent variables are orthogonal and have been entered on the basis of a clear causal ordering are not appropriate in the current study. This caveat applies to all reported results.

* $p < .10$, one-tailed test
** $p < .05$, one-tailed test
*** $p < .01$, one-tailed test

Turnover

Table 7.3 shows the regression results for turnover. Each equation reached significance at conventional levels, and the control variables generally had the expected signs and significance levels. Although employee skills and organizational structures were consistently negative and significant, employee motivation was not significant in either model. This result is less surprising when it is recognized that the use of incentive compensation systems may actually encourage employees who are performing poorly to leave a firm.

I next estimated the practical significance of the impact of High Performance Work Practices on turnover, from the results of the third equation shown in Table 7.3. With all other variables held at their means, firms with employee skills and organizational structures and employee motivation scores three standard deviations below the mean exhibited 21.48 percent turnover, but firms with scores three standard deviations above the mean had 15.36 percent turnover. This 40 percent decrease of course would be the maximum expected effect of High Performance Work Practices, because it implies that a firm has moved from the total absence of any effective human resource programs to complete participation across all dimensions. A more representative estimate can be made by calculating the effect of a one-standard-deviation increase in each practice scale on turnover. Each such increase reduced turnover 1.30 raw percentage points, or 7.05 percent relative to the mean. Considering that this model controls for firm size, the impact of unions, and employee compensation (selling, general, and administrative expenses), this effect is practically as well as statistically significant. In fact, this specification provides a highly restrictive test of the impact of High Performance Work Practices on turnover, as the inclusion of selling, general, and administrative expenses controls not only for employee wage levels but also for any direct costs associated with the implementation of these practices. Removing this variable and thus allowing the effect of High Performance Work Practices on compensation to be reflected in the direct effect of such practices increased the magnitude of their impact on turnover by more than 20 percent.

Productivity

Table 7.4 presents the regression results for productivity. As above, each equation reached significance at conventional levels, and the control variables generally had the expected signs and significance levels. When employee skills and organizational structures and employee motivation were entered individually (models 4 and 5), each was positive and significant at conventional levels. In model 6, which includes both employee skills and organizational structures and employee motivation, only the coefficient for the later remained significant. This finding graphically demonstrates the need to adopt a system perspective in evaluating the links between High Performance Work Practices and firm-level outcomes and the way in which focusing on a subset of human resources management practices may overstate their effects. In fact, these analyses are likely to understate the biases associated with a focus on individual High Performance Work Practices, as I focus here on the impact of omitting an entire facet of these practices, rather than a single practice.

To estimate the practical significance of the impact of High Performance Work Practices on productivity, I next calculated the impact of a one-standard-deviation increase in each practices scale on the numerator of productivity (net sales) while holding total employment and all other variables at their means. These analyses were based on model 6 from Table 7.4. The findings indicate that each one-standard-deviation increase raises sales an average of $27,044 per employee. This substantial figure represents nearly 16 percent of the mean sales per employee ($171,099). However, this is a single-period estimate, and spending on High Performance Work Practices should be thought of as an investment that can reasonably be

TABLE 7.4 *Results of regression analysis for productivity*

Variables	Model 4		Model 5		Model 6	
	b	s.e.	b	s.e.	b	s.e.
Constant	10.919***	0.227	10.899***	0.225	10.899***	0.225
Logarithm of total employment	−0.123***	0.018	−0.119***	0.017	−0.123***	0.018
Capital intensity	0.399***	0.025	0.404***	0.025	0.403***	0.024
Firm union coverage	0.000	0.001	0.001	0.001	0.001	0.001
Industry union coverage	0.001	0.003	0.001	0.003	0.000	0.003
Concentration ratio	−0.240**	0.146	−0.251**	0.145	−0.251**	0.145
Sales growth	0.105***	0.024	0.100***	0.024	0.101***	0.024
R&D/sales	−0.771**	0.457	−1.004***	0.457	−1.002**	0.457
Systematic risk	0.083	0.087	0.042	0.087	0.043	0.087
Turnover	−0.003**	0.001	−0.003**	0.001	−0.003**	0.001
Employee skills and organizational structures	0.073*	0.050			0.046	0.051
Employee motivation			0.160***	0.041	0.154***	0.041
R^2	0.490***		0.498***		0.498***	
ΔR^2	0.001[a]		0.010[a]		0.010[a]	
F for R^2	2.100		15.448***		8.136***	
N	855		855		855	

[a] These statistics reflect the incremental variance accounted for when employee skills and organizational structures and employee motivation, respectively, are added to the complete specification for each model. The impact of High Performance Work Practices on the dependent variable is underestimated by this statistic because the assumptions that the independent variables are orthogonal and have been entered on the basis of a clear causal ordering are not appropriate in the current study. This caveat applies to all reported results.
  * $p < .10$, one-tailed test
 ** $p < .05$, one-tailed test
*** $p < .01$, one-tailed test

assumed to produce gains for longer than a single year. If the effects of increasing such practices are arbitrarily assumed to accrue for a five-year period at an 8 percent discount rate, the present value increase in sales will be $107,979 per employee. It should be noted that the assumption underlying this specification is that High Performance Work Practices increase sales for a fixed number of employees rather than increase efficiency (lower employment) given a constant level of sales. Otherwise identical specifications that modeled sales as a function of total employment produced very similar results.

Corporate Financial Performance

Table 7.5 presents the results for Tobin's q, and Table 7.6 shows the same specifications for the gross rate of return on assets. Each equation reached significance at conventional levels, and the control variables generally had the expected signs and significance levels. The results for q showed the employee skills and organizational structures and employee motivation

TABLE 7.5   Results of regression analysis results for Tobin's q

Variables	Model 7 b	Model 7 s.e.	Model 8 b	Model 8 s.e.	Model 9 b	Model 9 s.e.	Model 10 b	Model 10 s.e.
Constant	0.672*	0.505	0.515	0.495	0.642	0.502	-2.166*	0.995
Log of total employment	0.065**	0.040	0.082**	0.039	0.067**	0.040	0.106***	0.041
Capital intensity	-0.125***	0.054	-0.115**	0.054	-0.119**	0.054	-0.251***	0.063
Firm union coverage	0.000	0.002	0.004	0.003	0.004*	0.003	0.003	0.003
Industry union coverage	-0.002	0.007	-0.003	0.007	-0.003	0.007	-0.005	0.007
Concentration ratio	-0.443*	0.326	-0.469*	0.325	-0.471*	0.324	-0.400	0.321
Sales growth	0.205***	0.053	0.195***	0.053	0.198***	0.054	0.172***	0.054
R&D/sales	2.354***	1.009	1.935***	1.013	1.937**	1.013	2.198**	1.005
Systematic risk	-0.039	0.194	-0.115	0.194	-0.112	0.194	-0.099	0.192
Employee skills and organizational structures	0.215*	0.113			0.165*	0.113	0.135	0.112
Employee motivation			0.297***	0.090	0.277***	0.091	0.221***	0.091
Turnover							-0.007***	0.003
Productivity							0.27***	0.078
R²	0.138***		0.146***		0.148***		0.167***	
ΔR²	0.004ᵃ		0.012ᵃ		0.014ᵃ		0.033ᵃ	
F for ΔR²	3.635*		10.842***		6.483***		7.781***	
N	826		826		826		826	

ᵃ These statistics reflect the incremental variance accounted for when employee skills and organizational structures, employee motivation, turnover, and productivity, respectively, are added to the complete specification for each model. The impact of High Performance Work Practices on the dependent variable is underestimated by this statistic because the assumptions that the independent variables are orthogonal and have been entered on the basis of a clear causal ordering are not appropriate in the current study.

   * p < .10, one-tailed test
  ** p < .05, one-tailed test
 *** p < .01, one-tailed test

TABLE 7.6 Results of regression analysis for gross rate of return on assets (GRATE)

Variables	Model 11 b	s.e.	Model 12 b	s.e.	Model 13 b	s.e.	Model 14 b	s.e
Constant	-0.126**	0.072	-0.159**	0.072	-0.125***	0.072	-0.588***	0.140
Log of total employment	0.019***	0.006	0.023***	0.006	0.019***	0.006	0.025***	0.006
Capital intensity	0.011*	0.007	0.012*	0.008	0.011*	0.008	-0.009	0.009
Firm union coverage	0.000	0.000	0.000	0.000	0.000	0.000	0.000	0.000
Industry union coverage	0.000	0.001	0.000	0.001	0.000	0.001	0.001	0.000
Concentration ratio	-0.077**	0.046	-0.075**	0.046	-0.076**	0.045	-0.065*	0.046
Sales growth	0.008	0.007	0.008	0.007	0.008	0.007	0.004	0.008
R&D/sales	-0.213*	0.144	-0.202**	0.146	-0.201**	0.145	-0.153**	0.145
Systematic risk	-0.050*	0.027	-0.049*	0.028	-0.048*	0.027	-0.048	0.027
Employee skills and organizational structures	0.041**	0.016			0.043**	0.016	0.040*	0.016
Employee motivation			-0.003	0.013	-0.008	0.013	-0.015	0.013
Turnover							0.000	0.000
Productivity							0.044***	0.011
R^2	0.117***		0.109***		0.117***		0.137***	
ΔR^2	0.008[a]		0.001[a]		0.008[a]		0.027[a]	
F for ΔR^2	6.649***		0.680***		3.356***		6.157***	
N	826		826		826		826	

[a]These statistics reflect the incremental variance accounted for when employee skills and organizational structures, employee motivation, turnover, and productivity, respectively, are added to the complete specification for each model. The impact of High Performance Work Practices on the dependent variable is underestimated by this statistic because the assumptions that the independent variables are orthogonal and have been entered on the basis of a clear causal ordering are not appropriate in the current study.

* $p < .10$, one-tailed test
** $p < .05$, one-tailed test
*** $p < .01$, one-tailed test

scales to be significant in each equation. For GRATE, employee skills and organizational structures were positive and significant in each model but employee motivation was not. Although the diversity in these results reinforces the importance of researchers' considering multiple outcomes when evaluating the impact of human resources department activities (Tsui, 1990), the structure of incentive systems in many firms may help to explain them. Given the numerous problems associated with the use of accounting measures of firm performance in incentive compensation systems (Gerhart and Milkovich, 1992), many firms have begun to explicitly link employee compensation with capital market returns. This shift may help to explain why employee motivation has a much stronger impact on the market-based performance measure than on the accounting returns–based measure.

I next assessed the practical significance of the impact of High Performance Work Practices on firm profits. To do so, I estimated the impact of a one-standard-deviation increase on the numerator of both Tobin's q and GRATE while holding their denominators and all other variables at their means. These analyses were based on models 9 and 13 from Tables 7.5 and 7.6, respectively. In terms of market value, the per employee effect of increasing such practices one standard deviation was $18,641 (relative to q). Such an increase in market value is not likely to occur immediately, however. A more likely scenario is that investments in High Performance Work Practices create an asset that provides an annual return. If one assumes (again, arbitrarily) that these returns accrue over a five-year period at an 8 percent discount rate, then such an investment would provide an annuity of $4,669 per employee per year.

Estimates of the practical effects of increasing use of these practices can also be made on the basis of annual accounting profits. Relative to GRATE, each one-standard-deviation increase in High Performance Work Practices increased cash flow $3,814. These figures are remarkably close to the five-year annuity values calculated above.

Summary of financial performance results   In short, although there is strong support for the hypotheses predicting that High Performance Work Practices will affect firm performance and important employment outcomes, the results are not completely unambiguous. Notably, the significant effects found are also financially meaningful. Moreover, where these effects are meaningful their magnitude is consistent across very different measures of financial performance. For example, a one-standard-deviation increase in High Performance Work Practices yields a $27,044 increase in sales and a $3,814 increase in profits. The ratio of these variables (cash flow to sales) at 14 percent is very near the sample mean of 10 percent. And assuming that the market value of a firm reflects the discounted net present value of all future cash flows, the present value of these cash flows ($15,277 at 8 percent for five years) is remarkably close to the estimated per employee impact on firm market value of $18,614. The point of these analyses is to demonstrate that High Performance Work Practices have impacts of similar magnitude on each dependent variable of interest. In fact, these results show a remarkable level of internal consistency, especially given the fact that they are based on measures of firm performance that are only moderately intercorrelated.

Sources of the Gains from High Performance Work Practices

The next series of analyses examined the processes through which High Performance Work Practices affect corporate financial performance. Specifically, Hypothesis 1b states that employee turnover and productivity will mediate the relationship between systems of work practices and corporate financial performance. Following Baron and Kenny (1986), I first regressed the mediating variables (turnover and productivity) on the practices scales (see Tables 7.3 and 7.4). The next step was to regress each dependent variable on those scales (see models 7, 8 and 9 in Table 7.5 and models 11, 12, and 13 in Table 7.6). The significant effects shown in each case are necessary but not sufficient conditions to establish that mediation exists. Finally, as an estimate of the magnitude of any mediation effect, I regressed the dependent variables on the work practices scales and the mediating variables. These results are shown in the final models in Tables 7.5 and 7.6. Here, the decrement in the coefficients for the employee skills and organizational structures and employee motivation scales as turnover and productivity are entered into the profitability equations providing an estimate of the degree to which the effects of High Performance Work Practices on firm performance can be attributed to these factors.

As expected, the coefficient on each practices scale becomes smaller once turnover and productivity have been entered into the models. The magnitude of this effect can be shown by calculating the proportionate change in the impact of High Performance Work Practices on corporate financial performance that can be attributed to the inclusion of turnover and productivity. Although, on the average, the coefficients on the two scales fall by approximately 20 percent each when turnover and productivity are entered into the models, the joint effect is to reduce the estimated financial impact of High Performance Work Practices on q by 74 percent and on GRATE by 77 percent. This effect is sizable and suggests that a significant proportion of the impact of High Performance Work Practices on corporate financial performance is attributable to either lower turnover or higher employee productivity, or to both. The fact that turnover and productivity are temporally antecedent to my measures of firm profits and that the contemporaneous estimates of the profitability effects were highly similar increases my confidence in these results.

Evidence of Complementarity

The final phase in the analyses was to evaluate the influence of internal an external fit on the dependent variables. Owing to space constraints, I focus here on firm profits, but the results for turnover and productivity were similar.

Internal fit as moderation   The first measure of fit I developed was the interaction between the degree of human resources policy consistency and each of the scales measuring High Performance Work Practices. These results were uniformly nonsignificant. Conversely, the second measure of internal fit, the interaction between the employee skills and organizational structures and employee motivation scales, was positive and significant for both Tobin's q and GRATE.

Internal fit as matching   The internal fit-as-matching variable, which assesses the degree to which a firm adopts the same level of High Performance Work Practices throughout its operations, was negative and significant for GRATE but nonsignificant for q.

External fit as moderation   The first external fit-as-moderation variables reflect the interaction between the proportion of sales associated with differentiation and focus strategies and the employee skills and organizational structures and employee motivation scales respectively. These results were uniformly nonsignificant.

The second measures of external fit as moderation reflects the interaction between firms' scores on the strategic HRM index and the practices scales. With the exception of the interaction between this index and employee motivation for GRATE, these analyses were also uniformly nonsignificant.

External fit as matching   Finally, the fit-as-matching variables for external fit show the coefficient for q to be positive – in the unanticipated direction – and significant, but nonsignificant elsewhere.

In summary, most of the coefficients on the fit measures had the expected signs, and the interaction of employee skills and organizational structures and employee motivation was consistently positive and significant. But despite the strong theoretical expectation that better internal and external fit would be reflected in better financial performance, on the whole the results did not support the contention that either type of fit has any incremental value over the main effects associated with the use of High Performance Work Practices.

[. . .]

Discussion

Prior work in both the academic and popular press has argued that the use of High Performance Work Practices will be reflected in better firm performance. This study provides broad evidence in support of these assertions. Across a wide range of industries and firm sizes, I found considerable support for the hypothesis that investments in such practices are associated with lower employee turnover and greater productivity and corporate financial performance. That my results were consistent across diverse measures of firm performance and corrections for selectivity and simultaneity biases lends considerable confidence to these conclusions.

The magnitude of the returns for investments in High Performance Work Practices is substantial. A one-standard-deviation increase in such practices is associated with a relative 7.05 percent decrease in turnover and, on a per employee basis, $27,044 more in sales and $18,641 and $3,814 more in market value and profits, respectively. These internally consistent and economically and statistically significant values suggest that firms can indeed obtain substantial financial benefits from investing in the practices studied here. In addition, these estimates imply a constant level of investment in such practices each year. If an increase requires only a one-time expense (as perhaps could be the case with recruiting or selection costs), these values will be underestimates of the impact of High Performance Work Practices on firm performance. Moreover, these calculations only include a firm's portion of the gains from increasing use of these practices. Presumably, some of the value created by adopting more effective HRM practices will accrue to employees, in the form of higher wages and benefits (Becker and Olson, 1987). Since higher levels of High Performance Work Practices lead to lower turnover, and presumably greater employment security, there appears to be considerable justification for encouraging firms to make such investments from a public policy perspective.

The impact of High Performance Work Practices on corporate financial performance is in part due to their influence on employee turnover and productivity. The identification of some of the processes through which these practices affect firm profits helps to establish the plausibility of a link with corporate financial performance. However, some of their influence on firm profits remains unaccounted for, and the source of these remaining gains is an important topic for future research.

But despite the compelling theoretical argument that better internal and external fit will increase firm performance, I found only modest evidence of such an effect for internal fit and little evidence for external fit. These findings are in fact consistent with recent attempts to model fit in the organizational strategy literature (Venkatraman, 1989), and they are perhaps unsurprising given the preliminary nature of the measures of fit I developed. And given the substantial main effects associated with systems of High Performance Work Practices, one might conclude that the simple adoption of such practices is more important than any efforts to ensure these policies are internally consistent or aligned with firm competitive strategy. However, the theoretical arguments for internal and external fit remain compelling, and research based on refined theoretical and psychometric development of these constructs is clearly required before such a conclusion can be accepted with any confidence. The very large theoretical literature in the fields of human resources management based on the premise that fit makes a difference cries out for more work in this area, and the primary import of the current findings may in fact be to call attention to this important line of research.

Finally, the reader is cautioned to recognize the limitations associated with the use of cross-sectional data when an attempt to draw conclusions about causality is made. Although the use in this work of simultaneous equations, corrections for response bias, measures of current and subsequent years' profits, extensive control variables, and a large and diverse sample mitigate many of the traditional methodological concerns, longitudinal data on both High Performance Work Practices and firm performance are needed to conclusively replicate the findings presented here. But such data are extremely costly to generate and are as yet unavailable.

This caveat is not intended to obviate the central conclusions of this study, however. Although traditional economic theory would suggest that the gains associated with the adoption of High Performance Work Practices cannot survive into perpetuity (because the returns from these investments will be driven toward equilibrium as more and more firms make them), the substantial variance in the HRM practices adopted by domestic firms and the expectation that investments in such practices help to create firm-specific human capital that is difficult to imitate suggest that, at least in the near term, such returns are available for the taking.

Appendix: Components of the Strategic Human Resources Management Index[*]

1. Match the characteristics of managers to the strategic plan of the firm.
2. Identify managerial characteristics necessary to run the firm in the long term.
3. Modify the compensation system to encourage managers to achieve long-term strategic objectives.
4. Change staffing patterns to help implement business or corporate strategies.
5. Evaluate key personnel based on their potential for carrying out strategic goals.
6. Conduct job analyses based on what the job may entail in the future.
7. Conduct development programs designed to support strategic changes.

[*]Adapted from Devanna et al. (1982).

Notes

1 10-K reprints are informational documents filed with the Securities and Exchange Commission.

2 A particular focus of this chapter concerns estimation of the financial impact of HRM practices. Huselid uses two measures of financial performance: Tobin's q and GRATE. Tobin's q is the ratio of the market value of a company to the

estimated replacement cost of its assets. It can be interpreted as a measure of the strength of competitive advantage held by a firm. GRATE (gross rate of return on capital) is the ratio of cash flow to gross capital stock, and is an accounting-based measure of return on assets.

References

Arthur, J.B. (1992) 'The link between business strategy and industrial relations systems in American steel minimills', *Industrial and Labor Relations Review*, 45: 488–506.

Bailey, T. (1993) 'Discretionary effort and the organization of work: employee participation and work reform since Hawthorne'. Working paper, Columbia University, New York.

Baird, L. and Meshoulam, I. (1988) 'Managing two fits of strategic human resource management', *Academy of Management Review*, 13: 116–28.

Baron, R.M. and Kenny, D.A. (1986) 'The moderator-mediator variable distinction in social psychological research: conceptual, strategic, and statistical considerations', *Journal of Personality and Social Psychology*, 51: 1173–82.

Becker, B.E. and Olson, C.A. (1987) 'Labor relations and firm performance', in M.M. Kleiner, R.N. Block, M. Roomkin and S.W. Salsburg (eds), *Human Resources and the Performance of the Firm*. Washington, DC: BNA Press. pp. 43–85.

Becker, B.E. and Olson, C.A. (1992) 'Unions and firm profits', *Industrial Relations*, 31: 395–415.

Begin, J.P. (1991) *Strategic Employment Policy: An Organizational Systems Perspective*. Englewood Cliffs, NJ: Prentice-Hall.

Boudreau, J.W. (1991) 'Utility analysis in human resource management decisions', in M.D. Dunnette and L.M. Hough (eds), *Handbook of Industrial and Organizational Psychology* (2nd edn), vol. 2. Palo Alto, CA: Consulting Psychologists Press. pp. 621–745.

Butler, J.E., Ferris, G.R. and Napier, N.K. (1991) *Strategy and Human Resources Management*. Cincinnati: South-Western.

Cappelli, P. and Singh, H. (1992) 'Integrating strategic human resources and strategic management', in D. Lewin, O.S. Mitchell and P. Sherer (eds), *Research Frontiers in Industrial Relations and Human Resources*. Madison, WI: Industrial Relations Research Association. pp. 165–92.

Curme, M.A., Hirsch, B.T. and McPherson, D.A. (1990) 'Union membership and contract coverage in the United States', *Industrial and Labor Relations Review*, 44: 5–33.

Delaney, J.T., Lewin, D. and Ichniowski, C. (1989) *Human Resource Policies and Practices in American Firms*. Washington, DC: US Government Printing Office.

Devanna, M.A., Fombrun, C., Tichy, N. and Warren, L. (1982) 'Strategic planning and human resource management', *Human Resource Management*, 22: 11–17.

Gerhart, B. and Milkovich, G.T. (1992) 'Employee compensation: research and practice', in M.D. Dunnette and L.M. Hough (eds), *Handbook of Industrial and Organizational Psychology* (2nd edn), vol. 3. Palo Alto, CA: Consulting Psychologists Press. pp. 481–569.

Hall, B.H., Cummins, C., Laderman, E.S. and Mundy, J. (1988) 'The R&D master file documentation'. Technical working paper no. 72. National Bureau of Economic Research, Cambridge, MA.

Hirsch, B.T. (1991) *Labor Unions and the Economic Performance of Firms*. Kalamazoo, MI: W.E. Upjohn Institute for Employment Research.

Hirschey, M. and Wichern, D.W. (1984) 'Accounting and market-value measures of profitability: consistency, determinants, and uses', *Journal of Business and Economic Statistics*, 2: 375–83.

Huselid, M.A. (1993) 'Essays on human resource management practices, turnover, productivity, and firm performance'. Unpublished doctoral dissertation, State University of New York at Buffalo.

Ichniowski, C. (1990) 'Manufacturing businesses'. NBER working paper series no. 3449. National Bureau of Economic Research. Cambridge, MA.

Jackson, S.E. and Schuler, R.S. (1995) 'Understanding human resource management in the context of organizations and their environments', in J.T. Spence, J.M. Darley and D.J. Foss (eds), *Annual Review of Psychology*, vol. 46. Palo Alto, CA: Annual Reviews Inc. pp. 237–64.

Jackson, S.E., Schuler, R.S. and Rivero, J.C. (1989) 'Organizational characteristics as predictors of personnel practices', *Personnel Psychology*, 42: 727–86.

Jones, G.R. and Wright, P.M. (1992) 'An economic approach to conceptualizing the utility of human resource management practices', in K. Rowland and G. Ferris (eds), *Research in Personnel and Human Resource Management*, vol. 10. Greenwich, CT: JAI Press. pp. 271–99.

Kleiner, M.M. (1990) 'The role of industrial relations in firm performance', in J.A. Fossum and J. Mattson (eds), *Employee and Labor Relations*. Washington, DC: BNA Press. 4.23–4.43.

MacDuffie, J.P. (1995) 'Human resource bundles and manufacturing performance: organizational logic and flexible production systems in the world auto industry', *Industrial and Labor Relations Review*, 48: 197–221.

Milgrom, P. and Roberts, J. (1993) 'Complementarities and fit: strategy, structure, and organizational change'. Working paper, Stanford University, Stanford, CA.

Osterman, P. (1987) 'Choice of employment systems in internal labor markets', *Industrial Relations*, 26: 46–57.

Osterman, P. (1994) 'How common is workplace transformation and how can we explain who adopts it? Results from a national survey', *Industrial and Labor Relations Review*, 47: 173–88.

Porter, M.E. (1985) *Competitive Advantage: Creating and Sustaining Superior Performance*. New York: Free Press.

Pritchard, R.D. (1992) 'Organizational productivity', in M.D. Dunnette and L.M. Hough (eds), *Handbook of Industrial and Organizational Psychology* (2nd edn), vol. 3. Palo Alto, CA: Consulting Psychologists Press. pp. 443–71.

Schuler, R.S. (1992) 'Strategic human resource management: linking people with the needs of the business', *Organizational Dynamics*, 20: 19–32.

Tsui, A.S. (1990) 'A multiple-constituency model of effectiveness: an empirical examination at the human resource subunit level', *Administrative Science Quarterly*, 35: 458–83.

US Department of Labor (1993) *High Performance Work Practices and Firm Performance*. Washington, DC: US Government Printing Office.

Venkatraman, N. (1989) 'The concept of fit in strategy research: toward a verbal and statistical correspondence', *Academy of Management Review*, 14: 423–44.

Wright, P.M. and McMahan, G.C. (1992) 'Theoretical perspectives for strategic human resource management', *Journal of Management*, 18 (2): 295–320.

8   Playing God? The Performance of Appraisal

Tim Newton and Patricia Findlay

In both the private and public sector, the use of formal employee appraisal procedures appears to be growing. At the same time it is being applied to sections of the workforce (e.g., blue-collar) to which it had previously not been applied (Long, 1986). Yet while there has been a growth in its deployment, this has not been accompanied by similar developments in theorising about appraisal. This chapter aims to remedy this neglect by critically evaluating our existing knowledge of appraisal in the light of the contrasting theoretical perspectives provided by labour process theorists and by Michel Foucault. We also attempt to move beyond the narrow strictures in which performance appraisal is presently conceptualised and explore wider issues relating to performance management. Finally, while we find both labour process theory and Foucauldian themes particularly apposite to theorising appraisal, we are attentive to their limitations.

Existing Research

One way of highlighting the shortcomings of current research is to look at Long's (1986) large-scale study of appraisal practices, since its limitations are symptomatic of the problems that appear common to much appraisal research. In our view, Long's study is subject to four main weaknesses. First, there is little information on context: sectoral and ownership factors are only rarely referred to and workforce composition is virtually ignored, whether in terms of skill and education levels or in relation to gender, race or age. Yet there seems little point in analysing appraisal outside the context in which it operates and without reference to power relations within and without the organisation. Secondly, the report exhibits a clear bias towards the views of the appraisers; the experiences and responses of those who are appraised merit little attention. Thirdly, the emphasis within Long's report is on the techniques used to carry out appraisal rather than

Originally published in *Human Resource Management Journal*, 6 (3), 1996: 42–58 (abridged).

on the 'outcomes' achieved. There is a continuing lack of systematic evidence on the actual working of performance appraisal schemes in the longer term. Finally, the data analysis is cursory to say the least: much of the report draws on analyses of single variable frequencies, with the occasional cross-tabulation providing the most sophisticated form of analysis. The reader is given no outline of the questions asked and few details on the composition of the sample.

The limitations identified in Long's study are not atypical. It is interesting to speculate therefore on why such a situation has arisen. To some extent, those areas which are largely unresearched are those which present the greatest difficulties for researchers. However, this in itself is not a sufficient explanation. It is our contention that our knowledge of appraisal is deficient because most writers exhibit an (often unconscious) adherence to the assumptions and research methods of neo-human relations writers of the 1950s and 1960s, with the consequence that their work provides unitarist prescriptions that are generally insensitive to both context and outcome. We will suggest that it is this discourse which continues to set the terms of current debates, despite the evident limitations.

Appraisal and Neo-human Relations

In his oft-cited paper, McGregor (1957) laid out many of the concerns found in work on appraisal, including the problem of the conflicting roles of the appraiser as both a disciplinary 'judge' and yet a supposedly helpful 'counsellor':

> The modern emphasis on the manager as a leader who strives to help his subordinates achieve both their own and the company's objectives is hardly consistent with the judicial role demanded by most appraisal plans. (McGregor, 1957: 90)

The judge/counsellor conflict still forms a feature of more recent debates about appraisal (for example, Fletcher and Williams, 1985; Latham, 1986) as do many of the other issues which McGregor examined. Underlying McGregor's arguments was the neo-human relations vision of the need 'to approach the whole subject of management from the point of view of basic social values', drawing on 'our convictions about the worth and the dignity of the human personality'.

McGregor's arguments also incorporated the usual unitary approach of human and neo-human relations (Hollway, 1991) with its assumption that appraisal will automatically serve the supposedly common interest of employee and employer. He argued that appraisal should be a participative process, drawing on the human relations imperative that the appraisee should become 'an active agent, not a passive "object"'.

Because they are all working together, the appraiser in a participative appraisal process can be a true 'helper' rather than a judge.

> He [*sic*] is not telling, deciding, criticizing or praising – not 'playing God'. He finds himself listening, using his own knowledge of the organization as a basis for advising, guiding, encouraging his subordinates to develop their own potentialities. Incidentally, this often leads the superior to important insights about himself and his impact on others. (McGregor, 1957: 92)

Appraisal is thus about people learning about themselves and working together in order to help themselves and the organisation.

It seems relatively easy now to criticise the assumptions that underpin McGregor's arguments. To take an obvious one, it seems unlikely that an appraisee will view appraisal as a purely helping/counselling exercise where they may 'confide' their job difficulties and anxieties, when there is often the possibility (even if not stated) that the appraisal 'data' will be used in assessing promotion, transfer 'or even a demotion'. More generally, one must question the unitarist assumptions of human relations and its accompanying individualism: do employees really want to take responsibility for improving themselves through their 'active' participation in appraisal or, rather, might they view appraisal as a manipulation which places the burden of 'development' on the employees and encourages them to see themselves as a resource which they must polish and refine according to their employer's needs (Salaman, 1979). Finally, there is little concern that developments in appraisal technology might represent new possibilities for the surveillance and discipline of employees. In spite of such possible criticisms, most recent appraisal literature still conforms to the parameters set by neo-human relations writers.

In general, there is also a lack of scrutiny of the research base on which neo-human relations discourse (on appraisal) is founded. Thus, many current writers on appraisal accept the neo-human relations argument that appraisals will be more effective where destructive criticism is avoided and where the appraisee takes an active, participatory role (provided there is also a 'participatory culture'). Yet research supporting such arguments seems questionable. The original argument against 'destructive criticism' derives from the highly influential studies at General Electric reported by Meyer and colleagues (1965). However, this study appears fundamentally flawed because of the well-documented problem of 'criteria contamination' (Smith, 1976; Klimoski and Strickland, 1977). For example, Meyer et al. found that those who received 'above-average' criticisms in their appraisal subsequently 'showed less goal achievement' (1965: 126). However, the people who measured 'goal achievement' were the same people who made the 'above-average' criticisms – the manager of the appraisee (see pp. 126–7) – so that the later poor goal achievement results may have simply represented the avoidance of dissonance on the part of the managers doing the ratings. It seems surprising to us that such obvious limitations of the 'very influential' study of Meyer et al. have not received more attention in the appraisal literature.

Some of the problems with the research base that supports a partici-patory role for appraisees have been well documented, particularly its heavy reliance on experimental laboratory findings. A number of writers on appraisal have noted the drawbacks of such laboratory research, especially the poor simulation that it provides of 'real-life' appraisal practice (Latham, 1986). Despite such condemnation, however, participation is still a fairly standard prescription for effective appraisal and career development practice.

The Emergence of a Critical Debate

In sum, we argue that much of the appraisal literature remains faithful, whether consciously or unconsciously, to the neo-human relations discourse espoused by writers like McGregor, Meyer and Maier. In general, there has been a lack of questioning of the assumptions of this discourse, as well as limited criticisms even operating within its parameters. Yet recently, a more critical stance towards appraisal has been gradually emerging with the most notable 'openers' for such a critical position being the review provided by Townley (1989) and the research study of Barlow (1989).

Townley's starting point was to question why the 1970s and 1980s have witnessed an increasing use of appraisal, particularly with groups of employees who were not previously formally appraised. She rejected the idea that investment in appraisal is solely a consequence of the need to attend to labour costs. Instead, she argued that appraisal needs to be seen in the context of increasing levels of discretion and autonomy among employees which have made direct monitoring of them more difficult. Following Offe (1976), she suggested that management is attempting – through appraisal – to influence the normative orientations of workers so that employee discretion is enacted within the general line of managerial/ organisational interests. Thus, appraisal may not be solely or mainly concerned with measuring performance; rather, it may be more effective as a means of conveying implicit expectations.

Barlow's study also examined control through exploring the gap between the espoused aims of appraisal and its meaning in practice. He argued many organisations were unable or unwilling to undertake the enormously complex task of a rigorous appraisal, instead seeking expla-nations based largely on 'simple economic prescription' which, in them-selves, are fundamentally flawed (1989: 501). Yet given their limitations, why do organisations devote time and resources to appraisal schemes? Barlow suggests that appraisal systems legitimate managerial actions through demonstrating that human resources are being deployed in a rational and efficient way. In addition, their deficient operation allows more dominant power groups to continue to pursue their own agendas unchallenged. The appraisal system therefore merely provided the 'window dressing' of rational and efficient HRM, while the 'real' decisions (such as those regarding promotion) were based on social evaluations operating outside of the appraisal process.

In what follows, we shall try to build on this and later critical work through an exploration of two contrasting theoretical approaches: labour process theory and the work of Michel Foucault.

Labour Process Perspectives

Over the past decade, labour process thinking has moved on considerably from earlier attempts to identify universal management solutions to the problems of labour control (such as through deskilling). While there remains a central assumption of an accumulation and control imperative, it is now widely acknowledged that management have at their disposal a range of mechanisms through which control is sought. From this perspective, performance appraisal can be viewed as one important mechanism in management's control armoury and it seems surprising that it has received very little attention from labour process writers. Nevertheless, there have been a number of labour process critiques of the related issue of employee participation (Friedman, 1977; Ramsay, 1985) and these critiques are of direct relevance to work on appraisal. For example, many labour process writers would take issue with the positive sum view of employee participation as presented by the neo-human relations school. Rather, they suggest (following Fox, 1974) that participation is a device through which management control may be enhanced by appearing to disperse it and thus is a means of eliciting greater employee identification with managerial interests. They argue that an emphasis on employee participation may be of strategic benefit to employers when they are facing significant challenges, when organised labour has considerable bargaining power or when the costs of, or limitations to, more overt control methods are felt to be prohibitive. However, other commentators, such as Kelly (1985) also argue that in circumstances where the balance of power at the workplace favours employees, participatory forums can provide workers with some advantages.

There are a variety of other ways in which labour process themes seem relevant to appraisal. For example, appraisal can also be seen as a process through which previously collective issues (such as setting performance levels and allocating pay increases) are transferred to the level of the individual employee and their immediate superior. Similarly, where employees are unhappy with their appraisal, they are forced into what is largely an individual confrontation with their employer. Thus, as Offe (1976) argues, appraisal may serve to obscure the social and collective elements of work. From this perspective, appraisal appears to have less to do with performance management *per se* and more to do with legitimising management decision making, aided and abetted by its seeming fairness and objectivity.

Appraisal can also be seen as relevant to attempts to move beyond bureaucratic control of the labour process. For example, recent debates on HRM have suggested that, in order to rise to the challenges of recession, increasing global competition, technical change etc, employers must build on the capabilities and commitment of their workforces and therefore must adopt policies which elicit that commitment and encourage a joint problem-solving approach (Storey, 1989). In this light, Townley's (1989) work is of interest, particularly her argument that appraisal is increasing in use because changing production requirements demand greater employee autonomy and discretion.

To sum up from a labour process perspective, appraisal practices appear significant in attempting to influence worker subjectivity and in trying to reduce or diffuse conflict. Nevertheless, we should perhaps be careful not to exclude from our consideration those instances in which appraisal has another clearly defined and explicit agenda: that is, to monitor perform-ance levels more closely (Townley, 1989). Consequently, appraisal may operate at two levels: either as a direct intervention in the labour process which makes performance more visible and the employee more account-able, or, in terms of its influence in 'managerialising' worker subjectivity. This summary brings us to a discussion of Michel Foucault, since his work has an immediate relevance to both the surveillance and the subjectifying (or 'constitutional') implications of appraisal.

Foucauldian Perspectives

The emphasis on discipline and surveillance in Foucault's earlier concep-tualisation of power (most especially in *Discipline and Punish*, 1979) finds an easy application in performance appraisal. Appraisal can be seen as epitomising a desire for observation and surveillance, to make the employee a 'knowable, calculable and administrable object' (Miller and Rose, 1990: 5). It appears as one tactic working towards the notion of disciplinary power enshrined in Foucault's reference to Bentham's 'Panopticon', the model prison in which prisoners can always be seen.

It is easy to see the panoptic power of appraisal in the plethora of appraisal measures, such as the use of Likert scales, graphic rating scales, critical incidents, mixed standard rating scales, behaviourally anchored rating scales and so on. All such measures are designed to refine the observational assessment of the appraisee, to provide an unfettered gaze on their job performance and, particularly, to identify any inabilities they may have in meeting expected norms. Yet appraisal is not just about monitoring 'sub-standard' performance, but knowing why it occurred. Answering this question requires an ability to gaze on the subjectivity of the workers, to know their feelings, anxieties, their identity and their consciousness (Newton et al., 1995).

The rationale of appraisal is the examination of the employee and the 'learning' that can take place through the 'sharing' of difficulties. Yet as we have seen, this counselling role was acknowledged (even by human relations writers) as under threat because the appraiser is also a judge. The appraiser should not be someone who is 'telling, deciding, criticizing' but rather one who 'finds himself [*sic*] listening . . . advising, guiding, encouraging his subordinates to develop their own potentialities' (McGregor, 1957: 92). This participative vision of appraisal brings us close to the celestial vision of a 'god' who 'knows' and 'sees' and 'guides'. At the same time, it provides a remarkably neat example of Foucault's argument that modernity is characterised by a shift away from 'monarchic' and 'juridical' power towards other forms of power such as disciplinary, pastoral and 'bio-power' (Foucault, 1979, 1981). Power is no longer exercised by right or through judges who 'lay down the law'. Rather, for example, a disciplinary power can be seen to operate through observation and the ability:

> to qualify, measure, appraise, hierarchize, rather than display itself in its *murderous splendour*: it does not have to draw the line that separates the enemies of the sovereign from his obedient subject; it effects distribution around the norm. (Foucault, 1981: 144, emphasis added)

The parallel to neo-human relations prescriptions for performance appraisal is transparent. The appraiser is not the sovereign or the judge, but the observer (the 'listener') who must 'measure, appraise, hierarchize'. Appraisal technology uses the observational methods of personnel psychology to gauge where the appraisee 'stands', which can only be done with respect to some assessment of a norm.

Appraisal can also be seen as providing an example of Foucault's emphasis on the productiveness of power, and the way in which this productiveness can be both 'negative/repressive' and 'positive/creative' in its effects. For example, neo-human relations can be seen as productively 'constituting' appraisers and appraisees in a discourse which emphasises the 'learning' that can take place, through 'listening', 'sharing' and through 'solving problems together'. Not only can this lead to 'self-awareness' and a greater 'intelligibility' on the part of the appraisee or subordinate but also, as McGregor noted, it 'often leads the superior to important insights about himself and his impact on others' (1957: 92).

The most direct and detailed example of a Foucauldian perspective on performance appraisal has been provided by Townley (1992, 1993a, 1993b and 1993c) and consequently her work is worth examining in some depth. Townley undertook a textual analysis of performance appraisal documents (forms, notes of guidance and so on) employed by 30 UK universities (1993a and 1993b).

Townley conveys not just a productive view of power (in a Foucauldian sense) but one which tries to elevate the potential of power to be 'positive and creative' (Townley, 1993a: 224; 1993b). It is not that her interpretations deny the negative implications of the operation of power but that she sometimes appears overly concerned to locate the positive. At the same time her accounts secrete an image of power processes which appear as much, if not more, negative than positive in their effects. For example, she noted how performance standards in one appraisal committee were moving towards being set around a 'model' work output. This arose through casual suggestions that the 'troops' might 'get some idea of what was required' if the appraisal record of an academic with 'a particularly successful publication record that year' were circulated to 'subsequent appraisees'. Drawing on her Foucauldian account, Townley read this as an example of how 'a "norm" becomes established' (1993a: 232). But, this is not Foucault's norm since it is not the 'average' score implicit in Foucault's reference to norms and hierarchical assessment (Foucault, 1979). Instead, it is much closer to an 'outlier', to performance at the 'upper end of the scale' and, as such, the 'model academic' she describes is reminiscent of Taylor's 'first class' worker. But of course, if you want to maximise employee output, you set outliers as your model performance, not norms, so that in traditional labour process theory terms, you try to squeeze the last drop of surplus value out of your labour.

In sum, this example illustrates a view of power which appears somewhat more negative and constraining than positive and creative, and Townley's analyses can be seen as indicative of the difficulty of sustaining a positive notion of power when analysing performance appraisal. After all, as we have noted, job performance and its assessment is at the heart of the control of the labour process. If one's concerns are centred away from the employment relationship (as, for example, with the many modern notions of the self such as self-growth and psychotherapy), it is perhaps easier to shy away from the negative image of discipline as control because there is no wage–labour relationship (e.g., in psychotherapy it is the client who pays the therapist, not the other way round; there is no dependency for economic livelihood, even though there may be a perception that 'psychological livelihood' is at stake). But once one is focusing on the wage–labour relationship it is hard to ignore the kind of monarchic/juridical power that Foucault was keen to dispel (Foucault, 1981). While in the modern era, employers may no longer simply rule by right, with managers dictating exactly what employees will do, it can nevertheless be argued that the employer's right to punish and reward does create a lot of good old-fashioned coercive possibilities. Though this quasi-monarchic power of right is only occasionally publicly displayed in all its 'murderous splendour' (Foucault, 1981: 144; cf. the Scottish Timex dispute, 1993), it does still seem relevant to the way in which people toe the line, how they try to please and placate their superiors so that they may one day be granted favours just as kings and queens once rewarded their courtiers (Newton, 1994).

Grey (1994) has recently provided another Foucauldian analysis of performance appraisal which is particularly relevant to our arguments above because it can be (re)read to illustrate the importance of the need for 'courtly behaviour' in performance management. As with Townley, his study is worth examining in some depth and like Townley, Grey is at pains to stress that appraisal and career management should not just be seen as an example of an external and 'negative' disciplinary power, since the 'techniques of disciplinary power become constructed as benevolent aids to career development' (1994: 494). Thus, in his study of career management among trainee and chartered accountants, Grey illustrates how the 'panoptic gaze' provided by recruitment interviews, appraisal ratings and professional examinations are not seen by trainee accountants as regulatory disciplinary devices, but as a means to assist them 'in the maximisation of [their] career prospects' (1994: 494). Yet what is most interesting about Grey's study is that his use of 'career' as a metaphor for an 'enabling' power almost becomes redundant if his data is reinterpreted from the angle of a quasi-monarchic power where aspiring novices are seen to continually need to maintain 'civility'. For example, the 'royal court' provides a strong metaphor for Grey's analysis of the world of accountancy firms, where all those at lower levels of the hierarchy are continually begging favour from the managers and partners at the top of the hierarchy (Elias, 1978, 1982). The eventual goal of young accountants in their 'career' is to gain access to the inner elite of the 'accountancy court', the managers and partners who not only receive very good financial 'rewards' but who are also principally responsible for policing civil behaviour within the court. Thus all members may be criticised for inappropriate dress at the court such as 'having overly garish ties', while women 'universally wore skirts rather than trousers'. As very junior members of the court, trainee accountants are nevertheless 'expected to display enthusiasm and commitment at all times, regardless of the tediousness of the chores'. True aspiring members of the court will not see tedious mundane tasks as chores since 'through an (individualised) conception of career, their mundanity is transformed' (Grey, 1994: 486).

Re-interpreting Grey's analysis, 'career' for these (predominantly) white male middle-class courtiers becomes a metaphor for penetrating the inner circle of the court. Yet participation in court life is perilous. Not only are there the professional examinations to pass but there is also 'the cull', whereby a number of the novitiates are sacked for reasons of business expediency. With the appropriate grace of courtly language, the sacking of employees is officially termed 'counselling out', since it is 'a supposedly mutual career decision for the employee to leave the firm' (1994: 489). Yet the effect remains the same; the new courtier is continually aware that his seniors may entertain their royal prerogative in all its 'murderous splendour' and, in consequence, 'an ingenious game is played between the employees and the personnel staff in which the former seek to identify those who are liable to be "culled"'. As Grey noted (1994: 490), there are a number of signs of one's standing in the court, chief of which is the salary level attained by the courtiers which 'is seen as a "sign of grace"' (1994: 490; differential salary levels are paid to employees in the same grade). The use of such language as 'grace' is remarkable if only because of its strong evocation of the sense of patronage and attaining grace through civil and courtly behaviour (Elias, 1978). Performance appraisal in this context, though supposedly 'liberal' and participative, appears instead as the imposition of an almost 'royal decree'. First, it is directly linked to 'the cull' whereby those rated no better than 'satisfactory' are highly likely to be dismissed. Secondly, 'it is not a two-way process'. Although invited to comment on their ratings employees rarely do so since, in the words of a newly qualified accountant, 'it wouldn't be very good for your career' (Grey, 1994: 491). The sensible courtier knows her place.

Thus, what is fascinating about Grey's analysis of career management among accountants is that it can easily be (re)read as an example of *monarchic* discipline, not discursive discipline.

Summary

Our application of labour process and Foucauldian themes have provided a basis to contextualise and politicise appraisal practice. Attending to Foucault's work highlights the need to examine the way appraisal discourse has developed and the kind of objects it creates in terms of appraisers, appraisees and appraisal practice. Yet we remain critical of the treatment of Foucault by writers on appraisal. We have no quarrel with the conceptualisation of power in general as potentially positive, pleasurable and creative or with the argument that 'repression is not . . . fundamental and overriding' (Foucault, 1981: 73). However, it does seem to us that among some Foucauldians there is a tendency to attempt to continually rescue a positive image of power in the employment relationship and to downplay the way in which power/knowledge relations are likely to entail a mixture of negative and positive effects. In the context of appraisal this means that, as with any other organisational practice, we do need to look at appraisal discourse and practice as it is established within the employment setting. In the employment relationship, we are still observing a quasi-monarchic exercise of employer power enshrined in labour contracts and thus it seems likely to us that the terms of appraisal discourse and practice will be written in a manner that is broadly convenient to management and to the need to control the labour process (for example, as with the unitary images of a consensus of interest between employer and employee contained in neo-human relations discourse). In consequence, current formulations of labour process theory are of interest because of the kind of *foci* they provide in understanding the establishment of appraisal discourse and practice – for example, the way they direct our attention towards the individualisation of employment issues through appraisal and the diffusion of vertical conflict which appraisal may encourage. At the same time, we would argue that we need to be wary of any zero-sum view of appraisal and recognise that in certain (albeit limited) circumstances it can bring benefits to employees.

In the remainder of this chapter, we shall attempt to apply the foregoing theoretical discussion to a consideration of some current and future issues in researching performance appraisal. While the work of Foucauldians and of labour process writers are limited in certain respects, they can nevertheless help to illustrate some important issues concerning research into appraisal.

Research Issues

Manufacturing Consent

Perhaps the first point to note is that there is a danger in overstating the relevance of appraisal to the constitution of employees in a discourse favourable to management. It is important not to overstate capital's need for voluntary compliance from all employees and, more significantly, not to overstate the extent to which management is successful in achieving its aims of generating commitment and identification through appraisal. While we may consider it more likely that appraisal will work in favour of management groups, we should have no a prior assumptions about the outcomes of appraisal. On the one hand, appraisal does represent a greater emphasis on individualism in evaluating employee contribution and can be a route to greater intensification of work. Alternatively, it can in some circumstances, be likened to collective bargaining, in that areas of common interest exist and, when the times are right, can be capitalised on by employees. This view has often been the basis on which professional groups have accepted appraisal systems. Similarly Collinson et al. (1990) found that where the scope of appraisal is widened and where multiple sources of assessment are used, appraisal schemes may be viewed positively by employees. Thus, it must remain an open question as to how much of a zero-sum game appraisal represents.

We also need to recognise that the outcomes of appraisal may be affected by the way in which individual managers approach it. Longenecker (1989) has suggested that managers regularly inflate appraisal ratings in order to avoid confronting subordinates, damaging working relationships and creating written records which may later harm an individual's career. Not only is the appraisal system used in this overtly patronising fashion, managerial motives for so doing often suggest that they see their actions as a way of enhancing individual, unit and organisational performance (Longenecker, 1989). Thus, we see an informal subversion of the appraisal process in order to support formal organisational goals.

We must also be open to the possibility that no group may make significant gains: as Latham has pointed out, 'appraisers and appraisees in organisations perceive that there are literally no consequences whatsoever for a good or bad appraisal' (Latham, 1986: 134). In a similar vein, a recent survey by Bevan and Thompson (1991) indicated that there was no evidence to suggest a link between the operation of a formal performance management system and improved organisational performance in private sector organisations. These points together suggest the need for caution in evaluating appraisal largely on the basis of textual analysis (as, for example, in Townley's 1993a analysis). White it is crucially important to acknowledge the relevance of appraisal texts as an indication of management's formal or public stance on appraisal, it is clear from the limited literature which exists that appraisal schemes rarely work as their formal procedures suggest.

Performance Appraisal versus Performance Management

In approaching appraisal research, we also need to widen considerably the parameters in which appraisal discourse is currently constructed since there are a variety of means of observation and surveillance other than those currently considered by this discourse. For example, there now exist a range of sophisticated 'electronic surveillance' possibilities, illustrated by writers applying the work of Foucault such as Zuboff (1988) and Sewell and Wilkinson (1992). Zuboff presented a number of cases illustrating the panoptic power of recent innovations in information technology which potentially enables the chief executive to instantly appraise the performance of the lowliest employee. Sewell and Wilkinson (1992) illustrated electronic surveillance at a Japanese electronics plant where a 'final electronic test on the completed product instantly identified any defect and traced it to the individual operator responsible' (1992: 280). Such electronic capabilities mean that the performance of workers really does become naked in front of something that appears very close to a panoptic vision of an all-seeing, all-knowing power.

Attention to this panopticism also suggests another limitation of the way in which the appraisal discourse is framed. This is the tendency to see the appraisal interview as central to the appraisal process, overlooking the fact that a lot of surveillance takes place on a routine basis without any particular ritual enactment. For example, Ogbonna and Wilkinson (1990: 10), in their study of culture change in six major UK supermarket chains, observed how cashiers are encouraged to smile 'all the time and [note] that the customer is always right'. The ability to maintain this emotional labour is monitored in a variety of ways, such as through supervisors who 'have a chat' when they detect that 'a check-out operator is not smiling or even putting on a false smile'. It is not difficult to locate other examples of the surveillance of employees' emotion management. A large number of organisations also now employ the marketing 'strategy' of 'mystery shopping' whereby internal company 'observers' act as bogus customers and file reports on the service and 'quality' of individuals and departments.

The above examples question our image of appraisal as centrally enacted through the appraisal interview and they also question other aspects of this image, such as the 'observed' being a managerial or would-be managerial employee rather than a shop-floor worker or supermarket cashier. Given that the examples above share a common concern with the monitoring and surveillance of employees, it seems theoretically unwarranted to bracket them off from the mainstream literature on appraisal.

Human Agency

As our review of the existing critical literature on appraisal implicitly suggested, there is also a need to consider issues of human agency in performance management. Townley's (1989) article reproduces one of the major limitations of early labour process theory since, within her analysis, managers appear to act unreflectingly in the appraisal process (so that the effect of human agency seems limited). For example, there is no reference to the somewhat ambivalent views of appraisal held by many managers, nor to the range of outcomes which are possible. Similarly, in Barlow's account, the differing reactions of appraisees are not discussed sufficiently. On the one hand, Barlow suggested that the operation of the appraisal scheme 'served neither to motivate nor to control' managers (1989: 510). On the other hand, he suggested that some middle managers did accept the myth of rational routes to success. Elsewhere, though Barlow did suggest that 'subordinates typically abide by the boundaries of appraisal agendas with acceptance, collusion or cynicism', he provided no discussion of what underlies these differing kinds of reaction (Barlow, 1989: 502). As Barlow's research (implicitly) suggested, there is a need to consider why some employees internalise discursive regimes more than others and how they rationalise and act within these regimes.

Unfortunately, both of our theoretical frameworks – labour process and Foucauldian perspectives – are limited in analysing human agency. Despite the emphasis within labour process accounts on the social relations of production, there is little doubt that on the whole, the treatment of the subjective experiences of workers and the way in which they interpret these experiences has not been given sufficient attention. As Thompson and McHugh (1990) noted, the tendency within Marxist accounts to write off subjective experience as false consciousness has stunted analysis of the connection between structural and subjective factors.

Similar problems in accounting for human agency arise in Foucault's work. In part it arises because of the way in which human action is implicitly portrayed as the outcome of the identity of subjects being 'constituted' within particular discourses, such as appraisers and appraisees within neo-human relations discourse. While Foucault argued implicitly that subjects will be constituted in a discourse as much by their resistance to it as by their acceptance of it, he did not illustrate how individuals position themselves, negotiate and translate within discourse and practice, how they 'agonise' within the 'permanent provocation' of a 'field of possibilities' (Foucault, 1982: 23); i.e., he did not elucidate a history of human action in relation to discourse, so that there remains only a partial account of the relation between discourse and agency.

In sum, the neglect of human agency remains a limitation of both current labour process and Foucauldian perspectives. It is beyond the scope of this chapter to attempt to remedy this theoretical difficulty (which, after all, remains a significant 'bête noire' within social theory more generally). However, despite this limitation, it remains the case that labour process and certain Foucauldian accounts do provide a strong point of contrast to the neo-human relations text through which performance appraisal is still largely written and, in so doing, they significantly enhance our understanding of key issues in performance appraisal and point us towards interesting areas for further research.

Conclusion

This chapter stemmed from a concern that our existing knowledge on performance appraisal was seriously deficient: that the available literature neglects the context of appraisal, its outcomes and employee responses to it. We contend that such limitations are a consequence of the continuing dominance of neo-human relations assumptions in appraisal research, in particular, the view that appraisal can equally serve the appraiser and appraisee. We have attempted to progress the theoretical debate on appraisal (and consequently redirect empirical investigations in this area) through a discussion of the conceptual frameworks provided by the work of Foucault and by the body of work within labour process theory. We believe that there are gains to be made in seeing appraisal from a Foucauldian perspective in terms of discourse and the objects which the appraisal process creates, thus accepting Grint's (1993) view that appraisal both reflects and constitutes the individual. However, the emphasis by some Foucauldian writers on the positive aspects of the productivity of power, occasionally appears in danger of approximating the rather anodyne accounts provided by the mainstream neo-human relations approach. In addition, we would question the extent to which there has been a move away from monarchic or juridical forms of power in the employment setting.

For us, a greater understanding of the organisational context in which appraisal takes place and, consequently, of appraisal itself, requires an acknowledgement of the differences of interests between appraisers and appraisees, a project to which labour process theory is clearly relevant. Further, we need to identify the actual approaches to appraisal taken by both management and employees. With particular regard to employees, analysis of their attitudes towards appraisal may provide a useful insight into exactly how far values and attitudes have been 'transformed' in response to the newer management approaches of recent years, for example, towards greater individualism and active co-operation with management. We remain sceptical as to whether, through practices such as appraisal, employees have gained a sense of themselves as, say, 'entrepreneurial', 'autonomous' agents (Miller and Rose, 1990; Rose and Miller, 1992). Rather, we would argue that appraisal remains inextricably linked to the contested terrain of control and thus lies at the heart of the management of the employment relationship. In consequence, performance appraisal needs to be seen in the broader context of other forms of performance management, surveillance and accountability.

References

Barlow, G. (1989) 'Deficiencies and the perpetuation of power: latent functions in management appraisal', *Journal of Management Studies*, 26 (5): 499–518.
Bevan, S. and Thompson, M. (1991) 'Performance management at the crossroads', *Personnel Management*, November: 36–9.
Collinson, D.L., Knights, D. and Collinson, M. (1990) *Managing to Discriminate*. London: Routledge.
Elias, N. (1978) *The History of Manners: The Civilising Process* (Vol. 1). Oxford: Blackwell.
Elias, N. (1982) *State Formation and Civilisation: The Civilising Process* (Vol. 2). Oxford: Blackwell.
Fletcher, C. and Williams, R. (1985) *Performance Appraisal and Career Development*. London: Hutchinson.
Foucault, M. (1979) *Discipline and Punish*. Harmondsworth: Penguin.
Foucault, M. (1981) *The History of Sexuality* (Vol. 1). Harmondsworth: Penguin.
Foucault, M. (1982) 'Afterword: the subject and power', in H.F. Dreyfus and P. Rabinow (eds), *Michel Foucault: Beyond Structuralism and Hermeneutics*. Brighton: Harvester Press.
Fox, A. (1974) *Man Mismanagement*. London: Hutchinson.
Friedman, A. (1977) 'Responsible autonomy versus direct control over the labour process', *Capital and Class*, 1 (Spring): 43–57.
Grey, C. (1994) 'Career as a project of the self and labour process discipline', *Sociology*, 28 (2): 479–98.
Grint, K. (1993) 'What's wrong with performance appraisals? A critique and a suggestion', *Human Resource Management Journal*, 3 (3): 61–77.
Hollway, W. (1991) *Work Psychology and Organisational Behaviour*. London: Sage.
Kelly, J. (1985) 'Management's redesign of work', in D. Knights, H. Willmott and D. Collinson (eds), *Job Redesign*. Aldershot: Gower.
Klimoski, R.J. and Strickland, W.J. (1977) 'Assessment centres – valid or merely prescient?', *Personnel Psychology*, 30: 353–61.
Latham, G.P. (1986) 'Job performance and appraisal', in C.L. Cooper and I.T. Robertson (eds), *International Review of Industrial and Organizational Psychology*. Chichester: Wiley.
Long, P. (1986) *Performance Appraisal Revisited*. London: IPM.
Longenecker, C. (1989) 'Truth or consequences: politics and performance appraisals', *Business Horizons*, 32 (6): 76–82.
McGregor, D. (1957) 'An uneasy look at performance appraisal', *Harvard Business Review*, 35: 89–94.

Meyer, H.H., Kay, E. and French, J.R.P. (1965) 'Split roles in performance appraisal', *Harvard Business Review*, 43: 123–9.

Miller, P. and Rose, N. (1990) 'Governing economic life', *Economy and Society*, 19: 1–31.

Newton, T.J. (1994) 'Discourse and agency: the example of personnel psychology and "assessment centres"', *Organization Studies*, 15 (6): 879–902.

Newton, T.J. with Handy, J. and Fineman, S. (1995) *'Managing' Stress: Emotion and Power at Work*. London: Sage.

Offe, C. (1976) *Industry and Inequality*. London: Edward Arnold.

Ogbonna, E. and Wilkinson, B. (1990) 'Corporate strategy and corporate culture; the view from the checkout', *Personnel Review*, 19 (4): 9–15.

Ramsay, H. (1985) 'What is participation for: a critical assessment of labour process analyses of job reform', in D. Knights, H Willmott and D. Collinson (eds), *Job Redesign*. Aldershot: Gower.

Rose, N. and Miller, P. (1992) 'Political power beyond the state: problematics of government', *British Journal of Sociology*, 43: 173–205.

Salaman, G. (1979) *Work Organisations: Resistance and Control*. London: Longman.

Sewell, G. and Wilkinson, B. (1992) 'Someone to watch over me: surveillance, discipline and the just-in-time labour process', *Sociology*, 26: 271–89.

Smith, P.C. (1976) 'Behaviours, results and organisational effectiveness: the problem of criteria', in M.D. Dunnette and L.M. Hough (eds), *Handbook of Industrial and Organizational Psychology*. New York: Wiley.

Storey, J. (ed.) (1989) *New Perspectives on Human Resource Management*. London: Routledge.

Thompson, P. and McHugh, D. (1990) *Work Organisations*. Basingstoke: Macmillan.

Townley, B. (1989) 'Selection and appraisal: reconstituting "social relations"', in J. Storey (ed.), *New Perspectives on Human Resource Management*. London: Routledge.

Townley, B. (1992) 'In the eye of the gaze: the constitutive role of performance appraisal', in P. Barrar and C. Cooper (eds), *Managing Organisations in 1992*. London: Routledge.

Townley, B. (1993a) 'Performance appraisal and the emergence of management', *Journal of Management Studies*, 30 (2): 27–44.

Townley, B. (1993b) 'Foucault, power/knowledge, and its relevance for human resource management', *Academy of Management Review*, 18 (3): 518–45.

Townley, B. (1993c) 'Accounting for performance: strategies of governance', revised version of paper presented at Critical Perspectives on Accounting, New York, April.

Zuboff, S. (1988) *In the Age of the Smart Machine*. Oxford: Heinemann.

9 Performance-related Pay

John Storey and Keith Sisson

Two main types of individual PRP (performance-related pay) scheme are to be found: one involves the linking of pay to performance as measured by the achievement of specific individual objectives and the other – sometimes known as merit rating – assesses performance in terms of certain behavioural traits such as problem-solving, reliability, initiative, cooperation, and so on. A number of recent surveys, which are reviewed in Kessler (1993), confirm substantial growth in both types, especially among non-manual employees, many of whom have traditionally been paid salaries with automatic annual increments related to length of service. Unlike some previous trends in pay systems, the public sector as well as the private sector is affected; for example, among the 500,000 non-industrial civil servants, assessed performance is now integral to salary progression for most grades.

However, despite the outpouring of advice and consultancy that is available, the signs are that in many organizations individual PRP is leading to major problems. Not only is the introduction of PRP being badly handled. The near-obsession with individual PRP means that other features essential to performance management are being ignored or not being given the attention they deserve. We suggest that the single-minded determination to install individual PRP (despite the lack of firm evidence concerning its efficacy) is reflective of the wider move towards individualism and away from collectivism.

If one ignores for the moment the substantial body of evidence which casts doubt on the links between pay and performance, the case for individual PRP sounds very plausible. It is difficult to quarrel with the overall objective of performance pay which has been described as 'to improve performance by converting the paybill from an indiscriminate machine to a more finely tuned mechanism, sensitive and responsive to a company's and employees' needs' (Brading and Wright, 1990: 1). Equally, there appears to be nothing exceptional about the kinds of specific objectives which organizations are said to be looking for in introducing PRP (see Table 9.1),

Originally published in John Storey and Keith Sisson (1993) *Managing Human Resources and Industrial Relations*. Buckingham: Open University Press (abridged).

TABLE 9.1 *The logic of performance pay*

1	It focuses effort where the organization wants it (specified in performance plans, objectives or targets).
2	It supports a performance-orientated culture (pay for results not effort).
3	It emphasizes individual performance or teamwork as appropriate (group-based schemes foster cooperation, personal schemes focus on individual contribution).
4	It strengthens the performance planning process (the setting of objectives and performance standards will carry more weight).
5	It rewards the right people (high rewards to those whose performance is commensurately high).
6	It can motivate all the people (a well-designed scheme will be motivating to all participants).

Source: Brading and Wright (1990: 1)

especially if the possibility of group as opposed to individual PRP is taken into account.

However, as Kessler's (1993) review of the research evidence suggests, there is a significant gap between assumptions and reality in those many organizations which have introduced individual PRP. A common feature is a failure to think through the introduction of performance-related pay in a coherent manner. Thus, in many cases the establishment of formal performance criteria leaves a great deal to be desired – 'objectives' and 'behaviours' which bear little relationship to work practice are being engineered purely for the purposes of having an individual PRP scheme. In the performance assessment process, which lies at the heart of individual PRP, there are complaints about subjectivity and inconsistency which are often compounded by lack of attention to the training of managers in carrying out appraisal and to the administrative procedures for monitoring arrangements. The links between performance and the level of pay are not always clear and effective – in many cases, it is argued, the amount of the incentive element is far too small to make any material difference. It has also been noted that excessive emphasis on extrinsic motivation in the form of pay can result in damage to intrinsic motivation (Deci, 1975). Motivation which comes from pride in work may be undermined.

Perhaps the most worrying aspect, however, is that individual PRP would seem to contradict or sit uneasily with a number of other policies and objectives which managers profess to be pursuing. One of these is the emphasis which many organizations are putting on teamwork. In many cases, notably where operations are inter-linked, individual PRP would appear to be totally inappropriate. Focusing on individual performance goals in such situations can undermine team spirit and cooperation. At the very least, employees may focus their attention on individual targets (especially if they are artificially contrived for the pay system) at the expense of the performance of the unit. Even so, there currently appears to be a widespread insistence on having individual PRP – come what may. Arguably, this clamour for the latest flavour of the month is as good an example as any of the kind of *lack* of strategic thinking in HR and industrial relations (IR).

Why? The discussion in Kessler (1993) is extremely helpful here. He identifies two analytical approaches to understanding managers' choices of pay systems which draw attention to the confusion of motives that appear to be present in many organizations. The first approach sees the choice of pay system as part of a relatively ordered and rational process in which managers pick the scheme which is appropriate to its needs. This, the contingency approach, has a long tradition in the writing about pay systems in the UK (Lupton and Gowler's *Selecting a Wage Payment System*, which was published as long ago as 1969, is a well-known example and is still probably the best guide there is). The second approach sees the choice of the payment system as a far less ordered or rational management process. Rather, it is a largely political or ideological process acquiring symbolic value to support particular interests or values. In this case the details of the scheme, and how it is introduced and monitored, are likely to be seen as largely irrelevant by decision makers. It is the message sent by the introduction of the scheme that matters most.

It is difficult to escape the conclusion that it is the second view that it is most appropriate to adopt, namely that individual PRP is being introduced for largely ideological reasons. The messages which senior managers would appear to be wishing to give are also fairly clear. First, there is to be a change in the culture of the organization. It is no accident, for example, that some of the most publicized individual PRP schemes have been in the newly privatized public utilities. Secondly, managers must manage. A key implication of individual PRP is that managers have to take responsibility for performance management: requiring them to take tough decisions about the payments that are going to be made to individual employees is seen as a critical element in the process. Thirdly, and perhaps most important, there is the focus on the individual; the implication, at the very least, is that trade unions and collective bargaining will play a lesser role in pay determination.

It is also possible to suggest two further and related considerations. One is the inherent belief of top managers – it seems to be almost an article of faith – that pay is the prime motivator in performance. The second is their conviction that not only is managing through the payment system the most effective means of managing HR and IR, but it is also sufficient for doing so. This last point is worth stressing because it has much wider implications. Much is made in the personnel management literature of different types of 'contract'. UK management, it seems, feels much more comfortable – largely because of historical reasons – with the cash nexus or subcontracting relationship than it does with the other forms of contract which carry mutual obligations.

Key Issues in Reward Management

There is no dispute about the overall significance of the reward system in performance management. In the words of Collins (1991: 78), the reward system is important in attracting and retaining employees of the required quality, underpinning the drive to improve performance, and supporting the ability to change.

However, as will be clear from reading any standard textbook (see, for example, Torrington and Hall, 1991), one of the great debates in personnel management is whether the system of rewards, in Herzberg's (1966) terms, is to be seen as a 'motivator' or 'hygiene' factor. Is the system of rewards, in other words, to be seen primarily as a positive incentive to greater performance or, if employees feel that it is unfair, as a source of disincentive? Our view is that it is sensible to start from the second position. This is because, in the head-long rush to individual PRP, there has been a tendency in many UK organizations to neglect other key components of reward systems. Certainly the research evidence suggests that there is considerable scope for improvement in a number of the areas involved.

An Appropriate Pay Structure

Two main aspects are involved. One relates to internal pay relationships or differentials; the other to external pay relationships or relativities. Both these are fundamentally important because they are inextricably tied up with notions of fairness. The problem is that fairness is not an absolute but a relative concept. Pay relationships provide the critical measure of the worth or status which the individual is accorded in the organization and in society more generally; their fairness is judged in comparison to others. If they are felt to be unfair, they can be a major disincentive. In Brown's words:

> The most ingenious of bonus systems and the best of supervision are of little use if the underlying pay structure is felt to be unfair. Consequently, the prudent personnel manager devotes far less time to devising new pay incentives than to tending old notions of fairness. (1989: 252–3)

The recommended method of setting the basis for pay differentials which are felt to be fair is job evaluation. This is simply a procedure for allowing comparisons between jobs in a systematic way. A variety of methods is available, but four main types can be found: ranking; paired comparisons; grading or job classification; and points rating (ACAS, 1988: 7–8; and NBPI, 1968).

Typically, UK companies have operated with a minimum of five or six grades. A number of the Japanese companies who have invested in the UK, notably Nissan, have chosen to work with only two major grades. If a major objective is to improve flexibility, it is argued, too many grades can present major obstacles – job evaluation, by definition, involves the preparation of job descriptions. The tighter these are drawn for the purposes of distinguishing one job from another, the greater the inflexibility.

External pay relationships or relativities, the second aspect of pay structure, have in the past been an issue of considerable controversy especially during the periods of incomes policy in the 1960s and 1970s. Currently, to return to the point made earlier about the ideological explanation of management behaviour, they are supposed to be a non-issue. The main considerations in pay determination, it is argued, ought to be the specific circumstances of the individual organization – the ability to pay, in other words, is of paramount importance. The problem is that the issue will not go away. Organizations have to have regard to what potential competitors for their employees are paying. Otherwise, they risk losing their best people. In the main they do this through market surveys. In the case of managers, for example, considerable use is made of the Hay system to judge the appropriateness of pay levels. In the case of manual workers the local employers' organization is very often the source of the data. In the public services, groups like the armed forces, senior civil servants, doctors, nurses, and teachers have formal review bodies responsible for making recommendations on the basis of comparisons.

Single Status

Most commentators accept that the division between manual and non-manual workers, which is grounded in history, cannot be justified and makes little sense. A key reason is that the very existence of these status differences makes it extremely difficult to win the kind of cooperation and commitment that organizations claim to be seeking. There is no defensible reason, for example, why a 50-year-old skilled craftsman, who has worked 30 years with an organization should have inferior sick pay or pension arrangements to his 18-year-old offspring who only recently joined as a junior. A second reason is that in many organizations it is increasingly difficult to distinguish on any objective basis between manual and non-manual jobs. A third reason is that, as the non-pay items increase in their cost, management want greater return from them. Indeed, in the USA the so-called 'cafeteria principle' is becoming increasingly important: in the attempt to draw attention to the costs and benefits of these elements, employees are encouraged to choose between different combinations of non-pay benefits instead of taking them for granted.

Such concerns have not been translated into practice, however, despite predictions about the decline of the status gap (Price and Price, 1993). Certainly throughout the 1980s there have been moves to harmonize some of the terms and conditions of manual and non-manual workers. Sick pay is a case in point. Examples of single status arrangements, however, remain the exception rather than the rule. In the ACAS survey of 667 workplaces in manufacturing and services in 1988, for example, of the respondents who used some form of job evaluation in determining payment, only one in eight reported that they had an integrated scheme covering manual and non-manual workers (ACAS, 1988: 7).

Admittedly, there are some major problems in moving towards single status arrangements. One is cost. Sizeable increases may be involved and many organizations are in no position to pay the bill. Especially important is the cost of security that would be involved in many organizations as a result of different notice provisions which would arise. Another is trade union opposition. Much of this has come in particular from non-manual unions who are afraid of losing their particular advantages or who fear that they will be 'held back' while others catch up. In many cases, there is a suspicion that managers simply do not perceive the status divide to be a major cause for real concern. On the contrary, the divide could be seen as bringing positive advantages to management. Rightly or wrongly, managements in some organizations feel that it enables them to enjoy the tactical advantage of playing one group off against another.

Group Performance Pay

Kessler's (1993) review of the recent surveys notes that the incidence of 'collective performance schemes, especially those which cover the unit or the company, is relatively low'. Indeed, the ACAS (1988: 18) survey referred to earlier suggested that just over half of the establishments in the sample had some form of group or collective bonus system. The majority of these affected the immediate work group only, however. A mere 13 per cent of workplaces had schemes which covered the workplace or the enterprise as a whole.

There is a widespread view that the direct incentive in group schemes is low because the performance–reward link is too remote. Even so, the relatively low incidence of such schemes is surprising for several reasons. First, there are a number of important variables which can be the basis of performance schemes such as output, cost reduction, sales and quality (for further details, see ACAS, 1985: 14–7, 34–7). Secondly, much work is team work and many of the problems associated with individual PRP schemes are overcome with appropriately designed group schemes – especially if the low level of the payment in many individual PRP schemes is taken into account. Thirdly, group bonus schemes are one of the most effective forms of communication to employees about such key issues as productivity, costs and quality.

Profit Sharing

A further possibility in the private sector is profit sharing. Profit sharing, which has received considerable support from the government in the form of tax incentives through the Financial Acts involves linking pay or some element of pay to profits either in the form of direct cash payments or shares.

The empirical evidence also provides a useful starting point here. There has, it is true, been a significant increase in the coverage of profit sharing since the early 1980s. It is by no means extensive, however. Only 36 per cent of the workplaces in the ACAS (1988: 20) survey which has already been quoted, reported some form of profit sharing and share ownership. Significantly too, in the light of the discussion above about the status divide, the majority of these schemes affected non-manual workers only, however. Only about one-third of the workplaces with profit-sharing schemes or between 12 per cent and 13 per cent of the total applied them to both manual and non-manual workers.

The nature of the Inland Revenue arrangements may have been a deterrent here. But this applies only to government schemes. Here too then there would appear to be considerable scope for improvement in the performance management stakes.

Conclusion

Any serious consideration of the topic 'managing human resources and industrial relations' inevitably involves a critical review of current practice. We have sought to continue this but, in addition, to switch the emphasis onto a positive, practical plane by showing how a practitioner, [. . .] might set about the process of reform at the organizational level. The practical steps outlined re-confirm [that] – there are no easy quick-fixes to be found for this realm of management. None the less, [. . .] there are a great many things that can be done to ensure that the adage that 'people are our most important asset' becomes something more than a shibboleth.

References

Advisory, Conciliation and Arbitration Service (ACAS) (1985) *Introduction to Payment Systems*. Advisory Booklet No. 2. London: ACAS.

Advisory, Conciliation and Arbitration Service (ACAS) (1988) *Developments in Payment Systems*. Occasional Paper No. 45. London: ACAS.

Brading, E. and Wright, V. (1990) 'Performance-related pay', *Personnel Management Factsheets*, No. 30. London: Personnel Publications.

Brown, W.A. (1989) 'Managing remuneration', in K. Sisson (ed.), *Personnel Management in Britain*. Oxford: Blackwell.

Collins, M. (1991) *Human Resource Management Audit*. Birmingham: North Western and West Midlands Regional Health Authorities.

Deci, E.L. (1975) *Intrinsic Motivation*. New York: Plenum Press.

Herzberg, F. (1966) *Work and the Nature of Man*. Cleveland, OH: World Publishing.

Kessler, I. (1993) 'Performance pay', in K. Sisson (ed.), *Personnel Management in Britain* (2nd edn). Oxford: Blackwell.

Lupton, T. and Gowler, D. (1969) *Selecting a Wage Payment System*, Research Paper 111. London: Engineering Employers' Federation.

National Board for Prices and Incomes (1968) *Job Evaluation*. Report No. 83. London: HMSO.

Price, E. and Price, R.J. (1993) 'The decline and fall of the status divide', in K. Sisson (ed.), *Personnel Management in Britain* (2nd edn). Oxford: Blackwell.

Torrington, D. and Hall, L. (1991) *Personnel Management: A New Approach*. London: Prentice-Hall.

10 Human Resources as Strategic Assets: An Evolutionary Resource-based Theory

Frank Mueller

This chapter deals with the theoretical issues and empirical evidence surrounding the relationship between human resources and competitive advantage. The basic argument is that existing theorizing within the SHRM domain needs to be complemented by an evolutionary perspective on the creation of human resource competencies. The chapter will argue that recent advances in the RBV [resource-based-view] can help us understand the conditions under which human resources become scarce, valuable, firm-specific, difficult-to-imitate resources, that is 'strategic assets' (SAs) (Amit and Shoemaker, 1993; Winter, 1987). The chapter will put forward five propositions, including the two main propositions: that strategic assets grow slowly over time, and that codified policies are typically easy to imitate. The chapter suggests developing the RBV in a direction where the focus is not only on the official but also unofficial, formalized as well as informal aspects of organizational life, not only codified but also tacit knowledge. From the evidence consulted it would appear that the preoccupation among both managers and researchers with explicitly formulated, codified HRM policies is a position for which there is neither sufficient theoretical nor empirical justification. In order to develop the chapter's main argument, I will first give my definition of SHRM; then I deliberate the theoretical issues involved, and provide discussion of the empirical evidence regarding the actual impact of SHRM. Following this I discuss reasons for strategic rationalizations by management. I then present an evolutionary resource-based theory which, arguably, avoids most of the persistent points of criticism of (S)HRM.

Originally published in *Journal of Management Studies*, 33 (6), 1996: 757–85 (abridged).

Strategic Human Resource Management and Competitive Advantage

I propose to take the following as the defining features of the 'orthodox notion of SHRM'. According to this notion a strategic utilization of human resources means that:

1 management is *active*, not reactive
2 there is high *integration* between policies
3 an orchestrational role is played by *senior* management
4 and there is *articulation* of policies by senior management.

[. . .]

The Impact of Strategic Human Resource Management: Empirical Evidence

The mainstream concept of SHRM is characterized by the importance placed, first, on the role played by senior management and, secondly, the role of strategic HR policy and planning activities. These two variables are obviously highly even though not perfectly correlated. The argument that better human resource planning is the basis of superior business performance has received support from various angles, even from authors whose overall work reflects a critical attitude to (some aspects of) SHRM. However, in spite of such proclamations, the stronger evidence seems to suggest that we do not actually *know* about the link between SHRM on the one hand, and improved business performance on the other hand (Whipp, 1992). First of all, what is seldom recognized is that the 'strategicness' as such has costs, which include additional decision complexity, commitments to organizational growth that are incompatible with industry conditions, employment security commitments which may turn out to be an unacceptable burden, or the allocation of resources to HR activities which may be too high (Lengnick-Hall and Lengnick-Hall, 1988: 455).

Indeed, over the last decade or so, there has been an intensifying debate over whether a senior management team and their policies can be a likely source of sustained competitive advantage. While Castanias and Helfat (1991) argued that top management can be the basis of competitive advantage, others pointed out that high visibility of top management's contributions leads to high imitability, either through hiring away senior managers or through imitation (Barney and Tyler, 1992; Wright et al., 1994). Udayagiri and Hunter (1995) state that human resource policies or practices are unlikely to be truly scarce and inimitable resources, but rather what constitutes a strategic asset is the higher-order capability of evaluating their contributions to performance. This could be rephrased as managerial knowledge about causal relationships which typically would reside in the higher management echelons. However, Wright et al.'s model would suggest that such a rare and valuable managerial knowledge base would be subject to attempts of poaching in the managerial labour market, and therefore unlikely to be the basis of sustainable competitive advantage. However, these questions are very much unresolved and subject to opposing points of view.

Storey (1989: 3) speaks of a 'lacuna in theoretical and conceptual discussion . . . and hard empirical data' regarding the impact of (S)HRM in those organizations that claim to practise it. Ferris et al. (1990) found that construction firms with higher levels of strategic, including HR, planning *have* achieved higher organizational performance (see also Cook and Ferris, 1986; Ferris et al., 1984). However, Capelli and Singh (1992) suggest that Ferris et al.'s finding could also be explained by forwarding the hypothesis that firms that are doing better have more resources to plan more for the future (p. 170), which poses the quite general difficulty of distinguishing between *cause* and *effect.* In this sense, Hendry and Pettigrew (1988) warn not to adopt 'simplistic views that training leads to improved business performance' (p. 41), because it is more likely that more successful companies will under certain conditions increase their training budget. Nkomo's (1987) statistical tests did not find significant differences between the performance of firms using formal human resource planning and firms that did not. Delaney et al. (1988: 157) surveyed US firms but could not establish a strong statistical correlation between HR programmes supported by senior management and company performance. Rather, they suggested that other – intervening – variables such as information sharing and profit sharing might influence the outcome. Other sectoral studies in the USA have not been able to remove such doubts (Dyer and Reeves, 1995; Katz et al., 1988; MacDuffie and Kochan, 1988).

While some authors have anticipated or interpreted this evidence as confirmation that managerial policies have no significant impact on a firm's economic performance over the medium term (McKelvey, 1982), there are others who are somewhat disinclined towards such an uncompromising interpretation: Purcell and Ahlstrand (1994) argue that planning has been *over*valued in its strategic significance, but they retain the importance of senior management choices as a differentiating factor, in particular its ability to 'step back from taken-for-granted structures and systems and think about the possibility for change' (1994: 39). Guest (1989) showed that the link between specific HRM policies and organizational performance is dubious, and must rely either on potentially unrepresentative case material or 'be based on inference from a range of indirect sources of evidence' (Guest, 1989: 41). Guest (1990) stated that there was no reliable survey evidence (not even) for the USA, because the available case study 'evidence' often refers to the same companies including Cummins Engine, Xerox, AT&T, Procter & Gamble, IBM, H-P, People Express: 'The important point is that they are the regular core of any list which is used to claim that American industry is moving towards HRM'.

SHRM says that competitive advantage can result if management is proactive in their approach to human resources, which requires the build up of an organization-specific knowledge base about costs and benefits. However, Dyer (1985) found that none of those companies under investigation which used employment security policies was in fact able to provide any *data* that could be used to evaluate the costs and benefits of such policies. Thus, overall there appears to be little evidence for stating a *direct* link between SHRM on the one hand, and a firm's performance on the other hand, a fact which Purcell (1989: 73) termed the 'ambiguity in human resource management', Brewster (1995) interprets this lack of evidence about the (S)HRM-performance link as primarily an objection against the 'US' model of (S)HRM, and suggests a 'European' model which takes greater account of the influence of factors such as ownership structures or the role of the State. Demands for management to embrace SHRM therefore do not appear to be actually based on knowledge of performance-enhancing effects of SHRM which led Dyer and Reeves (1995: 668) to speak of a 'strategic bandwagon' which is likely to continue to roll in spite of 'the rather fragile empirical undercarriage on which it currently rests'.

Strategic Human Resource Management and the Problem of Rhetoric and Rationalization

SHRM *as a Form of Rationalization?*

What are the reasons then for the apparent strong emphasis on high-level planning and the 'strategicness' of HR activities? One reason might be an *over-rationalistic view* inherent in (S)HRM, a view that is ignorant to the fact that (S)HRM would be particularly rewarding if the future were radically different from the past, but that the human capacity to predict the future adequately is highly unreliable – which is why the more keenly a firm needs (S)HRM the less capable it is of actually doing it competently. In the strategy literature, in particular in the context of incrementalist agendas, arguments have increasingly questioned whether long-range corporate planning should be regarded as a reliable method for creating competitive advantage. Mintzberg (1978, 1987a, 1987b, 1990, 1994; contrast Ansoff, 1991) criticized the 'superficial rationality' of planning and design school models, which can be seen in their argument that managers only know what they are doing if they make strategy highly deliberate.

Rather, Mintzberg attempts to show that an observable strategy is the logical pattern underlying the historical sequence of successful trials, and creating explicit strategies is not necessarily beneficial, because it can turn into a blinder that blocks out peripheral vision. Indeed, Mintzberg's arguments have been backed by empirical studies on the impact and role of (S)HRM: for example, in a study on small and medium-sized enterprises in Britain, Arthur and Hendry (1990) found that HRM planning approaches did *not* present a realistic picture, and that a process-centred view describing a less orderly world was more adequate. Based on a single case study of a multinational electronic instruments corporation in Britain, Webb and Dawson (1991: esp. 205) reached a similar conclusion. In this vein one could argue that markets are too hostile, competitors too dissimilar and managers too irrational for orthodox strategic planning to work (Whittington, 1993). Bamberger and Phillips (1991: 157) describe human resource strategy as an 'emergent pattern in a stream of human-resource-related decisions occurring over time'. One reason for this emerg-ent character is that centralized intelligence-gathering is limited by cogni-tive boundaries as well as information impactedness affecting an individual or a group of managers. Gioia and Chittipeddi (1991) suggest that strategic planning is often nothing but a metaphor employed by top management in order to *legitimize* emergent decisions and actions.

[. . .]

Rhetoric and Rationalization

In bridging the theoretical and practical gap between policy, practice and performance the most obvious route would be greater reliance on direct evidence given by participants in the change process. This would apply to researchers as much as to management, in so far as both may want to build a knowledge base about the effect of certain policies and practices. As we will see, this is prone to serious problems, which restrict building such a reliable knowledge base. To start with, actual events are rewritten and rendered differently in retrospective accounts especially those provided to researchers with the prospect of subsequent publications (Kanter, 1985: Chapter 10): initiatives largely pushed by one person may be retold to make other people *appear* involved and play a role: furthermore, in *post-hoc* accounts of change the prehistory of change – which is often only known to the participants – is normally lost. What appears as a first step is in actual reality always preceded by other important events. Also, change is bound up with the meanings attached to it, which makes it difficult to replicate the 'formula' elsewhere where those meanings are absent. In the case of Data General, Thomas West had played a dominant role in leading the engineering team towards development of the Eagle machine, but one of his chief lieutenants pointed out: 'When this is all over there are gonna be thirty inventors of the Eagle machine. . . . Tom's letting them believe that they invented it. It's cheaper than money' (quoted in Kanter, 1985: 284).

[. . .]

The belief that planned and formalized HRM policies are 'strategic', rational answers to specific problems and likely to lead to enhanced busi-ness performance, may partly be due to managerial rationalizations. Management rhetoric may be present, either where management represen-tatives write (Roots, 1988; Wickens, 1987) or where (senior) management responses – either in interviews or to questionnaires – are taken more or less at face value. Through *ex-post* rationalizations, managers often impute a strategic quality to changes which did not exist at the time of the event. If that is so then (S)HRM might learn important things from those areas of research where there has been much less emphasis on formalized managerial policies. In summary, policy initiatives on the one hand and performance outcomes on the other hand are separated by an *epistemic* and *practical* gap: epistemic because research has clearly not yet established a solid base of reliable knowledge about cause–effect relationships; practical, because managers themselves are prone to following fads without being able to evaluate their impact on business performance. Formal accounts of organizational change are subject to a variety of problems which restricts learning by researchers as well as imitation by competing firms. The 'rewriting of company history' can be motivated by the desire to:

- facilitate employee commitment by making employees feel part of the change process
- glorify one's own position in the change process
- espouse supreme confidence in the success of the change process
- to show to the outside world that organizational learning is taking place, even if it is superstitious learning [learning based on unproven assumptions]
- to obstruct the explication of hidden 'theories-in-use'.

One practical implication is that management is well advised to invest more time and effort into organizational capabilities of evaluating the impact of certain policies, instead of simply following latest fads. As far as theoretical implications are concerned, the points made thus far seem to suggest that only under certain conditions will (S)HRM policies lead to the creation of competitive advantage. In the following it will be necessary to discuss to what extent emergent features play a role in the creation of strategic assets.

Human Resources as Strategic Assets: Outlines of an Evolutionary Theory

Resources have been defined as 'those (tangible and intangible) assets which are tied semipermanently to the firm' (Wernerfelt, 1984: 172), including skilled manpower, reputation, brand image, ability of managers to engage in teamwork, technological know-how and expertise, efficient working practices, trade contacts, and machinery. Firms within the same strategic industry group have overlapping, but also unique resources. Lippman and Rumelt (1982) argued that even under fully competitive conditions, there might be persistent differentials in profitability, if for other reason than that the 'factors responsible for performance differenti will resist precise identification' (1982: 418). Otherwise, rational management in competing firms would clearly make sure that the crucial resources were also available to them. But because of causal ambiguity, imitation of competing firms is often *not* a short-cut to competitive advantage. Thus, unique resources can provide competitive advantage if they are non-tradeable, non-imitable and non-substitutable (Dierickx and Cool, 1989; Grant, 1991; Teece et al., 1990). *Sustained* competitive advantage requires that the state of resource heterogeneity be relatively durable over time, in order to add significant value (Barney, 1986, 1991). This means that resource mobility barriers (RMBs) are crucial for limiting attempts at imitation (Peteraf, 1993). Barney (1986) showed that corporate culture can be a source of sustained competitive advantage if the corporate culture is valuable, rare, and imperfectly imitable, and if it cannot result from a planned process of change by an imitating firm. Because, if it was open to rational planning and manipulated change processes, and involved only the application of codified knowledge, then it could be imitated by competitors and thus could not be the basis of sustained competitive advantage. Put differently, for a firm to have built a superior resource position, there must be limits on the mobility of resources across firm borders. If other firms can imitate a competitor's resources (and policies) without major problems, then these resources or policies will lose their differentiating value. Two implications of the RBV are therefore that resource mobility barriers are crucial for a firm's ability to build competitive advantage from its human resources, and that formalized strategic HR planning is unlikely to be an effective RMB. The introduction of the concept of RMBs is thus an – even if indirect – answer to the somewhat plausible criticism that HRM is little more than rhetoric if it tries to create the impression that excellent companies can be created anywhere, independent of specific existing contexts. For the concept of (S)HRM to be theoretically promising, it would have to explain why some HR initiatives can add value in a particularly unique and difficult to imitate way, while other firms' initiatives cannot. This would include an explanation of why other firms did not imitate an apparent 'route to success'. Thus, the question that needs to be addressed is which scarce resources enabled certain companies to embrace successful HR initiatives.

The discussion has thus touched upon one of the current debates in strategic management, namely whether management policy is a sufficiently 'strong' independent variable to satisfy our desire for the explanation of a certain company's competitive advantage, or whether management policy is in fact simply an intervening variable that needs to be accounted for in terms of other independent variables. Wright and McMahan (1992) hint at this when they define the RBV as primarily focusing on the relationships among strategy, HR practices and the HR capital pool. The human capital pool as a whole is more likely to be a SA [strategic asset] than a single team, such as the senior management team. The question is also touched upon by Pettigrew and Whipp (1991) with their emphasis on the managerial process of balancing various demands, management's ability to mobilize resources, and limits to imitation. Indeed, even the doyen of the 'management policy' approach in strategic management has found it necessary to redefine his position, and focus on analysing resource mobility barriers. Going beyond his own analysis of competitive strategies (Porter, 1980, 1981, 1985), Porter (1991) acknowledges that an analysis of competitive strategies needs to be complemented by an analysis of which scarce resources enabled certain companies to embrace successful competitive strategies. Arguably, without such a recourse to resource constellations it is difficult to explain why, for example, successful differentiation strategies are not simply being imitated across the industry.

In the same way, even if formalized HR exercises are *insufficient* for the creation of SAs, then they can still perhaps play a role in conjunction with other changes or already existing resources. One way of achieving some sort of synthesis is by saying that while senior management *can* make a difference, the preoccupation with senior management's codified policies is barely justified when accounting for the creation of SAs and, rather, we need to look for non-codified aspects of behaviour in order to find truly effective RMBs. Often such RMBs might be somewhat hidden from view, and it might *appear* as if certain HR policies had made all the difference in terms of resulting competitive advantage. I propose an evolutionary approach according to which the development of strategic human resources:

- happens as a slow, incremental, evolutionary process that requires patience (Proposition 1)
- is facilitated by the existence of 'persistent intent', an example of which would be a continuous improvement attitude (Proposition 2)
- draws on underlying processes of skill formation which can be facilitated or accelerated but not substituted by HRM development activities (Proposition 3)
- draws on established patterns of 'spontaneous co-operation' (Proposition 4)
- is particularly effective if HRs work in concert with other resources, that is if there is resource interdependency (Proposition 5).

Proposition 1

SAs often 'grow' in a slow, incremental, highly uncertain evolutionary process, and the social patterns that result from this is what is meant by 'social architecture'. It is these very characteristics that make the process scarce and difficult to imitate. The medium to long-term horizon required protects against easy imitation. The RMBs are represented by the fact that few in management will have the stamina to see through a long drawn-out process with often no clear pay-off in sight; that the executive incentive structure may reduce senior management's motivation in pursuing such a course of action; that few management personnel will be able to mobilize the various stakeholders behind an agenda with uncertain outcomes. Thus, corporate prosperity not seldom rests in the social architecture that has emerged incrementally over time, and might often even predate the tenure of current senior management.

Adopting such a view would allow us to resolve certain 'paradoxes' identified by the HRM literature: it has been argued that the greater the need for a clan, the worse the condition for its creation through formal HRM policies (Alvesson, 1993; Alvesson and Lindkvist, 1993). Similarly, Lobel (1990) found that cross-cultural training is most effective for those managers who need it least, that is who possess already substantial cross-cultural competence. By implication, the benefits from training might rise disproportionately over a certain period for those managers where a basic competence needs to be built up first. Not surprisingly, Lobel suggests assessing training effectiveness 'through controlled, longitudinal studies' (1990: 42). This obviously suggests that it is misplaced to have any expectation of a quick fix through HRM or quick return on investment. Although this point has been made before, it would appear that the implications have not been sufficiently elaborated. Some HRM scholars but especially consultants have created the expectation among management that any investment into human resource development and adoption of HRM programmes will pay off: Martell, Carroll and Gupta concluded that certain executive HRM practices may 'pay off in the general business population by outperforming alternative policies' (1992: 19).

Proposition 2

Strategic intent which describes the determination of a firm to pursue a certain strategic option *persistently* (as used, for example, by Prahalad and Doz, 1987), can also be regarded as a potentially valuable SA, in so far as the persistent pursuit of a certain strategic policy can be regarded as an important condition for making it succeed. While, generally speaking, imitability of senior management actions is relatively high because they are highly formalized and thus open to diffusion through the normal channels, the persistent pursuit of these policies over a substantial length of time can in itself represent a significant RMB. Similarly, while any single formalized policy initiative is open to imitation, a continuous improvement (CI) *attitude* spanning a range of diverse initiatives and policies is not open to easy imitation, and is another case of an institutionalized persistent strategic intent. This is because CI is composed of a large number of detailed – but on their own, not highly visible – processes which makes CI a highly complex phenomenon (Suzaki, 1993). CI requires the full co-operation and commitment of a large number or even all of the employees, a feat which can typically only be achieved through a sustained and ongoing effort rather than any single initiative. Furthermore, the realization of CI requires an established stock of 'tacit knowledge' which can be *nurtured* by the persistent application of HRM policies, but is unlikely to be solely *created* by any one such initiative.

Proposition 3

Knowing one's job entails having the appropriate routines in one's repertoire, knowing what routines to perform, knowing when to perform routines (Nelson and Winter, 1982). The routinization of activities can be regarded as the locus of operational knowledge in an organization. Blueprints will be drawn upon only when a routine breaks down. Therefore, skills also need to be scripted into the routines, because this is where most of the organization's knowledge is stored. Knowledge that is stored only in theoretical blueprints is likely to be forgotten unless it is *regularly activated*, which suggests the importance of 'skill formation' activities. Skill formation encompasses formal knowledge acquisition and development activities, but also informal and incidental learning in the workplace (Marsick and Watkins, 1990). Skill formation refers to tacit knowledge, action-centred skills, learning from mistakes, learning from interactions with others, learning-by-doing, and can happen as a by-product of another activity. Often, these learning processes happen in semi-autonomous teams, in cross-functional teams or as part of a work-related interaction. Thus, skill formation describes ongoing processes of employees activating knowledge by applying it to specific problems guided by a willingness to learn. By implication, skill formation presupposes the embeddedness of learning into daily work routines and it refers therefore less to isolated formalized training measures. In fact many skills can only be learnt by doing (Odagiri, 1994: 68). Indeed, unless a skill becomes part of operational work routines it is likely that it will be unlearnt again, which is why skills are mostly 'work-related' (Nordhaug and Gronhaug, 1994). This is, of course, an experience managers often go through when returning from an executive development programme. Therefore, HR policies such as employee training and management development are unlikely to be the basis of the creation of SAs, unless they tie into subsequent or contemporaneous skill formation activities, including ongoing daily operational routines. Ongoing skill formation activities result in a 'reservoir' of skills, a certain part of which will not explicitly be recognized as such by management, that is a 'hidden reservoir'. However, HRM policies can play a role as part of a process aimed at preventing the obsolescence of skills by re-activating (part of) the reservoir.

Proposition 4

Many industrial sociologists have, over the past four decades, dealt with the conflict of formal goals and informal motivations. The common message of these arguments is that the organization has an institutional own life, which is notoriously difficult to control and manage (Reed, 1988).

In contrast to institutional economists, who see the collective order of governance structure most threatened by the potentially always present opportunism of agents (e.g., Williamson, 1988), organizational sociologists see the organization's formalized collective rationality challenged by other forms of *collective* rationality (Maitland et al., 1985): commitment to sub-unit goals, games played by groups (Crozier and Friedberg, 1979), power accumulated by departments (Hickson et al., 1971). This whole research tradition dealing with the informal side of organizations, the daily forms of bargaining, exchanges, tit-for-tat, negotiations, and resistance questions the prudence of concentrating too much on formalized policies and rules. However, while some of them were guided by an implicit functionalist framework, especially authors like Selznick, nowadays we are able to view informal practices in a different – often positive – light: strategic assets may be the largely unintended result of many patterns of informal and unofficial behaviour which are explicitly goal-directed, not at the organizational but at the group level. In particular since the 1980s, the case of Japanese companies has demonstrated what had been stated before, namely that deviancy with regard to means does not imply deviancy with regard to underlying goals (Katz and Kahn, 1978: 73; Lincoln and Kalleberg, 1990).

Therefore, HR policies need to be in accordance with the forms of spontaneous co-operation that are embedded into daily operational routines. This means that while HRM policies cannot *substitute* for the potential that resides within established patterns of co-operation, they can *help exploit* this 'hidden reservoir'. Organizational culture has been identified as perhaps the most difficult to overcome RMB, partly because attitudes and beliefs are so difficult to change, but more importantly because huge change efforts often presuppose the existence of those very positive features which the change effort attempts to create in the first place (Fitzgerald, 1988). In fact, 'social architecture' might be a more useful concept in that it refers to behavioural patterns, while the notion of culture often refers to deep-seated values which makes its usefulness to HRM doubtful (Ogbonna, 1992; Smircich, 1983). In the iceberg model used in organization development courses, underlying norms and values are difficult to change, and can only slightly be influenced by formalized HRM policies. Similarly, Wilkins and Ouchi (1983) argued that a strong clan-based culture requires a long history and stable membership; absence of institutional or value alternatives so that the taken-for-granted is not challenged; and frequent interactions among all members across all dividing lines. Some of these can be encouraged through the creation of non-specialized career paths through HRM policies. Wilkins (1984) and Solberg (1985) lay great emphasis upon the role of stories and ceremonies which represent shared organizational knowledge, and can thus transmit the company philosophy to new members. However, the considerable advantage of the concept of 'social architecture' is that it allows for the *constructive role of deviance*, while culture needs conformity in order to become a SA. [. . .] What develops from deviant events from the bottom up is much less visible to the outside, and therefore much more difficult to imitate compared to formal HRM policies. Thus, the most promising avenue for future research seems to be one which sees HRM policies and existing forms of spontaneous co-operation interacting dynamically with each other, so that some of the co-operative behaviour will be channelled into more formalized paths, as shown for example by Whipp (1991) and Mueller (1994a). This provides a preliminary answer with regard to the relationship between policy and practice: the reconciliation between the original plan and the actual practical realities will be achieved continuously in a dynamic context, and thus represents a non-trivial RMB (Mueller, 1995).

Proposition 5

Human resources alone seldom constitute sufficient RMBs, because of the possibility of poaching. While they may play a dominant role in creating competitive advantage, they can often only sustain it in concert with other RMBs, such as trademarks, patents and industry standards. This is why HR policies are likely to be effective mainly if undertaken in concert with (policies affecting) other SAs. Thus, instead of espousing high expectations with regard to employee development and training policies (e.g., Beer et al., 1984: 177–83; Thurley, 1991) one would be well advised to devise development policies while keeping the principle of resource interdependence in mind. It is the complexity typically associated with resource interdependence that can act as an effective RMB.

Empirical analyses conducted within an RBV framework have shown that in fact most companies value their company and product reputation – even though they are obviously sustained by employees – as their most important assets, followed in third place by employee know-how (Hall, 1993). It is difficult to see, for example, what could be more important for Glaxo than its patents, or for British Airways its landing slots at London Heathrow Airport. Clearly, people are prerequisites for this, but so are legal rights, or corporate reputation. Often, people alone cannot *sustain* the success of the 'super stars' of corporate performance: the Microsoft, Intel and Glaxos of this world. Otherwise, once the extraordinary success of a company has become apparent to the outside world, competitors could and would take the requisite steps to poach crucial staff. In fact, in all three cases it is legal rights and brand reputation – combined with industry standards and people – that sustain exceptional corporate performance (see also Cusumano and Selby, 1995; D'Aveni, 1994: 103–4; Kay, 1993).

This chapter argues, therefore, that it is more fruitful to look at how different strategic assets sustain each other, rather than engage in a sterile debate about which are analytically prior or more important. Thus, human resources have to be seen within the *context of the firm's broad array of resources*: employees are central for a firm to retain its valued product reputation, but also vice versa; a highly reputable company will find it easier to attract highly qualified employees (Itami, 1987; Mueller, 1993). To state any special status for human resources is analytically imprecise, unless specifically justified in a particular context. A more realistic model of HRM has to take such considerations into account, which also means that it is of little use to state that human resources are a certain company's most important assets, unless it is specified how these assets in interdependence with other assets sustain the company's resource position and competitive advantage. Further empirical research could perhaps aim at distinguishing certain types of typical resource interactions. One type might be where outstandingly skilled and talented people create the basis of exceptional corporate performance, which can then be made sustainable through use of industry standards and legal rights.

Conclusions and Implications for Research

Even though valuable collections and accounts by Blyton and Turnbull (1992) and Storey (1989, 1995) have shown the difficulties of developing the field of (S)HRM, they have not provided a coherent theoretical explanation that would either explain the existence of these problems or show us a way out of them. Thus, there appears to be an ideal situation of complementary needs: on the one hand, while precise theoretical formulations of the RBV exist, there is a need for applications to specific fields of management and organization theory (Grant, 1991); on the other hand, research into the effects of human resource strategies on organizational effectiveness argu-ably suffers from a lack of 'conceptual sophistication' (Dyer and Reeves, 1995: 668). Indeed, the ideas of the RBV have become more popular recently, but only a few papers (Kamoche, 1994; Mueller, 1994b; Wright and McMahan, 1992; Wright et al., 1994) have attempted an integration with contributions to SHRM. The chapter built on these foundations, and put forward five propositions. While they are 'loosely' based on existing research, their primary purpose is to guide *future* empirical research.

The chapter argued that SHRM can lead to competitive advantage only under those conditions described by an evolutionary resource-based approach, namely if effective RMBs exist. One implication of the foregoing is that truly valuable strategic assets are unlikely to result from senior management's codified policies alone. Rather, what is truly valuable is the 'social architecture' that results from ongoing skill formation activities, incidental or informal learning, forms of spontaneous co-operation, the tacit knowledge that accumulates as the –often unplanned – side-effect of intentional corporate behaviour. Thus, corporate prosperity typically rests in the social architecture that emerges slowly and incrementally over time, and often predates the tenure of current senior management.

The social architecture is created and re-created not only or even primarily at senior management levels in the organization, but at other levels too, including at workgroup level on the shop-floor. Given the low visibility of such spontaneous co-operation, it is even more likely to be resistant to easy imitation and therefore a valuable strategic asset. While this suggests a more balanced view of management's role, management policies are far from unimportant: management needs to take action, either through policies or through changed managerial behaviour in order to facilitate the corporate utilization of the hidden reservoir of skills and social architecture. Thus, while our argument denies HRM the status of a sufficient condition, it can still leave a *necessary* role for HR policies in order to provide a stimulus for change and start a process that results in a more extensive tapping of the organization's 'hidden reservoir'.

References

Alvesson, M. (1993) *Cultural Perspectives on Organizations*. Cambridge: Cambridge University Press.

Alvesson, M. and Lindkvist, L. (1993) 'Transaction costs, clans and corporate culture', *Journal of Management Studies*, 30 (3): 427–52.

Amit, R. and Shoemaker, P.J.H. (1993) 'Strategic assets and organizational rent', *Strategic Management Journal*, 14: 33–46.

Ansoff, I. (1991) 'Critique of Henry Mintzberg's "The design school: reconsidering the basic premises of strategic management"', *Strategic Management Journal*, 12 (6): 449–61.

Arthur, M.B. and Hendry, C. (1990) 'Human resource management and the emergent strategy of small to medium sized business units', *International Journal of Human Resource Management*, 1 (3): 233–50.

Bamberger, P. and Phillips, B. (1991) 'Organizational environment and business strategy: parallel versus conflicting influences on human resource strategy in the pharmaceutical industry', *Human Resource Management*, 30 (2): 153–82.

Barney, J.B. (1986) 'Organizational culture: can it be a source of competitive advantage?', *Academy of Management Review*, 11: 656–65.

Barney, J.B. (1991) 'Firm resources and sustained competitive advantage', *Journal of Management*, 17 (1): 99–120.

Barney, J.B. and Tyler, B. (1992) 'Top management team attributes and sustained competitive advantage', in L.R. Gomez-Mejia and M.W. Lawless (eds), *Advances in Global High-Technology Management* (Vol. 2). Greenwich, CT: JAI Press, pp. 33–48.

Beer, M., Spector, B., Lawrence, P.R., Mills, D.Q. and Walton, R.E. (1984) *Managing Human Assets*. New York: Free Press.

Blyton, P. and Turnbull, P. (eds) (1992) *Reassessing Human Resource Management*. London: Sage.

Brewster, C. (1995) 'Towards a "European" model of human resource management', *Journal of International Business Studies*, 26 (1): 1–21.

Capelli, P. and Singh, H. (1992) 'Integrating strategic human resources and strategic management', in D. Lewin, O.S. Mitchell and P.D. Sherer (eds), *Research Frontiers in Industrial Relations and Human Resources*. Madison, WI: Industrial Relations Research Association, pp. 165–92.

Castanias, R.P. and Helfat, C.E. (1991) 'Managerial resources and rents', *Journal of Management*, 17: 155–77.

Cook, D.S. and Ferris, G.R. (1986) 'Strategic human resource management and firm effectiveness in industries experiencing decline', *Human Resource Management*, 25 (3) Fall: 441–58.

Crozier, M. and Friedberg, E. (1979) *Actors and Systems: The Politics of Collective Action*. Chicago: University of Chicago Press.

Cusumano, M.A. and Selby, R.W. (1995) *Microsoft Secrets: How the World's Most Powerful Software Company Creates Technology, Shapes Markets, and Manages People*. New York: The Free Press.

D'Aveni, R.A. (1994) *Hypercompetition: Managing the Dynamics of Strategic Maneuvering*. New York: The Free Press.

Delaney, J.T., Ichniowski, C. and Lewin, D. (1988) 'Employee involvement programs and firm performance', *Industrial Relations Research Association Series*, Proceedings 41st Annual Meeting, New York, 28–30 December.

Dierickx, I. and Cool, K. (1989) 'Asset stock accumulation and sustainability of competitive advantage', *Management Science*, 35 (12): 1504–11.

Dyer, L. (1985) 'Strategic human resources management and planning', in K.M. Rowland and G.R. Ferris (eds), *Research in Personnel and Human Resources Management* (Vol. 3). Greenwich, CT: JAI Press.

Dyer, L. and Reeves, T. (1995) 'Human resource strategies and firm performance: what do we know and where do we need to go?', *International Journal of Human Resource Management*, 6 (3): 656–70.

Ferris, G.R., Schellenberg, D.A. and Zammuto, R.F. (1984) 'Human resource management strategies in declining industries', *Human Resource Management*, 23 (4) Winter: 381–94.

Ferris, G.R., Russ, G.S., Albanese, R. and Martocchio, J.J. (1990) 'Personnel/ human resource management, unionization, and strategy determinants of organizational performance', *Human Resource Planning*, 13 (3): 215–27.

Fitzgerald, T.H. (1988) 'Can change in organizational culture really be managed?', *Organization Dynamics*, Autumn.

Gioia, D.A. and Chittipeddi, K. (1991) 'Sensemaking and sensegiving in strategic change initiation', *Strategic Management Journal*, 12 (6): 433–48.

Grant, R.M. (1991) 'The resource-based theory of competitive advantage: implications for strategy formulation', *California Management Review*, 33 (3) Spring: 119–35.

Guest, D.E. (1989) 'Human resource management: its implications for industrial relations and trade unions', in J. Storey (ed.), *New Perspectives on Human Resource Management*. London: Routledge, pp. 41–55.

Guest, D.E. (1990) 'Human resource management and the American dream', *Journal of Management Studies*, 27 (4): 377–98.

Hall, R. (1993) 'A framework linking intangible resources and capabilities to sustainable competitive advantage', *Strategic Management Journal*, 14: 607–18.

Hendry, C. and Pettigrew, A. (1988) 'Changing patterns of human resource management', *Personnel Management*, 20 (11): 37–41.

Hickson, D., Hinings, C., Lee, R., Schneck, R. and Pennings, J. (1971) 'A strategic contingencies theory of intra-organizational power', *Administrative Science Quarterly*, 16: 216–29.

Itami, H. (1987) *Mobilizing Invisible Assets*. Cambridge, MA: Harvard University Press.

Kamoche, K. (1994) 'A critique and a proposed reformulation of strategic HRM', *Human Resource Management Journal*, Summer.

Kanter, R.M. (1985) *The Change Masters*. London: Unwin Paperbacks (first published by Allen & Unwin in 1983).

Katz, D. and Kahn, R.L. (1978) (1st edn 1966) *The Social Psychology of Organizations*. New York: Wiley.

Katz, H.C., Kochan, T.A. and Keefe, J.H. (1988) *Effects of Industrial Relations on*

Productivity: Evidence from the Automobile Industry. Brookings BPEA 2:88 (Paper).

Kay, J. (1993) *Foundations of Corporate Success.* Oxford: Oxford University Press.

Lengnick-Hall, C.A. and Lengnick-Hall, M.L. (1988) 'Strategic human resource management: a review of the literature and a proposed typology', *Academy of Management Review*, 13 (3): 454–70.

Lincoln, J.R. and Kalleberg, A.L. (1990) *Culture, Control, and Commitment: A Study of Work Organization and Work Attitudes in the United States and Japan.* Cambridge: Cambridge University Press.

Lippman, S.A. and Rumelt, R.P. (1982) 'Uncertain imitability: an analysis of interfirm differences in efficiency under competition', *Bell Journal of Economics*, 13: 418–38.

Lobel, S.A. (1990) 'Global leadership competencies: managing to a different drumbeat', *Human Resource Management*, 29 (1): 39–47.

MacDuffie, J.P. and Kochan, T.A. (1988) 'Human resources, technology, and economic performance: evidence from the automobile industry', *Industrial Relations Research Association Series*, Proceedings 41st Annual Meeting, New York, 28–30 December.

Maitland, I., Bryson, J. and Van de Ven, A. (1985) 'Sociologists, economists, and opportunism', *Academy of Management Review*, 10 (1).

Marsick, V.J. and Watkins, K.E. (1990) *Informal and Incidental Learning in the Workplace.* London: Routledge.

Martell, K., Carroll, S.J. and Gupta, A.K. (1992) 'What executive human resource management practices are most effective when innovativeness requirements are high?', in L.R. Gomez-Mejia and M.W. Lawless (eds), *Advances in Global High-Technology Management* (Vol. 1). Greenwich, CT: JAI Press, pp. 3–30.

McKelvey, W. (1982) *Organizational Systematics.* Berkeley, CA: University of Berkeley Press.

Mintzberg, H. (1978) 'Patterns in strategy formation', *Management Science*, 29 (9): 934–48.

Mintzberg, H. (1987a) 'Crafting strategy', *Harvard Business Review*, 65 (4): 65–75.

Mintzberg, H. (1987b) 'The strategy concept', *California Management Review*, 30 (3): 11–32.

Mintzberg, H. (1990) 'The design school: reconsidering the basic premises of strategic management', *Strategic Management Journal*, 11: 171–95.

Mintzberg, H. (1994) 'The rise and fall of strategic planning', *Harvard Business Review*, Jan.–Feb.

Mueller, F. (1993) 'Understanding technological leadership: observations from the automobile industry', *Technology Analysis and Strategic Management*, 5 (2): 15–26.

Mueller, F. (1994a) 'Teams between hierarchy and commitment: change strategies and the internal environment', *Journal of Management Studies*, 31 (3): 383–404.

Mueller, F. (1994b) 'Strategic human resource management and the resource-based view of the firm: toward a conceptual integration'. Aston University Business School Working Paper.

Mueller, F. (1995) 'Organizational governance through employee cooperation: can we learn from economists?', *Human Relations*, 48 (10) October.

Nelson, R. and Winter, S. (1982) *An Evolutionary Theory of Economic Change.* Cambridge, MA: Harvard University Press.

Nkomo, S.M. (1987) 'Human resource planning and organization performance: an exploratory analysis', *Strategic Management Journal*, 8 (4): 387–92.

Nordhaug, O. and Gronhaug, K. (1994) 'Competences as resources in firms', *International Journal of Human Resource Management*, 5: 89–106.

Odagiri, H. (1994) *Growth Through Competition, Competition Through Growth: Strategic Management and the Economy in Japan.* Oxford: Clarendon Press.

Ogbonna, E. (1992) 'Organization culture and human resource management: dilemmas and contradictions', in P. Blyton and P. Turnbull (eds), *Reassessing Human Resource Management*. London: Sage, pp. 74–96.

Peteraf, M.A. (1993) 'The cornerstones of competitive advantage: a resource-based view', *Strategic Management Journal*, 14: 179–91.

Pettigrew, A. and Whipp, R. (1991) 'Managing change and corporate performance', in K. Cool, D. Neven and I. Walter (eds), *European Industrial Restructuring in the 1990s*. London: Macmillan, pp. 227–65.

Porter, M.E. (1980) *Competitive Strategy*. New York: The Free Press.

Porter, M.E. (1981) 'The contributions of industrial organization to strategic management', *Academy of Management Review*, 6: 609–20.

Porter, M.E. (1985) *Competitive Advantage*. New York: The Free Press.

Porter, M.E. (1991) 'Towards a dynamic theory of strategy', *Strategic Management Journal*, 12: 95–117.

Prahalad, C.K. and Doz, Y. (1987) *The Multinational Mission: Balancing Local Demands and Global Vision*. New York: The Free Press.

Purcell, J. (1989) 'The impact of corporate strategy on human resource management', in J. Storey (ed.), *New Perspectives on Human Resource Management*. London: Routledge, pp. 67–91.

Purcell, J. and Ahlstrand, B. (1994) *Human Resource Management in the Multi-Divisional Company*. Oxford: Oxford University Press.

Reed, M.I. (1988) 'The problem of human agency in organizational analysis', *Organization Studies*, 9 (1): 33–46.

Roots, P. (1988) *Financial Incentives for Employees*. BSP Professional.

Smircich, L. (1983) 'Concepts of culture and organizational analysis', *Administrative Science Quarterly*, 28: 339–58.

Solberg, S.L. (1985) 'Changing culture through ceremony: an example from GM', *Human Resource Management*, 24 (3) Fall: 329–40.

Storey, J. (1989) 'Introduction: from personnel management to human resource management', in J. Storey (ed.), *New Perspectives on Human Resource Management*. London: Routledge, pp. 1–18.

Storey, J. (ed.) (1995) *Human Resource Management: A Critical Text*. Oxford: Blackwell.

Suzaki, K. (1993) *The New Shop Floor Management*. New York: The Free Press.

Teece, D.J., Pisano, G. and Schuen, A. (1990) 'Firm capabilities, resources and the concept of strategy'. Working Paper No. 90–8, Berkeley, CA: University of Berkeley Press.

Thurley, K. (1991) 'The utilisation of human resources: a proposed approach', in C. Brewster and S. Tyson (eds), *International Comparisons in Human Resource Management*. London: Pitman, pp. 15–32.

Udayagiri, N. and Hunter, L.W. (1995) *Holding onto Brainpower: Managing Experts' Turnover in High-Tech Firms*. Mimeo. Philadelphia, PA: Wharton School.

Webb, J. and Dawson, P. (1991) 'Measure for measure: strategic change in an electronic instruments corporation', *Journal of Management Studies*, 28 (2): 191–206.

Wernerfelt, B. (1984) 'A resource-based view of the firm', *Strategic Management Journal*, 5: 171–80.

Whipp, R. (1991) 'Human resource management, strategic change and competition: the role of learning', *International Journal of Human Resource Management*, 2 (2) September: 165–92.

Whipp, R. (1992) 'Human resource management, competition and strategy: some productive tensions', in P. Blyton and P. Turnbull (eds), *Reassessing Human Resource Management*. London: Sage, pp. 33–55.

Whittington, R. (1993) *What is Strategy – And Does It Matter?* London: Routledge.

Wickens, P. (1987) *The Road to Nissan: Flexibility, Quality, Teamwork.* Basingstoke: Macmillan.

Wilkins, A.L. (1984) 'The creation of company cultures: the role of stories and human resource systems', *Human Resource Management*, 23 (1) Spring.

Wilkins, A.L. and Ouchi, W.G. (1983) 'Efficient cultures: exploring the relationship between culture and organizational performance', *Administrative Science Quarterly*, 28: 468–81.

Williamson, O.E. (1988) 'The economics and sociology of organizations: promoting a dialogue', in G. Farkas and P. England (eds), *Industries, Firms, and Jobs. Sociological and Economic Approaches.* New York: Plenum Press.

Winter, S. (1987) 'Knowledge and competence as strategic assets', in D.J. Teece (ed.), *The Competitive Challenge: Strategies for Industrial Innovation and Renewal.* Cambridge, MA: Ballinger, pp. 159–84.

Wright, P.M. and McMahan, G.C. (1992) 'Theoretical perspectives for strategic human resource management', *Journal of Management*, 18 (2): 295–320.

Wright, P.M., McMahan, G.C. and McWilliams, A. (1994) 'Human resources and sustained competitive advantage: a resource-based perspective', *International Journal of Human Resource Management*, 5 (2): 301–26.

11 Checking Out Service: Evaluating Excellence, HRM and TQM in Retailing

Patrice Rosenthal, Stephen Hill and Riccardo Peccei

Products, technology and price are vulnerable to emulation by competitors. Thus many companies choose now to differentiate themselves on something that they assume is less easy to copy: quality of customer service. The role of the *deliverers* of the service – those employees with direct customer contact – is thought to be crucial in the quality management and applied business literature (Bowen and Schneider, 1988). The problem for managers is how to ensure the quality of the personal treatment their customers receive from employees. From a sociological perspective, Fuller and Smith (1991) argue that neither simple and direct control by managers, nor bureaucratic solutions that standardise the service transaction by means of rules, are likely to elicit the required levels of responsible autonomy and sensitivity to interactional dynamics.

The alternative route to service quality that is widely canvassed in managerial circles is through the attitudes and orientations of employees. Internalisation of quality norms is a prescription of the quality management literature, which emphasises the development of a culture of quality among all organisational members. It is also found in the emphasis of the human resource management literature, that managers should pursue policies that increase employee commitment, motivation and flexibility, in place of control and standardisation.

In this chapter we examine the impact of this alternative route on employees.

Principles and Debates

A number of the principles expounded in contemporary management thought underpin most recent attempts to improve service quality. At the

---

Originally published in *Work, Employment & Society*, 11 (3), 1997: 481–503 (abridged).

centre is the individualising philosophy of the contemporary enterprise culture, in particular the values of self-actualisation, freedom and 'respect for the individual'. This philosophy informs the 'excellence' approach to organisations, which in turn influences human resource and quality management. A second principle is that of the full utilisation of human resources as a basis for obtaining competitive advantage, through high employee satisfaction, commitment and productivity. A third is the notion of assigning more discretion and responsibility ('empowerment') which is central to all approaches. Fourth, there is the weight given to customer satisfaction achieved through continuous improvement and service excellence. Finally, there is the emphasis placed on the need to integrate individual and organisational goals through the creation of 'strong' performance-oriented corporate cultures.

Discussions of quality management and HRM have a tendency to polarise. The optimistic position is that the principles underlying the approaches are genuine, being both realisable and genuinely held by managers, and that quality management and HRM benefit both firms and employees alike. The critical stance is that quality and human resource management, and the broader ideas of enterprise and excellence, increase the subjection of employees. One view is that greater subjection results from the refinement of techniques of surveillance that permit enhanced control, while the other is that it arises out of the manipulation of meaning. New managerial fashions therefore contain a large element of sham in terms of what they claim to deliver to employees. The control approach has its roots in the labour process tradition, while some recent variants of control develop the 'panopticon' element of the Foucauldian perspective on power. Panopticonism increases the potential for management to control individuals via the deployment of techniques of individualisation and enhanced surveillance. Those concerned with the manipulation of meaning suggest that, in structuring meaning, corporations manage to influence how their employees think about and interpret 'reality'. Structuring may take place either via ideologies or discursive practices, following different theoretical perspectives, and the effect is to create norms and meanings that are congruent with corporate interests.

Within the control approach, the claim is that participation in decisions and the amount of autonomous decision-making are trivial (Delbridge et al., 1992; Parker and Slaughter, 1993; McArdle et al., 1995). Sewell and Wilkinson (1992) regard quality management as individualising accountability and so, in conjunction with improved technologies of surveillance in the modern panopticon, as increasing managerial control. The threat of the sack if performance is inadequate is what gives surveillance its disciplinary force in this account. Surveillance techniques are both technical and social, the first being the deployment of information technologies in order to monitor the quality performance of employees, the second being the way members of work teams come to monitor the quality of each other's work.

In a similar vein, Fuller and Smith (1991) identify customer feedback, one of the tools of quality management, as a technique for monitoring, evaluating and disciplining interactive service workers such as checkout staff. A final criticism of programmes that claim to increase discretion or empower is that they lead to effort intensification (Dawson and Webb, 1989; Sewell and Wilkinson, 1992; Parker and Slaughter, 1993).

There is a more pragmatic approach, which indicates that an increase in discretion and employee involvement/participation may occur, albeit within a limited and managerially defined agenda (Hill, 1991, 1995; Wilkinson et al., 1991, 1992, 1997; Rees, 1995; Collinson and Edwards, 1996).

The second approach within the critical tradition is concerned with the structuring of meaning within organisations. Following the publication of *In Search of Excellence* (Peters and Waterman, 1982), issues of meaning and identity, in particular how these are socially constructed, have been emphasised. The claim that 'excellent' organisational cultures lead employees to identify with the objectives of their employers informs the corporate fascination with cultural engineering. 'Improving' organisational culture, by channelling identity and behaviour in ways that align with corporate objectives, is a central prescription of excellence and of quality and human resource management. The managerialist position is that excellence and quality go with the grain of human nature and therefore cultural change is not manipulative. Indeed, in several versions of quality management it is the re-education of senior managers that has primacy, the issue being to persuade the people at the top to create the conditions for employees to express their own human nature. This concern with structuring meaning and identity has of course been widely discussed in the critical literature, first in the analysis of ideology and later of discourse (see du Gay, 1996).

The traditional notion of ideology indicates that managers try to shape the values and beliefs of others, in effect by means of propaganda. For example, the rhetoric of markets, customers and enterprise in the excellence approach has been described as an ideology that attempts to establish the moral superiority of the private sector and its managers in popular consciousness (Webb and Cleary, 1994). Quality management has been similarly characterised as ideological, in this case as an attempt by management to create new forms for controlling subordinate staff that establish hegemonic control of their thoughts and so substitute consent for coercion (Tuckman, 1995). HRM has been described by Keenoy and Anthony (1992: 235) as an 'ideological script' that attempts to redefine the meaning of work for employees and how they relate to their managers. Against the post-structuralist views of the inseparability of language and practice and the discursively constituted nature of reality, ideology assumes an objective reality that is in principle knowable provided people cut through the propaganda that attempts to obscure this.

Other critics have taken a post-structuralist, specifically a Foucauldian, position that privileges both 'discourse' and the construction of identity. The analysis of contemporary management by Deetz (1992) is that, through their monopoly of the systems of discourse which mould meaning, language and personal identity, corporations have the opportunity to 'produce' their employees (workers and managers alike). Discursive monopoly, in alliance with disciplinary power, means that corporations greatly influence what employees internalise as 'common sense, self-evident experience and personal identity' (Deetz, 1992: 37). The strong cultures advocated in the excellence approach have hegemonic power; thus employees willingly accept the views of reality and the personal identities promoted by their corporations. The potential for totalitarianism arises because, when they root out ideas and practices among employees that do not reinforce the corporation's own values, managers suppress cultural diversity and promote a monocultural world.

The various accounts of the manipulation of meaning are long on the content of ideological or discursive messages and on theories of identity. They are short, however, on the substantiation that managerial ideologies or discourses do indeed work in the ways that they allege. Little evidence has been presented for the view that corporations have substantial effects on the attitudes, beliefs or identities of their employees. There is a long-established criticism of the older sociological use of ideology, that people are not cultural dupes and see through attempts to manipulate their thoughts in favour of the socially powerful (Abercrombie et al., 1980). Moreover, within the post-structuralist perspective, Foucault's own view that identity remains unsettled and is never finally determined, because individuals are subject to a variety of discourses, some of which conflict, indicates that corporate cultures are unlikely to operate quite as indicated above.

The Intervention

The organisation under investigation (hereafter referred to as Shopco) is one of the three major supermarket companies in the UK.

[. . .]

Service Excellence Training

Training of management, supervisory and front-line staff in the 'new' definition of customer service was seen as an integral part of the programme. Its purpose was to educate staff in Shopco's new customer service values and to find ways of translating those values into individual behaviour. The 'message' of Service Excellence training was one of a new freedom (and responsibility) in staff dealings with customers. The old, 'scripted' style of service (for example, greeting every customer with the same obligatory smile and form of words) was to give way to a new authenticity, a new freedom to respond in ways that seem natural and appropriate to the individual employee and customer (for example, to call a customer 'love' if that is the natural form of address). Sensitivity to individual customer requirements was stressed: employees were to continually search for ways to *exceed* these requirements and expectations.

Employee Empowerment

The objective of the training was to inculcate service quality values and competences among staff. Obstacles to the *use* of these competences on behalf of customers were to be removed through the empowerment of employees. This was to encompass changes in the nature of front-line jobs and of supervision.

A stated purpose of this new autonomy was to increase the scope for continuous improvement in regard to service quality. It was also anticipated that the programme would make jobs more varied and interesting. The increased discretion and variety in job design was seen, in turn, to require the development of hierarchical trust.

[. . .]

The new customer-oriented values and behaviour desired of employees were seen to be inconsistent with the 'command and control' style of managing traditionally practised within Shopco. 'Managerial Excellence' was thus explicitly formulated and required of individual managers, and these requisite behaviours became criteria used in assessment and reward. 'Excellent' managers were to function as role models, demonstrating their commitment to customers through their personal behaviour on the selling floor. Changes in attitudes and behaviour towards *employees* were presented as a vital aspect of the cultural shift.

Data and Discussion

The critical view is that initiatives such as Shopco's, although presented in a positive light by management, are either designed, or tend in practice, to greater subordination of employees. If management's objectives are realised, they are achieved through some combination of work intensification masquerading as 'empowerment', increased control and surveillance and the manipulation of meaning.

[. . .]

Front-line Reaction to Service Excellence

Both our interview and survey data indicate a strong endorsement of Service Excellence by front-line staff. In the interviews, no one spoke

TABLE 11.1 *Descriptive statistics*

Measures	Time 1		Time 2	
	Mean	Std Dev.	Mean	Std Dev.
Employee Internalisation of Service Excellence (SE):				
Understanding of SE	4.21	0.77	4.14	0.79
Value for future of store	4.48	0.67	4.43	0.70
Personal commitment to SE	4.00	0.85	3.98	0.86
Commitment to Customer Service	3.89	0.55	3.90	0.57
Job Autonomy	3.73	0.74	3.71	0.82
Supportiveness of Supervision	3.34	0.96	3.32	0.96
Job Pressure	3.58	0.76	3.64	0.78

No statistically significant differences between Time 1 and Time 2 means.

negatively about the value of the initiative or questioned the goal of better service, and the majority were enthusiastic. Based on survey data at Time 1, employees reported a high level of understanding of the Service Excellence initiative (mean=4.21); a positive assessment of its value for the future of their store (mean=4.48); and a high level of personal commitment to it (mean=4.00). Nor was there any erosion of these positive views six months later at Time 2 (see Table 11.1).

Front-line reaction to the 'idea' and aims of Service Excellence was, and remained, strongly positive. However, Shopco management was looking for something more than an endorsement of the initiative. The ultimate objective was the provision of a more personalised, flexible and innovative service, this achieved through employee commitment to customers. Commitment to customer service (CCS) was measured in the survey by a set of questions tapping the extent of employees' (self-reported) effort and continuous improvement on behalf of customers. The mean CCS rating at Time 1 was 3.89, with no significant change six months later at Time 2.

Does this level of customer-oriented behaviour represent the success of the programme? The mean score is relatively high, but the absence of benchmark data from comparable organizations makes evaluation more difficult. Our survey data do, however, enable us to provide an overall picture of the situation in Shopco prior to the implementation of Service Excellence and to trace broad shifts in CCS over the lifetime of the programme. Employees were asked whether Service Excellence had changed the way they did their job. We can therefore identify a subgroup of employees who, by their own account, already showed a strong customer orientation prior to the implementation of the programme. These were individuals who reported a high level of CCS in the first survey (i.e., who scored 4 or above on the CCS scale) but at the same time, said that Service Excellence had not changed the way they did their job. This group of 'pre-committed' employees (N=144) accounted for 20 per cent of our sample at

Time 1. Prior to the implementation of Service Excellence, therefore, about one in five Shopco employees already engaged (or claimed to engage) in the kind of customer-oriented behaviour management was seeking to elicit through the programme.

This 20 per cent figure provides an important benchmark for assessing overall changes in CCS as the programme unfolded. Our data indicate a positive shift in CCS following the launch of the programme. By the time we conducted the first survey, six months after the initiative, the number of employees reporting a high level of customer orientation had more than doubled, with exactly half the workforce saying it was strongly committed. Thereafter the situation appears to have stabilised. The proportion of highly committed employees remained at 50 per cent in the second survey carried out six months later (i.e., a year into the programme).

Three background points stand out. First, employees appeared strongly to endorse the idea and aims of the programme. Secondly, there was a sharp increase in customer orientation among employees in the early stages of the initiative, after which the system appears to have stabilised. And thirdly, front-line staff, by and large, reported relatively high levels of the kind of customer-oriented behaviour sought by management.

[. . .]

The enlargement of discretion cannot be disputed. There has been an advance over the virtual absence of discretion under the old regime, and this is not trivial in the eyes of store staff. On the other hand, we would assess this empowerment as being fairly limited. Jobs have been redesigned by the introduction of more discretion and, as we show below, by task enlarging flexibility. Service Excellence has also modified the organisation of work, because the company has reduced the number of supervisors and redefined their role to become more managerial with less direct intervention in operations, reflecting the new situation of greater discretion among staff. In general, the more the constraints deriving from an existing design of jobs and organisation of work are relaxed, the greater the possibilities for empowerment. However, Shopco did not consider even more far-reaching redesigns, such as introducing the self-managing teams found in some quality programmes. Nor do the documentary and interview material suggest increased participation by hourly paid staff in the decisions made by those above them in the hierarchy, which is the other dimension defined in the literature.

[. . .]

Our interview data do not support a view that Shopco's customer service programme has intensified effort. None of the interview respondents suggested that the new customer service requirements have made the work physically, intellectually or emotionally harder.

[. . .]

Individuality is a key value of the excellence and HRM literature, and the training programme uses the language of individual freedom and self-expression to convey how it wishes its staff to behave in their dealings with customers. The majority of our interview respondents did indeed feel freer to 'be themselves' when relating to customers and positively welcomed the opportunity for greater self-expression afforded by the programme. Many of them commented favourably on the fact that now they could be more 'natural' in their dealings with customers, and contrasted this new freedom with the constraints and artificiality previously imposed by the need to adhere to pre-set company rules and scripts governing every aspect of their interaction with customers.

[. . .]

Thus the Shopco case suggests that the new management discourse of quality can indeed have a substantial effect on aspects of employee consciousness, and also resonate with pre-existing attitudes and orientations on the shopfloor. It lends little support, though, to arguments about the hegemonic qualities of managerial discourses and their homogenising effects.

Indeed, our data allow us to point to an unexpected and critical potential of the quality discourse, when it is used by staff to bring managers into line with *their* expectations. Many people said that they evaluated actions by other individuals or groups on the basis of whether or not they conformed to the espoused values of the programme. Any actions that were not deemed to do so were seen to be illegitimate. The most frequent examples given concerned lapses by managers into the 'old' authoritarian mode of issuing commands or behaving disrespectfully or condescendingly towards employees. If managers were to behave in ways that did not follow the guidelines on how to treat staff (or, less typically, customers), employees apparently felt that they could use the language of the programme to express their displeasure with management and the company. Indeed, the language seems to have given many a new confidence in their dealings with Shopco, because it provides a clear and legitimate yardstick by which to assess managerial actions. This may be an unanticipated consequence of training people to become more confident. If the internalisation of the language and concepts of customer service really is a form of manipulation, then it certainly does not work to smother discontent under a hegemonic and discursive blanket. On the contrary, some staff now apparently feel empowered to scrutinise their managers and supervisors, to see whether they will manage in an 'appropriate' way. The discourse of quality and customer service may be a double-edged sword which can be used as much by employees to 'reconstitute' management, as by management to 'reconstitute' employees.

Conclusion

This investigation provides no support for the view that, if a company's objectives of improving service quality are realised, they are achieved through some combination of sham empowerment, work intensification and increased surveillance. From senior management's perspective, the programme does appear to have had a positive impact in Shopco. First, a large majority of employees strongly endorse Service Excellence, and there is a substantial level of support for the values and concepts of service quality and internalisation of the language. This endorsement has survived into the second year of the programme. Secondly, half of the staff say that they engage in the sort of customer-oriented *behaviours* that the programme was seeking to elicit. As 20 per cent were apparently pre-committed to customer service, the programme seems to have had a positive effect on 30 per cent of staff. This can be seen as a fairly substantial impact within a system as large as Shopco.

It is particularly significant for our argument that high levels of customer service are neither achieved through, nor associated with, disempowerment or work intensification. The discretion people have at work has increased rather than decreased and is not trivial, although this empowerment has a limited scope. The same applies with respect to freedom of expression on the job. In the interviews, people report greater opportunities for self-expression with customers. At the same time, they recognise that constraints on their freedom of action remain; but they do not see these as illegitimate or as contradicting the message of Service Excellence. Finally, there is no evidence that the attempt to improve customer service via the programme has led to a systematic intensification of work at store level. Thus, within clear limits, the optimism of the management writers and others is better supported here than the pessimism of the control school.

Given these results, it is worth considering what specific features may have contributed to the Shopco outcome, following the contingency approach noted earlier. First, Service Excellence was explicitly designed to give store staff more discretion and, moreover, this was a policy decision of top management, in contrast to schemes where increased discretion is not a design feature or where the sponsoring managers show no particular commitment to the objective. Secondly, middle management manipulation or resistance, which is a feature of some initiatives where TQM [Total Quality Management] disturbs the political system within management or because of the changes it brings to relations with subordinates, was noticeably absent in Shopco. Top managers made compliance with Service Excellence one of the criteria to be used in rewards and assessments, giving store-level managers a good reason to toe the line. Thirdly, the upgrading of supervisory work and a reduction in their numbers, created the space for enlarged jobs and more discretion among the staff.

Fourthly, the intervention occurred within the context of a predominantly female workforce engaged in direct interaction with customers. In interviews, many people suggested they had already possessed the skills required for the 'emotional labour' (see, for example, Hochschild, 1983; Ashforth and Humphrey, 1993) in which they are engaged, and therefore chafed under the artificiality imposed by the company script. Thus, the demands imposed by the new quality regime were not seen as particularly onerous, and the greater freedom in customer interaction was positively welcomed. Finally, the management style previously practised within the firm was relatively authoritarian and employee discretion closely delimited. With this as a starting point, even a modest shift towards a more open and supportive management style would be expected to make a substantial positive impression on employees. In short, the nature of the work, the workforce and employee relations provided fertile ground for the intervention.

What of the role of discourse in the overall process of change within Shopco? Was the new managerial discourse of quality instrumental in (re)shaping the consciousness of employees? There seems to have been a strong initial impact. The interviews showed that many employees took on the language of Service Excellence and appeared to structure their representations of work activity in its terms. The survey indicated that systematic exposure to the new quality discourse through structured training had a significant effect on employees' attitudes towards customer service. Indeed, normative re-educative training appeared to have more of an effect than prior orientation to the quality message.

This suggests that managerial discourse did have an effect on how employees viewed certain aspects of their organisational world. It lends little support, though, to more radical arguments about hegemony and cultural homogeneity. First, there was considerable variation in how receptive people were to the message of Service Excellence and in the strength of their customer orientation: some employees were more resistant than others to the 'dominant' discourse. Secondly, there was no sign that the longer the programme lasted the more people endorsed the aspects that we were able to measure. Indeed, the qualitative evidence may suggest some decline in the language of Service Excellence.

Thirdly, there was the unanticipated consequence of Service Excellence, that employees used its language and concepts to try to bring managers into line with worker expectations. The deeper implications of our evidence for the use of managerial rhetoric against its instigators are of course subject to interpretation and debate. One view would interpret this as a rational and instrumental action on the part of workers, because they know that it is less easily resisted by managers. In this account, language is calculatedly turned back on managers to the potential benefit of employees: through such action they are better able to resist peremptory treatment from supervisors or managers. Thus management has ceded some control. An alternative view might interpret our evidence as signalling the *greater* subjection of employees. Here, the 'turning back' of rhetoric would illustrate what is seen to be management's increasing ability to dictate the parameters of possible dissent. Service Excellence contributes to management's project of totalising control, through the displacing of other and more significant points of resistance from the consciousness of employees.

Confirmation of either position is beyond the bounds of our data. However, two points are worth noting. First, it was management's treatment of staff, as opposed to customers, that employees typically said they resisted through the language of Service Excellence. Thus the quality discourse had not had the effect of replacing employees' self-concern with a monolithic attention to customers (a more desirable arena for dissent from management's point of view). Secondly, existing arenas of potential conflict, such as collective bargaining over pay and conditions, are not affected by the programme. Given this, it is difficult to see that the increased scrutiny of managerial behaviour described by employees in fact represents a totalising of management control within Shopco. More generally, therefore, it can be argued that managerial discourse did have an effect on employee meanings within Shopco, but this was neither a 'blanket' nor a 'blank cheque'.

References

Abercrombie, N., Hill, S. and Turner, B.S. (1980) *The Dominant Ideology Thesis*. London: Allen and Unwin.

Ashforth, B. and Humphrey, R. (1993) 'Emotional labour in service roles: the influence of identity', *Academy of Management Review*, 18 (1): 88–115.

Bowen, D. and Schneider, B. (1988) 'Service marketing and management: implications for organizational behaviour', *Research in Organizational Behavior*, 10 (43): 43–80.

Collinson, M. and Edwards, P. (1996) 'Empowerment or constrained involvement? The place of employers in quality management'. Unpublished paper, Warwick Business School, University of Warwick, Coventry.

Dawson, P. and Webb, J. (1989) 'New production arrangements: the totally flexible cage', *Work, Employment and Society*, 3 (2): 221–38.

Deetz, S. (1992) 'Disciplinary power in the modern corporation', in M. Alvesson and H. Willmott (eds), *Critical Management Studies*. London: Sage.

Delbridge, R., Turnbull, P. and Wilkinson, B. (1992) 'Pushing back the frontiers: management control and work intensification under JIT/TQM factory regimes', *New Technology, Work and Employment*, 7 (2): 97–106.

Fuller, L. and Smith, V. (1991) 'Consumers reports: management by customers in a changing economy', *Work, Employment and Society*, 5 (1): 1–16.

du Gay, P. (1996) *Consumption and Identity at Work*. London: Sage.

Hill, S. (1991) 'Why quality circles failed but total quality might succeed', *British Journal of Industrial Relations*, 29 (3): 541–68.

Hill, S. (1995) 'From quality circles to TQM', in A. Wilkinson and H. Willmott (eds), *Making Quality Critical: Case Studies in Organisational Change*. London: Routledge.

Hochschild, A. (1983) *The Managed Heart: Commercialization of Human Feeling*. Berkeley, CA: University of California Press.

Keenoy, T. and Anthony, P. (1992) 'HRM: metaphor, meaning and morality', in P. Blyton and P. Turnbull (eds), *Reassessing Human Resource Management*. London: Sage. pp. 233–55.

McArdle, L., Rowlinson, M., Proctor, S., Hassard, J. and Forrester, P. (1995) 'Total quality management and participation: employee empowerment or the enhancement of exploitation?', in A. Wilkinson and H. Willmott (eds), *Making Quality Critical: Case Studies in Organisational Change*. London: Routledge.

Parker, M. and Slaughter, J. (1993) 'Should the labour movement buy TQM?', *Journal of Organizational Change Management*, 6 (4): 43–56.

Peters, T. and Waterman, R.H. (1982) *In Search of Excellence*. New York: Harper and Row.

Rees, C. (1995) 'Quality management in the service industry: some case study evidence', *Employee Relations*, 17 (3): 99–109.

Sewell, G. and Wilkinson, B. (1992) 'Empowerment or emasculation: shopfloor surveillance in a total quality organization', in R. Blyton and P. Turnbull (eds), *Reassessing Human Resource Management*. London: Sage.

Tuckman, A. (1995) 'Ideology, quality and TQM', in A. Wilkinson and H. Willmott (eds), *Making Quality Critical: Case Studies in Organisational Change*. London: Routledge.

Webb, J. and Cleary, D. (1994) *Organisational Change and the Management of Expertise*. London: Routledge.

Wilkinson, A., Allen, P. and Snape, E. (1991) 'TQM and the management of labour', *Employee Relations*, 13 (1): 24–31.

Wilkinson, A., Godfrey, G. and Marchington, M. (1997) 'Bouquets, brickbats and blinkers: TQM and EI in practice', *Organizational Studies*.

Wilkinson, A., Marchington, M., Goodman, J. and Ackers, P. (1992) 'Total quality management and employee involvement', *Human Resource Management Journal*, 2 (4): 1–20.

Part III

THE EMERGENCE OF NEW ORGANIZATIONAL FORMS AND RELATIONSHIPS

So far in this volume, we have been exposed to various analyses of the nature of strategic human resource management (SHRM), its location within different economic and social contexts, and the link between SHRM and business performance. In this section we turn to a series of chapters which shift the focus towards the link between structures and relations. As we noted in the overall introduction to this volume, it has been traditional to treat employment relationships and organizational structures as distinct domains. The former has conventionally been the province of writers on industrial relations, whereas the latter has been within the territory of organization theory. Increasingly, however, in tune with significant developments in practice, analyses have tended to blur that traditional demarcation. Quite simply, transformations in organizational forms have impacted simultaneously upon both structures and relationships. The chapters in this section reflect that fact.

The chapter by Homa Bahrami captures the excitement surrounding the emergence of the new flexible and agile enterprises in the knowledge-based industries. Basing his analysis upon a study of 37 high-technology firms in Silicon Valley, California, he brings to life rather vividly the radical reshaping of the traditional organizational landscape. He shows how a loose, hands-off management style is integral to redesigning relationships to fit the new forms. Notably, Bahrami reveals how this new management requires a negotiation between the divergent pressures of control and autonomy. A balance has continually to be struck therefore between innovation and maintaining focus; between rapid response and the avoidance of duplication; between a focus on future products and meeting time-to-market criteria; and between long-term vision and the importance of performance today. Creativity is prized and required but not at the expense of chaos. In managing these tensions the new forms in Silicon Valley have moved towards structures and relationships characterized by semi-permeable boundaries where strategic alliances and collaborative partnerships are a crucial component of the system; by 'organizations' which break from centralized hierarchies to federations and constellations of multiple business units; where line and staff distinctions are blurred and the focus shifts to front-line orientation, resulting in a claimed fusing of strategic and operational roles.

In their chapter, Ewan Ferlie and Andrew Pettigrew reassess the central idea of network forms in a public-sector and British context – some distance one might judge from high-tech firms in Silicon Valley. Focusing upon a study of the National Health Service, they examine the extent to which a deep-seated shift has occurred from hierarchies to networks and, in so far as this has happened, they try to assess the implications for managers. These authors suggest that the period between 1900 and the 1970s can perhaps, in retrospect, be seen as a distinct period when large vertically integrated organizations producing mass-produced goods and services was the prevailing and dominant organizational model. 'Fordism' was the exemplar in the private sector while the Welfare State bureaucracies were the analogues in the public sector. Towards the end of the twentieth century Ferlie and Pettigrew detect signs of a long-term reversal, signalling a possible shift to network-based organizations as the preferred form. Drawing mainly upon their own empirical study in the NHS but also upon a wider literature, they suggest that the transition is as yet partial. The consequence seems to be a period when mixed modes operate simultaneously. The long-term significance of the network form is open to some question at this stage but already, they suggest, the form is of sufficient importance to deserve close and continuing scrutiny.

Thomas Kochan and Paul Osterman address the issue of relationship structuring in a rather different way. In their chapter, the focus is upon a new kind of enterprise whose foundations are built upon the principles of what they term 'mutual gains'. This concept refers to the implicit contract between the range of stakeholders who, together, constitute an enterprise. This analysis therefore shifts attention to the underlying expectations, understandings or 'deals' upon which enterprises or organizations of any kind are dependent. Kochan and Osterman maintain that long-term sustainability of competitive advantage requires a set of work relationships which are recognized to benefit all parties. Based on an empirical study of a number of leading American firms, these authors have constructed a model (the mutual gains enterprise) which they suggest offers a beacon for other businesses which aspire to long-term sustainable competitiveness. In this chapter, Kochan and Osterman develop the three levels of reform (strategic, functional and workplace) which are necessary to effect this transformation. The chapter also marshals the evidence to date, indicating what economic effects can result from the pursuit and establishment of the new model of restructured relationships.

Some of these points are picked up in the next chapter authored by David Guest. However, whereas Kochan and Osterman in effect champion a particular model (albeit with full recognition that the detailed paths towards the achievement of that model can vary), Guest adopts a rather different mode of analysis. At the heart of this chapter is the sheer *variety* of options facing managers and others in the design of employment strategies and the associated patterns of relationships. What is especially interesting about this chapter is the cross-cutting of human resource management and industrial relations possibilities, thus giving rise to four main types of relationship pattern: (i) a 'new realism' which combines a significant emphasis both upon HRM policies and industrial relations (this therefore allows both an emphasis upon collective and individual relations); (ii) traditional collectivism where priority is given to industrial relations but with little attention if any to HRM policies; (iii) individualized HRM − that is where high priority is given to HRM but not to industrial relations; and (iv) the 'black hole' scenario where an employer addresses neither human resource management nor industrial relations. Thus, in laying bare these four different patterns and by indicating the various strands of evidence which support the existence of each in turn, Guest makes a valuable contribution to the understanding of the complexity of contemporary conditions and punctures the multitude of gurus and evangelical texts which blithely disregard the evidence on the ground.

The chapter by Nicolas Bacon and colleagues redresses the long-standing neglect of employment relations in small firms. Relatively little is known about the impact of the new human resource management and employment agenda on the small business sector. Drawing upon an extensive study of 560 companies, Bacon and his colleagues reveal a surprisingly high take-up of the new management agenda among small businesses. Moreover, they also show that having adopted the new practices there is considerable evidence that small businesses sustain their usage. The chapter serves to question the 'black hole' and 'bleak house' scenarios of recent times which have tended to suggest that employment policies in the 1990s tended towards the cost-cutting, minimalist options.

Finally, in this section, the chapter by Ray Jacques puts all that has preceded it into a much broader historical context. Jacques reveals that a great deal of the language associated with the 'new management' of corporate restructuring and new employment relations was in fact widely rehearsed by the classical writers and industrialists of the end of the nineteenth century and the early part of the twentieth century. Many of the platitudes about the requirements for 'managing in the twenty-first century' are shown by Jacques not only to have been articulated before but, more seriously, to be based on rather suspect logic. Jacques makes a strong case for more critically reflective practice.

12 The Emerging Flexible Organization: Perspectives from Silicon Valley

Homa Bahrami

Many enterprises are in the midst of fundamental changes in organizational designs and management practices. Pioneering and traditional companies alike are experimenting with novel organizational structures and management processes in order to accommodate the fast pace of technological change, global competition, and the emergence of a knowledge-based economy. These developments are collectively precipitating a move away from monolithic and rigid organizational designs which were geared for repetitive transactions and routine activities. The resulting impetus is toward flexible and agile organizational forms which can accommodate novelty, innovation, and change.

This chapter describes some of the organizational features of the emerging flexible enterprise and is based on field studies of 37 high-technology firms in California's Silicon Valley. These firms are experimenting with new organizational arrangements and are at the forefront of experiencing the challenges of the information era. Their business foundations are anchored in knowledge-based industries. Many compete in global markets and face global competition. They employ educated, young, and mobile professionals with high expectations. Some enter, or even, create pioneering markets and develop as yet untested products without the benefit of existing role models and blueprints for success. Moreover, they must manage novelty and continuous changes in products designs, competitive positions, and market dynamics. As Bill Joy, a co-founder of Sun Microsystems, observes:

> High-technology obeys the iron law of revolution . . . the more you change, the more you have to change . . . you have to be willing to accept the fact that in this game the rules keep changing.[1]

Originally published in *California Management Review*, 34 (4), 1992: 33–48 (abridged).

The Changing Organizational Landscape

An extensive array of organizational experiments have been under way in many firms during the past decade. Some of these developments have turned out to be transient fads, whereas others point to fundamental shifts in organizational design and management practice. Some of the more prevalent developments include delayering, team-based networks, alliances and partnerships, and a new employer–employee covenant.

The delayering and down-sizing trend was initially triggered by the need to reduce costs. However, it also reflects the administrative impact of information and communication technologies. Increased use of technologies, such as electronic mail, voice mail, and shared databases, has, over time, reduced the need for traditional middle management, whose role was to supervise others and to collect, analyze, evaluate, and transmit information up, down, and across the organizational hierarchy. The potential consequences of delayering are intended to be, in part, faster response to competitive and market changes, larger spans of control, increased workloads, and a broader range of assignments and roles for individuals and groups. One of the expected benefits of flatter hierarchies is the organization's ability to become flexible and responsive by reducing the time lag between decision and action – enabling faster response to market and competitive dynamics.

In an attempt to manage cross-unit projects and to reduce time-to-market, many firms are increasingly relying on multi-functional, multi-unit teams. Indeed, during the last decade 'teams' and 'groups' have become part of our managerial vocabulary and are now viewed as a central organizational building block. A key advantage of teams is their intrinsic flexibility. They can be formed, re-formed, and disbanded with relative ease; they can by-pass the traditional hierarchy; and their composition can evolve over time in order to blend different skills and address changing priorities.

Reliance on sub-contracting has been prevalent in a number of industries for some time. Recently, however, there has been a substantial increase in alliances which affect core business activities – such as product development, distribution, and financing. This trend is giving rise to complex organizational forms and business relationships. A number of reasons have been put forward to explain the rapid diffusion of such 'hybrid' organizational forms. These include 'changing environmental conditions, the limits of large-scale organization, and the importance of speed and information' (Powell, 1987). As Evans (1982) suggests, collaborative partnerships are a flexible mode of blending capabilities, sharing risks, and generating options.

Recently, we have also witnessed a major re-assessment of the implicit lifetime contract between employers and employees. Many firms have re-examined their employment policies – initiating early retirement programs and other incentives to reduce the size of their workforce. As pointed out in other studies, the critical tradeoff in this context is between 'corporate flexibility and individual security' (Kanter, 1989: 357). Many corporations rely on temporary workers, specialized vendors, and consultants in order to flexibly deal with unique contingencies. Additionally, this trend points to a fundamental shift in the foundation of employer–employee relationship, away from the traditional patriarchal orientation toward what may be characterized as a peer-to-peer relationship. This sentiment is echoed in the following comment which encapsulates the implicit relationship between Apple Computer and its employees: 'You own your own careers; we provide you with the opportunities'.[2]

Collectively, these and other changes point to a somewhat radical re-shaping of the traditional organizational landscape. As current trends indicate, contemporary firms need flexible and agile organizations that can effectively function in environments of continuous and kaleidoscopic, rather than periodic and paradigmatic, change.

Flexibility: The Emerging Imperative

Historically, the term 'flexibility' has been used rather loosely – referring to a blend of capabilities and attributes that facilitate adjustments to change. However, as suggested in previous studies, flexibility is a polymorphous concept whose meaning varies according to the situational context (Evans, 1991). For example, flexibility means 'being agile' – fast on one's feet, able to move rapidly, change course to take advantage of an opportunity or to side-step a threat. This capability is critical for enabling 'time-based' competition, facilitating rapid response, and reducing product development cycles. It also refers to the ability to quickly redefine a position and re-focus in the midst of a dynamic engagement – such as an acquisition, new product introduction, or legal proceedings.

Flexibility, however, is not just synonymous with agility. It also implies the ability to be 'versatile' – able to do different things and apply different capabilities depending on the needs of a particular situation. For example, employees with diverse capabilities are versatile in that they can readily switch between different assignments.

On the 'defensive' side of the spectrum, flexibility also refers to qualities which enable an enterprise to endure when negatively affected by change. This attribute is reflected in concepts such as 'robustness' or 'resilience'. The former characterizes the capability to absorb shocks and withstand perturbations – for example, by having excess slack or liquid assets. The latter refers to the ability to come back from the brink of disaster without bearing permanent scars or disabilities. Sometimes the events which trigger the need to change can be anticipated ahead of time. More often than not, however, firms need to respond to changes which are typically unexpected.

The point is that all these different attributes – spanning both offensive and defensive qualities – are needed in a truly flexible enterprise. The concept of flexibility, in an organizational context, refers to the ability to precipitate intentional changes, to continuously respond to unanticipated changes, and to adjust to the unexpected consequences of predictable changes. Put simply, strategic flexibility 'is the ability to do things differently or do something else should the need arise' (Hart, 1937: 272).

In view of these challenges, a number of innovative organizational experiments have been under way in many high-technology firms in Silicon Valley and elsewhere. Some pioneering moves have also been initiated by established corporations in the process of metamorphosis and transformation.

Building Blocks of Flexible Organizational Designs

High-technology firms face significant organizational tensions in spite of their relative youth. Irrespective of their size or stage of development, they need to remain disciplined, lean, and focused, requiring minimal duplication of effort, stringent accountability, and effective control and coordination. However, a loose, hands-off management style is needed to manage expectant professionals, maintain a conducive environment for creative thinking, and provide the capability for rapid response to competitive and market developments. As depicted in Table 12.1, they need flexible organizational systems which can balance dialectical forces – facilitating creativity, innovation, and speed, while instilling coordination, focus and control, and the staying power to withstand periods of adversity.

The following comments capture the essence of some of the dialectical tensions facing these firms: 'We want an environment that enhances individual creativity, but we do not want chaos . . . we want people involved in decisions that affect their work and we want teamwork, yet we want our employees to have a bias toward action . . . we want small groups of dedicated workers (decentralization) but such groups may feel aimless or may be charging in the wrong direction with hidden agendas . . . we want people to stretch to reach tough goals, so our real emphasis is on easily measured short-term growth and profits – but we should also have time to develop our employees for the longer haul, to promote from within, to monitor the atmosphere for creativity'.[3]

A *Multi-polar Organization*

The traditional model of the industrial enterprise has been one of an all-powerful center with various subsidiaries. The center has historically formulated the strategic direction, consolidated and integrated divisional plans, allocated resources, and monitored performance. For example, in the classic multi-divisional structure, senior corporate management – assisted by their staff – have set the long-term direction while the divisions have implemented the plans.

TABLE 12.1 *Organizational dilemmas*

Control	Autonomy
Focus	Innovation
Global products	Local recipes
Less duplication	Rapid response
Time-to-market	Future products
Today's performance	Long-term vision

Managing Opposing Tensions

This model of the omnipotent center which functions as the enterprise's brain has been subjected to much pressure as business enterprises have had to think and act quickly, re-calibrating their strategies continuously in fast-moving conditions. Under these circumstances, the traditional approach has several drawbacks:

- Rapid change demands quick reactions and continuous re-calibration. Separating the brain (the center – which plans a response) from the muscles (the line units – which enact the response) can lead to slow response and result in information distortion through hierarchical filtering processes.
- The executives with the most up-to-date understanding of evolving market realities are typically in the trenches. They are thus best-positioned to strategize *and* execute the necessary actions in real time as new imperatives unfold.
- Line managers in knowledge-based companies have the professional expertise and the educational background to undertake much of the strategizing and analytical work; assisted by new technologies, they can minimize their reliance on corporate support groups.

The emerging organizational system of high-technology firms is more akin to a 'federation' or a 'constellation' of business units that are typically interdependent, relying on one another for critical expertise and know-how.

Apple Computer is a case in point. Its main line units – although varying in size, scope, and style – have a peer-to-peer relationship with one another and with the center. The heads of the line units – Apple Products, Apple USA, Apple Europe, and Apple Pacific – are represented on its top management team together with the leaders of the corporate functions – finance, human resources, and legal and administrative services. Members of the different units collectively participate in setting and implementing the corporate direction: worldwide meetings (held twice a year) of the top 400 or so executives provide focused opportunities for discussing critical challenges; and the extensive movement of people between the units ensures that personal relationships are forged to enhance inter-unit cooperation.

Dualistic Systems

Many observers may have the impression that the organizational systems of high-technology companies are in a continuous state of flux: that formal structures – in the sense of clear reporting relationships, grouping of skills, and concise assignment of responsibility, authority, and accountability – do not exist in their organic setting. Such an impression, however, only reflects one dimension of the organizational reality. Many firms we observed were both *structured and yet chaotic*; they had evolved dualistic organizational systems, designed to strike a dynamic balance between stability on the one hand, and flexibility on the other.

A good case in point is the structural evolution of ROLM Corporation, a pioneering telecommunications company which was acquired by IBM in 1984. During its 15 years as an independent company, ROLM went through four major re-organizations of its bedrock structure, although it formed and disbanded many temporary groups and project teams. As depicted in Table 12.2, the first major structural change was initiated in 1973 (four years after its founding) when it entered the telecommunications business. This involved a fine-tuning of its functional structure to embrace the new venture. The second re-organization occurred in 1977 when three autonomous divisions were set up to focus on different businesses: mil-spec computers (its original business), telecommunications products, and a new venture (later discontinued) in the energy management field. The third re-organization (which was largely confined to the telecommunications business) was initiated in 1981 when a hybrid structure was created to consolidate its end-user sales and service organization and to focus on the new initiative in office systems. A further re-organization was completed in February 1984, prior to the IBM acquisition. It resulted in a partly functional superstructure and divisional substructures devised to ensure effective coordination of its telecommunications and office products.

Such dualistic systems enable high-technology firms to deal with a widely felt tension: how to create a relatively stable organizational setting within whose boundaries people and resources can be flexibly deployed. Bedrock structures are the relatively stable base units. Temporary teams are the flexible, rapid deployment overlay. They enable the organization to pool together different individuals at short notice, put them to work on diverse projects, and disband them once their task has been accomplished.

Front-line Orientation

Historically, organizational roles and departmental activities have been divided into staff and line positions. The first category comprises functions whose power and influence are based on advisory or monitoring roles, with 'the right to advise, rather than the power to decide' (Mintzberg, 1983). Typically, these groups have limited direct control over line operations, and

TABLE 12.2 *Organizational evolution of ROLM Corporation: 1973–83*

Year	Revenue (m$)	Business	Organization
1973	3.6 million	Mill-Spec Computers New Venture: PBX	Functional
1977	30.0 million	Mil-Spec Computers Digital PBX; New Venture: Energy Management	3 Stand-alone divisions
1981	294.5 million	Mil-Spec Computers PBX Systems; New Venture: Office Systems	Hybrid: partly functional/partly divisional
1983	502.6 million	Mil-Spec Computers PBX Office System	Functional super-structure; divisional sub-structure

hence over revenues and profits. Functions such as personnel, planning, and MIS, among others, have historically belonged to this category. By contrast, line functions, such as sales, manufacturing, or product development, have the 'power to decide' with direct control over, and accountability for, revenues and profits. Critics have long argued that as a result, staff functions have been cushioned from the harsh realities of the 'market'.

This instrumental distinction between staff and line functions is becoming increasingly blurred, not just in high-tech companies, but also in many traditional organizations. The impetus for change has largely come from competitive pressures to reduce costs. Many staff functions are becoming directly exposed to the 'front-line' realities of their internal customers – funding their operations by selling their services to the line units.

In many high-technology companies, support groups are also typically responsible for undertaking what would have traditionally been viewed as advisory assignments and are held directly accountable for the results. For example, an employee relations expert may deal with a disgruntled employee, and the training staff may actually design and deliver many courses. Other staff functions, such as strategic planning and business development, are more support-oriented, rather than control-oriented. These groups typically view their role as facilitators, consultants, and process managers, rather than as formulators of strategies and overseers of line activities.

Cosmopolitan Mindset

Many technology firms become global very early in their development. For example, it is not unusual to find young companies – less than ten years old – with manufacturing, research, and distribution facilities in the USA, Europe, Japan, and the Pacific Rim. Moreover, many generate more than half of their sales outside the USA, and have a large population of non-American employees.

Such a rapid process of globalization makes it necessary to develop a cosmopolitan mindset that incorporates different cultural assumptions and premises. This is a significant challenge since it requires balancing strong corporate values (which typically reflect the 'home' culture) with a broad perspective (which accommodates the diverse viewpoints of global customers, employees, and competitors). Despite the inherent challenges, however, a pluralistic culture can provide considerable versatility by drawing on diverse perspectives, approaches, and solutions.

Apple Computer is a good case in point. Its executives have attempted to manage Apple not as an American entity, but as a global company: 'we want to look and feel like a local company to our customers while successfully competing with worldwide corporations that rapidly leverage expertise and resources wherever they are located'.[4] Apple strives to create a cosmopolitan organization – not with one heart rooted in US culture, but with 'multiple hearts which beat as one' reflecting the diversity of its markets and employees.[5] It has attempted to create a pluralistic organization and a cosmopolitan culture in a number of ways:

- Its top management team is composed of different nationalities. Until 1990, a French-born executive was in charge of worldwide product development, manufacturing and R&D. A German-born national is its current President and an Australian has been in charge of the Asia-Pacific group. The composition of this team sends a strong symbolic message to its employees, partners and customers, reinforcing the value of cultural diversity.
- Workforce diversity is an important part of Apple's human resource strategy. It is a key component of its recruiting plans, promotion policies, and management training and development programs.
- Apple is also focusing on other initiatives to further strengthen its global orientation. These include 'dispersed expertise to leverage unique local talent, global dissemination of knowledge and skills partly through communication forums which bring together groups with similar interests, consistent treatment of global accounts with local look and feel, global account management information systems, integrated databases and networks, and global telecommunications facilities.[6]
- Simultaneous product launch in key global markets is another goal. For example, Claris Corporation, Apple's software subsidiary, has set out to develop the US and international versions of its products at the same time, so they can be distributed in its global markets soon after their US introduction.

Capability-based Organizations and Multi-talented Employees

Andrew Grove, the President and CEO of Intel Corporation coined the expression: 'Our assets have legs; they walk home every day.' Indeed, the core capability of high-technology companies is their know-how, which resides in people. The organization can thus be characterized as a montage of individual capabilities and informal networks and relationships, rather than a series of pre-determined roles and positions and formal hierarchical relationships.

The pivotal importance of informal networks in high-technology companies is due to the fact that the productivity of knowledge-based entities depend on employees' capabilities, commitments, motivations, and relationships. They cannot be programmed around pre-determined roles and positions in a machine-like hierarchy. Moreover, continuous change typically renders institutionalized roles and positions somewhat obsolete. An individual's effectiveness in getting things done is based on results and credibility, perceived reputation, and network of relationships, rather than on formal authority, job descriptions and position in the hierarchy. In this context, titles, seniority, spans of control, formal power, and hierarchical position are not necessarily significant determinants of individual success and organizational power.

Moreover, in contrast to the specialized orientation of traditional entities, many high-technology companies build versatility into their organizations by leveraging their employees in different capacities, depending on their situational needs. This is reflected in the following comments which were made by the founder of a medical electronics firm: 'I want to recruit people who are absolute experts in a given area but who can also apply their talents to other areas; "A" class players in their field, but also "B" and "C" class players in other fields.'[7] Effective employees have the flexibility and the confidence to leverage their knowledge and capabilities across different areas as and when conditions change and new needs arise.

Developing versatile employees by exposing them to different experiences is not new or unique to the high-tech sector. As early as the 1970s, Royal Dutch Shell used its corporate planning group as a vehicle for broadening its line managers' perspective and giving them a bird's eye or 'helicopter' view of Shell's global operations. Similarly, job rotation programs at companies such as IBM, Hewlett Packard, and many Japanese corporations have been a key component of their career planning systems for some time. What is different in the emerging high-tech sector is that employees need to possess a flexible mindset and the ability to adjust unexpectedly and quickly to the demands of a new assignment, without going through extensive training or being assigned the responsibility as part of a systematically planned career management program.

Semi-permeable Boundaries

Much has been written in recent years about the rise of strategic alliances and collaborative partnerships. The consensus seems to suggest that such alliances are a novel form of 'hybrid' organizational arrangement, provide a mechanism for pooling complementary capabilities, addressing rapid product development cycles, reducing risks, and providing strategic flexibility (Borys and Jemison, 1987; Doz, 1987; Evans, 1991; Kanter, 1989;

Mowery, 1988; Ouchi and Bolton, 1988; Powell, 1987). Moreover, in recent years they have proliferated into various forms, and are continuously evolving.

High-technology companies have been at the forefront of initiating and managing many types of strategic partnerships. These vary in form, scope, and longevity. Many companies have forged their fundamental business proposition and organizational infrastructure around partnerships. Apple, for example, collaborates with third-party software developers, dealers, distributors, and resellers, and sub-system and component suppliers.

While such 'leverage' models of business partnership are at the extreme end of the alliance spectrum, others may have a more limited objective. They may be used for financing purposes – as is the case with many Japanese investments in new start-ups. They may give the parties reciprocal access to geographic markets, or they may provide an effective way of pooling know-how and sharing risks in developing technologically advanced products. In many instances, they are an extension of the traditional supplier–customer relationships. Irrespective of their purpose, scope, or form, their continuous formation has broken down the solid walls which have historically separated the firm from its external stakeholders.

The emergence of these semi-permeable boundaries in the high-technology sector is organizationally apparent in a number of ways. Many firms have access to their partners' internal information systems through electronic mail networks. For example, Apple gives its partners – including software developers, consultants, dealers and resellers, and sub-system suppliers – access to its internal electronic mail system. This facilitates communication between the different groups and gives them timely information on new product releases, press announcements, and re-organizations, among other items. Additionally, it is a common practice for engineers working on joint development projects to be assigned to a strategic partner. The employee in question becomes a temporary employee of the partner for a limited period of time – forging crucial relationships and gaining access to vital information about the partner's culture and *modus operandi*.

In summary, the key organizational challenge facing many high-technology firms is balancing several opposing tensions: selling and servicing existing products while developing and bringing new ones on stream; remaining disciplined, focused, and frugal, while continuously learning, experimenting, and re-calibrating; generating consensus, yet ensuring timely decisions; balancing individual contribution and teamwork; ensuring short-term profitability in the context of a long-term vision. The modern high-technology enterprise needs diverse capabilities and multi-faceted organizational arrangements to flexibly deal with these complex tensions. As depicted in Table 12.3, their organizational building blocks have evolved in order to address these tensions, and to provide different forms of flexibility.

TABLE 12.3 *Organizational attributes: a comparison*

Traditional model	Emerging model
Single center	Multiple centers
Self-contained	Steeples of expertise
Independent activities	Interdependent units
Vertically integrated	Multiple alliances
Uniform structure	Diverse structures
Parochial mindset	Cosmopolitan mindset
Emphasis on efficiency	Emphasis on flexibility

The Emergence of a Bi-modal Organization

Many firms appear to have walked a tightrope between these tensions without having allowed any one imperative to dominate the strategic and organizational context. These attempts cannot be described in monolithic, unidimensional terms, as simple recipes and 'either/or' solutions. Their organizational systems were by no means chaotic, but neither were they in total control. They were not frugal although a cost-conscious mentality pervaded their style. The management teams were not mavericks, yet an entrepreneurial zeal and anti-bureaucratic sentiments were frequently observed. They focused on generating short-term results but did not lose sight of their long-term mission. The resulting organizational systems can be best depicted as 'bi-modal' – in that they could accommodate opposing tendencies and yet function as coherent and cohesive concerns. Signs of bi-modality were commonly observed in broaching three types of tension: centralization versus decentralization, stability versus dynamism, and uniformity versus diversity.

Centralization and Decentralization

The organizational system of many high-technology firms clearly tran-scends the centralization–decentralization spectrum. On the one hand, it needs to remain loose, decentralized, and differentiated in order to provide the capability for creative initiatives and rapid responsiveness. On the other hand, tight centralized direction is needed to maintain strategic cohesion, manage interdependencies, and reduce the time lag between decision and action. This imperative is reflected in the following: 'we like the idea of small, decentralized units . . . with focused accountability . . . but our products have to play together . . . our customers buy an integrated system . . . there is a major element of success that depends on coordination and close cooperation between the units'.[8]

Centralizing tendencies can be observed in visible and involved leaders whose passion, vision, and charisma are critical in charting the direction, generating cohesion, defining the boundaries, and motivating the troops. Moreover, top management teams are typically involved in new, risky projects during the formative stages and participate side-by-side with the troops in the development process. For example, a co-founder of ROLM was directly involved in the development of its office systems products during the early 1980s, even though he was an executive vice president and a member of ROLM's top management team.

However, strong leadership and directed moves do not imply that leaders are the sole source of the corporate vision, or that strategies and decisions are imposed from the top. The scenario portrayed by individual contributors is one of a 'great deal of autonomy', a 'lot of room for initiatives', and 'doing whatever it takes to get the job done'. Indeed, those who are promoted and rewarded are typically champions of major initiatives and doers who have made things happen. Such levels of autonomy have historically been associated with decentralized structures.

The resulting organization can be best characterized as both centralized *and* decentralized. It is centralized in that top management teams are a critical force behind charting the strategic direction and defining the boundaries for individual and team initiatives. It is decentralized in that front-line personnel can exercise discretion in dealing with new imperatives as they arise – within broad, yet well-defined, strategic and cultural parameters. The critical catalyst in creating this alignment is reliance on formal and informal bridging mechanisms which establish direct communication channels between the leaders and the doers. These include electronic-based communication, planning sessions and review meetings, informal opportunities for interaction, educational forums, and open access protocols. Regular communication ensures that impending changes in market realities and strategic priorities can be quickly discussed, evaluated, and implemented.

Stability and Dynamism

Bi-modality is also manifest in the tradeoffs made between stability and change as reflected in the following remark: 'we want to be flexible and respond to market changes without *creating chaos and confusion amongst our people.*' Indeed, the priorities facing many high-technology firms are in a state of flux, resulting in continuous change and frequent re-calibrations. For example, one month the focus may be on launching a new product; another month it may shift over to volume manufacturing and procurement; and in the third month, product re-design, based on lead-users' feedback, may be on top of the business agenda.

Dynamism and change are accommodated through extensive reliance on project teams, micro re-organizations, and re-deployment of core employees in various capacities. Moreover, many high-technology firms seek to improve their flexibility by relying on temporary workers, specialist vendors, and consultants and contractors. Reliance on such a variable talent pool enables them to undertake different assignments without incurring the fixed cost and the long-term commitment expected by core employees.

However, constant change can also be threatening and de-motivating for individuals, and disruptive and unproductive for the organization. It is not surprising to find that many firms strive to create anchors of stability around which everything else can change. Some attempt to clarify and articulate a clear sense of purpose and a few overarching values which define the broad boundaries within which changes take shape. For example, the mission of Conner Peripherals, a disk drive manufacturer and one of the fastest growing companies in US corporate history, is described as follows: 'Identify customers' needs sooner and fill them faster than the competition' (Conner Peripherals, 1992). Moreover, their recruiting practices and orientation programs help set the employees' expectations and thereby ensure an effective fit between personal and organizational goals.

Uniformity and Diversity

There is a clear sense of corporate purpose and cultural identity associated with pioneering high-technology companies, yet their style professes to value diversity. Inculcating diversity enables these firms to become versatile, pool together different capabilities, and nurture the ability to address different contingencies.

Many high-technology companies attempt to become 'diverse' by blending various management styles and cultural perspectives. For example, they may recruit inexperienced college graduates as well as experienced professionals with extensive track records. They also recruit people from different cultures and ethnic backgrounds to blend together different cognitive orientations. A young company in the network server business, for example, consciously sought to recruit a woman chief financial officer from a different cultural background in order to provide a role model for its women professionals and develop the capability base to deal with clients and partners from other cultures. In this case, after a period of extensive search, they recruited an Asian woman as their chief financial officer.

Composition of top management teams can also send an important symbolic message and further reinforce the importance of diversity. A well-known case is the complementarity between David Packard's business style and Bill Hewlett's technical orientation. Other famous examples include the late Noyce–Moore–Grove troika at Intel, and Oshman, Maxfield, and Chamberlain at ROLM. These teams represent unity through their shared values and overarching sense of purpose. Diversity is promoted in that they have complementary skills and management styles.

Recently, a number of high-technology firms have also set out to sensitize their employees to cultural diversity through in-house training and educational programs. A few companies have made strong commitments to internal training programs that prepare executives for global assignments and strive to build cultural awareness in all employees. The crucial value of diversity further highlights the importance of distinctive corporate values.

These spell out a few boundary conditions within which everything else is free to operate. They define the limits and set the constraints for individual and team initiatives.

Summary and Conclusion

Developing flexible organizations is critical for business enterprises in the 1990s. Flexibility is a multi-dimensional concept – demanding agility and versatility; associated with change, innovation, and novelty; coupled with robustness and resilience, implying stability, sustainable advantage, and capabilities that may evolve over time.

A critical challenge facing many business entities is how to transform their traditional organizational systems and management practices in order to become more flexible. This task requires identifying and implementing those approaches, processes, and tools that can be used to manage a bi-modal – rather than a monolithic – organization. This poses a major challenge because our existing organizational systems and managerial mindsets have evolved to address uni-dimensional imperatives, rather than the new, rampant multi-dimensional tensions.

Moreover, our expectations, norms of behavior, vocabularies, and frames of reference have evolved around the traditional themes of stability rather than change, uniformity rather than diversity, and optimality rather than flexibility. We need to forge new attitudes and behavior patterns by deploying educational programs, incentive systems, and communication protocols, among others, to support and reinforce the importance of flexibility, diversity, and dynamism. If the experience of the high-technology sector is indicative of broader trends, the 1990s is likely to be a decade of organizational experimentation and managerial innovation, and one likely to bring forth novel organizational systems and management approaches. This challenge requires focused attention, a readiness to experiment, and the willingness to share ideas and learn from different corporate experiences.

Notes

1 Speech given by Bill Joy, a co-founder of Sun Microsystems, at the Churchill Club, Palo Alto, California, 1990.

2 Speech given by K. Sullivan, Senior Vice President, Apple Computer, to the author's MBA class on Organizational Behavior at the University of California, Berkeley, April 1991.

3 Internal memorandum from the Executive Vice President of a $700 million high-technology firm on its business philosophy, 26 May 1981.

4 Internal presentation, Apple Computer, 23 September 1988.

5 M. Spindler, in a speech given to Apple's worldwide sales force, March 1987.

6 Internal document on Apple's New Enterprise Project, 1988.

7 Personal communication, W. New, Managing Director, August 1989.
8 Interview with R. Maxfield, Executive Vice President and co-founder ROLM Corporation, April 1985.

References

Borys, B. and Jemison, D.B. (1987) 'Hybrid organizations as strategic alliances'. Working paper 951r, Graduate School of Business, Stanford University, Stanford, CA.
Conner Peripherals (1992) 'Managing at Conner', *Internal Employee Orientation Handbook*. Conner Peripherals.
Doz, Y.L. (1987) 'Technology partnerships between larger and smaller firms', *International Studies of Management and Organization*, 17 (4).
Evans, J.S. (1982) 'Strategic flexibility in business', SRI Business Intelligence Program, Report No. 678. Menlo Park, CA, December.
Evans, J.S. (1991) 'Strategic flexibility and high-technology maneuvers: a conceptual framework', *Journal of Management Studies*, January.
Hart, A.G. (1937) 'Anticipations, business planning and the cycle', *Quarterly Journal of Economics*, February.
Kanter, R.M. (1989) *When Giants Learn to Dance*. New York: Simon and Schuster.
Mintzberg, H. (1983) *Structure in Fives: Designing Effective Organizations*. Englewood Cliffs, NJ: Prentice-Hall.
Mowery, D. (1988) *International Collaborative Ventures in Manufacturing*. Cambridge, MA: Ballinger.
Ouchi, W. and Bolton, M. (1988) 'The logic of joint research and development', *California Management Review*, Fall.
Powell, W. (1987) 'Hybrid organizational arrangements', *California Management Review*, Fall.

13   Managing through Networks

E. Ferlie and A. Pettigrew

Hierarchies, markets and networks have been described as three basic and indeed alternative modes of organizing (Thompson et al., 1991), each of which may call for distinctive managerial orientations and styles. Thus managers in market-orientated organizations may take on the persona of an entrepreneur; managers in a vertically line-managed organization take on the persona of military personnel; while managers in network-based organizations may take on the persona of a diplomat.

The question arises as to whether there is now a deep-seated shift underway away from organizational forms based on markets and hierarchies and towards more network-based forms of organization. One suspects that this concept of the N-form organization often remains at the level of a slogan (Nohria and Eccles, 1992), and that detailed studies of how N-form organizations function (Pettigrew et al., 1995) – or how non-N-form organizations make the transition to N-form mode – remain scarce.

One view is that 1900–1970 can be seen as a distinct period in terms of preferred organizational form, dominated by large and vertically integrated organizations which produced mass volume standard products. Within the private sector, the Ford Corporation is seen as an exemplar of this organizational form (sometimes indeed termed 'Fordism').

Within the public sector, the post-1945 nationalized corporations or Welfare State bureaucracies (such as in the NHS in the UK) can be seen as an analogue of the Fordist Corporation, where hierarchical 'command and control' methods of resource allocation and management were dominant, at least within the administrative subculture. Such managerial styles indeed assumed greater importance in the NHS of the 1980s with the creation of general management and of a single line-managed organization with a pronounced performance orientation.

Yet in the 1990s, there are some signs – as we shall explore – that this seemingly long-term trend may be going into reverse with a shift evident to network-style organizations. The management implications of the growth

Originally published in *British Journal of Management*, 7 (special issue), 1996: 581–99 (abridged).

of such network-based organizations is also emerging as an important area for investigation.

The purpose of this chapter is to assess the significance of these broader developments with reference to changing managerial practice within a major UK organization (the NHS). It seeks to access the developing theory of network-based organizations; to assess empirically the significance of these developments for managerial practice within public-sector organizations such as the NHS; and to consider the organizational and managerial implications and challenges which arise, such as HRM strategy. There have so far been few studies which have taken public-sector settings for study or which have sought to connect network theory to practice (but see Moss Kanter and Eccles, 1992).

The next section will review more generic and theoretic literature on network-style organizations, accessing different accounts which might explain the growth of such network-based organizations.

The third section will outline the changing organizational and managerial context of the NHS over the last decade, suggesting that three rather different streams of centrally sponsored activity have been evident which have had different consequences for the received managerial style evident at local level.

The fourth section makes explicit the methodology used in our empirical study designed to investigate some of these themes, and in the following section, we will outline our empirical results.

The final part of this chapter considers the implications of these findings both for theory and for managerial practice within the NHS.

Network-based Forms of Organization – Some Recent Literature

Since the 1970s, increasing evidence has been accumulating of a shift towards more flexible 'post-Fordist' modes of organizing. The 'new competition' literature (Best, 1990) points to the growth of small entrepreneurial firms, of industrial districts and of new high-tech sectors which relate to each other on a network basis. In response to more intense global competition and a faster pace of change, a general move from inflexible pyramids to more flexible network-style structures was detected in the 1980s (Miles and Snow, 1986, 1992). Such network-style organizations were also found to pose distinctive management challenges of their own.

Partly in response to such trends, Nohria (1992) argues that the network perspective is of rising importance in organization theory. It has moved from being the province of a few mathematically inclined sociologists in the 1950s to much more mainstream status. The network perspective redirects our attention away from formal structure and policy to the importance of patterns of social relationships within organizations, including (perhaps especially) informal ties. It conceptualizes market processes in highly relational and socially embedded terms. Concepts of trust, reciprocity and reputation move centre stage. As such it offers a powerful perspective and language at a meta-level, quite different from that (say) of the neo-classical economists so influential in the 1980s. However, as there is now a danger of the perspective becoming over fashionable and faddish in its turn, we need to develop both conceptual rigour and an empirical base.

Certainly many large organizations are currently unbundling them-selves into loosely coupled flotillas of smaller organizations. The Italian textile industrial districts are sometimes taken as a leading-edge example (Lazerson, 1993). Co-ordination here takes place through the agreement or the contract more than through the hierarchy. Within the post-1990 quasi market in health care, the contract has indeed replaced the command as the prime mode of co-ordination. Signs and symptoms of this more general shift include such interrelated developments as de-layering, down-sizing, outsourcing, the growth of joint ventures, strategic alliances and strategic networks (Jarillo, 1988). Within the public sector, questions of interagency co-operation and networks are also assuming greater prominence (Marsh and Rhodes, 1992) as it has become clear that the implementation of many policies requires agencies and tiers of government to co-operate.

Why are Network-based Forms of Organization Emerging?

There is always a danger that any new management style will be seen as a universal panacea or assume the status of a management fad. Network-based forms of organization may be functional for certain types of work flow but possibly not for others (such as high volume, stable and standard-ized forms of production). So what factors are seen as driving the adoption of network-based forms of organization?:

– an increased requirement for *flexibility and learning*: many products or services are now designed for more specialist markets, or may display short product life cycles. Within the public sector, too, there is increased empha-sis on greater service variety, on service innovation and greater user choice. Under these circumstances, organizations may need to develop more flexible modes of production, to accelerate the pace of internal change and to increase the rate of organizational learning.

A move to network-based organizations can open up access to more numerous sources of information than is possible either with a self-contained vertically-run organization or an atomized market where infor-mation is conveyed through prices, offering a richer set of interactive and reciprocal learning opportunities. This is particularly the case when it comes to the exchange of sophisticated technological knowledge that is tacit in character and difficult to codify (as in health care) (Grabher, 1993).

– *reducing market uncertainty*: many industrial markets are in fact characterized by stable long-term relationships between firms rather than faceless transactions. This is because (Johanson and Mattson, 1990) suppliers and customers need extensive knowledge about each other, if they are to carry out important business. They need knowledge not only about price and quality (which in itself may be difficult to obtain) but also more intangible factors such as levels of service and reliability. Much of this tacit knowledge can only be gained through the experience of repeated transactions. Moreover, the participants need knowledge about each others' resources, organization and development possibilities in order to assess possible future developments.

As a result, long-term exchange relationships emerge within the market in order to reduce the level of uncertainty to a tolerable level. The emergence of such relational contracting within the health care quasi market will be explored in the next section.

– *managing joint production*: Johnston and Lawrence (1991) argue that there is an empirically observable move within industrial organization from a pattern of large, vertically integrated companies to a new form of value adding partnerships (VAPs), where a set of independent companies work closely together to manage a flow of goods and services along an entire value-added chain. Low-cost computing and communications systems are seen as tipping competitive advantage to such partnerships of smaller companies, each of which performs one function within the value-added chain and co-ordinates its activities with the rest of the chain. Within public-sector care, too, there are an increasing number of 'joint production' processes, where the NHS joins with Social Services, the voluntary and informal sectors in producing joint goods. These VAPs are not just technology driven, but depend on the development of trustworthy relationships which stop the VAP from devolving into anarchy or moving back to the vertically integrated giant (Johnston and Lawrence, 1991).

– *a high-tech base*: Bahrami (1992) detects strong moves to de-layering, team-based networks, alliances and partnerships within high-tech organizations such as in California's Silicon Valley. These organizations are anchored in knowledge-based industries. They employ educated, young and mobile professionals with high career expectations. They create innovative products and must manage novelty and continuous change.

In knowledge-based sectors such as biotechnology (Grabher, 1993), organizational forms are changing as large chemical corporations are increasingly linking up with business start-ups and small firms that possess entrepreneurial commitment and new expertise. Health care, too, can be seen as a knowledge and science-based form of work organization where these arguments apply.

– managing cultural diversity: one of the areas in which the network paradigm has made most impact has been in the study of the internationalization of firms and the management of multi-national corporations (MNCs) which cross national boundaries and contain different cultures.

Bartlett and Ghoshal (1989) suggest that many MNCs are physically dispersed in different milieux; that they are highly differentiated internally and possess a complex variety of internal linkage and co-ordination mechanisms. As a result, they can now be seen as moving towards inter-organizational networks, where the subsidiaries play an important role as well as the centre.

Many MNCs operate across national cultures. Martinez and Jarillo's (1989) review suggests a growing interest in informal and culturally based means of co-ordination within MNCs. How is this cultural diversity managed? They see increasing attempts to develop a strong organizational culture that includes a deep knowledge of the company's policies and objectives and shared values and beliefs.

Critics have seen this as an attempt to create a cosmopolitan 'master culture' which overrides local national cultures in a crude fashion. Hofstede (1994) instead writes about alternative linking mechanisms such as the 'corporate diplomat' who is experienced in living and functioning in various foreign cultures.

Some Lead Theoretic Questions

So far we hope to have established that there is at least prima-facie evidence of a shift towards network forms of organization and to have reviewed some explanatory accounts.

In interrogating such evidence, Nohria (1992) suggests four lead questions should be kept in mind:

Power and influence in network-based organizations   Power is a central question in organization theory. So what happens to the nature and distribution of power in network-based organizations? As far as the nature of power is concerned, is there a shift from the use of positional power to other sorts of power or influence?

Is power in network-based organizations concentrated or dispersed? Network theory suggests that being central in a network may convey a source of power. However, network-based organizations are also seen as more polycentric and diffuse in nature than the vertically integrated organization.

Organizing efforts   What is the nature of the organizing efforts required to build network-based organizations? How are new organizations created or

– perhaps even more difficult – old ones transformed? Such institution-building processes may require a high level of skill and energy sustained over a long period from product champions and innovators (Sarason, 1976).

Of particular interest is the nature of such organizing efforts in public-sector contexts when organizational change is often imposed from the top. Is there ownership of the agenda at local agency level or are local managers only paying lip service to the new order?

Strategic alliances Network theory would certainly expect to encounter organizations which place great emphasis on the construction of strategic alliances. However, it would argue that it is only possible to understand the strategic behaviour of the organization in the context of the overall network in which it is embedded. Single alliances may interconnect to bind the organization into a complex web of relationships. The inherited pattern of alliances may in turn shape future behaviour. An analysis of the interorganizational set – and how ties are constructed and maintained thus emerges as a focal point of analysis.

The new competition and the network form As we have indicated, the rise of the 'new competition' is often seen as associated with the emergence of the N-form organization as a new organizational form. This perspective is theoretically controversial and requires elaboration.

For Powell (1990), this concept of networks as a novel organizational form gets beyond treating them as a collection of middle-ground hybrids lying in the middle of the markets/hierarchies spectrum as proposed by the new institutional economics (Williamson, 1975). It also represents an alternative perspective from those in the new economic sociology who have tried to recast the notion of markets in a more relational or socially-embedded direction (White, 1981; Granovetter, 1985).

What is the distinctive logic of collective action in the network form (Powell, 1990)? How do such networks manage to sustain themselves over the long term? This directs attention to the analysis of factors which help sustain and regulate these networks. These mechanisms lie on a focal/diffuse spectrum ranging from individual animators and brokers (Thorelli, 1990), through linking institutions and rules for governance to diffuse norms which underpin transactions.

We shall return to these theoretic questions in the final section.

Recent Policy and Management Developments in the NHS

Before reviewing some evidence from the NHS, it may be helpful to remind readers of the distinctive nature of public-sector settings where the network paradigm has remained relatively undeveloped. It must be remembered that health authorities are bodies established by statute, accountable through the regional tier of management to the NHS executive, ministers and eventually Parliament. As public-sector organizations, they face more constraints on their actions than many private corporations. Local agendas are to an important extent mandated or enforced by central government, although also renegotiated locally.

There have been a series of top-down management reform efforts apparent in the NHS in the last decade. No one consistent agenda has been pursued by the centre over this time period, but perhaps three rather different streams of activity can be distinguished.

The Vertically Integrated Organization

Between 1983 and 1990, the emphasis was on the strengthening of the general management function and the construction of a single vertically managed organization. This agenda continued into the early 1990s, with the bringing in of the regional tier into the Civil Service in 1993 and the emergence of a strong performance management orientation. These reforms were associated with a strengthening of 'command and control' styles of management, reinforced through techniques such as Performance Related Pay (PRP), personal objective setting and a move away from nationally agreed to individual contract-based forms of employment.

The Internal Market

In the early 1990s, central policy shifted to the adoption of an internal market model whereby the NHS disaggregated into purchasers and providers. Health authorities evolved as macro purchasers, and GP fundholders (GPFHs) as micro purchasers operating with developed budgets. On the providing side, NHS trusts competed with alternative private and voluntary sector providers. The two sides were aligned through the contracting process, which was still subject to internal regulation (neither side had right of access to the courts in cases of alleged breach of contract).

The Emergence of Relational Contracting

As the internal market matured, crude classical models of contracting increasingly gave way to models of relational contracting. This model of markets developed out of the concerns of marketeers. It was felt that the conventional view of an active marketeer, passive consumers and an atomistic market restricted understanding of what actually happened in markets. The classical view of markets assumes that markets are populated by individuals or simple firms, yet economic life is often dominated by a small number of large and complex firms which behave in a different way.

A number of important implications follow from seeing markets in more relational terms. Unlike individual consumers, corporate buyers might often interact with sellers. The relationship between organizations in a

relational market might display a complex history of adapt
ment, trust and conflict.

The interaction process is not seen as solely revolving around
service exchange, but also includes important processes of social exc
which may reduce uncertainty and build trust. There is a tendency to 'k
things in the family' so that buyers – once locked into a set of relationships
– may be relatively inert in seeking new sources of supply. There may be
periodic competition *for* markets, but little competition *within* markets.

Proponents of this model argue that much of the buying and selling
engaged in by the large private-sector companies is of this nature. Large
companies, such as Marks & Spencer or J. Sainsbury, for instance, are
likely to develop enduring relationships with their subcontractors, and
those providing professional services frequently retain their clients over
long periods of time and many discrete episodes of service provision.

The New Network-based Agenda of the mid-1990s

The emergence of relational contracting would in any case have highlighted
the importance of informal interorganizational networks in the NHS. In
the mid-1990s, the centre launched or supported a number of new policy
initiatives which (at the very least) are consistent with more network styles
of management and the formation of strategic inter-agency alliances within
the public sector and across to the private sector ('healthy alliances'). There
is a related cluster of developments emanating from a variety of directions
rather than one single causal factor.

At the local level, health authorities are struggling to digest multiple
initiatives which may be of secondary significance when taken individually
but when taken together have real force. There are anecdotal reports of
attempts to reshape managerial culture towards a more network-based
direction.

Methodology

Informed by these important developments in theory and in policy, the
authors were commissioned by the NHS Executive to undertake a one-year
study of the management by networks phenomenon (1994–1995) within the
NHS. An initial and wide-ranging literature review highlighted the move to
network-based forms of organization in parts of the private sector as well
as the public sector.

This initial review was used to construct a semi-structured interview pro
forma to test these arguments empirically. Visits were undertaken to nine
purchasing organizations across the country which were nominated by
experts at the Department of Health as having the reputation of being at
the 'leading edge' of development. A typical programme consisted of 4/5
interviews at HQ in the morning, combined with visits to two innovative

A spread of respondents from different func-
:essed (about 70 in total). As the researchers
:resting people in innovative localities, the data
t be typical of practice at the NHS, but rather
ving at its leading edge. The data are of course
nce of purchasers rather than trust providers.

the NHS

ι Exists

The first and confirmatory conclusion of our empirical work was that
network-based styles of management should now be seen as of substantial
and rising importance within NHS purchasing organizations when assessed
against both hierarchical and market-based forms of management. This
represents, however, a shift of emphasis rather than total displacement of
one mode by another and respondents talked of the need to operate in
different modes in different circumstances. The possible implications of
such mixed modes of management will be discussed further in the next
section.

Nevertheless, most respondents agreed that networking with external
stakeholders was now a key managerial skill. Some felt that this had
always been the case, citing traditional negotiations with other autonomous agencies (such as local authority social services departments) about the
boundary between social and health care, or the historic need to persuade
clinicians or politicians before managerial action could take place. Under
these circumstances, influencing had always been a more functional tactic
than the exercise of positional power.

When asked to define the characteristics and skills needed within
network-based forms of management, 'trust', 'reciprocity', 'understanding'
and 'credibility' all emerged as important basic concepts in use. There is
thus an important interpersonal component to network-based forms of
management, which can make it vulnerable to turnover of key people.

However, the alignment of incentives at an agency level is also important
as it is unlikely that decision makers from different agencies will co-operate
unless a 'win-win' situation can be established. As coercive or manipulative
forms of behaviour are unlikely to be successful, achieving such interorganizational trust may be considerably more difficult than building
interpersonal trust, yet vital if alliances are to survive the departure of key
individuals.

But what are networks for? A major concern expressed about unplanned
moves to network-based management was that the means could displace
the ends – all process and no output. The co-existence within the NHS of
network-based management and a strong performance management

orientation may be uneasy in the short term but in the long term may be helpful in exposing the question: what flows through the network? What are these networks for?

In response, it has long been apparent that health in a broad sense cannot be seen just as a province of the NHS. The purpose of networks may thus be defined as follows: (i) to transfer ownership of a health agenda to wider groupings (e.g., helping local communities to take ownership of health issues); (ii) to engage in the production of joint goods with other producers (e.g., improved housing may be associated with improved health); (iii) to clarify responsibilities and patient flows so as to produce 'seamless care' across a complex web of organizations (e.g., post discharge planning).

In the rest of this section, we outline an initial typology of the various types of network-based management uncovered in our fieldwork.

Changing Internal Management Structures and Styles

The networking phenomenon has internal as well as external consequences. A number of respondents reported recent moves within their own purchasing organizations away from reliance on established functional hierarchies and towards network-based or matrix management styles of working. An active organization development (OD) function was at work in some of the sites, trying to reshape organizational style in this direction. A move from organizing along uni-functional or professional lines to more team-based and multi-disciplinary approaches was also widely reported.

As a result, respondents were expected to operate with a much more mixed portfolio of tasks ('matrix hoppers'). Some managers reported problems with the resulting lack of a clear structure, particularly at middle management level where the pace and complexity of work had been 'upped'.

Such matrix management approaches depend on strong channels of informal communication to make them work, and movement away from the 'meeting culture' which had previously been dominant in these organizations. The introduction of e-mail is seen as having a helpful decentralizing effect. Critics argued that sometimes these organizations were changing their internal management style less in practice than they proclaimed in theory.

Evolving CEO Role and Style

What might be the role of the CEO in network-based forms of organization? One role is clearly to help build and maintain networks, through the selection and development of key staff, through external contacts and by retaining an overview across the multiplicity of networks. The CEO might take a view about the value added from each network, deciding to boost involvement in one network, while withdrawing from another. Such meta-level management of the network can not of course be decreed from above but needs to be enacted in negotiations with key partners.

The consequence may well be less time spent in the office and a lessened ability to react immediately to the short-term crises that constantly flare up in the NHS. The CEOs interviewed felt themselves to be highly 'outwards facing' – one estimated that she spent only 25 per cent of her time at HQ.

A second key role is to give the network strategic direction, to reinforce core purposes and tasks, to ensure corporacy and to assess performance against key objectives. The CEO may well embody a strong performance management focus within the network. There was a concern expressed that network-based forms of management might degenerate into perpetual 'talking shops', and that key purposes could be lost. A key role of the CEO could thus be to ensure that network participation remains purposeful.

A third role of the CEO could be to institutionalize strategic alliances by moving on from a reliance on interpersonal trust to a deeper level of interorganizational trust. CEOs may act to construct win-win situations, to broaden channels of communication and joint working and to build an internal culture more receptive to alliances. At present, however, many of the alliances studied remained at the interpersonal level and have not progressed on to the inter-institutional level.

The Operation of Clinical Networks

NHS networks could be seen as polycentric and diffuse rather than concentrated in nature. A variety of different networks were in operation, some of them clinical in nature which were difficult for management to penetrate. So network-based forms of management in the NHS are too important to be left solely to managers.

The role of the public health function Public health displayed a networking function in all the commissions visited, although the extent to which it had achieved a truly strategic role at the core of the organization varied. The personal qualities, career history and organizational 'clout' of the Director of Public Health (DPH) in particular determined the profile of the function at corporate level.

While good quality data and analysis remain central to the public health function, DPHs also reported the need to operate as 'persuaders', communicating effectively with a variety of different groups. They need to be able to manage and secure change in practice, not only within the public health function but much more broadly. DPHs were in this respect seen as needing generic skills, flexibility and an ability to switch networks and tasks in a 'reed like' way.

DPHs face a difficult dilemma. As DPHs move from a specialist function to a more corporate role, so they may well increase their influence at a corporate level. However, by becoming more corporate, they may also lose their status as an independent advocate of the public health, cherished by many DPHs.

[. . .]

Multi-disciplinary Settings

Within multi-disciplinary teams, leadership roles are subject to more negotiation than in vertically line-managed organizations and cannot be imposed in a purely top-down manner. The exercise of positional power is complemented by other sources of authority, such as sapiential wisdom or demonstrated competence.

While multi-disciplinary working is well established in fields such as psychiatry, it is of increasing importance in other service sectors such as primary care and also in operational management mechanisms such as locality commissioning.

In order for such mixed teams to work, a shared model of practice and clear objectives had to be negotiated within the team across conventional occupational boundaries. Achieving such an inter-professional consensus will be difficult in settings where each professional group remains rigidly attached to inherited and uni-professional modes of working. Thus great care needs to be taken in selection into these teams. However, hierarchy does not give way to a purely collective mode of working: co-ordination roles were usually found to be necessary and one community-based team which had not appointed a co-ordinator reported real difficulties in maintaining a focus.

[. . .]

A Web of Inter-agency Alliances

Health commissions were actively engaged – with varying degrees of success – in establishing alliances with a wide variety of local agencies. We are not so much dealing with a single strategic alliance directed from the top but rather a dense web of inter-agency alliances was being constructed, with different leaders and sometimes with players playing multiple roles.

While the frontier between health and social care might superficially be seen as the easiest to cross, given a 20 year pre-history of interorganizational collaborative machinery (joint planning and finance structures were set up in 1976), difficult issues remain, given a problematic national context and continuing differences at local level between the priorities, decision-making systems and cultures of the two organizations.

The NHS has withdrawn from long-term care, placing a greater burden on social care. While extra money has been made available centrally to support Social Services Departments (SSDs), demand has often proved greater than predicted, and a number of SSDs reported severe loss of financial control in 1994/1995. While there is the potential danger of inter-agency 'cost shunting' breaking out in relation to grey areas (such as care for people with strokes or Alzheimer's disease), it is interesting to note that relations generally are mature. One NHS respondent said; 'we must not allow this to drive us apart.'

Health's perception was that the purchaser/provider split was at an earlier stage in SSDs, which were still organizations in transition. SSDs were also seen as characterized by a hierarchical and centralist culture, in particular with elected members being much more interested and active in operational matters than NHS Non-Executive Directors (NEDs).

The lead role for interfacing with the SSD was sometimes undertaken by a senior manager who had built up years of experience in the community care field and could understand – if not always agree with – SSD culture. Occasionally the NHS might poach a 'bright' manager directly from the SSD.

At operational level, NHS/SSD links were seen as more advanced. Broker roles were emerging in some localities, with personnel able to cross conventional boundaries. A district nursing sister in Bournemouth had also trained as a SSD care manager and was able to access the SSD care budget in one flexible area (but not elsewhere).

Alliances with local voluntary groups   The voluntary sector represents both a source of community activity and information but increasingly also a service delivery mechanism. The experience of such organizations of the introduction of 'contract culture' varied markedly. In some areas, good relations had been established, particularly where health commission money had been used to expand the range of voluntary sector provision. Voluntary organizations were sometimes staffed by ex-NHS workers, perpetuating a highly stable informal interorganizational network.

In one locality, however, the arrival of contacting was seen as heralding a retreat from an open and community orientated Family Health Services Authority (FHSA) to a health commission driven much more by perform-ance management criteria. The SSD was seen as taking more time to discuss matters with the voluntary sector than the NHS ('the Health Commission is too busy to listen'). The commission could display arro-gance, for example, cancelling meetings at short notice.

Alliances with local councils   Joint working with local councils was of enhanced importance given the need to build local ownership of controversial strategies of change in health care, such as plans to reorganize acute services. Where such alliance building had not taken place, plans for restructuring could founder on the rocks of local opposition. There was sometimes a need to secure a 'turnaround', given a legacy of mistrust.

As such joint working moved up the agenda, enhanced regular face-to-face contact at senior level (chairs, CEOs, party leaders) could be built on to construct local joint alliances for the delivery of new forms of outposted health care run from non-clinical venues. Behind formal statements of opposition (particularly in Labour areas), informal understandings could sometimes emerge.

[. . .]

Alliances with higher education institutions The requirement for a skilled workforce in the NHS, the development of the NHS R&D strategy, the expansion of higher education over the last five years (particularly the new universities) and the requirement to move towards evidence-based purchasing have all resulted in increased emphasis being placed on the development of links with higher education institutions. In some inner city localities, in particular, academic networks have long been of central importance, given the importance of medical schools. Recent developments move beyond such traditional alliances with medical schools to the development of new links with other institutions which offer skills in health services research, including some business schools.

Participation in centrally prescribed inter-agency fora A number of localities reported NHS involvement in centrally constructed inter-agency fora, such as *city challenge*, with very significant budgets to spend. Many of the old community development projects of the 1970s were seen as failing because they tried to promote social development without economic development. More recent *city challenge* initiatives link these two agendas in a much more explicit way, spanning the environment, employment, crime and also health. A separate board is usually set up to administer *city challenge* programmes, typically involving the Department of the Environment, TECs, local business people and leading councillors.

There is evidence in these programmes of at least some joint working between the NHS and the private sector. Some senior private sector personnel now staff the boards of many local non-elected agencies, providing another point of contact. Senior NHS managers may themselves sit on boards of other public agencies or socially minded businesses.

Alliances with local employers Health promotion campaigns are sometimes workplace-based, dependent on winning the co-operation of local employers (e.g., workplace-based '*look after your heart*' campaigns). The link between unemployment and poor health also means that job centres may provide an important focus for an inter-agency alliance.

Alliances with the EU EU funding now represents a source of very substantial additional financial support for local initiatives in some deprived areas (such as Merseyside). Councils and health authorities are here beginning to develop supra-national networks with the EU in order to win these significant sums to help their work towards meeting public health targets.

[. . .]

In summary, NHS purchasing organizations are having to manage relationships with a range of external stakeholders, ranging from local community groups, through other agencies, up to the Department of Health and indeed the EU. They are involved in a number of inter-agency fora as well as single-agency alliances. Clinical as well as managerial networks play an important role. A small group of key people play multiple roles in a number of these settings, reflecting the rise of a new public-sector elite. It is thus sometimes difficult to attribute leadership in network construction, as actors may be operating with multiple roles and mixed motives. The network can thus be seen as a dense web of interlocking ties – many of which are inherited – rather than as a deliberately constructed strategic alliance between NHS management and management in another agency.

Rather than one single trigger, there is a variety of network-based initiatives and streams of work observable, propelled by different ideas and sources of leadership. The network phenomenon is polycentric and diffuse in nature. As CEOs do not automatically stand as central to many of these networks, their power base cannot be assumed but has to be won. Few would have predicted the revival, for instance, of the community development tradition with its emphasis on highly local forms of mobilization and collective leadership.

Concluding Discussion

Analytic Points

Public sector settings Few previous studies of network-based forms of management have taken account of the distinctive properties of public-sector settings (but see Marsh and Rhodes, 1992, for an analysis more focused on structure than process). Such public-sector settings are both highly professionalized and highly politicized. In the case of the NHS, clinical networks exercise an important role in interorganizational communication as well as managerial networks, and remain outside direct managerial control. The professional college represents a traditional mode of organization in health care and one which continues in importance.

NHS networks are thus diffuse in nature rather than concentrated on a focal managerial network. There is also a dense web of interconnections with other public-sector agencies, and also some private-sector firms and personnel. A small public-sector elite has emerged which occupies multiple roles in a number of different organizations within a locality.

NHS senior managers do not necessarily stand in a nodal position in these key networks, nor are they automatically accorded influence in situations where they can no longer exercise crude positional power. They thus have to win and enact influence in negotiation with others.

In politicized settings, organizations are sometimes instructed to enact top-down changes at a local level. These changes may indeed be mandated by legislation. This strategy of top-down and power-led change was increasingly evident in the 1980s. It is a paradox that some of the forces observable at local level which promote the adoption of more network-based forms of management have been mandated by the centre. Few sustained organizing efforts were found which might have acted to institutionalize and sustain the new styles of management (Nohria, 1992). Without such sustaining organizing efforts, the life cycle of these initiatives may be short indeed.

So is network-based management no more than the latest top-down fad? Is there genuine local ownership of network-based management? Will this agenda be suddenly dropped as further issue succession takes place?

The new competition and the N-form   The wider literature on the post-Fordist 'new competition' (Best, 1990) operates at a high level of generality. This wider literature sometimes suggests a paradigmatic transition to the N-form organization is underway at least in certain settings (Miles and Snow, 1986). The empirical evidence from the NHS by contrast suggests a more complex and contradictory picture, with several alternative models of management practice co-existing. Some of these changes may have been imposed on local agencies by the centre, rather than emerging organically. There is the possibility of rapid regression as well as forward movement. Moves to N-form organizations may be no more than cynical relabelling exercises (March and Olsen, 1983; Brunsson, 1989), so that ingrained behaviours re-emerge 'once the heat is off'.

Developments within the NHS certainly need to be tracked over a longer time period before it can be safely concluded that a major transition to the N-form is occurring rather than tactical compliance with a new set of central initiatives.

Mixed modes of management   The literature on strategic change of the 1980s (Pettigrew, 1985; Johnson, 1987) represented a useful correction to the presumption of incremental change so evident in the 1960s and 1970s. Long periods of incremental change were increasingly seen as interspersed by periodic moments of system-wide, paradigmatic or 'frame breaking' change (Miller and Friesen, 1984; Tushman et al., 1988). This literature on organizational transformation sometimes invoked the notion of a paradigm shift, the cognitive moving from one internally coherent model to a second.

However, we have to ask: is this notion of a managerial paradigm too fixed? Following Rorty (1991), Tsoukas (1995) suggests that sets of beliefs should be seen in somewhat looser terms as 'webs'. Such webs are constantly being rewoven to reflect new experiences, either on an incremental (first order) or substantial (second order) basis, achieving equilibrium in the web (i.e. coherence).

The present evidence from the NHS suggests that a pure paradigmatic transition is less likely than a period where different modes of management co-exist. Diversity is more likely than consistency; and pluralism than hegemony. The question is whether such a mixed mode period is better characterized by co-existence or by contradiction.

In their study in the substantive field of organizational participation, Dachler and Wilpert (1978: 2) construct an intriguing general argument about the consequences of ideological pluralism. They noted the divergence of theoretical ideas, inherent contradictions, and heterogeneity in approaches and purposes apparent in managerial literature and practice. Divergence and contradiction may be seen as important components of many social and organizational phenomena. Contradictions may grow out of socially produced change which then stands in contradiction to the established social order. Furthermore, since social production is imperfectly co-ordinated, it results in multiple and often incompatible social forms. Any higher order and convergent framework must be able to encompass such divergence and contradictions.

The competing values framework (Quinn and Rohrbaugh, 1983; Quinn, 1988; O'Neill and Quinn, 1993) represents an example of such an approach. This model emerged as an articulation of the underlying cognitive structures that experts used to make sense of organizational effectiveness criteria. Four models could be discerned: (i) the hierarchical internal process model; (ii) the organic open systems model; (iii) the task and performance orientated rational goal model; (iv) the interpersonal human relations model.

O'Neill and Quinn (1993) suggest that the four models should not necessarily be seen as contradictory and that these apparent opposites can be reconciled. Rather, it broadens the repertoire of approaches available to managers as they move from one situation to another, given that responses may well be context specific.

Against this view, Greenwood and Hinings' (1993) discussion of alternative organizational archetypes highlights four tracks:

- inertia: most organizations can be expected to gravitate to a design archetype and remain there for a lengthy period;
- 'aborted excursion': after limited or temporary movement, there is regression back to the original archetype;
- reorientations or organizational transformations where radical movement takes place between one archetype and another;
- unresolved excursions: there is here sustained movement from a coherent archetype without attaining a reorientation. Incomplete decoupling occurs without completed recoupling, leading to failed or resisted attempts at reorientation. As a result, an organization remains in an intermediate category over a long period of time.

A less optimistic view is that there are inherent contradictions between hierarchical, market-based and network-orientated styles of management.

In particular, engineering a transition to a new network-based style of management will be dependent on sustained organizing efforts including norm and standard setting. The NHS may be an example of an 'unresolved excursion', where attempts at reorientation are partial and resisted. In the absence of clear and consistent signals about what constitutes acceptable managerial behaviour in the new network-based form of organization, a pure transition is unlikely to be sustained. Rather, a period of disequilibrium ensues, characterized by a never-ending succession of reform efforts as each in turn fails to establish a unifying managerial paradigm.

Managerial Problems and Challenges of Network-based Organizations

Even if fully implemented, network-based styles of management should not be seen as a universal panacea. While they may solve some old management problems, they may also produce some new ones in their turn. What might these problems and challenges be?

Networks and performance A major criticism encountered in the field was that network-based forms of management were highly time consuming, and did not necessarily lead to tangible output. What, in other words, are these networks for? There is a danger that the means of managerial process could drive out the end of delivering better services.

Moreover, the combination of network based forms of management and also the strong performance orientation – with its focus on quantification and short-term target setting – now evident in the NHS might represent an uneasy and volatile combination. The problems of operating in such a mixed management mode have already been commented on.

Some commented that networks could easily proliferate, soaking up a lot of time while delivering very little. Is there a danger of engagement with too many networks? Who retains an overview to ensure that different networks do not duplicate work and that there is effective communication across network boundaries? How can one assess success and is it sometimes necessary to withdraw from non-productive networks? Network-based forms are thus perceived as diffuse and polycentric in nature, with many networks and sources of leadership interacting simultaneously.

There was a related concern about lack of clarity in network forms. While senior management often welcomed moves to network-based forms of management, middle management was reported as feeling under threat. A high level of turnover at middle management level was apparent in some organizations.

A key question was how to ensure a clarity of purpose in network-based forms of organization. Individual objective setting and personal development plans were felt to offer one way forward to give staff a greater sense of purpose.

Network sustainability   An important question relates to the sustainability of some of these networks, which were time consuming to create and maintain but could also collapse if they were not seen as delivering by participants. Networks can also rapidly disintegrate if known players are pulled out; 'a face that you know and recognise is key' said one respondent. Networks may represent a volatile form of organization, with short life-cycle effects.

How is it possible to keep interest and commitment over a long period once initial enthusiasm has worn off? There is a need to be realistic about demands on participants' time. If it is possible to deliver some early successes, then further participation in the network may be secured. The institutionalization of the network is then an important activity.

Many of the networks studied needed a focus or a 'broker' to animate and sustain them (Thorelli, 1990). The question of who is filling these broker roles is critical. Are people with networking skills coming forward or is the pack of existing personnel simply being reshuffled without much thought being given to selection against job and skill specifications?

Networks and change   A heavy reliance on pre-existing or 'closed' networks is often associated with continuity and maintenance management rather than innovation or change. Network-based management may then tend towards conservatism, yet NHS purchasing organizations face a high change agenda and will be assessed on their ability to deliver change. So far, NHS purchasing organizations can be seen as relatively closed in nature and as dominated at a strategic level by the new public-sector elite.

So players may need to engage far more openly than hitherto in network-building activity to open up networks and bring in new players. Initially, they may need to 'sell' participation in the network to partners not previously involved. While reciprocity is a fundamental norm in networks, NHS respondents may find that they need to give (and to create new relationships) before they can take.

The uncertainty of network-building processes   Network-building is a long-term, emergent and development process. It is not possible to predict in advance the outcome of work in this field and initiatives may indeed have unintended consequences. Substantial developmental work may have to be undertaken if traditionally powerless and disengaged partners are to participate more effectively in decision-making. Even if forward movement is secured, there may be rapid regression if key players are pulled out or if the national or local context deteriorates.

Such a long time-scale and indeterminacy as to output may well conflict with short-term and task-orientated approaches to management.

Moving along the diffusion curve   We consider that our sample should be seen as at the 'leading edge' and not as typical of the whole population. Using concepts found in the diffusion literature, it may be that a relatively small number of innovators/early adopters are reporting moves in the direction of network-based forms of management (Rogers, 1983; Stocking, 1995). Some of those interviewed reported unusual career paths, and this reinforces our view that so far only a small and atypical group of innovators has been studied.

Many of the early experiments were reported from relatively simple and contained settings with good prehistories. There is therefore a major question as to how – indeed whether – these experiments can be rolled out to an indifferent middle ground and perhaps hostile tail.

HRM Implications and Issues

The HRM implications of the move to network-based forms of management have not yet been fully addressed. In particular, we need to ask: what sort of skills and attributes are needed to make these forms of organization work?

When asked, respondents were able empirically to identify key networking attributes and skills meaningful to the field, including:

> strong interpersonal, communication and listening skills; an ability to persuade; a readiness to trade and to engage in reciprocal rather than manipulative behaviour; an ability to construct long-term relationships.

A mutual orientation and reciprocity emerge as key concepts in network-based organizations. The exercise of positional power gives way to influencing skills, such as an understanding of how best to manage group decision-making (Moss Kanter, 1989). It may be important to foster relational sentiments (e.g., indebtedness and obligation) so that exchanges are not seen as one-off transactions but take place 'in the shadow of the future' and the past (Powell, 1990). Such norms of obligation and co-operation imply the continued existence of a community of shared values across the NHS. Within such 'clannish' organizational fields (Ouchi, 1991), contractual opportunism is unlikely. Associated with such clan cultures is the importance of relationship-building and exhibiting trustworthy behaviour (Grabher, 1993). Such social exchange processes grow and increase in scope through mutual reinforcement over a long period of time (Blau, 1968).

> The ability to cross a variety of occupational, organizational, social and political boundaries; an ability to 'speak different languages'; an ability to act as interpreter between different groups; to be credible with a range of different groups.

A single master culture does not appear to be emerging within the NHS, but rather it continues to be characterized by a collection of very different subcultures. In Hofstede's (1994) terms, participants in such polycentric organizations will need to be adept at crossing conventional boundaries and at managing intercultural encounters. This requires them to be cosmopolitan and multi-cultural in nature, able to speak different languages in the different subcultures. They also need to possess highly developed analytic and diagnostic skills so that they are aware when they are crossing subcultural boundaries and are able to switch language and behaviour pattern as appropriate.

> Tolerance of high levels of ambiguity and uncertainty; a long-term as well as a short-term view; a good strategic sense, vision and ideas; an ability to reflect on experience and to conceptualize; a capacity to learn quickly and to adapt in new situations.

Managers in network-based organizations have often been seen as coping with higher levels of uncertainty and ambiguity, a greater pressure to innovate and hence as needing to demonstrate an accelerated capacity to learn. Some writers see joint ventures as a 'race to learn' (Hendry, 1994), where the alliance is no more than a transitional stage and where the interorganizational relationship is a bargain which obsolesces. This is a more predatory characterization of strategic alliances than the more co-operative accounts found elsewhere in the literature and may reflect the forms of European experience of joint ventures with Japanese corporations.

Is learning explicitly recognized as an objective in network-based organizations? How do HRM policies contribute to an effective learning organization? How can internal learning groups be established? Such learning processes also depend on the capacity of individuals to reflect on their experience, to conceptualize experimental knowledge and to adopt new skills and behaviours.

> An ability to impart knowledge to others; to act as teacher and mentor; an ability to transfer knowledge from one setting to another; an ability to convey requisite standards and attitudes to others inside and outside the organization (norm setting).

Concluding Remarks

We hope in this chapter to have accessed recent literature on moves towards network-based organizations and to have applied it to a major UK organization (the NHS) through an empirical study of purchasing organizations. This focus on a public-sector organization, and specifications of the implications for management style and development, are useful additions to the literature.

The transition is as yet partial, with the result that mixed modes of management may be emerging. It is still unclear whether centrally sponsored initiatives consistent with network-based approaches will be sustained or whether networking will be no more than a faddish phase. Interesting and potentially significant developments are occurring within the NHS, although further tracking is needed before we can begin to assess their long-term significance and scale.

References

Bahrami, H. (1992) 'The emerging flexible organization: perspectives from Silicon Valley', *California Management Review*, 34 (4): 33–52. (Also Chapter 12, this volume.)

Bartlett, C. and Ghoshal, S. (1989) *Managing across Borders*. London: Hutchinson.

Best, M. (1990) *The New Competition*. Cambridge, MA: Harvard University Press.

Blau, P. (1968) 'The hierarchy of authority in organizations', *American Journal of Sociology*, 73: 453–514.

Brunsson, N. (1989) 'Administrative reforms as routines', *Scandinavian Journal of Management*, 5 (3): 219–28.

Dachler, H.P. and Wilpert, B. (1978) 'Conceptual dimensions and boundaries of participation in organisations: a critical evaluation', *Administrative Science Quarterly*, 23: 1–38.

Grabher, G. (ed.) (1993) *The Embedded Firm: On the Socio Economics of Industrial Networks*. London: Routledge.

Granovetter, M. (1985) 'Economic action and social structure – a theory of embeddedness', *American Journal of Sociology*, 91 (3): 481–510.

Greenwood, R. and Hinings, C.R. (1993) 'Understanding strategic change: the contribution of archetypes', *Academy of Management Journal*, 36 (5): 1052–81.

Hendry, C. (1994) *Human Resource Strategies for International Growth*. London: Routledge.

Hofstede, G. (1994) *Cultures and Organisations*. London: HarperCollins.

Jarillo, J.C. (1988) 'On strategic networks', *Strategic Management Journal*, 9: 31–41.

Johanson, J. and Mattson, L.G. (1990) 'Internationalisation in industrial systems – a network approach', in D. Ford (ed.), *Understanding Business Markets*. London: Academic Press.

Johnson, G. (1987) *Strategic Change and the Management Process*. Oxford: Basil Blackwell.

Johnston, R. and Lawrence, P. (1991) 'Beyond vertical integration – the rise of the value adding partnership', in G. Thompson, J. Frances, R. Levacic and J. Mitchell (eds), *Markets, Hierarchies and Networks*. London: Sage.

Lazerson, M. (1993) 'Factory or putting out: knitting networks in Modena', in G. Grabher (ed.), *The Embedded Firm: On the Socio Economics of Industrial Networks*. London: Routledge.

March, J.G. and Olsen, J.P. (1983) 'Organizing political life – what administrative reorganization tells us about government', *American Political Science Review*, 77: 281–96.

Marsh, D. and Rhodes, R.A.W. (1992) *Policy Networks in British Government*. Oxford: Clarendon Press.

Martinez, J.I. and Jarillo, J.C. (1989) 'The evolution of research on coordination mechanisms in multi-national corporations', *Journal of International Business Studies*, 20 (Fall): 489–514.

Miles, R.E. and Snow, C.C. (1986) 'Organizations: new concepts for new forms', *California Management Review*, 28 (3), Spring: 62–73.

Miles, R.E. and Snow, C.C. (1992) 'Causes of failure in network organizations', *California Management Review*, 34 (4): 62–73.

Miller, D. and Friesen, P.H. (1984) *Organizations: A Quantum View*. Englewood Cliffs, NJ: Prentice-Hall.

Moss Kanter, R. (1989) *When Giants Learn to Dance*. London: Unwin.

Moss Kanter, R. and Eccles, R.G. (1992) 'Making network research relevant to practice', in N. Nohria and R.G. Eccles (eds), *Networks and Organizations – Structures, Form and Action*. Boston, MA: Harvard Business School Press.

Nohria, N. (1992) 'Is a network perspective a useful way of studying organizations?', in N. Nohria and R.G. Eccles (eds), *Networks and Organizations – Structures, Form and Action*. Boston, MA: Harvard Business School Press.

Nohria, N. and Eccles, R.G. (1992) *Networks and Organizations – Structures, Form and Action*. Boston, MA: Harvard Business School Press.

O'Neill, R. and Quinn, R.E. (1993) 'Applications of the competing values framework', *Human Resource Management*, 32 (1), Spring: 1–7.

Ouchi, W. (1991) 'Markets, bureaucracies and clans', in G. Thompson, J. Frances, R. Levacic and J. Mitchell (eds), *Markets, Hierarchies and Networks*. London: Sage.

Pettigrew, A.M. (1985) *The Awakening Giant*. Oxford: Basil Blackwell.

Pettigrew, A.M., Conyon, M. and Whittington, R. (1995) 'The N form corporation', successful proposal to the ESRC, Centre for Corporate Strategy and Change, University of Warwick.

Powell, W.W. (1990) 'Neither market nor hierarchy: network forms of organisation', in G. Thompson, J. Frances, R. Levacic and J. Mitchell (eds), *Markets, Hierarchies and Networks*. London: Sage.

Quinn, R.E. (1988) *Beyond Rational Management: Mastering the Paradoxes and Competing Demands of High Performance*. San Francisco: Jossey-Bass.

Quinn, R.E. and Rohrbaugh, J. (1983) 'A spatial model of effectiveness criteria: towards a competing values approach to organisational analysis', *Management Science*, 29: 363–77.

Rogers, E. (1983) *The Diffusion of Innovations*. New York: The Free Press.

Rorty, R. (1991) *Objectivity, Relationism and Truth*. Cambridge: Cambridge University Press.

Sarason, S. (1976) *The Creation of Settings and the Future Societies*. London: Jossey-Bass.

Stocking, B. (1995) *Initiative and Inertia in the NHS*. London: Nuffield Provincial Hospitals Trust.

Thompson, G., Frances, J., Levacic, R. and Mitchell, J. (eds) (1991) *Markets, Hierarchies and Networks*. London: Sage.

Thorelli, H.B. (1990) 'Networks: between markets and hierarchies', in D. Ford (ed.), *Understanding Business Markets*. London: Academic Press.

Tsoukas, H. (1995) *The Ubiquity of Organisational Diversity: A Social Constructivist Perspective*. University of Warwick, Warwick Business School.

Tushman, M., Newman, W. and Romanelli, E. (1988) 'Convergence and upheaval: managing the unsteady pace of organizational evolution', in K.S. Cameron, R.L. Sutton and D.A. Whetten (eds), *Readings in Organisational Decline*. Cambridge, MA: Ballinger.

White, H. (1981) 'Where do markets come from?', *American Journal of Sociology*, 87: 517–47.

Williamson, O.E. (1975) *Markets and Hierarchies: Analysis and Antitrust Implications*. New York: The Free Press.

14   The Mutual Gains Enterprise

Thomas Kochan and Paul Osterman

What kind of enterprise can help restore the American economy? There is remarkable consensus among a wide range of scholars, management writers, consultants, labor leaders, and human resource professionals regarding the fundamental principles needed to achieve competitiveness in individual enterprises.

One reason for this consensus is that these principles are not derived only from academic theory or from the mistaken glorification of a single organization's economic success. The consensus is the product of both theoretical and empirical research and more than a decade of trial and error and comparison of traditional and transformed human resource and organizational practices. What sets this consensus apart is that no single practice is seen as the silver bullet or simple solution. Rather, it is the combined and mutually reinforcing effects of *a broad-based and deep commitment to these principles followed by effective implementation* that add up to a new system of employment relations. We review these principles in this chapter by drawing on the experiences of a variety of companies that have led the way in this experimental phase and whose valuable experience sharpened our understanding. We demonstrate that the foundations for this new system have already been laid in practice.

Generic Principles of Mutual Gains Enterprises

Many terms have been used to describe firms that treat human resources as a source of competitive advantage and do so in a manner that preserves high standards of living: 'high commitment', 'excellent', 'best practice', 'high performance', 'salaried', or 'transformed'. We use the term 'mutual gains' because it conveys a key message: achieving and sustaining competitive advantage from human resources require the strong support of multiple stakeholders in an organization. Employees must commit their

Originally published in Thomas Kochan and Paul Osterman (1994) *The Mutual Gains Enterprise*. Boston, MA: Harvard Business School Press (abridged).

TABLE 14.1 *Principles guiding the mutual gains enterprise*

Strategic Level
  Supportive business strategies
  Top management commitment
  Effective voice for human resources in strategy making and governance

Functional (Human Resource Policy) Level
  Staffing based on employment stabilization
  Investment in training and development
  Contingent compensation that reinforces cooperation, participation, and contribution

Workplace Level
  High standards of employee selection
  Broad task design and team work
  Employee involvement in problem solving
  Climate of cooperation and trust

energies to meeting the economic objectives of the enterprise. In return, owners (shareholders) must share the economic returns with employees and invest those returns in ways that promote the long-run economic security of the work force. And everyone involved in decision making must behave in ways that build and maintain the trust and support of the work force.

Table 14.1 summarizes the generic principles that characterize the mutual gains approach. It is important to realize that these are broad principles applied differently in different settings. They do not translate into a universal set of 'best practices', but rather stand as generic requirements that can be met in ways that conform to particular cultural or organizational realities.

Table 14.1 organizes the principles according to the three-tiered model developed in some of our research. We distinguish among the workplace, personnel policy making, and the strategic levels of enterprise activity. The central argument is that policies at these different levels must reinforce one another to produce sustained support for a mutual gains enterprise and for the system to achieve the benefits necessary to be competitive at high standards of living.

Workplace Policies

We start at the bottom of the model with workplace policies because this is where most organizations began experimenting with new employment practices. This should not be surprising because introducing change at this level doesn't threaten the existing power structure of top management or, in unionized settings, of the collective bargaining process and contract.

By the workplace level we mean the day-to-day interactions of employees with their co-workers, supervisors, and jobs. Here we see several principles as critical. Clearly, a mutual gains workplace system starts with high recruitment standards. Potential employees must be selected not only for their education, skills, and training, but also for their ability and willingness to engage in further training and development and to work effectively with others in group settings. Thus both objective indicators of skill and subjective evidence of new recruits' attitudes are important.

[. . .]

Mutual gains firms will require of future recruits a higher level of technical, analytical, and behavioral skills and attitudes toward work. If we fail to supply new entrants with the characteristics needed for mutual gains systems to function effectively, we will make this approach too expensive to adopt in this country and these jobs will migrate to countries that do provide entry-level talent.

The second essential principle for a mutual gains workplace system is that the education and skills of employees be fully utilized on the job. The job design principles that continue to dominate in too much of American industry were developed around the turn of the century for an uneducated immigrant labor force undisciplined in the ways of mass production.

[. . .]

A third principle at the workplace level deals with opportunities for employees and their representatives to engage in problem solving and decision making in matters that involve their jobs and their work environment – what Edward Lawler referred to as job involvement, and what more recently has been referred to as employee 'empowerment' (Lawler, 1986).

There is a long and checkered history of employee involvement efforts in the United States, dating back to the early experiments with job enlargement and rotation in the 1960s and through the quality of work life and quality circle fads of the late 1970s and early 1980s to the more recent popularity of total quality management (TQM) programs. Each cycle of innovation brings new labels and new approaches to employee involvement, but over time none have survived, even though some have been quite widely adopted. For example, a 1985 survey showed that more than 50 percent of large firms and one-third of all employees in a nationally representative survey had some experience with employee involvement at their workplace. A 1990 survey suggested that the number of firms with some experience had increased to 70 percent; however, within these firms, on average, less than one-third of the work force actually participated in involvement programs (Lawler et al., 1992).

[. . .]

The fourth and final workplace principle relates to the quality of relationships between employees, their representatives, and managers. A high-conflict/low-trust relationship is incompatible with the task of building and maintaining the psychological and social climate needed to produce and sustain mutual gains. This does not mean that all conflicts between employees and employers wither away. Indeed, we assume that conflicting interests are a natural part of the employment relationship. But such conflicts cannot be so all encompassing that they push out potential for effective problem solving and negotiations. It is not conflict *per se* that matters, it is how effectively and efficiently the parties resolve conflicts which naturally occur that really matters.

Some industrial relations specialists and union leaders view employment relationships in which employees have independent union representation or other sources of independent voice or protection as an inherent competitive advantage. Although formal union representation may not be the only means by which conflicts can be aired openly and conflict resolution achieved expeditiously, some surrogate for this traditional form may be needed in settings where employees lack formal representation.

The Personnel Policy Level

Moving to the personnel policy level, we suggest three additional principles that are critical to a mutual gains enterprise. First, staffing policies must be designed and managed so that they reinforce the principle of employment security and thus promote the commitment, flexibility, and loyalty of employees. This does not imply guarantees of lifetime employment, but it does imply that the first instinct in good times and bad is to build and protect the firm's investment in human resources, not indiscriminately add and cut people as knee-jerk responses to short-term fluctuations in business conditions. Put differently, the firm – and its stockholders – should be willing to incur significant costs before resorting to layoffs.

Lee Dyer, Felecian Foltman, and George Milkovich of Cornell University surveyed firms that avoided such knee-jerk reactions in the 1970s and 1980s (Dyer et al., 1985). Table 14.2 lists the practices they followed in coping with declines in product demand or technological change without resorting to layoffs. Clearly, implementing such strategies as avoiding certain contracts or business opportunities of short duration requires organizational discipline that can be achieved only through a strong concern for human resource issues at the top of the firm. This condition was present at firms such as Control Data Corporation, IBM, Hewlett-Packard, Eli Lilly, and others included in the Dyer–Foltman–Milkovich study, until some of them experienced significant losses in market share and profitability.

This last point deserves more discussion. Many of the firms known for their use of the employment stabilizing techniques listed in Table 14.2 have had to resort to layoffs in the 1980s or 1990s as their market share shrunk, competition from lower-cost producers in maturing markets took its toll, and Wall Street analysts intensified their criticism of these 'full employment practices'.

TABLE 14.2 *Actions to maintain employment security*

When output is increasing	When output is variable	When output is declining
Avoid business that appears to be short-run or cyclical.	Call in vendored work.	Call in vendored work.
Gear up slowly.	Move work to people.	Produce for inventory.
Vendor some work.	Stretch productivity improvement programs.	Create work.
Add new jobs as a last resort.	Pressure suppliers for more reliable deliveries.	Freeze hiring.
Use overtime.	Move people to work.	Cut overtime.
Hire temporaries.		Share work.
Increase training.		Encourage voluntary leaves, retirements, and severance.
		Cut pay.
		Tighten performance standards.

Source: Dyer et al., 1985

We do not believe that it is possible or feasible for any firm to guarantee lifetime job security, nor do we necessarily advocate that firms make iron-clad pledges of employment continuity (although, as noted, we believe that firms and their stockholders should be willing to incur costs before laying off employees). Instead, we emphasize that we have what is sometimes referred to as a 'market failure' or 'public goods problem'. Individual firms find it extremely difficult and perhaps too costly to provide long-term employment security if surrounded by or competing with firms that follow short-term employment practices. Yet, if a sufficient number of firms adopt long-term employment practices, the costs of these practices to individual firms decline, making them more economically efficient and likely to endure.

Closely related to employment security practices are employee training and development strategies. Indeed, recognition that iron-clad employment security guarantees are seldom feasible makes training all the more important. Long-term employment security in today's economy lies not with a lifetime job in a single firm but in procuring and keeping current general skills that can transfer across firms as needed over the course of a career. Similarly, firms that seek competitive advantage through human resources must make the necessary investments to ensure that their employees have the appropriate skills and training not only to meet short-term job requirements, but also to anticipate changing job requirements over time. Both employers and employees must be prepared to adopt the concept of lifelong learning.

The third critical principle at the human resource policy level concerns compensation. It is very simple: if we are to stabilize employment (quantity of labor), we must have greater flexibility regarding the price of labor. Achieving this is far from simple.

There is little agreement among experts or little convincing empirical evidence to indicate that there is a single, best contingent compensation program or strategy. Profit sharing, employee stock ownership, stock options, and other equity- or profit-based plans may work better for higher-level executives who can see directly the relationship between their efforts and these outcomes; however, one must be careful not to warp management incentives in ways that lead people to maximize their own short-run compensation at the expense of overall organizational goals or long-term interests. Group incentives obviously make more sense than individual incentive plans when team work, task interdependence, and internal mobility across jobs and departments are critical to a firm's success. But where individuals work alone or their performance is not dependent on others – for example, salespersons with separate districts or products – or lawyers or consultants with separate clients, or athletes in individual sports such as tennis or golf (but not basketball!), individual incentive plans may still be appropriate. Suffice it to say that the number of settings where individuals work independently in organizations appears to be declining and, therefore, so too does the scope for individual incentive pay systems or contracts.

Strategic-level Requirements

A third group of mutual gains principles relates to decisions that traditionally were thought to lie beyond the legitimate domain of human resource professionals, employees, or labor union leaders. This is no longer the case, since these high-level or 'strategic' decisions have a profound effect on employment relations; they are part of the domain of human resource and labor–management relations practitioners.

Of all the important considerations at this level, perhaps the most central are a firm's competitive strategies. It is essential that the firm not depend solely on low costs, especially not on low wages, salaries, and benefit levels, but rather on such sources of competitive advantage as affordable quality, innovation, flexibility, speed, and customer service. Consider, for example, the difference between the strategies adopted after industry deregulation by Continental and Delta airlines. In 1983, Frank Lorenzo, the CEO of Continental, announced that the company was shifting its competitive strategy. It was determined to become the low-cost carrier and compete on the basis of low fares. Lorenzo used loopholes in Chapter 11 bankruptcy proceedings (later closed by Congress, partly in response to Lorenzo's actions) to cancel labor contracts with his employees, cut wages by 25 to 50 percent for different work groups, decertify his employees' unions, and thereby achieved the low labor costs needed to implement his strategy. Clearly this did little to build employee commitment or trust and obviously did not include employee participation or labor–management cooperation.

Compare this strategy to Delta's. Delta was known in the industry for its conservative financial strategies, its commitment to high-quality service to customers, and its commitment to its employees. For example, Delta was the only major US airline to avoid layoffs during the steep recession the industry experienced in the early 1970s. In return, its employees pooled their funds to purchase a Boeing 767 for the company! Consistent with its historical approach, Delta decided not to push for lower labor costs in the wake of industry deregulation and as a result retained its reputation for both quality of service and quality of employee relations. Over time, however, it did end up in the unhappy position of being the carrier with the highest labor costs, but at the same time it achieved the most consistent service quality and profitability record in the industry.

Delta is not, however, free of problems. In fact, in 1993 it had to resort to layoffs of pilots because they refused to take pay cuts to help cover losses the company, like most other airlines, experienced following the fare wars of 1992. But this merely serves to reinforce the point we are making: conflict with its employees, which may threaten the high level of trust and commitment Delta built up with them, emerged precisely when the company was forced to give greater weight to price and wage reduction as competitive weapons.

The lesson is clear. High employee commitment is impossible to sustain over time unless a company has a competitive strategy that requires the commitment and loyalty and motivation of its employees to succeed. The resulting differences in employee relations at Continental and Delta over the first ten years following airline deregulation are evident. Indeed, in airlines or other service industries where employee interactions with customers are so crucial to customer satisfaction, these differences may be essential to long-term competitiveness.

[. . .]

Xerox stands out as a company that has maintained its support for mutual gains principles for more than a decade under the leadership of three different CEOs. One feature that has been critical is that the company always has had various means for giving voice to employee and human resource interests in strategy formulation and organizational governance.

[. . .]

Obviously, the principles we have outlined are idealized organizational practices. No organization is expected to meet all of them perfectly or through the same practices. Nonetheless, we are suggesting that when these principles are properly operationalized they will come together in the form of an integrated system that, other things equal, will produce globally competitive business results as well as globally competitive standards of living for employees.

Evidence: Effects of Mutual Gains Practices

What are the effects of mutual gains practices on firm performance to date? We have at least three kinds of evidence: (1) self-reports of managers or union leaders of the results of their experiences, (2) case studies, and (3) quantitative assessments. As researchers, we would like to place the greatest reliance on the third kind, less on case studies, and relatively little weight on the parties' self-reports. Unfortunately, the bulk of the evidence to date comes in the opposite order: most of the evidence is self-reports; there are a limited number of in-depth case studies; and only a handful of quantitative evaluations have been conducted. Among all the studies, a small number of familiar leading examples are routinely reported, including such well-known companies as Xerox, Motorola, NUMMI, Saturn, Hewlett-Packard, Federal Express, Corning, and Steelcase. Boxes 14.1–3 provide capsule summaries of some of these 'best practice' cases put together by the Department of Labor.

Moreover, reviewing the quantitative evidence presents a real paradox. On the one hand, our theory argues that these practices reach their full potential when they are combined in a comprehensive system. Employee participation, for example, is unlikely to survive for long in an organization whose business strategies rely primarily on minimizing costs and there is little or no commitment to employment security. Although we do not necessarily believe that organizational decision makers fully comprehend this point when first considering innovations, they do come to understand it as they are forced to deal with inconsistencies among different organizational practices over time. For example, it became quite clear to Xerox executives that their 1982 fledgling employee involvement program could not be sustained unless they stopped laying off workers who took the risks of cooperating with their employee involvement experiment! Similarly, in the late 1970s the United Auto Workers made it clear to GM that the union's support for quality of working life efforts in current plants would not be sustained unless the company abandoned its 'southern strategy', i.e., opening new nonunion plants in the South. Yet most existing organizations cannot and do not transform their practices completely all at once. Instead, they tend to experiment with incremental changes in one or more practices at a time and then, as was the case at Xerox, deal with demands for additional change as problems arise. Usually it is only when designing a greenfield site or making a major technological or physical change in an existing facility that the parties can easily introduce entirely new systems of work organization and related human resource practices.

So it is not surprising that most empirical studies of human resource practices tend to focus on single or small sets of innovations. Indeed, research that is generally judged by accepted standards of social science to be the most rigorous and credible generally seeks to isolate the 'independent' effects of specific practices, holding constant or controlling for all other potential determinants of the outcome of interest. Researchers want to know, controlling for everything else, just what does an employee participation process add to productivity or quality? Our theory suggests this is the wrong question and the wrong test. We argue that employee participation cannot and will not be divorced from other human resource

---

BOX 14.1

Company: Saturn Corporation
Location: Springhill, Tennessee
Industry: Automobiles
Union: United Automobile Workers (UAW)
Size: 6,800 employees

Saturn has made an enormous investment – both financially and philosophically – in people. At each managerial level, from the president on down, and within each staff function, a UAW counterpart shares decision making equally with Saturn managers. All employees are part of at least one team. On the production floor, workers are formed into teams of five to fifteen people who manage themselves, from budgeting to scheduling to hiring and training. Decisions are made by consensus. There are no time clocks, no privileged parking spots, and no private dining rooms.

The whole system is undergirded by enormous amounts of training. Each new employee at Saturn goes through a week of orientation training before he or she hits the floor. Even then, workers work only part time for the first two or three months, as their time is split between classroom and on-the-job training. Production workers can expect to spend half their training time learning 'soft skills' such as conflict resolution, problem solving, presentation, and communication. While at Saturn, employees can expect to spend 5 percent of their time annually in training. The company guarantees 95 percent of their base wages and does not pay the remaining 5 percent unless everybody meets this training goal. The first-quarter goal was 155,687 hours; Saturn employees logged more than 300,000.

Saturn reduced work classifications and thereby increased the company's flexibility to deploy workers. The company has one classification for production workers and five for skilled trades. Everyone is on salary, and lifetime employment is guaranteed to 80 percent of its work force, barring 'severe economic conditions' or 'catastrophic events'.

From 1986 to 1992, there were only seven formal grievances at Saturn. There have been improvements to quality, productivity, cost savings, reduction of waste, communication, labor–management relations, and morale. From 1985 to 1990, Saturn reduced defects from 3.5 to 1.5 per vehicle. In 1991, Saturn sold more cars per dealer than any other manufacturer, including Honda – the first time in fifteen years that a US car maker claimed the number one spot. In a survey by *Popular Mechanics*, it was reported that 83.4 percent of Saturn owners would buy another Saturn.

---

practices and organizational strategies. The implication of this argument is that we need to look at the total set of organizational strategies and assess their effects on performance.

Since it is harder to measure empirically all these organizational practices, this approach encourages broader, more qualitative case studies and self-reports of the parties' experiences with these innovations, and their own assessments of the results. Because these approaches often involve

---

BOX 14.2

Company: Federal Express
Location: Memphis, Tennessee
Industry: Freight transportation
Size: 90,000 worldwide

In 1987 Federal Express instituted a pay-for-performance/pay-for-knowledge system, recognizing that programs rewarding outstanding performance and superior job knowledge translate into outstanding customer service. Federal Express rewards customer-contact employees with higher pay and promotions for superior job knowledge and performance. The system is built around job-knowledge testing, measuring how well an employee knows his or her job. The measuring system includes performance evaluations of how well the knowledge is applied.

Because of FedEx's far-flung locations, most training is provided through an interactive video disk (IVD) system. For example, FedEx developed an IVD course to teach its mechanics how to troubleshoot and repair electrical problems. The course allows mechanics to take readings, test components, replace equipment, and evaluate procedures. FedEx has more than 900 employees working officially in a training capacity. The company devotes 3 percent ($225 million) of its annual expenses to training.

Employees are grouped into teams as part of a performance-improvement and quality-enhancement program. One team analyzed and redesigned the minisort process, which re-sorts and redirects mail that arrives late or is misdirected by earlier operations. This redesign saved FedEx $1 million yearly and reduced the number of employees needed from 150 to 80. Federal Express established one cross-functional team for each component (12 in all) of its Service Quality Indicators program and a formal Quality Improvement Process (QIP) has been instituted throughout the company. The objective of the QIP is to achieve a 100 percent service level, increase profits, and make FedEx a better place to work.

In 1990 the company won the Malcolm Baldrige National Quality Award and in 1992 was awarded the RIT/USA Today Quality Cup for service. FedEx was also awarded *Distribution* magazine's number one quality ranking in the air express carrier category in 1991.

---

descriptions of firms that have been judged to be successful, we are too often left with several serious questions. First, how many failures go unreported? Second, which, if any, of the practices of these organizations accounts for the firm's success? And third, how do we know what is cause and what is effect? Put differently, would the same performance results be achieved if another organization in a similar product and labor–market environment copied exactly these practices? This kind of total organization research often cannot answer this question.

Our resolution of this dilemma, and the one we urge professionals and policy makers to follow, is to be open to considering all kinds of quantitative and case study research and testimonials of the parties involved, but at the same time to be skeptical of it, always asking the researcher to 'show

BOX 14.3

Company: Shenandoah Life Insurance Company
Location: Roanoke, Virginia
Industry: Insurance
Size: 220 employees

Insurance underwriting tasks at Shenandoah Life were redesigned around autonomous work groups of four to seven employees each. Work teams have responsibility for scheduling work and vacations, final selection of new members, designing office space, determining the basics of the compensation system, interacting with managers and other units, and discipline and training. With the advent of these self-directed teams, teams no longer have direct supervisors; instead they report to two managers who have responsibility for twenty-plus employees each. Instead of first-line supervisors, the company now has advisers who act as technical support for specific work teams.

Employees who work on teams receive training in group dynamics, brainstorming, conflict resolution, decision making, planning, and team functioning, in addition to task-related training. By moving to self-directed work teams, Shenandoah has benefited through higher efficiency and stream-lined operations. The employees have benefited through gaining more responsibility and more interesting work lives.

With the move to self-directed teams, the company instituted a pay-for-knowledge compensation system, which rewards employees on the basis of their knowledge of a number of different tasks. The cross-training provided to the employees has resulted in more creativity and better utilization of manpower. From 1985 to 1987, the number of people employed in the teams declined by 15.6 percent while the volume of work increased by 28.5 percent. Complaints from customers have decreased, and the supervisor/employee ratio has declined from 1:7 to 1:37.

Shenandoah Life has been so successful in implementing its team-based structure that it has established a for-profit consulting subsidiary.

us' the results. With these caveats in mind, let's look at what the evidence to date has to say.

[. . .]

The evidence on the effects of innovations in compensation, employment security, and training on economic performance and worker welfare is limited. The findings of the studies conducted on these issues seem to indicate that in isolation, single innovations have at best limited positive impacts. When combined with workplace innovations discussed in the previous section, their effects become stronger.

This point is best illustrated by the studies done on the effects of contingent, i.e., variable, compensation arrangements. Variable-pay systems range from individual bonus systems to group-based incentive plans, to organization-wide profit-, productivity-, or equity-based gain-sharing plans. Such plans as piece-work systems tend to be limited to production workers; annual bonuses tend to be largely limited to high-level executives; and merit-pay systems tend to exist mostly among middle managers.

A number of studies have found, after holding constant occupation and technology, that piece-rate workers earn more than straight hourly wage earners do. This higher pay presumably reflects higher productivity as well as a risk premium. The literature on executive pay is murkier, primarily because of difficult technical issues: how to measure performance (e.g., accounting versus stock market rates of return), how to hold constant general industry effects versus firm effects, and whether to examine short- or long-term bonus-pay systems. The bulk of the literature looks at short-term compensation–performance relationships (e.g., this year's pay and next year's performance) rather than such arrangements as long-term stock options.

The overall conclusion is that there is a modest relationship between executive-pay systems and firm performance. For example, Cornell's John Abowd finds that if a firm were to increase the bonus-to-pay ratio by one standard deviation, it would increase economic rates of return by between 5 and 16 percent of one standard deviation (Abowd, 1990). Other studies report even weaker results (Leonard, 1990). The best conclusion is that there is evidence that a properly designed executive-compensation system can improve firm performance, but the magnitude of the effect is most uncertain.

Under a typical gain-sharing plan, a base level of output and wages is determined, as is a method for valuing additional – or reduced – output. All members of the group receive pay increases, or decreases, depending on whether output increases or decreases relative to the base. Although there is considerable variation in how plans are organized, surveys suggest that the typical plan pays benefits on a monthly basis, focuses on reducing labor costs, and shares more than 50 percent of gains with employees. Profit sharing is similar to gains sharing in that it links pay to firm performance, although in this case the outcome variable is profit rather than a more direct measure of productivity gain.

Much of the evaluation evidence on gain-sharing plans comes from case studies. However, a few statistical studies are available and these, along with the case studies, paint a positive picture. For example, in a study of more than a hundred firms that introduced a gain-sharing program known as Improshare, Roger Kaufman found that the average cumulative productivity improvement was 15 percent three years after initial implementation, compared with an average 6 percent increase in comparable manufacturing firms without gain-sharing programs. A substantial portion of the gains resulted from the reduction in defects and downtime (Kaufman, 1992). Similarly, the US General Accounting Office in its survey found that those firms with gain-sharing plans in place for more than five years averaged an annual 29 percent reduction in labor costs (Lawler et al., 1990). This seemingly precise estimate should be viewed with some caution, however, given the limitations of the survey on which it is based (Ehrenberg and Milkovich, 1987). However, a more comprehensive study of a number of gain-sharing plans by Michael Schuster of Syracuse University also found positive effects on labor costs and productivity, although these gains tended to plateau after a period of time (Schuster, 1984).

[. . .]

Strategic-level Innovations

If the evidence on the effects of innovations at the workplace and in supporting human resource practices is thin, the evidence on the effects of strategic-level innovations is nearly nonexistent. This is partly because we have little experience with labor–management consultation or worker representation in strategic managerial activities in [the USA]. We know of no studies that systematically analyze the effects of integrating human resource considerations and employee concerns into strategic managerial decision making. On this issue, the rhetoric and the aspirations of human resource executives and worker representatives continue to be far ahead of organizational reality.

There have, however, been a few relatively recent studies that attempt to test whether the full range of human resource practices employed by firms affect their financial performance. For example, Mark Huselid at Rutgers University has conducted the most comprehensive such study to date. He examined the relationship of a bundle of 'progressive' human resource practices similar to those listed in Table 14.1 to four different measures of firm profitability and shareholder returns in a sample 700 firms in different industries. He found that, compared with all the rest, the firms with the most progressive practices (those in the top 25 percent) experienced more than twice as high a return on capital, higher total shareholder returns (share price growth plus dividends), higher gross profit margins, and higher market values. The effects of these human resource practices remained significant after controlling for industry effects and other relevant variables (Huselid, 1993).

Similarly, Barry Macy and his colleagues at Texas Tech University recently completed a massive review of virtually every individual quantitative study since 1960 of the effects of the workplace, human resource, and strategic level principles shown in Table 14.1. They found that the most significant positive effects of these practices on firm financial performance measures were reported in cases involving multiple or more systemic innovations containing more than one practice introduced in conjunction with changes in technology, human resources, and organizational strategies and structures (Macy et al., 1993). Once again, the systemic effects seem more powerful than those of individual practices.

Summary and Conclusions

This chapter has provided a thumbnail sketch of the principles underlying the mutual gains enterprise and the evidence to date on the economic effects of these principles in action. As example after example has shown, there is no single set of best practices for implementing these broad principles. Instead, there appears to be a variety of ways in which American managers and, where they are present, union leaders are implementing these principles. Nor, outside the case of greenfield facilities, is there strong evidence that the parties are implementing the full range of principles all at once. Instead, what we have observed is piecemeal, experimental phasing in of these practices, even though the empirical evidence to date from managers' testimonials, case studies, and quantitative assessments all suggest that the cumulative and combined effects of integrating these principles with equivalent innovations in manufacturing and service delivery systems produce the biggest payoffs.

References

Abowd, John (1990) 'Does performance-based managerial compensation affect corporate performance?', *Industrial and Labor Relations Review*, 43 (3, special issue): 52–73.

Dyer, L., Milkovich, G. and Foltman, F. (1985) 'Contemporary employment stabilization practices', in T.A. Kochan and T.A. Barocci (eds), *Human Resource Management and Industrial Relations*. Boston, MA: Little, Brown. pp. 207–9.

Ehrenberg, Ronald G. and Milkovich, George (1987) 'Compensation and firm performance', in Morris Kleiner, Richard Block, Myron Roomkin and Sidney Salsverg (eds), *Human Resources and the Performance of the Firm*. Madison, WI: Industrial Relations Research Association. pp. 87–122.

Huselid, Mark A. (1993) 'Human resource management practices and firm performance', unpublished paper, Institute of Management and Labor Relations, Rutgers University.

Kaufman, Roger T. (1992) 'The effects of Improshare on productivity', *Industrial and Labor Relations Review*, 45 (January): 311–22.

Lawler III, Edward E. (1986) *High Involvement Management: Participative Strategies for Improving Organizational Performance*. San Francisco: Jossey-Bass.

Lawler III, Edward E., Mitchell, Daniel J.B. and Lewin, David (1990) 'Alternative pay systems, firm performance, and productivity', in Alan Blinder (ed.), *Paying for Productivity*. Washington DC: Brookings Institute. pp. 15–94.

Lawler III, Edward E., Mohrman, Susan Albers and Ledford Jr., Gerald E. (1992) *Employee Involvement and Total Quality Management: Practices and Results in Fortune 1000 Companies*. San Francisco: Jossey-Bass.

Leonard, Jonathan (1990) 'Executive pay and firm performance', *Industrial and Labor Relations Review*, 43 (3, special issue): 13–29.

Macy, Barry et al. (1993) 'A meta analysis of organizational innovations', unpublished paper, Center for Quality of Work Life, Texas Tech. University.

Schuster, Michael H. (1984) *Union–Management Cooperation: Structure, Process, Impact*. Kalamazoo, MI: W.E. Upjohn Institute for Employment Research.

15   Human Resource Management, Trade Unions and Industrial Relations

David E. Guest

The rising interest in human resource management (HRM) throughout the 1980s coincided with a steady decline in the significance of industrial relations as a central feature of economic performance and policy. It also coincided with a decline in the membership and influence of trade unions – during the 1980s, trade union membership declined from 53 per cent to 33 per cent. Industrial conflict displayed a similar decline, so that in the early 1990s, strikes were at their lowest level for many decades.

It was tempting in the 1980s to seek an association between the apparent rise of HRM and the decline of trade unions and industrial relations. Part of the temptation lay in the knowledge that the early models of HRM were drawn mainly from successful American non-union firms. In the [late] 1990s the emerging evidence paints a much more complex picture. To begin to understand it, we need to set both HRM and industrial relations within the wider economic and political system.

The central thrust of economic, industrial and legislative policy in the UK for well over a decade has been to create a market-driven economy. From an industrial relations perspective, the most telling feature of this policy has been the successive pieces of legislation designed to limit the role and rights of trade unions. This legislative programme has moved the unions in particular, and industrial relations in general, from the centre to the periphery of corporate concern. For many firms, industrial relations are no longer a contingent variable, helping to shape their business policy in the way they might have done ten or fifteen years earlier.

Organizations now have more choice about industrial relations. Do they also have a choice about HRM? If we follow the new market philosophy, then HRM should be driven by market factors. The point to emphasize here is that innovation, and more particularly, quality-based strategies, require for their success a workforce that is committed to the organization. To take a well-known example, an airline competing through quality must,

Originally published in J. Storey (ed.) (1995) *HRM: A Critical Text*. London: International Thomson (abridged).

at the point of customer contact, have staff with the autonomy and motivation to provide the kind of high-quality service that will 'delight' the customer. This will require enthusiasm and initiative on the part of the staff, and trust to permit autonomy on the part of the organization. This 'psychological contract' is a core element of the concept of organizational commitment. But if commitment is a central concept in an HR strategy for managing the workforce, where does this leave industrial relations? Commitment is an essentially unitarist concept. Is it possible to be committed to both a company and a trade union, or is such dual commitment impossible? To understand the possible relationships between HRM and industrial relations and the role of trade unions in this market-driven economy, we must explore in more detail the concept of commitment and the feasibility of dual commitment.

The third strategy for competitive advantage, based on cost leadership, fits well with the political drive to present the UK as a cheap manufacturing base. The underlying assumptions are more pluralist in nature, to the extent that management will seek to minimize labour costs, while workers may well seek to maximize them. The context is therefore ripe for traditional industrial relations and apparently less suitable for the kind of HRM which has as its core the concept of organizational commitment. This certainly tends to be the conclusion of those writing from a strategic perspective. However, the legislation that has freed up the market has also extended the choice for employers. They may believe they can reduce costs more effectively without a trade union. The choice is therefore no longer HRM versus industrial relations; the new alternative is to have neither, and to get rid of all the expensive baggage with which each is associated. It follows that we need to incorporate this wider range of options in any review of trends in HRM and industrial relations.

Many of the strategic options available to management appear to challenge the role of trade unions and offer a potentially bleak view of their future. In some workplaces they may survive because they have always been there. Since they are built into the system, they can be accommodated as long as they are not a drain on resources. But whenever a major strategic review occurs – for example, in the context of a takeover, or a rationalization programme – their role is likely to be challenged. The logic of a market-driven HRM strategy is that where high organizational commitment is sought, unions are irrelevant. Where cost advantage is the goal, unions and industrial relations systems appear to carry higher costs. If possible, it will be preferable to do without them. This scenario is one of continuing gradual decline in membership and influence, unless the unions can respond with new strategies of their own. Paradoxically, HRM, far from threatening the union role, may present one basis for a new union strategy.

Following the themes raised in this introduction, the chapter is divided into two main parts. The first examines organizational commitment and dual commitment as a basis for considering the interaction between HRM

TABLE 15.1   HRM's *key dimensions*

Dimension	Industrial relations	Human resource management
Psychological contract	Compliance	Commitment
Behaviour referent	Norms, custom and practice	Values/mission
Relations	Low trust, pluralist, collective	High-trust, unitarist, individual
Organization and design	Formal roles, hierarchy, division of labour, managerial controls	Flexible roles, flat structure, teamwork/autonomy, self-control

and trade unionism. The second examines the evidence on the choices being made by employers in the UK about the type of HRM and industrial relations they wish to pursue.

Commitment and the Theory of Human Resource Management and Industrial Relations

Models of HRM (see, for example, Beer et al., 1985; Guest, 1987) place organizational commitment at their core. Indeed it is the central feature that distinguishes HRM from traditional personnel management/industrial relations systems. Furthermore, it has been suggested (Guest, 1989) that if the four key HRM policy goals are strategic integration, quality, flexibility and commitment, then only commitment to the organization need present a direct challenge to trade unionism. It provides the basis for the contrasting values and assumptions underpinning normative views of HRM and industrial relations which have been presented by Walton (1985), Guest (1987) and Storey (1992). The key contrasting dimensions are presented in Table 15.1.

Organizational commitment is central to [the HRM] approach for several reasons. First, by holding out the prospect that committed workers will be highly motivated and will go 'beyond contract', it promises higher performance. Secondly, committed workers can be expected to exercise responsible autonomy or self-monitoring and self-control, removing the need for supervisory and inspection staff and producing efficiency gains. Thirdly, committed workers are more likely to stay with the organization, thereby ensuring a return on the investment in careful selection, training and development. Finally, but central to the discussion of HRM and industrial relations, it is assumed that a worker who is committed to the organization is unlikely to become involved in 'industrial relations' or any type of collective activity which might reduce the quality and quantity of their contribution to the organization. This is aided by moving away from the traditional psychological contract of 'a fair day's work for a fair day's pay', thereby reducing the potential for the effort bargain to operate as a potential focus for conflict and grievance. The commitment contract implies that, instead, the staff will go that extra mile for the company.

Placing organizational commitment at the core of the definition of HRM acknowledges the deliberate attempt to win the hearts and minds of the workforce. The traditional definition of organizational commitment (Mowday et al., 1982), and the one most relevant to this analysis, defines it as consisting of three components: an identification with the goals and values of the organization, a desire to belong to the organization, and a willingness to display effort on behalf of the organization. Union commitment can be defined in precisely the same way (Gordon et al., 1980). The key issue then becomes the compatibility of the goals and values of the company and the union. If they are compatible, then it is possible to display high commitment to both company and union. At the same time, it raises fundamental questions about the role of the union and the nature of the values for which it stands. Alternatively, we need to consider how far workers can live with the inherent conflict and ambiguity of identification with two potentially opposing sets of values. Research by Reichers (1985, 1986), for example, has suggested that workers can express commitment to potentially conflicting targets such as work group, career and company. These issues have stimulated research on dual commitment to company and union.

The choices about commitment to company and union can be presented in a simple matrix:

		Commitment to company	
		High	Low
Commitment to union	High	1	2
	Low	3	4

A matrix of this sort is a useful starting point for analysis of commitment to company and union. It is important to bear in mind that it is an over-simplification in two important respects. The first is that there may be intermediate levels of commitment to both company and union, reflecting, perhaps, a kind of conditional approval of both. The second, building on the work of Reichers and others, is that there are other potential focuses of commitment. These include a career, a profession and the family. Commitment to any of these may also conflict with commitment to either company and/or union.

One important strand of research has examined the antecedents of commitment to company and union. If the factors that shape commitment to each are different, then it should be possible for them to coexist, since a change on a factor affecting company commitment need not influence union commitment. On the other hand, if they are caused by the same factor, either they operate from the same end of a continuum and become indistinguishable, which may be the case with some Japanese 'in-house' unions, or they operate from competing ends of the same continuum and therefore are incompatible. The first case might include the quality of working conditions, the second might be the right to hold union mass meetings in working time. The underlying theories are concerned with cognitive dissonance and role conflict. From the limited number of studies of the antecedents, the view seems to be emerging that union and company commitment, although psychologically similar constructs with similar classes of antecedent and outcome, are caused by different specific factors.

In one interesting study, Barling, Wade and Fullager (1990) had the opportunity to examine dual commitment in the aftermath of a strike. They found marked differences between those who viewed the industrial relations climate positively and negatively. In the former group, there was a correlation of 0.06 between commitment to a union and to the company but among those who perceived a poor industrial relations climate, the correlation was –0.52. This takes us one step further in suggesting that it is not just the existence of conflict but the way it is perceived and interpreted that influences the feasibility of dual commitment.

There has only been a limited amount of research on this topic in the UK. Guest and Dewe (1991), in a study of workers in three organizations in the electronics industry, found little evidence of dual commitment, where commitment was defined in terms of identification with company and union. Indeed, the predominant mode was commitment to neither company nor trade union. On the other hand, use of the same questions in other countries elicited evidence of higher levels of dual commitment in Sweden and West Germany, though, perhaps surprisingly, not in Japan (Guest and Dewe, 1991). The European evidence does provide further indirect support for the importance of the industrial relations climate.

If we accept the tenor of this research, and with it the implication that dual commitment is possible within a positive industrial relations climate, we then need to know something about the characteristics of this climate. As a minimum, if it is an industrial relations climate (Dastmalchian et al., 1991), this implies the legitimacy of a pluralist perspective, in which both company and union have distinctive roles. There is choice about how far these are grounded in legislation, as is the case in most of Europe, and how far they rest on the voluntaristic assumptions of those in key positions on both sides. Whatever the context, the role of the unions can vary considerably.

At least three models for the union role in the context of dual commitment can be identified. In the first, typified by some Japanese organizations, the role of the union at the local level is very much that of another arm of the company. One important manifestation of this is that the head of the union may move into a senior management position. A second approach, typified by Germany and Sweden, integrates industrial relations with the political system, and is therefore enshrined in legislation. One important element in this is the distinction between the issues dealt with at plant and company level and those handled at national level. In these countries, the more contentious issues, particularly those concerning pay and working hours, have mostly been handled at the national level. At the local level the works council has dealt with more operational issues, often issues of mutual concern.

The third model is the voluntaristic UK approach, now reshaped by the new legislative framework. The tradition of bargaining at company or even plant level has reinforced a pluralist perspective. At the same time, it is important to recognize that relations in most workplaces are relatively harmonious and that the propensity for industrial action has always been low. However, the absence of legislative or cultural forces encouraging dual commitment makes its presence more fragile and more susceptible to the choices and actions of the key stakeholders. The important point about this system is that it is inherently less stable and provides a less predictable basis for dual commitment.

[. . .]

The evidence of limited dual commitment presents challenges for the unions. It would be unwise for unions to rely on one of the traditional bases of commitment to the union, namely a presumed belief in trade unionism (Guest and Dewe, 1988). Unions must find a new basis for commitment. The apparent failure of many companies to generate enthusiastic commitment among their workforce suggests that opportunities for unions still exist. If management is tempted to pursue a 'hard' version of HRM, this might backfire, providing further scope for unions. These and other policy options for unions will be considered later in the chapter. First we analyse recent developments at the interface of HRM and industrial relations as a basis for understanding company policy and practice.

Developments in Industrial Relations and Human Resource Management

If we extrapolate from the discussion of dual commitment, which is essentially concerned with the response at the individual level, to the analysis of policy options facing organizations, we can present the broad alternatives in a similar way:

		HRM priority	
		High	*Low*
Industrial relations	*High*	1	2
priority	*Low*	3	4

Option 1 gives priority to both industrial relations and HRM, implies that dual commitment is feasible and assumes a positive industrial relations climate. It might be termed 'the new realism' and is reflected, for example, in recent publications from the IPA (1992). Option 2 represents the stereotype of the traditional UK approach. It assumes that trade unions are well established and that HRM has not figured significantly on the management agenda. This approach, a traditional collectivism, is probably most likely to be found in parts of the public sector. Option 3 represents the stereotype of individualized HRM, popularly associated with American electronics firms, where an individualistic philosophy assumes no need for trade unions or for any other type of collective activity. Option 4 reflects a view that cost advantage can best be achieved by avoiding both industrial relations and HRM. For those with a vested interest in industrial relations and HRM, and possibly for the workers affected by it, it represents a kind of 'black hole'. It is a neglected area of study which is just beginning to receive more attention. It is important because it helps to refocus a debate which can slip too easily into an analysis of the choice of either unions or HRM by suggesting the possibility of neither.

Within this framework we can analyse evidence on recent trends in industrial relations and HRM to determine developments in and between these options. Ideally, such evidence looks at industrial relations and HR trends together. This requires either sophisticated analysis of complex data sets or case studies. There are a number of both, although a lot of the evidence is more limited in scope. In this chapter we will emphasize developments in industrial relations, rather than in specific areas of HRM policy and practice.

In any analysis of trends in industrial relations related directly or indirectly to HRM, we might wish to look at evidence such as:

- union recognition and derecognition
- developments in the 'new' industrial relations, such as single table bargaining and no-strike deals
- the role of unions in any changes affecting industrial relations
- the importance of industrial relations as an issue
- the outcomes of industrial relations, including levels of conduct activity, any union mark-up and productivity.

We will analyse developments as they apply to each of the four options/ quadrants in the model.

1: The New Realism – a High Emphasis on HRM and Industrial Relations

Kochan, Katz and McKersie (1986), proclaiming the transformation of American industrial relations, cited a limited number of cases illustrative of a collaborative joint endeavour to shape a new relationship between management and union. It would be dangerous to over-emphasize the importance of any new emergent pattern of industrial relations in the USA. However, it is this type of pattern that we might expect in those organizations in the UK where attempts are made by managers to pursue an approach that integrates HRM and industrial relations.

Evidence about a joint approach can best be gleaned from case studies. There are a number of cases which appear to fit this pattern. One of the best known is Nissan (Wickens, 1987, 1993). He argues that the analysis developed initially by Walton (1985), which contrasts control/compliance and commitment philosophies, presents a false dichotomy. In the car industry, he suggests, you need both. He further argues that, by and large, leading Japanese organizations in Japan, and Nissan in the UK, have achieved this. He accepts the need for a representative system for workers and the need to promote workers' interests, and in particular to ensure job security. But he further emphasizes that this must be based on cooperation rather than confrontation. Wickens deserves attention as one of the small band of senior managers who have tackled these issues at both the intellectual and operational levels.

Many of the other examples of serious attempts at a joint approach – Rover being a case in point – come from the car industry, where the unions are very well entrenched but where market forces demand improvements in productivity and quality. Indeed the circumstances are similar to those in the cases cited by Kochan et al. (1986).

In new plants, one point at which high priority is given to both HRM and industrial relations is at the time of the so-called 'beauty contest', where unions have competed for recognition rights. From the union side, this constitutes a form of concession bargaining based on who promises an agreement closest to the management ideal. In some cases, such as the well-publicized ones of Toshiba (Trevor, 1988) and Nissan (Wickens, 1987) and the similar but less well-known case of the Japanese/American joint venture IBC Vehicles, the positive initial relationship has continued. However, negotiations and all important representative meetings take place between management and a works council. The council represents all the workforce and union shop stewards have to stand for election alongside non-union workers. There is, therefore, a pluralist system, based on a management agenda and the principle of mutuality, but one where the role of the union is somewhat ambiguous.

Another source of evidence about new collaborative arrangements comes from analysis of single-union and single-table bargaining. The third workplace industrial relations survey (WIRS 3) (Millward et al., 1992) found no evidence of major growth in these areas. Nevertheless such arrangements are almost always the result of employer initiatives, and both employers and unions seem satisfied with them. They have facilitated greater flexibility, more multi-skilling, the removal of union demarcations and improvements in quality. From a union perspective they have produced extensions in consultation and moves towards single status.

The cases described by Storey (1992) provide some of the best information on recent trends, although again we must note that many of the cases are drawn from large companies which are household names, or at least industrial relations names. Storey concludes that there is little evidence of any frontal attack on unions, but equally little attempt to involve the unions in the planning and implementation of change. In most cases where unions have been well established in the past, the two systems of industrial relations and HRM operate side by side but with a tendency for management to give increasing weight to systems of employee involvement, and in particular communication, which tend to by-pass the union.

Storey's (1992) finding that the two systems can coexist and remain relatively compartmentalized is not in doubt; but it does raise interesting questions about the impact of the systems and more particularly the HRM system. If industrial relations remain healthy in the context of HRM, there are at least five possible explanations. First, the HRM may be so ineffective that it is having a minimal impact on values and commitment. Secondly, the 'hard' version is being used, and this leaves a level of anxiety such that workers continue to support the traditional industrial relations system and the trade union as a safeguard and safety net. Thirdly, management, while supporting HRM, recognize the value of retaining collective arrangements because of their convenience, particularly in those establishments where large numbers are employed. Fourthly, it is possible that the system of mutuality is viable and a mutually beneficial collaboration between management and unions can operate, resulting in the maintenance of both systems. Fifthly, the industrial relations system may continue as a largely symbolic 'empty shell', insufficiently important for management to confront and eliminate, but retaining the outward appearance of health to the casual observer.

There are very few well-documented cases of a robust trade unionism in the context of enthusiastic HRM policies. As Storey notes of Rover, the unions were invited to the party, but some declined the invitation. At Ford, the party was of a rather different sort – an attempt to form a new partnership, but with less HRM and more concern for quality of working life, including a range of health and education programmes. This fits the American model described by Kochan et al. (1986) and which included Ford in America as one of its cases. The policy choice for the unions is whether they should decline the invitation, sulk at home and be ignored, or have their own party.

The implication of Storey's analysis and of other available data is that there has been little attempt by management and unions to forge a new partnership which gives high priority to both HRM and industrial relations through some process of integration. Instead, managers have taken a lot of piecemeal HRM initiatives, and in so doing have ignored or by-passed the industrial relations system. It continues to exist, accepted by management as having a legitimate, sometimes useful, but limited role. On the surface, it may appear that HRM and industrial relations both receive a high priority. Often, in the case of both, it will be an illusion.

2: Traditional Collectivism — Priority to Industrial Relations without HRM

The second main policy choice is to retain the traditional pluralist industrial relations arrangements within an essentially unchanged industrial relations system. The evidence from WIRS 3 (Millward et al., 1992) suggests that in many places where trade unions have been well established, the industrial relations system appears to continue to operate much as before. However, the empty-shell argument may apply with or without more vigorous HRM policies. Management may continue to use the industrial relations system, but accord it much less priority. Indeed it has been suggested (Smith and Morton, 1993) that from a management perspective it is safer to marginalize the unions than formally to derecognize them and risk provoking a confrontation; better to let them wither on the vine than receive a reviving fertilizer.

An alternative management view may be that it is easier to continue to operate with a union, since it provides a useful, well-established channel for communication and for the handling of grievance, discipline and safety issues. In its absence, management would need to develop its own alternative, which could be both costly and difficult to operate effectively. The trade union and the shop stewards remain a useful lubricant.

The anecdotal case evidence suggests that it is mainly in the public sector and some industries that have been removed from it, that traditional industrial relations continue to operate largely in the absence of HRM. In the privatized docks, the Transport and General Workers' Union has negotiated new working arrangements including, in some cases, worker cooperatives (Turnbull and Weston, 1993). However in some ports, derecognition has occurred and at Felixstowe the union members have conceded wage-cuts as part of a package to avoid derecognition. Large parts of the public sector, including the health service, the police service, local government and education, retain well-established industrial relations systems and, with a few exceptions, no real attempt to introduce HRM. The unions may play a less central role, but they are still significant players, as the response to a number of government initiatives in education and the police service has shown.

WIRS 3 contains mixed news about the traditional institutional industrial relations. Brown (1993) estimates that on the basis of the WIRS 3 data, only 47 per cent of the working population were covered by collective agreements in 1990, compared with 64 per cent in 1984 and 72 per cent in 1973. WIRS 3 also shows some decline in the number of shop stewards, more especially in those plants with modest or low union density, increasing the risk that they are drifting towards derecognition. Furthermore, it reveals a decline in the use of the union channel of communication and consultation and a marked decline in both the pre- and post-entry closed shop. Metcalf (1993) has reviewed the evidence on the union mark-up. Although it is hard to unravel, it does appear that the union mark-up – the extent to which a union presence results in higher wages, and therefore a major rationale for unions' existence – has declined.

The good news from WIRS 3 for the trade unions is that in most workplaces where trade unions have in the past been well established, trade union membership and organization has stood up well. Furthermore, any union presence was associated with positive benefits for the workforce. There was less wage inequality and less use of reward systems likely to engender greater inequality. There were more channels of communication, and more types of information were communicated. Workers in non-union plants were two and a half times as likely to be dismissed as those in unionized plants. Such evidence seriously challenges the empty-shell argument. Unions have been able to protect and promote workers' interests. Overall, WIRS 3 reveals that at 32 per cent of establishments, managers reported constraints on their ability to organize work as they wished, but this rose to 46 per cent in unionized workplaces.

3: Individualized HRM – High Priority to HRM with No Industrial Relations

One of the issues to address in considering the growth of HRM is whether companies are taking HRM seriously and, to the extent that they are, whether this includes operating without unions and an industrial relations system. We could debate what is meant by 'taking HRM seriously', but for many observers one criterion would be an attempt at strategic integration. However, a weaker test is to look at the way in which specific policy initiatives are implemented. A review of recent UK trends in selection, training and reward systems (Guest, 1993) and reports on developments in employee involvement (Marchington et al., 1992) suggest that the approach is essentially piecemeal and opportunistic.

It is interesting to note that in the UK, our models of companies successfully practising HRM are all becoming somewhat dated. Few new names have emerged to add to those of the mid-1980s. Analysis of new establishments in the WIRS 3 sample indicates that it is predominantly the North American-owned firms that appear to promote a high HRM non-union approach. In other new establishments there is a low likelihood of union recognition, but also no particular emphasis on HRM (Guest and Hoque, 1993).

Several companies in the oil industry – a sector which has always had a high reputation for innovation in industrial relations and personnel management – have recently taken steps to derecognize trade unions. The reasoning behind this appears to be that unions are a constraint on the kind of flexibility that market conditions demand, namely functional flexibility to increase productivity, and numerical flexibility, reflected in the use of more contract labour and fixed-term contracts. Despite the market focus on cost advantage, this strategy contains elements of an integrated HRM approach which the companies apparently believe is easier to achieve with a significantly reduced union presence.

4: The Black Hole – No HRM and No Industrial Relations

If HRM loses its attractions as a policy priority, or at best becomes no more than a set of piecemeal techniques, and there is no compelling reason to operate within a traditional industrial relations system, the alternative is to emphasize neither. In market terms this may imply a strategy based on cost advantage. Labour is viewed as a variable cost, perhaps resulting in increasing emphasis on short-term contracts.

There are several types of evidence which suggest that this option is becoming more prevalent. The first is the well-documented decline in trade union membership and trade union density. This decline continues to be partly structural, but is reinforced by two new factors. The first is a growth in partial or complete derecognition. The most convincing evidence for this comes from the recent company-level survey of industrial relations (Marginson et al., 1993), which shows that 19 per cent of the companies in the sample had partially or wholly derecognized unions at least at one site; this compares with 7 per cent where recognition had been extended.

The second type of evidence is the changing pattern of union recognition at new establishments. Disney et al. (1993), in their analysis of the work-place industrial relations surveys, have shown that the pattern of recognition at new plants has changed. They argue that the industrial relations climate at the time of the start-up is a crucial factor and that it was different in the 1980s compared with the previous decade. As a result, it was 28 per cent less likely, other things being equal, that a union would be recognized at a new establishment set up in the 1980s compared with one started in the 1970s. More specifically, WIRS 3 reveals that in 1990, only 24 per cent of establishments less than ten years old recognized a union. This compares with 45 per cent of establishments less than ten years old in 1980. It appears (Disney et al., 1993) that the trend away from recognition began prior to 1980, and apart from a minor hiccup in the late 1980s, has continued to gather strength.

All the evidence suggests that when confronted with a decision about whether or not to recognize a trade union, companies are increasingly deciding not to do so. It is possible to conclude that this is now the dominant pattern in new establishments; indeed, it raises the question of why unions are recognized at all. The available evidence indicates that a union presence elsewhere in the company is a key positive influence on trade union recognition at new establishments. One interpretation of this is that management accepts, on the basis of experience, that unions have some value.

If a union is not recognized, there is little evidence that management replaces it with an HRM strategy to obtain full utilization of the workforce, by gaining its commitment to company goals and values. Millward (1993) has begun to paint a picture of policy and practice in non-union firms, based on the WIRS 3 survey data. There are fewer procedures and fewer health and safety representatives. There are also fewer channels of information and consultation, less information from management and fewer personnel specialists. Although the workplace climate is described as better than in unionized establishments, there are more dismissals, more compulsory redundancies, more notices to quit and more low pay, alongside a greater dispersion of pay. Pay also appears to be both more often performance-related and more market-determined. For the workforce, this emerging non-union environment is bleak and insecure.

Despite the WIRS 3 evidence which reports a continuing growth in the influence of personnel departments, from which a case might be made for the effective promotion of either industrial relations or HRM, it seems more likely, as Marginson et al. (1993) emphasize, that a financial controller model is dominating board thinking about how to manage the workforce. This does not fit comfortably with an HRM strategy in which labour is a relatively fixed cost, or with an industrial relations perspective which sees labour as a countervailing force, with the power to negotiate additional wage costs. Returning to the four options presented at the start of this section, the trend is away from the traditional collectivism of a representative industrial relations system, but the drift is towards the black hole of no industrial relations and no HRM, rather than towards individualized HRM or the new realism.

References

Barling, J., Wade, B. and Fullager, C. (1990) 'Predicting employee commitment to company and union: divergent models', *Journal of Occupational Psychology*, 63 (1): 49–61.

Beer, M., Spector, B., Lawrence, P., Quinn Mills, D. and Walton, R. (1985) *Human Resource Management: A General Manager's Perspective*. Glencoe, IL: The Free Press.

Brown, W. (1993) 'The contraction of collective bargaining in Britain', *British Journal of Industrial Relations*, 31 (2): 189–200.

Dastmalchian, A., Blyton, P. and Adamson, R. (1991) *The Climate of Workplace Relations*. London: Routledge.

Disney, R., Gosling, A. and Machin, S. (1993) 'What has happened to trade union recognition in Britain'. CEP Discussion Paper No. 130. London: LSE.

Gordon, M., Philpot, J., Burt, R., Thompson, C. and Spiller, W. (1980) 'Commitment to the union: development of a measure and an examination of its correlates', *Journal of Applied Psychology*, 65: 479–99.

Guest, D. (1987) 'Human resource management and industrial relations', *Journal of Management Studies*, 24 (5): 503–21.

Guest, D. (1989) 'Human resource management: its implications for industrial relations and trade unions', in J. Storey (ed.), *New Perspectives on Human Resource Management*. London: Routledge.

Guest, D. (1993) 'Current perspectives on human resource management in the

United Kingdom', in C. Brewster (ed.), *Current Trends in Human Resource Management in Europe*. London: Kogan Page.

Guest, D. and Dewe, P. (1988) 'Why do workers belong to trade unions? A social-psychological study in the UK electronics industry', *British Journal of Industrial Relations*, 29 (1): 75–96.

Guest, D. and Dewe, P. (1991) 'Company or trade union; which wins workers' allegiance? A study of commitment in the United Kingdom electronics industry', *British Journal of Industrial Relations*, 29 (1): 75–96.

Guest, D. and Hoque, K. (1993) 'Are greenfield sites better at human resource management?'. CEP Working Paper No. 435. London: LSE.

Involvement and Participation Association (1992) *Towards Industrial Partnership: A New Approach to Management–Union Relations*. London: IPA.

Kochan, T., Katz, H. and McKersie, R. (1986) *The Transformation of American Industrial Relations*. New York: Basic Books.

Marchington, M., Goodman, J., Wilkinson, A. and Ackers, P. (1992) *New Developments in Employee Involvement*. Research Series No. 2. London: Employment Department.

Marginson, P., Armstrong, P., Edwards, P. and Purcell, J. (1993) 'Decentralization, collectivism and individualism: evidence on industrial relations in transition from the 1992 company level industrial relations survey'. Paper presented to the BUIRA Conference, York, July.

Metcalf, D. (1993) 'Industrial relations and economic performance', *British Journal of Industrial Relations*, 31 (2): 255–83.

Millward, N. (1993) 'Industrial relations in transition: the findings of the third workplace industrial relations survey'. Paper presented to BUIRA, York, July.

Millward, N., Stevens, M., Smart, D. and Hawes, W. (1992) *Workplace Industrial Relations in Transition*. Aldershot: Dartmouth.

Mowday, R., Porter, L. and Steers, R. (1982) *Employee–Organization Linkages: The Psychology of Commitment, Absenteeism and Turnover*. London: Academic Press.

Reichers, A. (1985) 'A review and reconceptualization of organizational commitment', *Academy of Management Review*, 10: 465–76.

Reichers, A. (1986) 'Conflict and organizational commitments', *Journal of Applied Psychology*, 71: 508–14.

Smith, P. and Morton, G. (1993) 'Union exclusion and decollectivization of industrial relations in contemporary Britain', *British Journal of Industrial Relations*, 31 (1): 97–114.

Storey, J. (1992) *Developments in the Management of Human Resources*. Oxford: Blackwell.

Trevor, M. (1988) *Toshiba's New British Company*. London: PSI.

Turnbull, P. and Weston, S. (1993) 'Cooperation or control? Capital restructuring and labour relations on the docks', *British Journal of Industrial Relations*, 31 (1): 115–34.

Walton, R. (1985) 'From control to commitment in the workplace', *Harvard Business Review*, 63 (March–April): 76–84.

Wickens, P. (1987) *The Road to Nissan*. London: Macmillan.

Wickens, P. (1993) 'Lean production and beyond: the system, the critics and the future', *Human Resource Management Journal*, 3 (4): 75–90.

16   It's a Small World: Managing Human Resources in Small Businesses

Nicolas Bacon, Peter Ackers, John Storey and David Coates

[This chapter analyses the outcome of] a major survey of 560 organizations in Leicestershire. The results indicated that small and medium-sized employers, as well as larger employers, claimed to be adopting new managerial approaches. To a remarkable extent, small organizations had experimented with new approaches such as culture change, devolved management, teamworking, flexibility and quality task forces. The fact that those organizations adopting elements of the 'new management' claimed they had *sustained* the initiatives enhances greatly the importance of these findings. Managers were not merely picking them up as 'flavours of the month'. Moreover, and perhaps even more significantly, these organizations were typically reporting some positive *outcomes* after implementing the initiatives. Considering these findings we explored in greater qualitative depth the new management agenda through a series of case study visits to small companies. In general, the findings reinforced the conclusions of the original survey and highlighted some important dynamics in the employment relations of small businesses. The analysis of these results will portray something of the developments in personnel management in small businesses that take us beyond the generalized 'bleak house' scenario.

The chapter has four main sections. In the first, we discuss the debate about employment management practices in small businesses. The second describes the take-up of the 'new management' agenda by small enterprises as revealed by the survey. In the third, we report qualitative data from thirteen small companies. The fourth explores the dynamics of change and considers the implications of these findings for our understanding of employee relations.

Originally published in *International Journal of Human Resource Management*, 7 (1), 1996: 82–100 (abridged).

Industrial Relations in Small Businesses

Small businesses have traditionally been marginalized in the study of UK employee relations. This position has gradually and partially begun to be redressed as the small business sector has become increasingly important economically and politically. Of the 2.7 million businesses in the UK, 96 per cent employ fewer than twenty people, representing one-third of the private sector work-force. During the 1980s the small firms sector grew at a faster rate in the UK than in the rest of Europe, Japan and the USA. In 1993 there were nearly 900,000 more small firms than in 1979 (DTI, 1994). The growth and importance of small businesses currently stands in stark contrast to the predominant view of the 1950–1960s when the growth in the size of organizations and the concentration of ownership made them appear anachronistic (Rainne and Scott, 1986).

For the nineteenth-century theorists of industrialization they were the 'sweat-shops' and sites of the worst excesses of exploitation and degradation of employees (Rainne and Scott, 1986). This view pertained until a renewal of interest in the late 1960s with optimistic views of employee relations in small businesses emerging (Stanworth and Gray, 1991). The Bolton Report (1971) and Ingham (1970) argued that employees were self-selecting a work environment with fewer economic rewards but more interesting work and satisfying social relations with colleagues and superiors. Small organizations, they argued, offered numerous advantages including: group working; direct communications; working rules to suit the individual; a more direct relationship between individual effort and the aims of the organization; more varied work roles; low labour turnover and infrequent industrial disputes. It was not until the late 1970s that Curran and Stanworth (1979a, 1979b, 1981a, 1981b) challenged this view. They argued that employees did not self-select their workplaces, that the pattern of social relations found in small businesses varied, and that small organizations had higher levels of labour instability and labour turnover. Alternative analyses have developed yet greater theoretical sophistication, with Scott et al. (1989) highlighting the 'informal routinization' of personal control in small organizations and the unitary view of authority held by managers. Rainne (1989) has also highlighted the importance of the position of each small business in its industrial sector and the economy as a whole as important influences on the way people are managed. Goss (1991) also notes there is not one but several different types of management control strategies in small businesses.

The large-scale industrial relations survey evidence of the 1980s and 1990s does little to dispel the sceptical view of human resource management practices in small businesses. However, there is some evidence from the USA to suggest that the picture may be changing. One study of 247 businesses in the Midwest concluded that the personnel practices of smaller firms are much more sophisticated than the literature would lead us to believe (Hornsby and Kuratko, 1990). They discovered that small businesses were in fact often concerned about the same human resource issues. As developments in HRM in the UK have closely shadowed those in the USA in other respects, could it also be that UK small business owners and managers would also be displaying greater sophistication in their techniques for managing people? A survey of employers in Leicestershire indicated that this may be the case.

The Leicestershire 'New Management' Survey

A team from the Human Resource and Change Management Research Unit at Loughborough University Business School constructed a questionnaire to survey 560 Leicestershire employers in March 1993. To allow a greater 'depth' in the data gathering and secure a high response rate we employed a survey company to interview respondents over the telephone. Conducted with 'the most senior manager on site responsible for human resource management', each interview lasted on average 30 minutes. The sample was constructed to allow representative coverage of employing organizations in all Standard Industrial Classifications and in terms of size of organization. The organizational size bands used were 15–24 employees, 25–199 employees and 200 plus employees. In reporting the results we will concentrate here on those organizations employing under 200 employees.

Previous large-scale studies have revealed that small organizations that are sub-divisions of larger groups are likely to be subject to policies made elsewhere and would therefore be more likely to have formalized personnel policies. It was therefore important to rule out subsidiaries, creating a group of independent operators who could determine their policies. It was this sector where we would least expect the take-up of aspects of the new management agenda. From a total sample of 560, there were 95 small employers (15–24 employees) and 134 small or medium-sized employers (25–199 employees). There were large numbers of companies for both size groups concentrated in the distribution sector, with significant numbers in the manufacturing sector, business services, other services and transport (see Table 16.1).

The survey allows exploration of some central hypothesized trends and developments. We asked many different questions to construct a profile of employment practices in small organizations. At the very heart of the questionnaire, however, was a table that encapsulates eleven critical initiatives. For each of these we sought, in essence, three types of information: (i) whether an initiative of this type had been launched and implemented within the past five years; (ii) whether it had been sustained, abandoned or operated only marginally; and (iii) whether the initiative had contributed to organizational objectives.

Tables 16.2 and 16.3 present a broad introductory summary of the findings on this core set of questions concerning the 'new management'. The main finding was the remarkable degree of take-up of the new

TABLE 16.1 *Organizations' standard industrial classification by size of organization (number of employees at site)*

	Number of employees	
	15–24 (%)	25–199 (%)
Energy	0.0	0.0
Processing	0.0	0.7
Manufacturing – metal	12.6	16.4
Manufacturing – other	28.4	24.6
Construction	5.3	9.7
Distribution	30.5	21.6
Transport	6.3	6.0
Business services	7.4	6.7
Other services	8.4	14.2
Agriculture	1.1	0.0
Sample bases	95	134

management practices by organizations employing below 200 people. Considering prolonged debate about the extent to which HRM is 'rhetoric' or 'reality', this is, on the face of it, a significant finding.

Given that the data depend upon self-reporting, there must obviously be some caution exercised in their interpretation. However, the questionnaire was carefully designed to allow some further checking of the initial basic claims. For example, the interviewer probed each initiative claimed in a number of ways. One significant 'test' was the question about the 'contribution to organizational effectiveness' which each initiative was judged to have made. In the main, respondents judged the initiatives such as teamworking and job flexibility to have made a high-level contribution. Moreover, the extent to which managers reported they had *sustained* the initiatives was also high.

It is evident first from these tables that the reported take-up of the eleven key initiatives is, on the whole, rather high. In the case of two of these initiatives – teamworking and increased flexibility between jobs – the adoption rates reported by organizations employing between fifteen and twenty-four people and those employing between twenty-five and 199 people were around three-quarters. Remembering that the question specifically asked about initiatives launched within the recent five-year period, this figure suggests a very significant movement in managerial practice. It indicates that this set of ideas in particular has now become the virtual orthodoxy. Also running at a relatively high rate of adoption were initiatives in team briefing; devolved management, that is, the pushing down of responsibility to lower managerial levels; performance appraisal extending across into non-managerial grades; and the harmonization of terms and conditions. Of the total sample of organizations with fewer than 200 employees, over 30 per cent had adopted each of these groups of initiatives.

TABLE 16.2   *The implementation of the new management agenda by organizations employing 15–24 employees*

	Initiative employed (%)	Initiative sustained (%)	'Considerable contribution' to objectives (%)
A culture change programme	23.2	54.5	40.9
Devolved management	56.8	81.5	61.1
Teamworking	74.7	83.1	69.0
Performance appraisals	44.2	71.4	61.9
A mission statement	14.7	100.0	92.9
Team briefing	61.1	82.8	67.2
Quality circles	20.0	78.9	57.9
Harmonized terms and conditions	33.7	96.9	65.6
Psychometric tests	3.2	0.0	0.0
De-layering	8.4	50.0	37.5
Increased flexibility between jobs	73.7	82.9	64.3

TABLE 16.3   *The implementation of the new management agenda by organizations employing 25–199 employees*

	Initiative employed (%)	Initiative sustained (%)	'Considerable contribution' to objectives (%)
A culture change programme	18.7	80.0	72.0
Devolved management	54.5	75.3	61.6
Teamworking	76.9	89.3	70.9
Performance appraisals	46.3	75.8	59.7
A mission statement	26.9	77.8	58.3
Team briefing	63.4	84.7	69.4
Quality circles	31.3	76.2	66.7
Harmonized terms and conditions	40.3	92.6	63.0
Psychometric tests	5.2	14.3	0.0
De-layering	14.2	68.4	68.4
Increased flexibility between jobs	74.6	89.0	79.0

Turning our attention to the least adopted initiatives, two in particular stand out as having seen a take-up of less than 20 per cent of the sampled cases: psychometric tests and de-layering.

What is of further note about the summary tables is the reported high level of sustainment of those initiatives that managers launched. On average, almost 80 per cent of respondents claimed that they maintained the initiatives adopted within the past five years and had neither abandoned them nor even let them 'operate only at a marginal level'. Among the top-scoring items here were teamworking, team briefing, a mission statement, harmonized terms and conditions and increased flexibility between jobs. The rate at which companies were sustaining these initiatives once adopted was approaching 90 per cent. Looking to the results from the final question reported in the summary tables, a pattern is clear. Those initiatives that had made a considerable contribution to the objectives of managers were the ones they were more likely to sustain.

The picture of innovation in small organizations that this survey presents is potentially highly significant. It suggests that the new management agenda has penetrated deep into the UK economy and that innovative and progressive employee relations practices are no longer restricted to large mainstream companies. The survey findings raise, of course, many further questions. Is this an accurate picture of small organizations or was the survey method itself at fault? How has this change come about if the findings are accurate? Follow-up research was necessary because there have been important differences between survey and case study data of HRM in large organizations. To answer these questions we conducted a series of qualitative case studies in small businesses intended not only to 'test' these results but also to explore their 'meaning'.

The 'New Management' in Practice: Case Study Evidence

A group of thirty small companies were selected from the survey sample with the intention of visiting around one-third of them. Those companies selected were spread across industrial sectors and were different sizes. The majority had claimed a high take-up of new initiatives. This would enable us to investigate whether there had been a degree of over-claiming. An organization was defined as having a high take-up of initiatives where it claimed to have introduced a minimum of five initiatives out of the eleven items of the new management agenda. In addition, the sample also included several organizations that claimed a low and moderate take-up of initiatives to explore the personnel agenda in those companies. A total of thirteen organizations agreed to participate further in the study and we visited them between June and August 1994. The majority of interviews took place with company directors who conformed to the owner/manager class of entrepreneurs. It is not possible to judge from our data to what extent there was a 'self-selection' of companies more interested in the new agenda than others, or who felt they had answered the original survey accurately.

Table 16.4 presents a summary of the case study research. Although it reveals an important amount of 'over-claiming' by these companies in the original self-reported survey, the take-up of new initiatives remains surprisingly high. Across the thirteen companies the survey method recorded a total of seventy-six new management initiatives. In reality, the case study approach reduced this to fifty-three after stringently checking these claims, a difference of twenty-three initiatives. This indicates that, despite some over-claiming, the take-up of new initiatives by small businesses remains significant. Not all small businesses in our sample had over-claimed to the

TABLE 16.4 *Short summary of results*

Dimension	Engineering Company	Nursing Home	Mail Order Company	Hotel	Motel	Printers	Transport and Haulage Contractors	Carton and Board Distributors	Decorating Merchants	Fruit and Veg Wholesalers	Carpet Retailers	Insurance Company	Clothes Manuf.
Survey new initiatives	9	8	8	7	7	7	6	6	6	5	5	4	1
Number new initiatives confirmed	7	9	5	0	8	6	3	4	6	2	0	2	1
A culture change programme	✓	✓	✓	✗	✓	?	✓	?	✓	✗	✗	✗	✗
Devolved management	✓	✓	✓	✗	✓	✓	✓	✓	✓	✓	✗	✓	✗
Teamworking	✗	✓	✓	✗	✓	✓	✗	✓	✓	✗	✗	✓	✗
Performance appraisals	✗	✓	✗	✗	✓	✓	✗	✓	✗	✓	✗	✗	✗
Mission statement	✗	✓	✗	✗	?	✓	✗	✗	✗	✗	✗	✗	✗
Team briefing	✓	✓	✓	✗	✓	✓	?	✓	✓	✗	✗	✗	✗
Quality circles	✓	✗	✗	✗	?	✗	✗	✗	✓	✗	✗	✗	✗
Harmonized terms and conditions	✓	✓	✗	✗	✗	✗	✗	✗	?	✗	✗	✗	✗
Psychometric tests	✗	✓	✗	✗	✓	✗	✗	✗	✗	✗	✗	✗	✗
De-layering	✓	✗	✗	✗	✓	✗	✗	✗	✗	✗	✗	✗	✗
Increased flexibility between jobs	✓	✓	✓	✗	✓	✓	✓	✗	✓	✓	✗	✗	✓

same degree. Two organizations, the Hotel and the Carpet Retailer, account for over one half of the over-claiming. At the Hotel we discovered people management ranked low on the business agenda. The culture change programme was, in reality, little more than 'trying to impress on the staff the importance of giving customers what they want'. Devolved management was 'if one of the girls starts to do a bit more, then that's fine, I'll leave her to it'. Teamworking was the notion that 'we are all a team and have to muck in together'. A performance appraisal was 'I'll keep my eye on those that are not doing what they should, if someone does that bit extra and really helps us out then I'll slip them a bit more money in their pay packet'. In such cases, where the respondent had interpreted the survey questions in a different manner from what we intended, then this cannot be taken as evidence of 'new initiatives'. Only where businesses were adopting consciously new initiatives and could provide documentary evidence and a clear understanding of the concepts did we interpret this as evidence of 'new initiatives'.

Although over-claiming had taken place, in most of our cases managers had adopted aspects of the 'new management agenda'. Two other organizations, the Nursing Home and the Motel, had even under-claimed the number of initiatives they had in the original survey.

The most popular initiatives in practice among our cases were devolved management (10 out of 13 cases), increased flexibility between jobs (9 out of 13 cases), team briefing and teamworking (both in 7 out of 13 cases) and culture change programmes (in 6 out of 13 cases). Across the sample, of eleven that had claimed to have five initiatives or more, six had done so in practice. The industrial sector to which they belonged did not explain the difference between the survey and the case study findings. The difference in results could in part, however, be explained by over-claiming on particular initiatives. Three initiatives in particular were more scarce in small businesses in practice than the survey had led us to believe. From our sample of thirteen cases, twelve had claimed in the survey to have teamworking but we discovered only seven examples in practice. Eight had claimed to conduct performance appraisals for employees of a non-managerial level but only four instances existed. Ten of our cases in the survey claimed to have harmonized terms and conditions but these existed in only two. These three initiatives alone accounted for over one half of the initiatives claimed which we could not find in practice. These results indicate that the meaning of these terms in the small business setting as our respondents understood them was quite different from how managers in larger organizations used the concepts.

To explore the change management agenda further we can consider a thumb-nail sketch of developments in these organizations. To what extent did these small organizations share common problems and dynamics, and what were the real extent and impact of changes taking place? For comparative purposes, the thematic analysis in Table 16.5 provides a feel for the thrust of the new management agenda in small businesses. This

TABLE 16.5   A schematic outline of change in the case organizations

Company	General theme	Elements of change
Printers	Formalized with growth. Hi-tech. Internal training.	Introducing professional managers. Task integration. Training and development.
Carton & Board Distributors	Culture change via professional manager as change agent. Formalization.	Devolving management. Teamworking and briefing. Performance appraisals.
Engineering Company	Professional management. Communication.	Culture change via communication and participation. Flexible working.
Decorating Merchants	Culture change and management development.	Devolving management and responsibilities.
Insurance Company	Formalization to professional IPD standards.	Professional recruitment and image raising.
Clothing Manufacturer	Management control.	None.
Fruit & Veg Wholesaler	Continued informality.	Devolving tasks to encourage the few
Hotel	Controlling 'temporary' staff.	None.
Transport & Haulage Contractors	Formalization and management development.	New MD. Culture change and devolved management by training and development.
Nursing Home	Professional development.	Culture management. Mission and Value Statements. Induction and recruitment.
Mail Order Company	Building informality.	Creating the informal culture with management control.
Motel	Professionalization.	Culture change, devolved management, de-layering. Flexibility.
Carpet Retailers	Informality. Market orientation.	Downsizing.

table emphasizes that the new agenda regarding people management has made a significant impact upon small businesses. Employee relations in the small business sector are undergoing considerable flux and change. One of the most interesting underlying themes within this welter of activity is the formalization of people management procedures. This stands in stark contrast to developments reported in large organizations that have been drifting away from proceduralization (Storey, 1992).

At first sight this development appears to conflict with the traditional picture of informality in small businesses where direct communications and the personal style of the owner or manager predominate. However, a superficial view is misleading. Managers were seeking to introduce more formal procedures alongside the informal culture and 'organic' nature of management in the small organization. There was little support among our cases for the notion that larger companies had a competitive edge through a more professional approach to human resource management. The wide range of new initiatives being adopted should not be seen as the search for a formalized strategic human resource management approach in the small business sector. Whereas in larger organizations managers design HRM-type change programmes to introduce informality and flexibility, smaller organizations generally already have these features. The challenge of introducing change in the small organization was managing the introduction of the formalization necessary to retain management control while not destroying the informality and culture of the small business. To explore further the people management agenda in small organizations it is helpful to adopt a thematic analysis of the data.

Meanings and Expectations

The standard of management was higher in the companies we visited than previous studies had led us to expect. This may be a sign that the type of person managing a small business is changing. Several of the managers we interviewed had left large organizations as they de-layered their strata of professional managers in the 1980s. These professional managers were taking with them the commitment to reaching professional business and service standards through people management. To give just one example of this, the manageress and manager (wife and husband) of the Motel had left jobs at the national Berni Beefeater chain. They identified their main task as changing the culture of their new workplace by 'instilling professionalism while trying to retain the unique social elements of running a hotel'. This involved concerted and multi-faceted attempts to 'make people more aware of what their job entailed and seek a greater contribution for all employees'. There had been a significant initial turnover of staff. This couple remained genuinely shocked by the lack of professionalism displayed by the previous owner, describing his style as the '"mine host" of pub management propping up the end of the bar running it like a social club'.

This description gives us an insight into the nature of new initiatives in small organizations. In describing this as a culture change programme we are not suggesting that small organizations have programmes as grand or complex as the more famous culture change programmes in large organizations. Small business managers in our sample argued that there was no time to create more formal programmes and that they communicated change to a small group of employees in a less structured manner. What is more important, they often explicitly rejected the formal approach to culture change itself. In the words of the manageress of the Motel, the culture change schemes of large employers in the hotel and catering industry tended to be of a Tayloristic nature:

> Because larger organizations are bureaucratic their schemes had a very 1980s script, with rules and instructions to staff on the hard sell. Companies trained waitresses to always give the same speech robotically, 'Hello, I'm your waitress for the evening, Kelly, what starter would you like?'

It is best to describe the culture change programmes in the smaller organization as attempts to change people by informal pressure and making explicit the changed expectations of managers. After purchasing a nursing home in 1988, a former NHS ward nurse and her husband were making significant attempts to introduce more professional standards, changing the culture of the organization. There had been a high initial turnover of staff as higher standards of care were introduced as the owners felt the home had been 'previously run more for the staff than for the residents'. When asked to draw a parallel between the changes in the private nursing home and the culture change programme currently being undertaken in the NHS, they rejected the more formal approach to culture change:

> The Government's NHS reforms are about putting money first and they are not driven by care issues. We have made our changes for the right reasons – to improve the quality of care for our residents, not just to reduce the budgets. Really, I'm a nurse first and a business owner second. Some of the NHS Trusts are being run by people who are business owners primarily, they just happen to be in health care.

In sum, the culture change initiatives in small organizations were linked to a wide range of other personnel initiatives, but managers deemed the informality of the entire process important. The schemes lacked the headline-catching names and slogans of the larger organizations, but managing culture change was *vital* to many of our cases. The intention of the culture change programmes was not to replace an informal culture with a formal one. It was to retain the informality and combine it with a more professional orientation to work, seeking higher commitment to the ends of the organization.

Work Organization

Out of the thirteen case organizations, ten had devolved management. This was a higher score than the WIRS 3 findings on the decentralization of management decision making (Millward et al., 1992: 355). Many small business owners reported it was exceedingly difficult to devolve manage-ment but it was nevertheless a widespread necessity in many small organ-izations. This was very much in evidence at the Decorators' Merchants.

The managing director sought to devolve management responsibility in an attempt to change the culture of the company. He found there had been 'no real management previously' with the shop run with 'the aim of closing for a one and a half hour lunch, not opening on Saturday and with the aim of closing at 4pm on Friday'. He had employed a whole range of HRM techniques, including team briefing and employee involvement, to change management attitudes, seeking to make managers more responsible for performance.

When control of the family-owned Transport and Haulage Company passed from the founder to his son, he introduced a new 'people-centred' orientation with paternalistic views on employee involvement. The two managers in the organization received training and completed management courses, generating a new management ethos in a largely traditional sector. As one of the managers explained:

> In this industry in the past most people management was done purely on the basis of strength of character and personality. The industry often attracted the strong and violent types to do a fairly rough job, so managers had to be able to handle rough characters. But this has changed for us. Now some of our drivers have been quite highly educated and they're willing to train. We have been consciously trying to recruit better people, so now we are able to let them do more for themselves.

Documentary evidence of this new approach existed in the newly created induction packs and drivers' manuals. The company also brought in outside trainers to develop the skills of its work-force.

Introducing devolved management into the sales-force was an important development at the Carton and Board Distributors. The directors who had established the company had found it difficult to delegate to the sales staff as the organization grew in size. Resisting employing professional consultants, they recruited a professional sales and marketing manager as a director who 'turned it all on its head'. The new director introduced individual incentives into the area sales teams where previously employees had split bonuses equally. Devolving responsibilities enabled the owners gradually to withdraw from the daily running of the business and reduce their workloads.

As for teamworking, in our original survey of organizations we found a reverse pattern to what we might have predicted. Small companies had been somewhat more active in developing teamworking than larger organizations in our sample. Managers interpreted the meaning of teamworking in reality very broadly among our cases. In general, it was not about creating formal work groups but maintaining the notion of 'all working together' at a time of increasing pressures to become more formalized. Pressure for change came from the demands of auditing for British Standard awards. At the Printers, the teenage employees with computer skills recruited directly from local colleges and schools were very different from the apprenticed craft-skilled printers traditionally associated with the trade. Managers ran the company as a tightly knit community. When recruiting new employees managers made extensive efforts to find out about the family details and friends of applicants. According to senior directors, this implied a very collective and informal management style.

Communication

The traditional image of communication in small companies is that informal channels predominate. Yet over one half of our case companies had formal team briefings, indicating that this picture may be changing. When the parent company of the Engineering Company went into receivership, it was subject to a management buy-out. In the first few months of business the director recalled that extensive 'communication to win the allegiance of staff was vital'. As the company's main customers are large engineering companies (Perkins, Cummins and Massey Ferguson) which have sought to get closer to their suppliers, it had become essential to inform employees not just about the condition of the business, but the need for world-class manufacturing standards. Yet, in small organizations, even formal briefing sessions have a large degree of informality. Having worked for several large concerns, the managing director pointed to the advantages small organizations have over the more formal communication systems of the large organization:

> It doesn't really matter if you have formal employee involvement schemes or not. The important thing is that there are team meetings taking place where people are asking 'what are your thoughts and ideas?' I think formal schemes like suggestion boxes can work and we do use them, but you don't just have to take that route. It tends to give you a select group who are the ones always producing ideas and participating, with others left out. If it can be done more organically in the small business, it's better.

At the Printers, employees were involved in competitions to create the company slogans. Managers everywhere regarded communication as important but the quality of shared information varied widely. However, it is grossly inaccurate to think of small organizations as universally dominated by poor communication because of the informal way in which managers transmit information.

Goal Setting, Appraisal and Pay

The cycle of pay determination remained rather traditional across our cases overall. Perhaps the reason for the lack of popularity among small businesses of performance-related pay is that they are not changing from a system of anything other than managerially determined pay. In comparison, large organizations have sought to move away from industry-wide settlements and negotiating change with trade unions. For two of our cases the relationship between the market and wages was quite direct. The Clothing Manufacturer used a computer-controlled piecework system and the Carpet Retailer monitored sales staff by a commission payment system. At the Nursing Home, the owners were gradually introducing a performance assessment scheme among senior staff before rolling it down to all employees. At the Motel senior managers appraised the most senior 15 per cent of staff. The owners of the Carton and Board Suppliers and the Printers ran the two extensive performance assessment schemes. The striking feature about performance management in smaller organizations was again the informal use of a formal scheme.

The Limits of the New Agenda

If we are to reappraise our view of the way some small organizations manage culture, work organization, communication and appraisals, it remains necessary to explain why our case organizations had not taken up the remaining aspects of the new management agenda. We came across only two mission and values statements (MVS). This issue brought a variety of responses from our cases, indicating that, even among the more formalized small businesses, if they could manage informally, then they are unlikely to seek to do otherwise. At the Transport and Haulage Company one manager explained there was a MVS 'in the MD's head', at the Carpet Retailers it was 'the removal of fixed costs', at the Hotel it was 'one of those postcards behind the bar' and at the Clothing Manufacturer a director explained 'we try to keep it friendly, things like that would scare them'. Generally, respondents emphasized the 'seat of the pants' nature of personnel management in small businesses preventing them developing such statements. As a manager at the Mail Order Company explained, the employment relationship in the small business can be highly instrumental:

> We don't actively try to manage the culture, it rubs off on people by being here, you can't tell people the culture, it's bollocks. We are here to make money and hopefully it benefits the staff. My Chairman's ethos is that there are more important things than work in people's lives, we should not try to pretend that working here demands their unswerving loyalty and commitment.

Small business managers reacted to the idea of quality circles by insisting communications remain informal. A director of the Fruit and Vegetable Wholesalers confessed that 'you tend to yell at them'. At the Carpet Retailers a manager commented simply 'if it makes your job easier, you change it'. In other companies managers usually dealt with such issues in staff meetings. The managers we interviewed generally thought psychometric tests involved too much work, that they were not trustworthy and less accurate than 'first impressions'. The issue of de-layering middle managers was not possible in organizations with very flat hierarchies.

Conclusions: the Dynamics of Change

The picture we have presented of the new management agenda in small businesses suggests that any wholesale categorization of this sector by the 'bleak house' notion is inaccurate. In concluding we need to explain how these organizations have adopted aspects of the new management agenda. Small organizations have many disadvantages in pursuing a new approach to managing people: they lack resources, management expertise and are less likely to be aware of developments in other companies. What therefore explains the dynamics of these changes in small businesses?

In the majority of our cases a change in ownership had been the key factor. Small businesses are more likely to closely reflect their owner and changes in control bring an important change opportunity. Developments at the Decorators Wholesaler illustrate this point well. The company had been family-owned since 1820 before undergoing two changes of ownership in the 1980s. The new owners were introducing professional management skills, new initiatives and substantial reorganization. A second important change mechanism in small companies was the introduction of professional management standards and skills that could occur with or without a change of ownership. At the Carton and Board Suppliers, the manager from a supplier company joined as a sales director. Acting as an agent for change, he radically altered the organization of work and payment systems in the sales-force. Among our sample only three interviewees had no work experience elsewhere, seven had broad non-management work experience in other companies and eight had broad managerial work experience in several companies.

A third source of new ideas and change in the small business sector has been internal management development. At the Insurance Company, an office manager had completed the Institute of Personnel Management training course. With the support of the directors she had begun to make the personnel strategy of the company more professional. Change has also started to occur in several of our companies because they were increasing in size. Managers regarded this in itself as signifying the end of informal and friendly ways of managing people, a process described by one director as 'drifting'. At the Carton and Board Suppliers, the small and informal sales business expanded in size, making it important to formalize procedures and practices. The financial director explained 'you have to change your philosophy and start to delegate'. Finally, a further important dynamic for change was pressure from customers. Increasingly, managers felt that companies needed British Standard accreditation to attract new customers. However, whereas the search for quality was the trigger to broader culture change in large organizations, in small organizations managers did not regard it as a catalyst for change but as a rubber stamp on what they already did. For instance, at the Printers, directors recruited a quality manager from a large engineering concern with the brief of helping the company secure BS5750 but not to change the way they did anything. Again, when faced with the need for formalization, small businesses tried to keep things informal.

It is now possible to construct a model of the dynamics of the new management agenda in small businesses. Whereas McKinlay and Starkey (1992: 108) and Storey (1992: 38) identify 'enhanced competition' as the main causes of the shift towards HRM in large organizations, changes in small businesses have had more specific triggers within each company. Managers had little understanding of HRM as a management theory. Nevertheless, small business owners were familiar with many of its components. There are several reasons why change in the management of human resources has not been more widespread than it has been in small businesses. The traditional structural features of small businesses within the economy, such as restricted finance and low turnovers, are undoubtedly important. However, there were also other major factors limiting the degree of change taking place. The life-world of the small business owner (Scase and Goffee, 1980) was still in many ways quite isolated. The most frequent source of new ideas remained practical experience. Only five respondents had drawn ideas on how to manage people from professional courses. Four people reported regularly using ideas from the trade press, chambers of commerce and other small companies. Given that there were pockets of managers in our sample largely untouched by the 'new management' agenda, it is not surprising that part of the small business sector remains insulated from new ideas.

Factors that contribute to the 'bleak house' sector appeared to include those workplaces where managers rely upon practical experience, those which are family-owned and have not grown so large that they need to recruit professional managers, and those managed by people with limited career experience outside the family firm. The small firms that had been most resistant to change in our sample were those in which a family kept firm control. Among these companies in particular, family business owners continue to regard professional managers with suspicion. In four of our cases there were no professional managers employed. In three of them family members had learned the necessary skills. Even among companies forced into recruiting professional managers there had been much agonizing and frequently the recruitment process had taken a very long time. Where companies had used consultants there had been a limited and frequently negative impact on personnel management. Employers sought more direct control through monitoring the work of staff through computerization rather than up-skilling staff.

Throughout this chapter we have presented evidence that points towards an important reappraisal of the human resource management practices of small businesses. Without doubt the issues and practices of personnel management in small firms are far from what the literature led us to believe. We have stressed that small organizations have been implementing many of the initiatives that we identify in larger organizations. The evidence presented in this chapter is at odds with the findings from the 1990 Workplace Industrial Relations Survey (Millward et al., 1992) that an investment approach to people is largely restricted to those workplaces with trade unions (Sisson, 1993). We do not wish to deny that there is an important dynamic at work whereby larger organizations are more likely to have the resources and technical knowledge and skills to implement large-scale change programmes and the latest HRM techniques. However, we have shown that, in a less formalized manner, small organizations are also implementing change programmes. Clearly we could justifiably attach the term 'bleak house' to many organizations, but the research presented here indicates that it would be inaccurate to assume they were the norm in the small business sector.

Finally, we would also like to draw attention to two broader implications of these findings for the study of HRM. First, the small business is in many ways the ideal site for the development of a HRM approach in two ways. Communications are more direct, people have to work more flexibly, the hierarchy is flatter, the impact of each employee on organizational performance is clearer and the greater insecurity makes the organization more responsive to changes in market and customer demands. Secondly, the nature of change programmes in small businesses appears to be much more informal and organic. As such, they carry greater meaning and indicate a more authentic approach than the relatively bureaucratic formal change programmes of larger organizations. This suggests that large organizations may have much to learn from the informal nature of change in small businesses. Rather than taking the absence of large formal programmes to be a weakness of HRM in small organizations, it may be the competitive advantage of the smaller organization. As a result of the internal power structure, when a small business manager decides to change things, she/he can more easily bring about change.

References

Bolton Report (1971) *Report of the Commission of Inquiry on Small Firms*, chaired by J.E. Bolton, Cmnd. 4811. London: HMSO.

Curran, J. and Stanworth, J. (1979a) 'Self-selection and the small firm worker – a critique and an alternative view', *Sociology*, 13 (3): 427–44.

Curran, J. and Stanworth, J. (1979b) 'Worker involvement and social relations in the small firm', *Sociological Review*, 27 (2): 317–42.

Curran, J. and Stanworth, J. (1981a) 'Size of workplace and attitudes to industrial relations in the printing and electronics industries', *British Journal of Industrial Relations*, 19 (1): 14–25.

Curran, J. and Stanworth, J. (1981b) 'A new look at job satisfaction in the small firm', *Human Relations*, 34 (5): 343–65.

DTI (1994) *Competitiveness: Helping Business to Win*, Cm 2563. London: HMSO.

Goss, D. (1991) *Small Business and Society*. London: Routledge.

Hornsby, J. and Kuratko, D. (1990) 'Human resource management in small business: critical issues for the 1990s', *Journal of Small Business Management*, July: 9–18.

Ingham, G.K. (1970) *Size of Industrial Organisation and Work Behaviour*. London: Cambridge University Press.

McKinlay, A. and Starkey, K. (1992) 'Competitive strategies and organisational change', in G. Salaman (ed.), *Human Resource Strategies*. London: Sage.

Millward, N., Stevens, M., Smart, D. and Hawes, W. (1992) *Workplace Industrial Relations in Transition*. Aldershot: Dartmouth.

Rainne, A. (1989) *Industrial Relations in Small Firms: Small Isn't Beautiful*. London: Routledge.

Rainne, A. and Scott, M. (1986) 'Industrial relations in the small firm', in J. Curran, J. Stanworth and D. Watkins (eds), *The Survival of the Small Firm: Employment, Growth, Technology and Politics* (Vol. 2). Aldershot: Gower.

Scase, R. and Goffee, R. (1980) *The Real World of the Small Business Owner*. London: Croom Helm.

Scott, M., Roberts, I., Holroyd, G. and Sawbridge, D. (1989) *Management and Industrial Relations in Small Firms*. Department of Employment Research Paper No. 70. London: Department of Employment.

Sisson, K. (1993) 'In search of HRM', *British Journal of Industrial Relations*, 31 (2): 201–10.

Stanworth, J. and Gray, C. (1991) *Bolton 20 Years On: The Small Firm in the 1990s*. London: Paul Chapman.

Storey, J. (1992) *Developments in the Management of Human Resources*. Oxford: Blackwell.

17 Managing for the Next Century – or the Last?

Ray Jacques

> The revolution we started almost two years ago with the publication of
> *Reengineering the Corporation* [Hammer and Champy, 1993] continues . . .
> (Hammer, 1995: xi)

The New Revolutionaries

The subtitle of Hammer and Champy (1993) is 'a manifesto for business revolution'. Manifesto? Revolution? Ever since that underdog victory of 1776–84, we Americans seem to have been consistently revolting (so to speak), but today a curious 'radical' is emerging. No less a management-consulting supernova than Tom Peters announced in the preface to his 1987 book that it was 'about a revolution' (p. xi) . In 1989, Rosabeth Moss Kanter threw in with the cause, announcing 'a far-reaching revolution in business management' (p. 9). By 1992, Peters judged his previous work too reactionary, coopting the rhetoric of liberation theology for his new book, *Liberation Management* (p. xxxi). By 1993, Peter Drucker confidently announced the arrival of 'post-capitalist society'.

Peters, Kanter, Drucker; hardly a group of wild-eyed radicals. Yet they are talking revolution. And they are only three of the more visible voices in a growing chorus of prominent managers, consultants and theorists who claim today's organizations are changing in transformational, not merely incremental ways. These assorted voices are beginning to coalesce into a fairly standard litany about the conditions and challenges of so-called 'post-industrial' management. One aspect of these changes, we are told, has to do with changing markets and technologies (Box 17.1). Global markets, hypercompetition, smart technologies and so forth are transforming the environment external to the organization. Internally, we are told that this changing environment is producing a new employee, the proactive, self-managing, team-oriented 'knowledge worker', who embodies

Originally published in Ray Jacques (1996) *Manufacturing the Employee*. London: Sage (abridged).

BOX 17.1   *Themes in managing for the new century: changing markets and technologies*

Forty years of the most rapid growth in production, the doubling of the population, and the conquest of the international markets were accomplished with a decrease in the number of firms in the leading industries.[1] The stupendous wave of industrial consolidations which began in the late eighties . . . culminated at the climax of feverish speculation [and] was abruptly terminated in conditions verging on a panic.[2]

Americans, in the first flush of their international victories, may have assumed foolish airs of 'US first and the rest nowhere',[3] but if we wish to compete with products made in countries where lower wages prevail we shall need to make a superior article. Not only will there be a need in the future for fewer workers to produce a given amount of product but those workers will need to be highly skilled . . . there will be more specialists. . . . In less than ten years more than 2,000,000 people have been thrown out of employment in the United States. They are finding re-employment in relatively new kinds of work, mostly of the service type.[4]

---

1 Simons, A.M. (1912) *Social Forces in American History*. New York: Macmillan. p. 309.

2 Dewing, A.S. (1920) 'The early trust movement outlined', in R.E. Curtis (ed.), *The Trusts and Economic Control*. New York: McGraw-Hill. p. 14.

3 Lawson, W.R. (1903) *American Industrial Problems*. Edinburgh: William Blackwood & Sons. p. 5.

4 Struck, F.T. (1930) *Foundations of Industrial Education*. New York: John Wiley & Sons. pp. 16, 69, 72.

the firm's most valuable capital asset (Box 17.2). Look closely at Boxes 17.1 and 17.2. It's beginning to sound familiar, isn't it? It should; the newest observation in these lists is more than sixty years old! If management thought has been 'evolving,' as our textbooks almost universally claim, why does 'managing for the twenty-first century' look so much like managing for the twentieth?

The Industrial Logic of 'Post-industrial' Management Discourse

What is the key challenge to organizations in the upcoming decades? It is no longer radical to suggest that present-day organizations may be in the midst of transformational change. While the specific topics said to indicate this change vary widely – from multiculturalism and self-management to flexible manufacturing and business process re-engineering – there is an archetypal question structuring the way each issue is approached. That question, today's management mantra, could be phrased as: *how can organizations develop new and innovative ways of managing the employee to achieve world-class efficiency, productivity and competitiveness?* This is the key challenge to 'managing for the twenty-first century', right?

Wrong.

BOX 17.2 *Themes in managing for the new century: the new worker – 'making capital' from knowledge work*

The *mechanical* phase . . . [of industrial organization was followed by] the *organic* phase . . . [which] maintained that society ought to be regarded as a complex organism, or at least as analogous to an organism. . . . At the present time the discussion has entered on a third phase. . . . Neither [the mechanical nor organic views] is adequate, or carries us far enough.[5] In the industrial era just passed and now drawing to a close, it was to have been expected that employers, with their chief attention absorbed by questions relating to machines and methods, should neglect the greatest of all their assets . . . their employees. Our records show that the average employee in the average institution represents a capital-ized value of between $32,000 and $38,000 to his or her employer. [The organization must] protect that investment from depreciation and loss in every way possible [and] develop and increase its value.[6]

The increased competition that has come in recent years . . . will have to be met, if it is to be met successfully, through education.[7] [The] manager of the future will have to be first of all an educator. . . . The contest ahead of us is an educational rivalry.[8] The thoughtful observer of contemporary scientific affairs must have noticed the gradual dissolution of the artificial barriers between different realms of knowledge. There is considerable traffic over the borders of all disciplines.[9] *The greatest thought of this century is the transference of value from property to the human being.*[10]

Machines must more and more be made to do the work for which labor is becoming scarce. . . . But instead of workers being mated to a single machine . . . one individual will supervise the work of a chain of machines . . . requiring, instead of a brainless and emotionless automaton, a well-trained mind and a knowing touch.[11] The employer who does not avail him or herself of the natural, healthy love of work in employees as a motive for excellence loses much.[12] Women [especially], we find, are absolutely loyal. They do not work for us awhile and then quit, which is sometimes urged as one of the objections against woman workers.[13] It is an important part of [the manager's] duties to find out what [the workers'] ideas and opinions are . . . and thus to *make capital out of their originality and their suggestions.*[14]

5 Drever, J. (1929) 'The human factor in industrial relations', in C.S. Myers (ed.), *Industrial Psychology*. London: Thornton Butterworth Ltd. p. 26.

6 Blackford, K.M.H. and Newcomb, A. (1914) *The Job, The Man, The Boss*. Garden City, NY: Doubleday, Page & Co. pp. 22, 38, 60. [Values given in the original of $2,500 to $3,000 have been adjusted for inflation to amounts *c.* 1990.]

7 Struck, F.T. (1930) *Foundations of Industrial Education*. New York: John Wiley & Sons. p. 67.

8 Fagan, J.O. (1909) *Labor and the Railroads*. New York: Houghton Mifflin. pp. 26–7.

9 Moore, B.V. and Hartmann, G.W. (eds) (1931) *Readings in Industrial Psychology*. New York: D. Appleton-Century Company. p. 1.

10 Crowther, S. (1917) 'There's a solution for labor troubles, an interview with John D. Rockefeller, Jr', in A.W. Shaw Co. (ed.), *Handling Men*. Chicago, IL: A.W. Shaw Co. p. 90; emphasis added.

11 Link, H.C. (1924) *Employment Psychology*. New York: Macmillan. pp. 385–6.

12 Blackford and Newcomb (op. cit.), pp. 50, 51, 57.

13 Ommer, W.I. (1917) 'Why we are replacing men with women', in A.W. Shaw Co. (ed.), *Handling Men*. Chicago, IL: A.W. Shaw Co. p. 54.

14 Edison, T.A. (1917) Aphorism cited in A.W. Shaw Co. (ed.), *Handling Men*. Chicago, IL: A.W. Shaw Co. p. 81; emphasis added.

This sentence has the 'ring of truth' because it is a familiar platitude supported by 'common sense'. On examination, it reflects many key assumptions of industrial, not post-industrial, societies. Precisely because they are assumptions, these beliefs are not available for examination. Before one even begins a discussion of managing in the post-industrial future, one is locked into a phenomenological factory, a factory of the mind. Consider the above platitude phrase by phrase:

Organizations must develop new and innovative ways. . .   Who or what is 'the organization'? Suppliers, customers, and society are not conventionally thought to be part of 'the organization'. Employees are most often conceptualized as contractors who exchange their labor with 'the organization' for compensation. Management as a group is often identified with 'the good of the organization', but this mandate is contingent upon the claim that managers act as stewards for the stockholders; examples can easily be found, both of managers acting in their self-interest (golden parachutes, poison pills, greenmail) or of stockholders treating managers as disposable employees. For that matter, is the board of directors itself synonymous with the interest of the stockholders in the large organization? How much proportional representation does the proverbial hundred-share grandmother in Hoboken really have? There appears to be *no* concrete entity necessarily represented by 'the organization'. Indeed, as long ago as 1932, Adolf Berle and Gardiner Means, a lawyer and an economist affiliated with Harvard University, saw clearly that:

> Grown to tremendous proportions, there may be said to have evolved a 'corporate system' [within which] . . . [p]hysical control over the instruments of production has been surrendered in ever growing degree to centralized groups who manage property in bulk, *supposedly, but by no means necessarily, for the benefit of the security holders. . . .* Since the corporation is a distinct legal identity, separate and apart from the stockholders . . . the owners of passive property, by surrendering control and responsibility over the active property, have surrendered the right that the corporation should be operated in their sole interest. . . . They have placed the community in a position to demand that the modern corporation serve not alone the owners or the control but all of society. (Berle and Means, 1932: 1, 7, 221, 222, 355, 356; my emphasis)

Consider an example common in US business rhetoric. IBM manufacturing facilities in South Korea may be portrayed as creating jobs for the Korean people and 'developing' their economy. Simultaneously, Sony's purchase of Columbia Pictures could be (and was) represented as a Japanese 'attack' on Hollywood, depleting US wealth and threatening the US economy. These views are consistent with common sense, but they are incompatible with each other. Who or what constitutes 'the organization' changes fundamentally between one example and the other.

. . . of managing the employee . . .   Speaking of people in organizations as 'managers' and 'employees' will seldom raise an eyebrow. This distinction is

deeply ingrained in common sense. Yet, managers are also employees. When is one speaking about manager-employees and when is one speaking about managed-employees? Associating the *tasks* of management with the *persons* called managers makes invisible the numerous ways non-management employees also 'manage' work activities (see Fletcher, 1994; Jacques, 1992, 1993; Jacques and Fletcher, 1994). What is made invisible through this common sense is precisely what one wishes to understand when dealing with the increasing number of situations where worker self-management is desirable. Unless entrenched habits of thought are questioned, one is unlikely to notice the process described by Hollway (1991) through which the domain of management discourse has narrowed over several decades from the general problem of organizing the work of society to the much narrower – and decreasingly relevant – issue of controlling the worker at task-level actions.

. . . *to achieve world-class* . . . In the 1980s 'international management' became a hot topic in the USA. While management is highly international today, one might also ask 'why now?' The US *entered* industrial society as an international power in the late 1800s.[1] The US multinational was a dominating force in world markets in the decades immediately after the Second World War.[2] Could the drive to be 'world-class' simply represent the American response to the erosion of a temporary privilege enjoyed while the other major industrialized countries were being devastated by two World Wars? Industrial common sense focuses us on the question 'how can one become world-class?' but never challenges us to ask why the idea of being world-class has become an icon of success at this time.

. . . *efficiency, productivity* . . . It may seem self-evident that business must make efficiency and productivity its first priority, but history suggests that this also may be simply an industrial habit of thought. Economic analysis was once centered on the subject of *wealth*. This changed in the eighteenth century to analysis of *production*. A further shift from production to *productivity* did not occur in the USA until the later 1800s. Today, efficiency and productivity are often enshrined as timeless icons. One can literally not imagine a responsible challenge to their importance. But what of the need for organizational flexibility? Creativity? Social citizenship? Building and balancing a long-term web of relationships and commitments?[3] Might these or other values be necessary for achieving efficiency and productivity? Might the direct pursuit of efficiency and productivity be paradoxically *un*productive in at least some important instances? Industrial common sense makes it all but impossible to think in these terms, even as emerging organizational realities demand it.

. . . *and competitiveness* . . . In the USA, to question the goodness of competition is blasphemous, but organizations in market economies are hardly combatants. Systematic and exclusive focus on competitive action obscures a network of cooperative relationships essential to the success of any enterprise. These relational practices are familiar to anyone who engages in business, but they are marginal in both popular and academic management writing, which more often reinforces the 'common sense' notion that only competition need be analyzed. One would be surprised today to read of the degree to which the architects of the US industrial order – builders of quasi-monopolistic, government regulated, socially scrutinized empires, the likes of Andrew Carnegie, J.P. Morgan, and John D. Rockefeller – openly identified the advent of the industrial era with a shift from 'invisible-hand' style competition to industry-wide cooperation between employers (some might say collusion, but collusion is not competitive either). Paradoxically, many would support the observation that lack of awareness of the value of relationships is one of the main disadvantages of US business culture relative to that of Japan. But, how does one discuss cooperation as a competitive advantage and competition as a barrier to competitiveness? Industrial common sense gives the very thought an oxymoronic quality.

Walking away from the Wall

A co-worker once told me of a recurring dream she has. In this dream, she is facing a high wall. On the other side of the wall she hears a sound and knows, with the certainty of a dreamer, that it comes from a large, hostile animal. In fear, she begins to run along the wall, but the sound follows her as the animal runs along the wall on the other side. She runs faster and faster, her terror increasing until she is stunned awake. Only after she wakes up does she remember that she could have walked away from the wall!

The central idea [I am propounding] is that if management knowledge is to have relevance to the emerging post-industrial world(s), both managers and management scholars must learn to 'walk away from the wall'. But before we can do that, we have to see how current ways of knowing constitute running along the wall, our increasing terror prodding us to more of the same rather than to creative responses. How is it that our dialogue about a society increasingly called post-industrial, post-bureaucratic, postmodern – even post-capitalist – unintentionally reinforces patterns of thought and habits of practice that have been coalescing since the emergence of industrialized societies? How is it that we no longer even see the wall itself?

The management knowledge I trace is that of the USA, but like Coca Cola and Levi jeans, it is exported worldwide. In the USA, we must come to see the degree to which our knowledge of contemporary work is shaped by past eras and past problems. We Americans will be able to understand the specificity of other cultures only to the degree we are able to become reflective about the cultural assumptions structuring our own. For those of you outside the USA, studying the cultural roots of American knowledge may help to contextualize the role it will play as it is consumed abroad.

The Need for Critically Reflective Practice

Management has not been a philosophical discipline. The US business hero, real or fictional, has been the 'man [*sic*] of action'. Getting to 'the bottom line' is highly valued. Even management scholarship has aspired to the eminently pragmatic. In the founding issue of *Administrative Science Quarterly*, Thompson expresses a vision of administrative science as the applied arm of the social sciences 'as engineering stands with respect to the physical sciences, or as medicine to the biological' (1956: 103). During times of incremental change, this pragmatic approach allows one to focus one's efforts on solving concrete problems. Treating the work, the worker and the world as objects of common sense allows one to deal with what Thomas Kuhn (1962/1970) called puzzle-solving science. It facilitates the accumulation of knowledge within a well-defined domain. During times of transformational change, however, not only do new problems arise; old *ways* of understanding problems become problems *themselves*. To be successful, puzzle-solving must assume a certain structure of assumptions; thus it does not permit examination *of* assumptions. If present times are indeed times of discontinuous change, prudence suggests inquiring how puzzle-solving science may constitute a barrier to dealing with today's central issues.

Paradoxically, during times such as these, 'pragmatic' approaches to problem-solving are *obstacles* to solving concrete problems while questioning basic values and assumptions – philosophy – is pragmatic. Such times of transformation require critically reflective practice, a blending of the poles of the traditional theorist/practitioner dichotomy. Both practice uninformed by theoretical reflection and theory disconnected from the workplace are sterile and reinforce the *status quo*. All too often we see this manifested in theory which accepts as 'normal' an assembly-line or hardhat workplace that has been declining in importance since the 1930s. Correspondingly, practicing managers often accept, as given, management principles developed in the 1960s or before as well as workplace structures that emerged in response to the needs of industrialization a century ago.

In order to break this cycle of reliance on obsolete expertise, managers, consultants and management scholars must become, in a sense, applied philosophers. These critically reflective practitioners (both theoretical practitioners and practical theorists) must raise issues that were once of central importance to business writing, but have been dormant within mainstream managerial literature for decades: What is 'the organization'? Who is 'the employee'? What is the purpose of the organization in society? What are the rights, responsibilities and values of organization members? What power relationships currently structure the workplace? How are these relationships changing? What can/should be done about them?

The challenge to what Douglas McGregor (1960) called 'the human side of enterprise' is shown by the topics emergent in the last decade and a half – organizational culture, quality of work life, 'Japanese' management, gender and diversity, international management, business ethics, entrepreneurship,

Total Quality Management. These are not simply new topics which can be conveniently added to accumulated theory in behavioral science. Each represents a new 'root metaphor'[4] for viewing work, the worker and the world. Knowledge can no longer be treated as transparent; one must know *from* a specific perspective, incompatible with other perspectives.[5]

One might think that times of transformation would be exciting for theorists of organizing. Surprisingly, this is not the case. In the last decade major figures in organization theory have increasingly described the results of this effort as 'trivial', 'disappointing', 'meaningless', 'out of fashion', or even 'disintegrating',[6] but it is still fashionable, after a century, to state that organizational research is on the verge of producing a paradigmatic science. Accordingly, the mainstream of organizational research continues to call for more scientific rigor, more data, more draconian norms requiring conformance to already formulated theory (for example, Bettis and Donaldson, 1990; Mitchell and James, 1989; Pfeffer, 1993; Van de Ven, 1989; Webster and Starbuck, 1988). This puts organization science into a tight position. The last period of major theory development seems to have begun faltering in the early 1970s (Ashmos and Huber, 1987; Perrow, 1973). Indeed, it is only a slight exaggeration to say that what today's business student is taught about behavior in organizations represents what was known about the white, male, American (and sometimes British) assembly-line worker and college sophomore in 1960. Organizational science is caught in a 'truth-trap'. Scientific rigor dictates that knowledge be developed cumulatively, based on prior knowledge about a presumably stable system. Business needs for knowledge are based on an already turbulent world where the pace of change is increasing. Where rigor and relevance diverge, the norms of the field tend to favor rigor (see Staw, 1985). The presumption that current organizational knowledge represents a fledgling science leads researchers to cling more tightly to this past knowledge the more its relevance is questioned. As a result, old knowledge is recycled and applied in procrustean fashion to new problems.

Example: The 1980s (and continuing) infatuation with so-called 'Japanese' management has made Total Quality Management and its successor, Business Process Re-engineering, a deservedly 'hot' idea. But, W. Edwards Deming, the guru of TQM, is a statistical quality control engineer, born at the turn of the century; he started his career when the 'hot' management concept was Scientific Management. The Deming system was fully articulated before the Second World War. While TQM concepts can be valuable to today's organizations, what does it say about the state of knowledge development in organizational theorizing that the latest theory for organizing people at work comes from half-century-old ideas developed by a century-old engineer?

Example: Peter Senge became the celebrity author regarding post-industrial 'learning organizations' with his book, *The Fifth Discipline* (1990). Senge offers a number of tips that could be quite valuable to the reader, but his theoretical position rests on systems theory developed and popularized four decades ago. Theoretically, much of *The Fifth Discipline* could be viewed as application of Karl Weick's *The Social Psychology of Organizing*, first published in 1969.

To summarize, we are living through a curious moment when a 'revolution' is being announced whose *avant garde* sit at the heart of the current power elite and whose *internationale* is composed from minor variations on a nineteenth-century theme. One might be tempted to dismiss the whole show as a lot of empty noise except for the growing conviction that transformational changes of some kind are indeed sweeping the organizational world. How is one to make sense of these mixed messages?

Notes

1 This is, for instance, the subject of Lawson's *American Industrial Problems* (1903).

2 For instance, Jean Jacques Servan-Schreiber's *The American Challenge* (1967), foresaw the US dominating Europe.

3 One concrete example is the report prepared by Clegg et al. (1994) on the development of 'embryonic industries', in which corporate self-interest is intertwined with industry and cross-industry alliances as well as multinational social policies. To understand the nurturance of embryonic industries in terms of productivity would be *counter*productive when it is the health of the overall web of developing relationships that one must foster. This report affirms that it is 'decreasingly production costs' that are responsible for 'driving competitive success' (1994: 95).

4 Smircich (1983) has distinguished between views of organizational culture which treat culture as a 'variable', something to be tacked onto the current way of viewing organizations, and culture as a 'root metaphor', an altogether different way of viewing *everything* that goes on in organizations.

5 Burrell and Morgan (1979) still make this argument better than any other source with which I am familiar. While some continue to argue that divergent paradigmatic positions can be unified, my experience as a knower does not support this view. Learning about race, gender and philosophy (i.e., the ongoing process of learning that I am white, male and Western/modern) has led me to adopt assumptions that cannot be integrated with the views I once held. I can view my experience through a number of lenses, but each leads to conclusions that are incompatible with the others and only one at a time 'really' reflects my belief. Others may argue that *they* do not have this experience, but I cannot accept the argument from others that I do not.

6 Sequentially: Weick (1989), Daft and Lewin (1990), Webster and Starbuck (1988), Ashmos and Huber (1987) and Perrow (1981).

References

Ashmos, D.P. and Huber, G.P. (1987) 'The systems paradigm in organization theory: correcting the record and suggesting the future', *Academy of Management Review*, 12 (4): 607–18.

Berle, A.A. and Means, G.C. (1932) *The Modern Corporation and Private Property.* New York: Harcourt, Brace & World, Inc.

Bettis, R.A. and Donaldson, L. (eds) (1990) 'Theory development forum: market discipline and the discipline of management', *Academy of Management Review,* 15 (2): 367–535.

Burrell, G. and Morgan, G. (1979) *Sociological Paradigms.* Portsmouth, NH: Heinemann.

Clegg, S., Dwyer, L., Gray, J., Kemp, S., Marceau, J. and O'Mara, E. (1994) 'Leadership and management needs of embryonic industries'. A research report for Midgley & Company on behalf of the Industry Task Force on Leadership and Management Skills.

Daft, R.L. and Lewin, A.Y. (1990) 'Can organization studies begin to break out of the normal science straightjacket?'. An editorial essay, *Organization Science,* 1 (1): 1–9.

Drucker, P.F. (1993) *Post-capitalist Society.* New York: Harper Business.

Fletcher, J. (1994) 'Toward a theory of relational practice in organizations: a reconstruction of "real" work'. Unpublished doctoral dissertation, Boston University, MA.

Hammer, M. (1995) *Reengineering Management: The Mandate for New Leadership.* New York: Harper Business.

Hammer, M. and Champy, J. (1993) *Reengineering the Corporation: A Manifesto for Business Revolution.* New York: Harper Business.

Hollway, W. (1991) *Work Psychology and Organizational Behavior.* London: Sage.

Jacques, R. (1992) 'Re-presenting the knowledge worker: a poststructuralist analysis of the new employed professional'. Unpublished doctoral dissertation, University of Massachusetts, Amherst, MA.

Jacques, R. (1993) 'Untheorized dimensions of caring work: caring as a structural practice and caring as a way of seeing', *Nursing Administration Quarterly,* 17 (2): 1–10.

Jacques, R. and Fletcher, J. (1994) '"Getting disappeared": relational work and invisibility in organizations'. Presentation in the symposium 'Bringing work relationships into the foreground of organizational research', annual meeting of the Academy of Management, Dallas, TX.

Kanter, R.M. (1989) 'The new managerial work', *Harvard Business Review,* 67 (6): 85–92.

Kuhn, T.S. (1962/1970) *The Structure of Scientific Revolutions* (2nd edn). Chicago, IL: University of Chicago Press.

Lawson, W.R. (1903) *American Industrial Problems.* Edinburgh: William Blackwood & Sons.

McGregor, D. (1960) *The Human Side of Enterprise.* New York: McGraw-Hill.

Mitchell, T.R. and James, L.R. (1989) 'Situational versus dispositional factors: competing explanations on behavior', *Academy of Management Review,* 14 (3): 330–2, 401–7.

Perrow, C. (1973) 'The short and glorious history of organizational theory', *Organizational Dynamics,* (1) 1: 8–20.

Perrow, C. (1981) 'Disintegrating social sciences', *NYU Education Quarterly,* Winter: 2–9.

Peters, T. (1987) *Thriving on Chaos: Handbook for a Management Revolution.* New York: Knopf.

Peters, T. (1992) *Liberation Management.* New York: Knopf.

Pfeffer, J. (1993) 'Barriers to the advance of organizational science: paradigm development as a dependent variable', *Academy of Management Review,* 18 (4): 599–620.

Senge, P.M. (1990) *The Fifth Discipline: The Art and Practice of the Learning Organization.* New York: Currency Doubleday.

Servan-Schreiber, J.J. (1967) *The American Challenge*. New York: Atheneum.

Smircich, L. (1983) 'Concepts of culture and organizational analysis', *Administrative Science Quarterly*, 28 (2): 339–58.

Staw, B.M. (1985) 'Repairs on the road to relevance and rigor: some unexplored issues in publishing organizational research', in L.L. Cummings and P.J. Frost (eds), *Publishing in the Organizational Sciences*. Homewood, IL: Irwin.

Thompson, J.D. (1956) 'On building an administrative science', *Administrative Science Quarterly*, 1 (1): 102–11.

Van de Ven, A.H. (1989) 'Special forum on theory building: nothing is quite so practical as a good theory', *Academy of Management Review*, 14 (4): 486–9.

Webster, J. and Starbuck, W.H. (1988) 'Theory building in industrial and organizational psychology', in C.L. Cooper and I. Robertson (eds), *International Review of Industrial and Organizational Psychology*. New York: Wiley. pp. 93–138.

Weick, K.E. (1969) *The Social Psychology of Organizing*. Reading, MA: Addison-Wesley.

Weick, K.E. (1989) 'Theory construction as disciplined imagination', *Academy of Management Review*, 14 (4): 516–31.

Part IV

BUILDING ORGANIZATIONAL CAPABILITY

Managing people and change in order to build organizational capability has become an important, if not the dominant, hallmark of strategic human resource management; that which differentiates it from earlier conceptions of personnel management. In this final section we bring together three very distinct contributions, written from different cultural viewpoints, which explore the supposed relationship between human resources and organizational capability. The first chapter in this section challenges some of the ways in which conventional SHRM writers – European and North American – are mishandling the terms 'strategic' and 'human', arguing that unless these socio-theoretical issues are resolved the true meaning and attainment of organizational capability will not be realized – in anything other than a narrow managerialist fashion. The second is a reflective essay by two Scandinavian authors on the nature of reformation and change in organizations. Although the term 'human resource management' is not used, this strategic activity is never far from the surface. This is also the case in the third and final chapter which focuses upon knowledge creation and why Japanese companies are apparently better at it than most Western organizations.

On the face of it, the chapter by Ken Kamoche is altogether less playful than the two that follow it, but while the core argument of this chapter revolves around academic treatment of SHRM and, among other matters, the legitimacy of the HR function within organizations, its destination is not dissimilar. It is the author's contention that human resource management, by virtue of its increasingly strategic aspirations, is in danger of being locked into a way of thinking which simply reflects the dominance of the organizational imperative. So, for example, by striving for integration between organizational and HR strategies, there is a real danger that the asymmetrical agendas of managers and managed will be concealed. Kamoche rehearses a number of reasons why this is both ironic, given that SHRM is concerned with the *diversity* of human assets and their interests, and counter-productive, because competitive advantage relies on strategic assets which are able to operate in ways which are not easily copied or poached, and thus retain their rarity value. For him, it is this resource-based view that provides a way of reasserting or rescuing the developmental-humanistic roots of SHRM from the clutches of managerialist ideology and unitarist thinking. As he notes, this approach focuses on 'the subjectivity, ambiguity and creativity that characterise HRM . . . [and] emphasises that the skills of employees are conceived as a vital resource, which the firm is able to build upon rather than simply to exploit, rationally and ideologically'.

Nils Brunsson and Johan Olsen's concern is the familiar one of attempting to orchestrate change, or bring about reform, in an organization plagued by vague and/or inconsistent goals, where it is difficult to mobilize action, where the ability to exercise top-down control is limited and where the typical questions (should we structure for flexibility or stability?; should we focus on the well-informed present or the ill-informed future?; should we control things centrally or locally?) are raging. To this ready-made 'supply' of problems they offer some telling insights on the potential supply of solutions. First, they note that solutions, by definition, promise a redress of balance, a simplifying of the complex present and an improvement on the discredited present, and that, by and large, this is all rhetoric. Secondly, they explore some of the internal decision-making processes which serve to aid or avoid reform within organizations. And it is here, usually undiscussed, that organizational capability is forged: whether to undergo external reform while leaving internal ideologies untouched; whether to accept (and work with the inevitability of) inconsistent norms by allowing conflict structures or by tolerating hypocrisy (where what is said is different from what is decided, which is different from what is done); whether to encourage organizational forgetfulness or organizational learning.

Ikujiro Nonaka and Hirotaka Takeuchi are equally attentive to the ways organizations build their competitive capability, but, for them, the capacity for knowledge creation is that which separates those that are successful from those that fail. Their tone is far more prescriptive than that of Brunsson and Olsen, who are content to reflect rather than to advise: in this they remain faithful to their own commentary by offering 'a supply of solutions' to the inherent problem of organization reform. In contrast, Nonaka and Takeuchi are quite passionate about the superiority of knowledge creation, learning and innovation among Japanese corporations compared to their Western counterparts. Again, this brief extract (from two chapters of a much more extensive treatise) cannot do justice to their argument, but it allows them to develop a telling list of contrasts between the two styles, or philosophies, of learning. While Western managers are characterized as relying upon quantifiable data, codified procedures and explicit information processing, Japanese managers are said to derive knowledge from highly personal intuitions, to work at internalizing their discoveries and then to find ways of migrating this tacit knowledge into the wider organization such that personal and corporate renewal can take place. This contrasting device between East and West perhaps spills into caricature on occasions. However the value of their chapter is the recognition that everyday mundanities reveal a mindset, and this mindset is one which either revels in, or eschews, inexactitude, ambiguity and creativity, and it is from this tolerance that organizational capability is borne.

18   A Critique and a Proposed Reformulation of Strategic Human Resource Management

Ken Kamoche

Following the growth of interest in strategic analysis in the face of mounting competition in industry, it is not surprising that human resource management (HRM) has been identified as a potential source of competitive advantage (e.g., Tichy et al., 1982; Schuler and MacMillan, 1984; Beer et al., 1985; Hendry and Pettigrew, 1986, 1990; Guest, 1987; Schuler, 1992). Some proponents of strategic human resource management (SHRM) argue that like any other management function, the management of human resources must fit a suitable strategy (e.g., Tichy et al., 1982; Miles and Snow, 1984; Hendry and Pettigrew, 1986; Schuler, 1989).

This has important implications for the direction of SHRM. One vital point is that to a large extent the concept is an expression of intent and a definition of possibilities yet to be fully realised. This implies that there is scope to define an agenda for SHRM which fully embraces the objective of enhancing the socio-economic well-being of the employees. The second vital implication relates to the nature of SHRM itself and is the core argument of this chapter. It is argued here that flaws in the conception of 'strategy' and the treatment of 'human' might be encouraging an approach to 'resource management' which disregards the complexity of the discipline. The problematic nature of SHRM requires a reconsideration of the conception of this discipline giving particular attention to the issues of 'strategy' and 'human'. In this regard it is argued that the emergence of the discipline concerned with the management of employees comprises three key strands or themes:

- a concern with the complex and often ambiguous needs and expectations of employees, the 'humanising of work' and a concern with 'equitable' practices; Hendry and Pettigrew (1990) refer to this as *developmental-humanism*

Originally published in *Human Resource Management Journal*, 4 (4), 1994: 29–47 (abridged).

ration of the personnel function in a way that constitutes a
enhanced status for the function and the practitioners – hence

lation of managerial control through the retrenchment of a
leology – hence *managerial control*

These themes are not necessarily mutually compatible; indeed much of
the ambiguity within SHRM is attributable to the contradictions inherent
in its conception. The idea that contradictions exist within HRM is not
new. Legge (1989) has shown that these contradictions are mirrored in
fundamental contradictions within capitalism itself. It is suggested here
that in order to appreciate fully the paradoxes inherent in the conception
of SHRM, it is necessary to explore its philosophical underpinnings. In
this regard, it is necessary to locate the themes identified above within
their socio-theoretical context. We argue therefore that the organisational
imperative for performance and productivity, which draws from an
industry-based view of the firm and is informed by a rationalistic view of
human action, is encouraging a definition of 'strategic human resource
management' which ultimately gives prominence to the themes of status
and managerial control at the expense of developmental-humanism.

[. . .]

Themes in the Management of Human Resources

Developmental-humanism

This theme refers both to the concern with meeting the needs of employees
at work and to the creation of conditions and circumstances which
engender a sense of belonging. It also includes the behavioural aspects of
organisation and the effort to 'humanise' work. In a very general sense,
this organisational function which McGregor (1960) termed 'the human
side of enterprise' has served to counterbalance, and indeed to sustain the
so-called needs of capital. This is referred to here as the organisational
imperative. With its momentum of profitability, productivity and cost-
efficiency, the organisational imperative bears the ethos of the industry-
based view of the firm especially to the extent that it has been shaped by
external competitive forces.

Our purpose here is not to query the existence of the notion of the
organisational imperative, or even to consider its desirability as a rationale
for the existence of organisations; we are instead proposing that the notion
of the organisational imperative as defined above has continued to lend
itself to a definition of an agenda for organisational functioning. An
agenda based upon such criteria is likely to preclude a concern with functions and activities whose contribution to the fundamental objectives of the
organisation is considered to be either tenuous or simply indeterminate.

Where such activities are considered, their perceived centrality to the organisation's functional agenda can only be determined after these activities have been subjected to the acid test of the organisational imperative. The emergence of 'scientific management' as popularised by Frederick Taylor's time and motion studies represented one of the earliest attempts to apply the organisational imperative to the utilisation of labour. The human relations movement and welfarism are illustrative of the initial strands of the theme we refer to here as developmental-humanism. It is noteworthy, however, that at the core of these efforts (e.g., the Hawthorne studies) was the concern with productivity: human relations theorists were able to justify organisational concern with 'social man' by pointing to the favourable effect this had on productivity.

From a theoretical standpoint, it is evident that the efforts of developmental-humanism theorists to rationalise the 'humanising of work' in terms of the very criteria that they have set themselves against is not without some contradiction. However, this apparent contradiction is simply a reflection of the dominance of the organisational imperative. Furthermore, the unitarist frame of reference offers a convenient device to resolve the above contradiction and to eliminate the need to reconcile any latent or manifest differences between capital and labour. The 'matching' concept is, for example, an intuitively appealing interpretation of unitarism. When articulated in the form of the psychological contract, it seeks to formalise the notion of a congruence of interests by establishing 'mutual understanding' (e.g., Mumford, 1978). This idea is today echoed in Walton's (1985) development of a model of HRM based on 'policies of mutuality'. The 'matching' concept also finds expression in the socio-technical school of thought (e.g., Trist and Bamforth, 1951).

Another management conception in the developmental-humanism genre, the 'quality of working life', was concerned with the 'humanisation of work' as the key to devising appropriate employment and social policies (Davies and Cherns, 1975). The HRM discipline acquired further impetus in the 1980s through the so-called 'excellence' movement. The advocacy of a concern with culture and leadership style gave the theme of developmental-humanism a new lease of life. This theme has evidently had a long and chequered history, and the purpose of this discussion is to argue that this particular aspect of HRM is likely to find its significance diminished as a result of the dynamic interplay of the three themes.

Ideology and Managerial Control

This section considers the role of SHRM as a legitimatory device to reconfirm the status of HR practitioners and to reformulate managerial prerogative. SHRM thus signifies a reformulation of managerial control and an ideological form of labour regulation. Two interrelated sub-themes are identified here: the enhanced imperative for organisational performance and the rediscovery of unitarism through the search for integrative practices that are aligned to and which support the organisation's primary strategic objectives. The first sub-theme reflects the intensification of global competition, the world recession, and the emergence of a new entrepreneurialism which demands higher performance and increased productivity at all levels – from the individual to the industrial.

Traditional career advancement and compensation policies are, as a result, found to be incompatible with the increasing pressure to perform, giving rise to merit-based approaches and performance related pay, and a broad array of similar flexibility programmes. Subsequently, these changing patterns of employment and the organisation of work have been the subject of a more intensive form of financial rationalisation which constitutes both economic and ideological control. These in turn define our conception of managerial control.

Economic control for our purposes consists in subjecting organisational activities to the 'bottom line' logic, that is evaluating activities and performance on the basis of criteria that are underpinned by market considerations. While economic control has always been invoked to rationalise the organisational imperative, the emergence of contemporary HRM has accorded it a new complexion. Far from rejecting the significance of economic control, however, we are suggesting here that it is this very reality that has ensured that human resource issues remain an important part of the organisational agenda.

This agenda involves rationalistic forms of strategy analysis, for example portfolio theory, which represent a quest for management control in line with the organisational imperative. Given the use of such strategy techniques, it is clear why HRM might be seen to offer something new only to the extent that it has 'strategic value'. This discussion aims to shed some light on the issue by ascribing the appeal of the 'strategic dimension' to the very definition of what is considered strategic in the first instance, and secondly, by suggesting that such a definition is the product of the social structure found in organisations which is expressed in both ideological and rationalistic terms. We have argued that the rationalistic dimension is located within the human capital theory and orthodox economic theory.

The ideological dimension of managerial control is considered in the socio-theoretical model below. Our aim here is to indicate how the theme of managerial control features within SHRM. The ideological perspective has provided valuable insights into the nature of HRM, whereby such HRM initiatives as selection and appraisal serve as techniques of organisational control (e.g., Townley, 1989) and where HRM is a sophisticated form of managerial control (e.g., Horwitz, 1990).

HRM thus emerges as a form of labour regulation conducted in accordance with the underlying organisational imperative and brought about by a divergence in interests between managers and subordinates. It is suggested here that because the values, expectations and socio-economic objectives of managers and employees tend to be inherently asymmetrical, managers find they have to invent techniques and methods to regulate the human resource process. This regulation derives its motive force from the organisational imperative and ideological support from the denial of asymmetry of interests. As such, the unitarist framework provides the medium for the incorporation of employee and organisational interests through strategic integration.

The Quest for Status

This final theme considers whether SHRM might in some way constitute the search for an enhanced status for human resource practitioners and for the human resource function as a whole. The question is pertinent for two reasons: in the first case, this idea has found expression especially in the view that 'traditional' personnel management has declined in importance. The second reason is located within the dynamic circumstances that are the subject of the socio-theoretical model posited below.

Part of the justification for the emergence of HRM is the argument that personnel management lacked status and was merely concerned with administrative and procedural matters; that is it was operational rather than strategic (see, for example, Thurley, 1981; Manning, 1983). The concern with status has also been pinpointed by Guest (1990) who attributes it to the origins of personnel management 'as an extension of scientific management or a form of welfare management'. According to this argument, personnel management was perceived as a 'trash can' into which unwanted tasks could be dumped rather than a key element in the search for competitive advantage.

If we accept this argument, then the concept of HRM, and in particular its quest for boardroom attention, offers personnel practitioners the opportunity to emerge from the managerial doldrums. Alternatively, it may be argued that those who doubt the centrality of personnel in the 1980s may be positing just one definition of the concern of the discipline, and that the prominence of (adversarial) industrial relations in Britain for instance comprised the human resource agenda, including efforts to curtail trade union power. Furthermore, it would be erroneous to see personnel management as a uniform set of practices. Tyson and Fell (1986), for example, identify three models, 'clerk of works', 'contracts manager' and 'architect', which describe different ways in which personnel practitioners have approached their tasks. It is noteworthy that the sequential patterning of these models is not inconsistent with a hierarchy of status.

The quest for status in managerial circles is an ongoing phenomenon – functional managerial interests are not necessarily homogeneous. If the quest for status is tied to 'prestige' and 'esteem', then it is easy to see why this dynamism exists. Functional specialisms are in a constant state of disequilibrium: at various stages, different specialisms have caught the imagination of management theorists, practitioners and consultants. Financial expertise has always been fairly influential; for some time in the 1980s, information technology specialists stole the show. Are total quality management and HRM specialists the 'new corporate heroes'?

A Socio-theoretical Model

This section brings together the three themes discussed above and locates them within a framework of dynamic social forces which define organisational phenomena. This model enables us to explore the second main strand in this chapter: the socio-theoretical issues underpinning SHRM. An investigation into the basis of knowledge within SHRM might allow us to arrive at a more informed view as to what constitutes a suitable definition of strategic HRM. The following dimensions comprise the building blocks of this analytical model:

- stratification
- unitarism
- legitimacy

Figure 18.1 depicts the connection between the themes of HRM and the dimensions of the socio-theoretical model. Our proposition here is that by examining the three themes of HRM through the 'looking glass' of our socio-theoretical framework, we observe that the theme of developmental-humanism is under threat of being eclipsed by the other two through the powerful forces of the organisational imperative. The notion of SHRM resulting from this scenario contains only two elements: control and status, where the former is predominant. In simple terms, this means that the conception of SHRM that is underwritten by the organisational imperative is in danger of losing one of the fundamental strands of its *raison d'être*. An investigation of SHRM through the socio-theoretical model will enable us to ponder what forces are at play in the conception of SHRM and whether a new definition of 'strategy' is needed for the purposes of HRM and what this might look like.

Stratification

Stratification here serves as an analytical tool into the organisational dynamics that bring about the quest for status. It is suggested here that the quest for status defines a structure of managerial stratification which is at once a response to and a rationale for the organisational imperative. The functional theory of stratification (e.g., Davis and Moore, 1966) – though quite problematic itself – yields some interesting insights into the nature of the quest for status. Davis and Moore contend that:

> If the duties associated with the various positions were all equally pleasant to the human organism, all equally important to societal survival, and all equally in

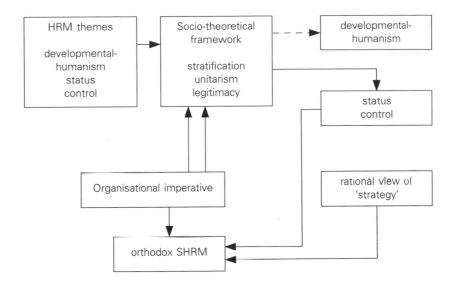

FIGURE 18.1 *The orthodox construct of* SHRM

need of the same ability or talent, it would make no difference who got into which positions, and the problem of social placement would be greatly reduced. But actually it does make a great difference who gets into which positions, not only because some positions are inherently *more agreeable* than others, but also because some require special talents or training and *some are functionally more important than others*. (Davis and Moore, 1966: 48, emphasis added)

These writers are concerned with two questions: why different positions carry different degrees of prestige, and how certain individuals get into those positions. In respect of the first question, the functional theory of stratification suggests that some positions are more important than others. This leads on to the second question and the view that society has a rational system of allocating rewards according to position, that is the possession of skills and scarcity of qualified personnel. Applying Davis and Moore's view at face value to our dynamic managerial milieu, it becomes evident that the human resource function has been treated as functionally less important than other functions such as finance, marketing, manufacturing and so forth.

We should, however, not construe the functional theory of stratification as an adequate explanatory tool. Ambiguity exists about how 'functional importance' is defined. This theory offers interesting insights into the way firms define status; however, it justifies putative inequality and ultimately becomes a self-fulfilling prophecy. Davis and Moore actually argue that:

If the rights and perquisites of different positions in a society must be unequal, then the society must be stratified, because that is precisely what stratification

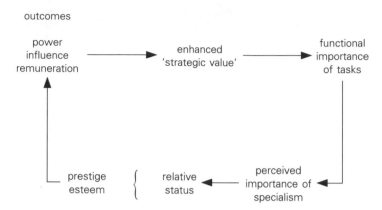

FIGURE 18.2   *The cycle of status ascription*

means. Social inequality is thus an unconsciously evolved device by which societies ensure that the most important positions are consciously filled by the most qualified persons. Hence every society, no matter how simple or complex, must differentiate persons in terms of both prestige and esteem, and must therefore possess a certain amount of institutionalized inequality. (1966: 48)

As Offe (1976) points out, this logic simply serves to legitimate privilege. The position maintained here is that managerial levels and functions are characterised by a form of stratification which the organisational culture justifies in terms of prestige and esteem: status. Status ascription is depicted in Figure 18.2. This shows what happens as managers in different functional specialisms jockey for position. HR managers have previously been unable to enjoy high prestige and its concomitant power and high remuneration because they have been unable to demonstrate the 'importance' of their functional specialism and the strategic value of human resources.

Unitarism

Our concern here is to illustrate how the notion of a 'fit' between human resource strategy and business strategy serves to revive the unitarist ethos of organisation in a way that underlines the congruence of purpose that is considered necessary for the functioning of the organisation. This section argues that the unitarist logic is enjoying a revival through the notion of strategic integration. Integration in this regard is defined in terms of establishing a 'fit', a notion that has been popularised by the 'matching' school of SHRM (e.g., Fombrun et al., 1984). Guest (1987) builds on this concept by advocating the strengthening of strategic planning through the integration of human resources into the corporate strategy, as well as the internal coherence of HR policies. In Boxall's (1992) evaluation, the primary emphasis here is on the view that choices in HRM should be governed by 'product market logic', that is HR strategy is often determined by the product market.

The re-working of the unitarist ethos in terms of strategic integration thus permits the rationalisation of human resource activities on the basis of the organisational imperative. This imperative overrides the interests of 'human resources', casts people in a reactive role and confers legitimacy on the pre-eminence of organisational functioning. The industry-based perspective leads managers to react to market forces through the adoption of policies that ensure tighter control over the labour process. In more politically palatable terms, this process involves the internal coherence of HRM policies and practices, and their 'integration' into the strategic process. This integration and 'matching' process is able to achieve the notion of congruence and conceal the asymmetry of interests. Ultimately, therefore, the use of techniques and methods to regulate the human resource management process becomes a matter of political expediency.

Legitimacy

The theme of control necessarily raises the question of the legitimacy of this control. We observed above that the incongruity of interests in organisations necessitates the adoption of labour regulation strategies in a way that is consistent with the organisational imperative. In this section we argue that in order to appreciate the socio-theoretical underpinnings of these strategies we must examine their legitimacy – and the way legitimacy is sought – because such strategies define and nurture power and exchange relations in organisational scenarios which are characterised by diversity of interests.

The Weberian conception of 'rational authority' provides interesting insights into the meaning of 'legitimation' at the sociological level. However, this is problematic in respect of the significance imputed to rationality itself and the belief in legality (see, for example, Habermas, 1976). For our purposes, the relevance of 'legitimacy' in the exercise of control exists at two levels: the management–labour interface and the HR *vis-à-vis* other managerial functions. This scenario is depicted in Figure 18.3.

Level 1 relates to the management–employee interface and its mediation through the definition of power and authority. At this level, the question of legitimacy arises in so far as management ideologies serve to support and legitimate authority (e.g., Bendix, 1966; Anthony, 1977). Level 2 has been elaborated under the theme of status and the dynamic jockeying for position in management circles. Legitimacy at this level has to do with the distribution of resources and the relative perceived 'importance' of the roles played by the managers. Figure 18.4 depicts how human resource specialists are seeking a more enhanced role for themselves and a more critical role for HRM. The organisational imperative cuts across these diverse functions and provides an overriding rationale of what is the accepted practice and

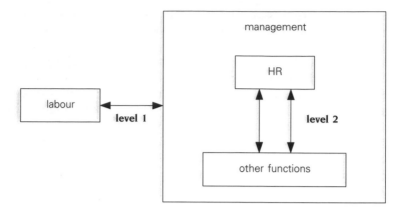

FIGURE 18.3   A *legitimacy struggle at two levels*

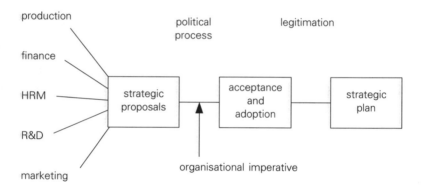

FIGURE 18.4   *Legitimation through acceptance*

how authority is conferred differentially on the constituents of the management functions. Two important questions arise from this scenario: how is the organisational agenda drawn up?; and who participates in the exercise? The first question refers to the processual, dynamic strategy formulation exercise which is reflected in a typical 'organisation chart'.

The second question is more problematic but deceptively straightforward. Decision making is a manifestly political exercise (e.g., Wildavsky, 1964; Pettigrew, 1973; Pfeffer, 1981; Kakabadse, 1983). The weight of the contributions of senior managers is a function of many factors, including personality, the perceived importance of their functional domains, and so forth. The final decision is arrived at through persuasion and bargaining, involving concessions and compromise. Eventually, the adoption of the strategy, whether by consensus or fiat, implies acceptance. The strategy therefore acquires legitimacy at management level through acceptance and adoption. In analysing the legitimation of power in social settings, Pfeffer

(1981) argues that activities which are accepted and expected within a context are said to be legitimate within that context.

The political process in strategy formulation involves negotiations regarding the distribution of resources. The participation of HRM specialists in strategy formulation, where this happens, represents a plea for the acceptance of a human resource agenda. Since strategy formulation and implementation eventually amount to a budgetary process – that is resource allocation – acceptance of any functional, business or divisional agenda or proposal is likely to depend on expected economic contribution. SHRM continues to strive to meet criteria determined on the basis of the organisational imperative, that is to be accepted as an important organisational function. This is exemplified in 'human resource accounting' (e.g., Flamholtz, 1985) which was the ultimate quest for legitimacy through quantification. Thus we find that the unseen, albeit ubiquitous, organisational imperative lies at the bottom of the entire exercise of seeking legitimation for SHRM. This is illustrated in Figure 18.4.

Toward a New Research Paradigm for Scripting SHRM

In this section we advance the argument that given the relatively embryonic nature of SHRM, there is wide scope to set a clear agenda and sense of direction for this concept before it crystallises into a rigid structure of propositions, misconceptions and practices. Our position in this regard constitutes a preliminary stage in what we see as a much more detailed reformulation of the concept of SHRM, the need for which has been identified in this chapter. Clearly, more research is needed to determine how the differences in perspectives as well as the contradictions inherent in the constituent elements and objectives of the variants of SHRM can be reconciled.

An important starting point is the concept of strategy itself, which we have observed to be problematic in respect of its application to the management of people. SHRM does not simply consist of 'integrating' the human resource dimension into the business strategic planning process. Such a position begs the question: what does it mean to integrate? Boxall (1992) suggests that in developing credible analytical frameworks, the relationship between strategic management and HRM should be explored as extensively as possible. It is often the case, however, that the viability of SHRM is mediated by short-term horizons and the degree to which strategic management is itself evident (Kamoche, 1992).

We need to have a clear understanding of what strategic management and SHRM really mean, and to ensure that the relationship between them is indeed tenable on socio-theoretical grounds. We have observed above that the orthodox definition which draws from economic theory and is underpinned by an assumption of rational man is unlikely to capture the essence of human nature in all its diverse manifestations.

Therefore efforts to apply the tools and techniques that have worked well for other resources to human resources are likely to create a credibility problem. We suggest that a definition or interpretation of 'strategy' for the purposes of SHRM might draw from a conception of a resource-based view of the firm as opposed to the industry-based view which engenders the dominant notion we have referred to as the organisational imperative. This concept sees the firm as a collection of resources and capabilities that play a vital role in a firm's profitability (see, for example, Wernerfelt, 1984; Barney, 1991; Conner, 1991; Amit and Schoemaker, 1993). When these resources and capabilities are rare, appropriable, non-substitutable and difficult to imitate, they become a potential source of sustained competitive advantage.

These conditions apply to human resources, making the resource-based view particularly relevant to the analysis of SHRM (Kamoche, 1993; Wright et al., 1994). This emergent research paradigm should enable us to take account of the nature of human resources by focusing on the subjectivity, ambiguity and creativity that characterise HRM. The complexity of human resources is found within the firm's socio-historical circumstances which define the values and management styles as well as the day-to-day routines and policies relating to training, socialisation, and so forth. Similarly, this research paradigm emphasises that the skills of employees are conceived of as a vital resource, which the firm is able to build upon rather than simply to exploit, rationally and ideologically. Therefore the full potential of HRM can be realised and can be a key determinant in a firm's performance, without the a priori imposition of the organisational imperative. Such an approach to the management of employees which is cognizant of the diversity and complexity of human nature and is unfettered by an organisational imperative could bring us closer to a conception of strategy whereby the theme of developmental-humanism is at the heart of strategic human resource management.

Conclusion

This chapter has sought to characterise and examine critically the dynamic social circumstances as well as the socio-theoretical issues underpinning the evolution of strategic HRM. It has identified three strands that constitute the ethos and practice of HRM: developmental-humanism, status, and control. It has argued that the emergent view of SHRM is in danger of losing the human component due to the dominance of organisational forces – the organisational imperative – which have defined the organisational agenda and are expressed in rationalistic and ideological terms.

The organisational imperative has in turn moulded a view of strategy which ignores the complexity of human nature and is therefore largely inappropriate in the management of employees. This chapter has suggested, therefore, that by giving careful attention to the definition of strategy and the nature of human resources, recognising the socio-theoretical motive forces behind managerial action, and shifting the level of analysis from industry to resource, we might arrive at a much more meaningful rapprochement of strategic management and human resource management.

References

Amit, R. and Schoemaker, P.J.H. (1993) 'Strategic assets and organizational rent', *Strategic Management Journal*, 14: 33–46.

Anthony, P.D. (1977) *The Ideology of Work*. London: Tavistock.

Barney, J.B. (1991) 'Firm resources and sustained competitive advantage', *Journal of Management*, 17 (1): 99–120.

Beer, M., Spector, B., Lawrence, P., Mills, D. and Walton, R.E. (1985) *Managing Human Assets*. New York: The Free Press.

Bendix, R. (1966) *Work and Authority in Industry*. New York: John Wiley.

Boxall, P.F. (1992) 'Strategic human resource management: beginnings of a new theoretical sophistication?', *Human Resource Management Journal*, 2 (3): 60–79.

Conner, K.R. (1991) 'A historical comparison of resource-based theory and five schools of thought within industrial organization economics', *Journal of Management*, 17 (1): 121–54.

Davies, L.E. and Cherns, A.B. (eds) (1975) *The Quality of Working Life* (Vols 1 & 2). New York: The Free Press.

Davis, K. and Moore, W.E. (1966) 'Some principles of stratification', in R. Bendix and S.M. Lipset (eds), *Class, Status and Power*. London: Routledge and Kegan Paul.

Flamholtz, E. (1985) *Human Resource Accounting*. San Francisco: Jossey-Bass.

Fombrun, C., Tichy, N.M. and Devanna, M.A. (1984) *Strategic Human Resource Management*. Chichester: Wiley.

Guest, D. (1987) 'Human resource management and industrial relations', *Journal of Management Studies*, 24 (5): 503–21.

Guest, D. (1990) 'Human resource management and the American Dream', *Journal of Management Studies*, 27 (4): 377–97.

Habermas, J. (1976) *Legitimation Crisis*. London: Heinemann.

Hendry, C. and Pettigrew, A. (1986) 'The practice of strategic human resource management', *Personnel Review*, 15 (3): 3–8.

Hendry, C. and Pettigrew, A. (1990) 'Human resources management: an agenda for the 1990s', *International Journal of Human Resource Management*, 1 (1): 17–43.

Horwitz, F.M. (1990) 'HRM: an ideological perspective', *Personnel Review*, 19 (2): 10–15.

Kakabadse, A. (1983) *The Politics of Management*. Aldershot: Gower.

Kamoche, K. (1992) 'HRM: an assessment of the Kenyan Case', *International Journal of Human Resource Management*, 3 (3): 497–521.

Kamoche, K. (1993) 'Strategic human resource management within a resource-capability view of the firm'. Working Paper, Birmingham University Business School.

Legge, K. (1989) 'Human resource management: a critical analysis', in J. Storey (ed.), *New Perspectives on Human Resource Management*. London: Routledge.

McGregor, D. (1960) *The Human Side of Enterprise*. New York: McGraw-Hill.

Manning, K. (1983) 'The rise and fall of personnel management', *Management Today*, March: 74–7.

Miles, R. and Snow, C. (1984) 'Designing strategic human resource systems', *Organizational Dynamics*, 12: 36–52.

Mumford, E. (1978) 'Job satisfaction: a method of analysis', in K. Legge and E. Mumford (eds), *Designing Organisations for Satisfaction and Efficiency*. Farnborough: Gower.

Offe, C. (1976) *Industry and Inequality: The Achievement Principle in Work and Social Status*. London: Edward Arnold.

Pettigrew, A. (1973) *The Politics of Organizational Decision Making*. London: Tavistock.

Pfeffer, J. (1981) *Power in Organisations*. London: Pitman.

Schuler, R.S. (1989) 'Strategic human resource management and industrial relations', *Human Relations*, 42 (2): 157–84.

Schuler, R.S. (1992) 'Strategic human resource management: linking people with the strategic needs of business', *Organizational Dynamics*, 21 (1): 18–32.

Schuler, R.S. and MacMillan, I.C. (1984) 'Gaining competitive advantage through human resource management practice', *Human Resource Management*, 23 (3): 241–55.

Thurley, K. (1981) 'Personnel management in the UK: a case for urgent treatment?', *Personnel Management*, August: 24–8.

Tichy, N.M., Fombrun, C.J. and Devanna, M.A. (1982) 'Strategic human resources management', *Sloan Management Review*, Winter: 47–61.

Townley, B. (1989) 'Selection and appraisal: reconsidering social relations?', in J. Storey (ed.), *New Perspectives on Human Resource Management*. London: Routledge.

Trist, E.L. and Bamforth, K.W. (1951) 'Some social and psychological consequences of the Longwall Method of goal getting', *Human Relations*, 4 (1): 3–38.

Tyson, S. and Fell, A. (1986) *Evaluating the Personnel Function*. London: Hutchinson.

Walton, R.E. (1985) 'From control to commitment in the workplace', *Harvard Business Review*, March–April: 77–84.

Wernerfelt, B. (1984) 'A resource-based view of the firm', *Strategic Management Journal*, 5: 171–80.

Wildavsky, A. (1964) *The Politics of the Budgetary Process*. Boston, MA: Little, Brown.

Wright, P.M., McMahan, G.C. and McWilliams, A. (1994) 'Human resource management and sustained competitive advantage', *International Journal of Human Resource Management*, 5 (2): 301–26.

19   Reform as Routine

Nils Brunsson and Johan P. Olsen

Administrative reforms are often presented as dramatic, unique changes in organizations. In this chapter we argue that reform can be regarded as an aspect of organizational stability rather than of organizational change. Reforms are common in large, modern organizations; reform is often a standard, recurring activity. Reforms are routines rather than interruptions in organizational life. Many studies claim that reforms are difficult to implement. We argue that it is fairly easy to initiate reforms. Indeed, the very ease with which reforms can be launched may be one of the reasons why so few are completed. Reformers often claim that reform is necessary to adapt the organization to important changes in its environment. We argue that both fairly mundane, common and stable aspects of internal organizational life and various stable and common features of organizational environments can also produce reforms. One of these factors is reform itself: reforms tend to generate reforms.

There are four common basic attributes of administrative reforms which, together with certain organizational characteristics discussed below, aid the introduction and pursuit of reforms in organizations. The first is simplicity and clarity: the ideas proposed in the reform are less complicated and more clear-cut than most organization members consider the current organizational practices to be. Reform ideas consist of principles rather than detailed descriptions, theories rather than perceptions, that is reforms present ordered ideas which cannot encompass all the complexity of the real world, but which therefore seem more clear than reality. Secondly, reforms are normative: they represent attempts to bring order into a chaotic reality rather than to report upon it. Thirdly, reforms tend to be one-sided: each reform invokes a single set of consistent values and perceptions of the world, in contrast to organizational practices which often have to deal with inconsistent values and perceptions. A fourth characteristic of reform is future-orientation: a reform is a process of idea elaboration, persuasion and implementation rather than an immediate action, so it cannot be expected to produce instant results. Instead it

---

Originally published in Nils Brunsson and Johan P. Olsen (1993) *The Reforming Organization*. London: Routledge. pp. 33–47 (abridged).

promises future benefits, sometimes when implementation has been completed and sometimes much later.

Since reforms contain ideas concerning both problems and solutions, they are dependent upon an adequate supply of both. That supply may support more reforms if each problem can be addressed and each solution can be used several times, which is made possible by what we call organizational forgetfulness. The supply of problems, solutions and forgetfulness in organizations is discussed below.

The Supply of Problems and Solutions

Reforms benefit from problems. The perception of problems in the current functioning of an organization can initiate the search for reforms and offer a strong incentive for attempts to implement them, as well as providing arguments to convince those whose support is needed.

There tends to be an ample supply of perceived problems in modern organizations. A changing or malevolent environment can generate many problems, but there are also many internal sources. Administrative reforms can be proposed to remedy almost any such problem, including low profitability, increasing competition or poor management. Administrative reform, it can be argued, will make the organization more efficient, more profitable and more market-oriented, or it will make management perform better. But administrative reform is regarded in particular as the obvious response when an organization's problems are perceived as being administrative or directly concerned with its internal functioning. There is an ample supply of administrative problems in modern organizations.

A major source of administrative problems is the tension between the way an organization is presented and the way in which it actually works (Brunsson, 1989). When presenting their organizations to the outside world, organizational leaders tend to stress unity, coherence, consistency, action and control. The organizations are portrayed as working towards a single goal or a set of consistent goals, as systems for producing action in accordance with these goals, which are maintained by managements' control over people and action at the lower organizational level.

However, organizations tend not to live up to these descriptions. The literature describing actual organizational processes tells us that organizations are commonly characterized by a higher degree of inconsistency, by greater difficulty in mobilizing action, and by a lesser degree of top-down control than is ever described in organizational presentations or desired by management. But the tension between presentations and intentions on the one hand and experiences of actual behaviour on the other provides an incentive for reform.

Even in organizations which achieve successful results, the tension between presentable ideas and actual behaviour may be strong. Thus even in successful organizations there can be widespread feeling that the organization is not working as it should, and that reforms are needed. Success may depend on an organization's capacity to adapt rapidly to changing circumstances in its environment, that is on its flexibility. But it has been suggested that organizational characteristics which lead to flexibility may also inhibit opportunities for manipulating the organization in a specific direction: 'changefulness' is not the same as 'changeability' (Brunsson, 1985).

Problems are a perceptual category. Some observers may perceive a situation as problematic, others not. Thus reformers may try to influence other people's perceptions of today's reality. But it may be easier to refer problems to an area in which we are not troubled by knowledge, namely the future. The future is especially important if things are going well now, so well-functioning, successful organizations need it more than others. The future provides particularly good arguments for reforms since reforms concern the future, not the present.

An organization's supply of problems is threatened in so far as it solves the problems. Therefore, the supply benefits from problems that cannot be solved. Organizations grapple with many problems that are insoluble in practice. These include those generated by conflicting demands, when it is impossible in practical terms to find any balance that could readily be regarded as exactly the right one. Any solution concerning these opposing elements is open to criticism for failing to satisfy one or the other of the needs sufficiently – or indeed both. For instance, centralized organizations tend to generate complaints about insufficient consideration to local knowledge and local needs for specialization and adaptation, while decentralized organizations discover that they are not paying enough attention to the benefits of co-ordination and standardization.

Solutions

Problems are not in themselves enough to trigger administrative reforms. A supply of ideas for solutions is also needed: more specifically, ideas for administrative solutions which deal with organizational structures, processes and ideologies, and which differ from the current solutions. Solutions can exert an attraction on reformers and reformees. Like problems, solutions can provide incentives to reform. And like problems, solutions can be produced by those who wish to pursue reforms, though the task of the reformers is made easier if there is a supply of more or less ready-made solutions.

Organizational scholarship is an important source of solutions. There are many different theories and ideas from Fayol (1916) onwards which argue that organizational form is important to management control and performance, and which also specify the forms that are best in different situations. Such theories provide both ideas for reform and elaborate supporting arguments.

But in order to initiate reforms, a supply of solutions is not in itself enough. The solutions must also appear to be better than those currently in use. It is not difficult to find these better solutions when designing reforms: current practice seldom appears as attractive as novel solutions; unlike current solutions, reforms promise to overcome both current and future problems. And if current practices are rather one-sided owing to an earlier one-sided reform, then a new, equally one-sided but reverse reform may seem very promising. If current organizational practices are perceived as highly complex, inconsistent and difficult to understand, reform can offer greater simplicity and consistency and can be much easier to understand. The proposed reform solutions may bring the organization closer to the presentation model of the organization, to the way in which it is presented by its management and the way people think organizations should be. If we set a simple, clear and good reform idea against our knowledge of the current situation with all its slack, *ad hoc* solutions, its ambiguities, inconsistencies, conflicts, compromises and complex relationships, then there is a good chance that the proposed solution will be more attractive. Simple principles can more easily attract enthusiasm and support than can complex descriptions of reality.

For reforms to occur, it is important not only that solutions exist and that they are seen as improvements on current practices, but also that they exist in considerable diversity. If there were only one perfect solution to an administrative problem, there would be no need for reform once that solution had been installed.

A diversity of solutions is provided in several ways. Fashion, as to both appropriate solutions and problems, is something that both reduces and increases the variety of available solutions. Fashion reduces the number of acceptable problems and solutions at any one time, but over time it also fosters diversity and provides a strong incentive to vary the targeted problems and proposed solutions. The existence of strong fashions guarantees that the practices of an organization will at least sometimes appear old-fashioned and in need of reform.

Management consultants play their part in helping to spread fashions. They also provide some variety within particular fashionable practices. As one of their means of competition is to offer slightly different solutions, they will effectively create variety in the supply of both solutions and problems. To improve their competitiveness, less successful consultants at least may seek to update their product by defining new solutions. Administrative experts within organizations can assume a role similar to that of management consultants; their task is to reform.

The theories that describe the causal effects of organizational form on control and performance have two characteristics that are important in providing diversity: they do not agree with one another and they are not entirely true. Since they disagree, an individual organization can draw on different theories at different times which can thus motivate many reforms. Since empirically no conclusive relationship can be proven between organizational form on the one hand and control and performance on the other, we find successful organizations with different organizational forms. Consequently, if an organization wants to imitate other successful organizations, it can usually find a number of alternative solutions to choose from.

Problems and Solutions in Institutional Environments

If the only driving force behind reforms was the urge to improve performance, we would risk a shortage of solutions. We generally know very little about the relationship between organizational form and performance; indeed there may often be little or no relationship. And if there was a close relation between forms and results, there would sometimes be few other organizations to learn from: the relation between forms and results would probably be specific for organizations with similar products, but organizations with similar products sometimes think of themselves as competitors and therefore have reason to conceal their forms that are successful.

Reform is far easier if ready-made standardized and general solutions are available, norms which directly prescribe appropriate forms for all, or a class of organizations. The supplies of both problems and solutions increase when organizational structures, processes and ideologies not only serve as means for improving performance but also take on independent values for the organizations' environments, and thus for organizations themselves. Even effective organizations with a consistently high demand for their products may find themselves in situations in which their structures, processes and ideologies fall foul of regulations or are seen as unjust, irrational or out of date.

General and ready-made norms about proper organizational forms free reformers from the need to find the most suitable forms for their specific organizations. they imitate rather than innovate. Reformers conform to established norms or imitate other organizations which maintain or redefine norms. The task of identifying new norms to imitate is made easy by the eagerness of other organizations to show off their forms. Institutional environments also create a supply of problems: there are widely held beliefs about what problems organizations have or should have; fashionable problems are suited to the solutions that are in fashion.

In short, it is not necessary to brood about the effects of new forms because it is not the effects which make a reform important. Rather, the reform is important in itself: it is not the means to an end, but has a value of its own. Sometimes the consequences are considered in conjunction with forms, but often they are assumed to be standardized effects which automatically result from the form. They provide arguments for the reform. For example, decentralization may be embarked upon to achieve fuller market adaptation, but rarely is anyone given the task of evaluating whether reformed organizations have actually achieved greater market adaptation. Appropriate problems, solutions and effects tend to come in prefabricated packages.

The organizational forms presented externally by organizations are often not those which govern their practices or 'inner life': the external image may become decoupled from internal operations. This decoupling means that it is easier to reform the structures, processes and ideologies intended for external use, since it reduces the risk that changes will affect operations. If there is a wide gap between external and internal practices, even the most radical reforms need not disturb internal operations. Thus, reformers need not feel intimidated by the possibility that they might disrupt or undermine the productive capacity of the organization. Moreover, such decoupling facilitates not only initiation but also other stages of reform: if there is no need to consider the demands created by actual operations, it is easier to determine the content of reforms; and if operations will not particularly be affected by reforms, they are less likely to meet opposition from operational departments. Introducing a new organizational structure in a well-decoupled organization is merely a matter of redrawing the organizational chart, which need not take long.

Inconsistent Norms

The norms and demands confronted by organizations are sometimes difficult or impossible to reconcile one with another as they may be mutually contradictory or inconsistent. There may be logical, technical or resource reasons for this inconsistency. There may be concomitant norms stating that organizations are to be centralized and demanding that organizations are to be decentralized. Some groups may demand democratic management processes and others authoritarian ones. It may be technically impossible to reconcile customers' preferences with norms for environmental protection. And there may not be enough money available to satisfy all the groups that call upon an organization for financial contributions.

Inconsistent norms are difficult to deal with; it can be difficult to conform to them simultaneously, and they are difficult to reconcile with co-ordinated action. Organizations often react to inconsistent norms by reflecting these inconsistencies in their structures, processes and ideologies, which then also become inconsistent. Inconsistent norms produce conflict structures, problem-oriented processes and hypocrisy (Brunsson, 1989). If it is important to reflect inconsistencies, conflict rather than consensus becomes the basis of organizational structure, and organizations will strive to recruit people who claim not to share the norms, values and opinions held by other members of the organization. Conflict is the structuring principle of parliaments, for instance, or of boards of directors on which trade unions are represented to meet the requirements of industrial democracy.

Inconsistent norms make it difficult to find solutions which satisfy everyone: solutions always run the risk of benefiting one party more than another. Many specific issues become problems simply because there are inconsistent norms involved. Discussions of the different aspects of a problem reflect different opinions. Organizations that confront inconsistent norms both have reasons to deal with difficult problems and are often forced to do so.

Organizations may also reflect norms ideologically, by producing talk and by taking decisions that are consistent with the norms. Inconsistent norms may be reflected in contradictory talk and decisions or by systematically constructing inconsistencies between talk, decisions and action, that is by producing hypocrisy. In such instances, talk may accord with one group of norms, decisions with another, and actions with yet a third. For instance, claiming that one of their ambitions is to save the environment is particularly important for a business or party whose operations create environmental problems.

When organizations respond to inconsistent norms with conflict, problem-orientation and hypocrisy, new reasons to reform arise. All these phenomena serve to uphold the belief that there is something better than the *status quo*, and satisfaction is avoided. It becomes clear that it is possible to do things differently or that they should be done differently; there are opponents who can point out that there are other solutions than the prevailing ones; they can claim that the existing problems should be solved; and they can argue that hypocrisy should be avoided – that promises should be kept, and that one should practise what one preaches. But as long as contradictory demands are being made on an organization, it will be impossible to banish hypocrisy: if the organization acts in a new way, it will encounter criticisms from elsewhere and will need to talk in accordance with such criticisms to compensate for its new action. All of this can create a great deal of frustration, and as it helps neither to implement new actions nor to replace management, it is easy to blame the organizational form. The demand for administrative reform will therefore be close at hand.

Conflict, problem-orientation and hypocrisy are also qualities which conflict particularly sharply with established notions of how organizations should function. This gives rise to powerful incentives to attempt reforms aiming towards greater consensus, action-orientation and consistency. But such reforms cannot succeed without posing threats to the legitimacy of the organization in an environment with inconsistent norms, and thus there will be continuous reform proposals and attempted reforms.

The Supply of Organizational Forgetfulness

Administrative reforms are often repetitions of earlier reforms. The ideas they contain may be roughly the same as in the previous reform, perhaps because the previous reform did not close the gap between what was desired and what was achieved, between aspiration level and practice, and was therefore deemed unsuccessful. The reform process may also be repetitive because it is oscillatory. The ideas may be the reverse of those contained in the previous reform but identical to those of an earlier reform, whose shortcomings the most recent reform was designed to correct.

Such repetitions may inhibit the initiation and pursuit of reforms. Proposing to reform an organization in the same way as on a previous occasion may encounter criticism: 'since we have to do it again, the earlier reform obviously did not succeed; and if the earlier reform did not succeed why should this one?' There may even be cynics in the organization who have experienced so many reforms that they have become sceptical about the very idea of reform itself as a means of solving problems or improving performance.

So reforms are facilitated not by learning but by forgetfulness, by mechanisms that cause the organization to forget previous reforms or at least those of a similar content. Reformers need a high degree of forgetfulness to avoid uncertainty as to whether their proposed reform is a good one. Forgetfulness also helps people to accept reforms. Reforms focus interest on the future rather than the present. Forgetfulness ensures that experience will not interfere with reform: it prevents the past from disturbing the future.

There are a number of mechanisms promoting such organizational forgetfulness, so clearing the path to reform. One such factor is high personnel turnover. Another is change among top management. A third is the use of management consultants: if they are fresh to an organization, consultants can easily repeat previous mistakes. Management consultants are generally expert at introducing reforms, but they are also normally too busy and too expensive to be involved in implementing them fully. When consultants are used in this way, they are systematically unlikely to learn that their reforms are not implemented and do not give the intended effects. They are therefore in a particularly good position for initiating and pursuing the same reform in new organizations with great enthusiasm and drive. Forgetfulness is their key competence.

Reforms Generate Reforms

Up to this point, we have argued that administrative reforms benefit from problems, solutions and forgetfulness, and that there tends to be a plentiful supply of these resources in modern organizations. Thus reforms tend to become common, indeed so common that in many organizations they virtually become routine. One further explanation of the frequency of reform is that reforms tend to generate new reforms. Reforms often result from previous reforms, and the outcome of reforms is often new reforms: reforms tend to be self-referential. The reason for this is that reforms tend to increase the supply of solutions, problems and forgetfulness.

Reforms may sometimes solve problems, but they may also trigger problems. This is true even of successful reforms. The successful implementation of a one-sided reform may well solve a particular problem while at the same time creating, reinforcing or drawing attention to other problems at which it was not aimed. For instance, successfully implemented reforms geared towards industrial democracy could produce new reforms aimed at increasing efficiency. Reform attempts aimed at addressing the insoluble problems mentioned above provide another set of examples: decentralizing a centralized organization, for instance, is a way of ensuring that the benefits of centralization will be discovered and sooner or later attended to. Reforms may therefore leave the organization oscillating between different solutions.

Reforms can also generate demands for further reforms aimed at the same problems and propagating the same solutions. This is the case when reforms generate more hope that they in fact fulfil, or even which they could ever fulfil. Reforms may be more productive in raising levels of aspiration than in achieving improvements. Reforms focus attention on the problems to be solved, and the process of promoting and trying to implement a reform can help to raise levels of aspiration, making people more eager to find solutions and to adopt higher standards about the kind of solutions they are prepared to accept. At the same time, it is often difficult to implement reforms. Or, even if one is implemented, in retrospect it may not be perceived as having been ambitious enough. For instance, a reform intended to promote democracy may be launched simply because the organization is extremely undemocratic. But that reform may lead to a considerably higher and more widespread appreciation of a preference for democracy, but only to a moderate increase in the actual level of democracy, thus making the lack of democracy and the need for further reform all the more evident.

In addition, reformers tend systematically to oversell what a reform can actually achieve. If overselling is an efficient technique in the acceptance and implementation of reforms, we can expect that reforms which have been accepted and implemented will also have been heavily oversold. And overselling may in turn help to raise aspiration levels even further.

Finally, reform constitutes a forgetfulness mechanism in itself. Reforms tend to be viewed very differently before and after the event, *ex ante* and *ex post*. At best, a reform proposal consists of a description of an expected future reality. Descriptions need to be simplified; and, as we have already noted, the descriptions associated with reforms tend to be greatly simplified. Reforms are often launched and sold in organizations mainly in the form of attractive principles. Simplicity *ex ante*, as mentioned above, is an important element in determining the likelihood of a reform being accepted. Reality *ex post*, when the reform has been implemented, tends not to be quite so simple. Opinions about the present are generally more complex than opinions about the future. Moreover, attempts to apply the simple principles to organizational realities in the course of reforms are usually characterized by a growing degree of complexity. As the level of complexity increases, difficulties, inconsistencies, conflicts and 'practical' problems become more evident. Attempts at implementing reforms tend to highlight these difficulties by making it obvious that the original ideas, which once seemed so attractive, no longer appear to be so simple, clear or precise; nor are they detailed enough for practical purposes, while making them practicable also makes them much less beautiful.

So just as comparison with today's chaotic reality makes the simple principles of a reform attractive, a reform which we have tried to implement will become less attractive than a reform that is new and still untried. Reforms tend not to deliver what they promise, but their promises are so good that people are easily persuaded to try again. As reforms lose their appeal over time, they become easy victims of proposals for new reforms.

So reforms can themselves be important suppliers of problems, solutions and forgetfulness, and thereby become important causes of new reforms. Reforms are both causes and effects of reforms. Reforms trigger new reforms, making the reform process a stable state.

Avoiding Reform

Reforms can be perceived as both positive and negative, from the point of view of both organizational insiders and external observers and stakeholders. They can be seen as important in encouraging repentance, hope and a tolerance of failure in a world where standards are and should be higher than it is possible to achieve in practice. They can also be regarded as futile and expensive attempts to achieve unrealistic goals.

Organizational legitimacy and survival may benefit from reforms, from maintaining belief in a future better than the present. If customers, financial institutions, state agencies or employees find the organization's present performance unsatisfactory, they may be persuaded not to withdraw their support by a reform that promises future improvement. But reforms are not a risk-free strategy from the point of view of organizational survival. We have argued here that reforms tend to be easy to initiate but more difficult to implement, so that they can focus attention on problems and increase levels of aspiration to a greater extent than improving performance. The main outcome is then that a reform reinforces the very perception of failure that was the initial reason for launching the reform. And since reforms are often directed to particularly problematic areas, they risk giving heightened importance to those very goals that an organization has greatest difficulty in achieving. While previous to a reform it might have been argued that the value to which the reform was geared was not very important or relevant to the organization, after the reform it may become an important criterion of evaluation. In some cases this can have a lethal effect on the organization.

In this way the reform of individual organizations may be a way of introducing more modern forms, not by changing the organizations undergoing reform but by bringing a quicker demise to those which cannot meet modern standards, thus hastening the adoption of modern forms in the total population of organizations. From the point of view of the individual organization there is reason to avoid these effects, if survival is considered more important than the meeting of high standards.

Strategies against Reforms

Organizations thus have reason not only to promote but also to avoid administrative reforms. The argument so far should encourage reformers: it seems to be fairly easy to initiate reforms. The task of those wanting to avoid reforms is more difficult, but there are a variety of threats to reform that can form the basis of their strategies. For instance, if problems or solutions or forgetfulness are lacking, reform is less likely.

It is difficult to imagine that a lack of problems could commonly form an obstacle to reforms in large organizations. However, one type of problem could actually block reform, namely problems that are acute. Since reforms take some time, they are more difficult to present as solutions to a threat of bankruptcy today than as solutions to future threat.

Reforms are threatened not only by a lack of problems, but also by alternative ways of responding to problems. Reforms imply a special approach to problems. They are aimed at action, changing and problem-solving. Problems should be solved by doing something about them, that is changing the situation so that problems disappear. Another way of reacting to problems is to ignore them. Problems may also be dealt with by increasing organizational slack (Cyert and March, 1963): instead of trying to solve problems by means of administrative reforms, an organization can try to increase its resources, perhaps by turning to more profitable products or improving its marketing.

Another way of dealing with problems is to administrate them, to live with them. People can analyse and discuss the problems without trying to find solutions in practice. Ignoring problems is difficult for a weak management unable to resist demands from lower levels of the organization for solutions to their problems. Living with problems instead of solving them is easier in organizations such as parliaments, which are judged more for their ability to provide a discussion of different opinions than for undertaking action.

A shortage of solutions may be experienced by a modern organization which has already introduced the latest structures, processes and ideologies. It is generally more difficult for innovators to find new solutions than it is for imitators. And if people have more than superficial knowledge of the solutions applied in other organizations, they may find themselves in shortage of real solutions: a deep understanding of the detailed, practical problems involved in implementing fashionable solutions, as well as too much experience with their results, tends to make these solutions less attractive. People with such knowledge may become reluctant to propose or accept available reforms. Learning about others' reforms has similar effects as does learning about one's own.

If reforms can be facilitated by the mechanisms of organizational forgetfulness, they can also be prevented by the mechanisms of organizational learning. Efforts to keep an established management in power, avoiding new recruitment and refraining from the use of external people like consultants are all possible strategies for avoiding reform.

If reforms contribute to a tolerance of present failure and hope for a better future, they can also expect competition from other methods of achieving these things. One such method is to emphasize the good intentions of an organization or its management, at the expense of descriptions of results. Another method is to emphasize the future rather than the past, that is to promise improvement (Brunsson, 1989). Goals describe both intentions and the future, and they can therefore produce both hope and tolerance. But all these methods may also lead to a demand for reform. Failure to fulfil intentions and goals is often blamed on administrative problems, and administrative problems in their turn provide arguments for administrative reform. And one way of increasing the credibility of references to a better future is to launch some reforms.

If reforms are much more attractive *ex ante* than *ex post*, attempts at implementing them will undermine their initial support. A relatively secure phase in the reform process is at the outset of implementing a reform, when it still looks promising. If reforms can remain at the stage where they have just been accepted but are still far from final implementation, they can survive for a long time. But if serious attempts are made to implement a reform, a stage may be reached where it is clear that the reform solution will not be so beautiful in practice, perhaps not even any better than the current practice. And if support falls off, perhaps the reform can be stopped.

So, paradoxically, attempts at implementing a specific reform may halt it. However, as we have seen, implementation can easily lead to a further reform with the same – or perhaps the opposite – characteristics. The same effect can arise from another important threat to reform: a proposal for another reform. Organizations cannot be expected to pursue several reforms in the same area at the same time. Proposing a reform to halt an existing one is most effective when the existing reform is at a weak stage in its life, when it has just been proposed and has not yet acquired too great a degree of commitment, or when it has gone far enough on the way to implementation for its less attractive *ex post* characteristics to have been revealed. It is then all too likely to be stopped by the proposal of a new reform presented in the more attractive *ex ante* version. Promising a new reform may even be the only practical way of halting one already under way.

Important strategies for anyone trying to stop reforms thus include providing arguments that easily lead to new reforms; further attempts to implement existing reforms; and proposing new reforms. The opponents of the reform following these strategies become reformers themselves! Even if it may be possible to put a stop to single reforms, it is difficult to stop the reforming process in general. So not only are reformers their own causes and effects, but attempts at avoiding reforms imply support for reform activities. Self-reference and opposition make routines of reforms.

The conclusion that may be drawn from our discussion up to this point is that it appears to be more difficult to resist administrative reforms than to initiate them. Generally, the difficulty lies not in persuading large organizations to reform but in preventing them from doing so. But it is one thing to initiate reforms and quite another to determine their content and succeed in implementing them.

References

Brunsson, N. (1985) *The Irrational Organization: Irrationality as a Basis for Organizational Action and Change*. Chichester: Wiley.

Brunsson, N. (1989) *The Organization of Hypocrisy: Talk, Decisions and Actions in Organizations*. Chichester: Wiley.

Cyert, R.M. and March, J.G. (1963) *A Behavioral Theory of the Firm*. Englewood Cliffs, NJ: Prentice-Hall.

Fayol, H. (1916) 'Administration industrielle et générale: prévoyance, organisation, commandement, contrôle', *Bulletin de la Société de l'Industrie Minérale*. Paris: Dunod.

20   The Knowledge-creating Company

Ikujiro Nonaka and Hirotaka Takeuchi

The Distinctive Japanese Approach to Knowledge Creation

There is a reason why Western observers tend not to address the issue of organizational knowledge creation. They take for granted a view of the organization as a machine for 'information processing'. This view is deeply ingrained in the traditions of Western management, from Frederick Taylor to Herbert Simon. And it is a view of knowledge as necessarily 'explicit' – something formal and systematic. Explicit knowledge can be expressed in words and numbers, and easily communicated and shared in the form of hard data, scientific formulae, codified procedures, or universal principles. Thus knowledge is viewed synonymously with a computer code, a chemical formula or a set of general rules. When Drucker (1993: 38) observes that 'within a few years after Taylor began to apply knowledge to work, productivity began to rise at a rate of 3.5 and 4 percent compound a year', he is actually referring to the application of quantifiable data to work. Similarly, Toffler (1990) uses the words 'data', 'information', and 'knowledge' interchangeably throughout his book 'to avoid tedious repetition'.

Japanese companies, however, have a very different understanding of knowledge. They recognize that the knowledge expressed in words and numbers represents only the tip of the iceberg. They view knowledge as being primarily 'tacit' – something not easily visible and expressible. Tacit knowledge is highly personal and hard to formalize, making it difficult to communicate or to share with others. Subjective insights, intuitions, and hunches fall into this category of knowledge. Furthermore, tacit knowledge is deeply rooted in an individual's action and experience, as well as in the ideals, values, or emotions he or she embraces.

To be more precise, tacit knowledge can be segmented into two dimensions. The first is the technical dimension, which encompasses the kind of informal and hard-to-pin-down skills or crafts captured in the term 'know-how'. A master craftsman, for example, develops a wealth of expertise 'at

Originally published in Ikujiro Nonaka and Hirotaka Takeuchi (1995) *The Knowledge-creating Company: How Japanese Companies Create the Dynamics of Innovation.* New York: Oxford University Press (abridged).

his fingertips' after years of experience. But he is often unable to articulate the scientific or technical principles behind what he knows.

At the same time, tacit knowledge contains an important cognitive dimension. It consists of schemata, mental models, beliefs, and perceptions so ingrained that we take them for granted. The cognitive dimension of tacit knowledge reflects our image of reality (what is) and our vision for the future (what ought to be). Though they cannot be articulated very easily, these implicit models shape the way we perceive the world around us.

The distinction between explicit knowledge and tacit knowledge is the key to understanding the differences between the Western approach to knowledge and the Japanese approach to knowledge. Explicit knowledge can easily be 'processed' by a computer, transmitted electronically, or stored in databases. But the subjective and intuitive nature of tacit knowledge makes it difficult to process or transmit the acquired knowledge in any systematic or logical manner. For tacit knowledge to be communicated and shared within the organization, it has to be converted into words or numbers that anyone can understand. It is precisely during the time this conversion takes place – from tacit to explicit, and, as we shall see, back again into tacit – that organizational knowledge is created.

Although Western managers have been more accustomed to dealing with explicit knowledge, the recognition of tacit knowledge and its importance has a number of crucially relevant implications. First, it gives rise to a whole different view of the organization – not as a machine for processing information but as a living organism. Within this context, sharing an understanding of what the company stands for, where it is going, what kind of a world it wants to live in, and how to make that world a reality becomes much more crucial than processing objective information. Highly subjective insights, intuitions, and hunches are an integral part of knowledge. Knowledge also embraces ideals, values, and emotion as well as images and symbols. These soft and qualitative elements are crucial to an understanding of the Japanese view of knowledge.

The Japanese have come to realize that tacit knowledge cannot be easily communicated to others. Everyone in Japan would agree that Shigeo Nagashima, nicknamed 'Mr Baseball' in Japan, is one of the greatest baseball players of all time. Having had the opportunity of meeting him in person, we asked him why he was so successful in rising to the occasion and hitting so many game-winning runs in tight moments. He used a lot of figurative language and body movement, but couldn't explain exactly what he meant. His words were not very logical or systematic. In the end, Nagashima simply said, 'You have to feel it.'

This episode questions the premise widely held in the West that knowledge can be taught through education and training. As Levitt (1991) points out, 'The most precious knowledge can neither be taught nor passed on.' Levitt uses another metaphor to drive home his point that not everything that is learned is done so consciously:

> A young child screams with pain upon touching a hot stove. A little comfort and mild medication soon makes things well, except for a small blister. That evening the parent, returning home, greets the child as usual: 'Hi – and what did you learn today?' 'Nothing,' comes the cheerful response. But never again will the child touch the burner, except cautiously, even when the stove is cold. (Levitt, 1991: 17)

In fact, the most powerful learning comes from direct experience. A child learns to eat, walk, and talk through trial and error; she or he learns with the *body*, not only with the mind.

Similarly, managers in Japan emphasize the importance of learning from direct experience as well as through trial and error. Like a child learning to eat, walk, and talk, they learn with their *minds* and *bodies*. This tradition of emphasizing the oneness of body and mind has been a unique feature of Japanese thinking since the establishment of Zen Buddhism. It stands in sharp contrast to the thinking behind the 'learning organization', a phrase that has become a conceptual catch-all of the new business organization. Peter Senge (1990), the apostle of the learning organization, utilizes 'systems thinking' to shift the mind from seeing the parts to seeing the whole. Systems thinking, according to Senge, is a conceptual framework, a body of knowledge and tools that has been developed over the past 50 years in the West to help people see the full patterns more clearly. The focus of the learning organization is clearly on learning with the *mind*, not with the body. Senge goes a step further and says that trial-and-error learning is a delusion, since the most critical decisions made in an organization have systemwide consequences stretching over years and decades, a time frame that makes learning from direct experience an impossibility.

The second implication of tacit knowledge follows naturally from the first. Once the importance of tacit knowledge is realized, then one begins to think about innovation in a whole new way. It is not just about putting together diverse bits of data and information. It is a highly individual process of personal and organizational self-renewal. The personal commitment of the employees and their identity with the company and its mission become indispensable. In this respect, the creation of new knowledge is as much about ideals as it is about ideas. And that fact fuels innovation. The essence of innovation is to re-create the world according to a particular ideal or vision. To create new knowledge means quite literally to re-create the company and everyone in it in an ongoing process of personal and organizational self-renewal. It is not the responsibility of the selected few – a specialist in research and development, strategic planning, or marketing – but that of everyone in the organization.

Creating new knowledge is also not simply a matter of learning from others or acquiring knowledge from the outside. Knowledge has to be built on its own, frequently requiring intensive and laborious interaction among members of the organization. New-product development team members at Canon, for example, hold 'camp sessions' at a local hotel over a weekend to brainstorm through a critical problem or issue. In this respect, the Japanese approach is at variance with the 'best' and 'benchmarking' practices carried out at companies such as GE, AT&T, Xerox, and Milliken, which are bent on learning from others. Milliken calls its practice SIS, for 'Steal ideas shamelessly'. The Japanese approach also runs counter to the basic premise of the 'modular' or 'virtual' corporation, which uses the knowledge of outside partners – suppliers, customers, rivals, and outside specialists – in lieu of its own. Companies in Japan believe that new and proprietary knowledge cannot be created without an intensive outside-inside inter-action. To create knowledge, the learning that takes place from others and the skills shared with others need to be internalized – that is, reformed, enriched, and translated to fit the company's self-image and identity.

A third important implication that can be drawn from the above discussion is that Western managers need to 'unlearn' their old view of knowledge and grasp the importance of the Japanese view. They need to get out of the old mode of thinking that knowledge can be acquired, taught, and trained through manuals, books, or lectures. Instead, they need to pay more attention to the less formal and systematic side of knowledge and start focusing on highly subjective insights, intuitions, and hunches that are gained through the use of metaphors, pictures, or experiences. Doing so will enable Western managers to understand what successful Japanese companies are doing right.

Making Tacit Knowledge Explicit: The Honda City Example

The explanation of how Japanese companies create new knowledge boils down to *the conversion of tacit knowledge to explicit knowledge*. Having an insight or a hunch that is highly personal is of little value to the company unless the individual can convert it into explicit knowledge, thus allowing it to be shared with others in the company. Japanese companies are especially good at realizing this exchange between tacit and explicit knowledge during the product development phase.

Take Honda as a case in point. In 1978, top management at Honda inaugurated the development of a new-concept car with the slogan, 'Let's gamble'. The phrase expressed senior executives' conviction that Honda's Civic and Accord models were becoming too familiar. Managers also realized that along with a new postwar generation entering the car market, a new generation of young product designers was coming of age with unconventional ideas about what made a good car.

The business decision that followed from the 'Let's gamble' slogan was to form a new-product development team of young engineers and designers (the average age was 27). Top management charged the team with two – and only two – instructions: first, to come up with a product concept fundamentally different from anything the company had ever done before; and secondly, to make a car that was inexpensive but not cheap.

This mission might sound vague, but in fact it provided the team with an extremely clear sense of direction. For instance, in the early days of the project, some team members proposed designing a smaller and cheaper version of the Honda Civic – a safe and technologically feasible option. But the team quickly decided this approach contradicted the entire rationale of its mission. The only alternative was to invent something totally new.

Project team leader Hiroo Watanabe coined another slogan to express his sense of the team's ambitious challenge: 'Automobile Evolution'. The phrase described an ideal. In effect, it posed the question: if the automobile were an organism, how should it evolve? As team members argued and discussed what Watanabe's slogan might mean, they came up with an answer in the form of yet another slogan: 'man-maximum, machine-minimum'. This captured the team's belief that the ideal car should somehow transcend the traditional human–machine relationship. But that required challenging what Watanabe called 'the reasoning of Detroit', which had sacrificed comfort for appearance.

The 'evolutionary' trend the team articulated eventually came to be embodied in the image of a sphere – a car simultaneously 'short' (in length) and 'tall' (in height). Such a car, they reasoned, would be lighter and cheaper, but also more comfortable and more solid than traditional cars. A sphere provided the most room for the passenger while taking up the least amount of space on the road. What's more, the shape minimized the space taken up by the engine and other mechanical systems. This gave birth to a product concept the team called 'Tall Boy', which eventually led to the Honda City, the company's distinctive urban car.

The Tall Boy concept contradicted the conventional wisdom about automobile design at the time, which emphasized long, low sedans. But the City's revolutionary styling and engineering were prophetic. The car inaugurated a whole new approach to design in the Japanese auto industry based on the man-maximum, machine-minimum concept, which had led to the new generation of 'tall and short' cars now quite prevalent in Japan.

Three Key Characteristics of Knowledge Creation

The story of the Honda City illustrates the way Japanese managers approach the process of making tacit knowledge explicit. It also suggests three other characteristics of knowledge creation that relate to how tacit can be made explicit. First, to express the inexpressible, heavy reliance is placed on figurative language and symbolism. Secondly, to disseminate knowledge, an individual's personal knowledge has to be shared with others. Thirdly, new knowledge is born in the midst of ambiguity and redundancy. We shall elaborate on each of these characteristics below. .

Metaphor and Analogy

First, the story of the Honda City suggests how Japanese managers use figurative language to articulate their intuitions and insights. Figurative language, which is especially prominent in product development, can take the form of metaphor or analogy. A metaphor or an analogy – such as 'Automobile Evolution', 'man-maximum, machine-minimum', or 'Tall boy' – is a distinctive method of perception. It is a way for individuals grounded in different contexts and with different experiences to understand something intuitively through the use of imagination and symbols. No analysis or generalization is needed. Through metaphors, people put together what they know in new ways and begin to express what they know but cannot yet say. As such, metaphor is highly effective in fostering direct commitment to the creative process in the early stages of knowledge creation.

An analogy is much more structured than a metaphor in making a distinction between two ideas or objects. It clarifies how the two ideas or objects are alike and not alike. In this respect, analogy is an intermediate step between pure imagination and logical thinking. In the Honda City example, recall how some team members proposed designing a smaller and cheaper version of the Civic. But the team quickly realized that this approach contradicted the rationale of its mission and decided to make a distinction by trying to invent something totally new. By exploring how the City and the Civic are actually alike and not alike, the team was able to postulate a breakthrough concept.

From Personal to Organizational Knowledge

Secondly, the story of the Honda City suggests how new knowledge always starts with an individual – Hiroo Watanabe in this case – and how an individual's personal knowledge is transformed into organizational knowledge valuable to the company as a whole (i.e., Tall Boy). Other examples of this sort of transformation may include a brilliant researcher's insight leading to a new patent or a shop-floor worker's long years of experience resulting in a new process innovation.

Although we use the term 'organizational' knowledge creation, the organization cannot create knowledge on its own without the initiative of the individual and the interaction that takes place within the group. Knowledge can be amplified or crystallized at the group level through dialogue, discussion, experience sharing, and observation. Recall how the new-product development team at Honda discussed what Watanabe's slogan might possibly mean before coming up with a metaphor of its own, 'man-maximum, machine-minimum'. This example illustrates the central role teams play in the knowledge-creation process – they provide a shared context in which individuals can interact with each other. Team members create new points of view through dialogue and discussion. This dialogue can involve considerable conflict and disagreement, but it is precisely such conflict that pushes employees to question existing premises and to make sense of their experience in a new way. This kind of dynamic interaction facilitates the transformation of personal knowledge into organizational knowledge.

Ambiguity and Redundancy

Thirdly, the story of Honda City suggests how certain organizational conditions can enhance the knowledge-creation process. It may sound paradoxical, but the confusion created within the product development team by the ambiguity of the mission handed down by Honda's top management provided an extremely clear sense of direction to the team. Ambiguity can prove useful at times not only as a source of a new sense of direction, but also as a source of alternate meanings and a fresh way of thinking about things. In this respect, new knowledge is born out of chaos.

Another organizational condition worth mentioning here is redundancy. To Western managers, the term 'redundancy', with its connotation of unnecessary duplication and waste, may sound unappealing. And yet, the building of a redundant organization plays an important role in management of the knowledge-creation process. Redundancy is important because it encourages frequent dialogue and communication. This helps create a 'common cognitive ground' among employees and thus facilitates the transfer of tacit knowledge. Since members of the organization share overlapping information, they can sense what others are struggling to articulate. Redundancy, which takes place primarily in information sharing, also spreads new explicit knowledge through the organization so that it can be internalized by employees.

The organizational logic of redundancy helps explain why Japanese companies manage product development as an overlapping process in which different functional divisions work together in a shared division of labor (Takeuchi and Nonaka, 1986). At many Japanese companies, redundant product development goes one step further. A product development team is divided into competing subgroups that develop different approaches to the same project and then argue over the advantages and disadvantages of their proposals. This redundancy encourages the team to look at a project from a variety of perspectives. Under the guidance of a team leader, the team eventually develops a common understanding of the 'best' approach.

The Key Players in Knowledge Creation

Who is responsible for creating new knowledge? Another unique feature of Japanese companies is the fact that no one department or group of experts has the exclusive responsibility for creating new knowledge. Front-line employees, middle managers, and senior managers all play a part. But this is not to say that there is no differentiation among these three roles. In fact, the creation of new knowledge is the product of a dynamic interaction among them.

Front-line employees are immersed in the day-to-day details of particular technologies, products, or markets. Most members of the Honda City development team were front-line employees who qualified as genuine car maniacs. Recalls Hiroshi Honma, 'It's incredible how the company called in young engineers like ourselves to design a car with a totally new concept and gave us the freedom to do it our way.' Giving them the freedom makes sense, since no one is more expert in the realities of a company's business than they are. But while these employees have an abundance of highly practical information, they often find it difficult to turn that information into useful knowledge. For one thing, signals from the marketplace can be vague and ambiguous. For another, employees can become so caught up in their own narrow perspective that they lose sight of the broader context. Moreover, even when employees do develop meaningful ideas or insights, they may find it difficult to communicate the importance of that information to others. People do not just receive new knowledge passively; they interpret it actively to fit their own situation and perspective. Thus what makes sense in one context can change or even lose meaning when communicated to people in a different context. As a result, there is continual confusion as new knowledge is diffused in an organization.

The major job of managers is to direct this confusion toward purposeful knowledge creation. Both senior and middle managers do this by providing employees with a conceptual framework that helps them make sense of their own experience. Senior managers provide a sense of direction by creating grand concepts that identify the common features linking seemingly disparate activities or businesses into a coherent whole. The Honda City project, for example, began with the slogan, 'Let's gamble'. These slogans provide employees with a sense of direction by establishing the criteria for estimating the value of the knowledge being created. Does the idea embody the company's vision? Is it an expression to top management's aspirations and ideals? Nobuhiko Kawamoto, the current president of Honda who was a vice president in charge of the City project at the time, kept on rejecting the team's too-conservative designs in the early phase of development. Recalls Hiroshi Honma, 'Senior managers are romantics who go in quest of the ideal.'

Middle managers serve as a bridge between the visionary ideals of the top and the often chaotic reality of those on the front line of business. Middle managers mediate between the 'what should be' mindset of the top and the 'what is' mindset of the front-line employees by creating mid-level business and product concepts. As team leaders of the product development team, for example, middle managers are in a position to remake reality according to the company's vision. Thus, at Honda, top management's vision of coming up with something completely new became a reality at the level of Hiroo Watanabe and his team in the form of the Tall Boy product concept.

Middle managers play a key role in the knowledge-creation process. They synthesize the tacit knowledge of both front-line employees and senior executives, make it explicit, and incorporate it into new products and technologies. It is people such as Hiroo Watanabe at Honda who actually manage the knowledge-creation process within Japanese companies.

Organizational Learning

The need for organizations to change continuously, which was emphasized by Drucker, has long been the central concern of organizational learning theorists. Just as with individuals, organizations must always confront novel aspects of their circumstances (Cohen and Sproull, 1991). The need is growing in this era of turbulent economy and accelerated technological change. It is widely agreed that learning consists of two kinds of activity. The first kind of learning is obtaining know-how in order to solve specific problems based upon existing premises. The second kind of learning is establishing new premises (i.e., paradigms, schemata, mental models, or perspectives) to override the existing ones. These two kinds of learning have been referred to as 'Learning I' and 'Learning II' (Bateson, 1973) or 'single-loop learning' and 'double-loop learning' (Argyris and Schön, 1978). From our viewpoint, the creation of knowledge certainly involves interaction between these two kinds of learning, which forms a kind of dynamic spiral.

Senge (1990) recognized that many organizations suffer from 'learning disabilities'. To cure the diseases and enhance the organization's capacity to learn, he proposed the 'learning organization' as a practical model. He argued that the learning organization has the capacity for both generative learning (i.e., active) and adaptive learning (i.e., passive) as the sustainable sources of competitive advantage. According to Senge, managers must do the following in order to build a learning organization: (1) adopt 'systems thinking'; (2) encourage 'personal mastery' of their own lives; (3) bring prevailing 'mental models' to the surface and challenge them; (4) build 'a shared vision'; and (5) facilitate 'team learning'.

Among these five 'disciplines', Senge (1990) emphasized the importance of 'systems thinking' as 'the discipline that integrates the disciplines, fusing them into a coherent body of theory and practice' (1990: 12). He also suggested that systems thinking is 'a philosophical alternative to the pervasive "reductionism" in Western culture – the pursuit of simple answers to complex issues' (ibid.: 185). He argues:

> At the heart of a learning organization is a shift of mind – from seeing ourselves as separate from the world to connected to the world, from seeing problems as

caused by someone or something 'out there' to seeing how our own actions create the problems we experience. A learning organization is a place where people are continually discovering how they create their reality. And how they can change it. (ibid.: 12–13)

Senge may not have intended to build a new synthesis between scientific and humanistic approaches to management, but he seems to be trying to overcome the Cartesian dualism. He says that 'Systems thinking may hold a key to integrating reason and intuition' (ibid.: 168) and that systems thinking fuses the five disciplines 'into a coherent body of theory and practice' (ibid.: 12). Judging from the entire argument of his book, more specifically from such terms as 'mental models', 'a shared vision', 'team learning', and the above quotation, his practical model of 'learning organization' has some affinity with our theory of knowledge creation. However, he rarely uses the word 'knowledge' and does not present any ideas on how knowledge can be created.

Despite the affinity with our own thinking, there are some critical limitations often found in the literature on 'organizational learning'. First, as seen in Senge (1990), organizational learning theories basically lack 'the view that knowledge development constitutes learning' (Weick, 1991: 122). Most of them are trapped in a behavioral concept of 'stimulus–response'. Secondly, most of them still use the metaphor of individual learning (Weick, 1991; Dodgson, 1993). In the accumulation of over 20 years of studies, they have not developed a comprehensive view on what constitutes 'organizational' learning. Thirdly, there is widespread agreement that organizational learning is an adaptive change process that is influenced by past experience, focused on developing or modifying routines, and supported by organizational memory. As a result, the theories fail to conceive an idea of knowledge creation. The fourth limitation is related to the concept of 'double-loop learning' or 'unlearning' (Hedberg, 1981) as well as to a strong orientation toward organizational development, which we will discuss below.

Following the development of Argyris and Schön's (1978) theory of organizational learning, it has been widely assumed implicitly or explicitly that double-loop learning – the questioning and rebuilding of existing perspectives, interpretation frameworks, or decision premises – can be very difficult for organizations to implement by themselves. In order to overcome this difficulty, the learning theorists argue that some kind of artificial intervention, such as the use of an organizational development program, is required. The limitation of this argument is that it assumes that someone inside or outside an organization 'objectively' knows the right time and method for putting double-loop learning into practice. A Cartesian-like view of organization lies behind this assumption. Seen from the vantage point of organizational knowledge creation, double-loop learning is not a special, difficult task but a daily activity for the organization. Organizations continuously create new knowledge by reconstructing existing perspectives, frameworks, or premises on a daily basis. In other words, the capacity for double-loop learning is built into the knowledge-creating organization without the unrealistic assumption of the existence of a 'right' answer.

A New Resource-based Approach to Strategy

A new paradigm of corporate strategy, which we call the 'resource-based approach', has emerged to help companies compete more effectively in the ever-changing and globalizing environment of the 1990s. In contrast to the structural approach, which we discussed under the science of strategy, the new approach sees competencies, capabilities, skills, or strategic assets as the source of sustainable competitive advantage for the firm. The literature on the resource-based approach to competitive strategy has been increasing in recent years, with Prahalad and Hamel's (1990) article on 'core competence' and Stalk et al.'s (1992) article on 'capabilities-based competition' representing the field. Conceptually, the new approach is rooted in Penrose's (1959) theory of the firm.

Proponents of the resource-based approach contend that the competitive environment of the 1990s has changed dramatically, making the structural approach, represented by Porter's (1980, 1985, 1990) competitive-forces framework, obsolete. Stalk et al. (1992) observed as follows:

> When the economy was relatively static, strategy could afford to be static. In a world characterized by durable products, stable consumer needs, well-defined national and regional markets, and clearly identified competitors, competition was a 'war of position' in which companies occupied competitive space like squares on a chessboard. . . .
>
> Competition is now a 'war of movement' in which success depends on anticipation of market trends and quick response to changing customer needs. Successful competitors move quickly in and out of products, markets, and sometimes even entire businesses – a process more akin to an interactive video game than to chess. In such an environment, the essence of strategy is *not* the structure of a company's products and markets but the dynamics of its behavior. (Stalk et al., 1992: 62, italics in original)

The dynamic nature of strategy was also emphasized by Teece et al. (1991), who developed the concept of 'dynamic *capabilities*,' or the 'ability of an organization to learn, adapt, change, and renew over time', which 'involves search, problem finding, and problem solving (at the organizational level)' (p. 20). Prahalad and Hamel (1990) provided a similar but less dynamic definition of core competence: 'the collective learning in the organization, especially how to coordinate diverse production skills and integrate multiple streams of technologies' (p. 82).

As the above definitions show, the distinction between core competence and capabilities has not been clear. Both concepts emphasize 'behavioral' aspects of strategy, namely 'how' a company chooses to compete rather than 'where' it chooses to compete. But whereas Prahalad and Hamel (1990) focused on corporatewide technologies and production skills that underlie a company's myriad product lines in defining core competence, Stalk et al. (1992) took a broader view of the skill base and focused on business processes, which encompass the entire value chain, in defining capabilities.

Prahalad and Hamel referred to the following examples to illustrate the importance of corporatewide technologies and production skills in gaining competitive advantage:

> In NEC, digital technologies, especially VLSI and systems integration skills, are fundamental. In the core competence underlying them, disparate businesses become coherent. It is Honda's core competence in engines and power trains that gives it a distinctive advantage in car, motorcycle, lawn mower, and generator businesses. Canon's core competencies in optics, imaging, and microprocessor controls have enabled it to enter, even dominate, markets as seemingly diverse as copiers, laser printers, cameras, and image scanners. (1990: 83)

According to Stalk et al. (1992), however, it is broader skills than can transform a company's key business processes into strategic capabilities, thereby leading to competitive success. Taking Honda as an example, they point out that the innovative designs of its products or the way they were manufactured are not the only factors underlying Honda's success. They believe that the company's ability to train and support its dealer network with operating procedures and policies for merchandising, selling, floor planning, and service management – its expertise in the 'dealer management' process – is equally as important. This expertise, which was first developed for its motorcycle business, has since been replicated in lawn mowers, outboard motors, and automobiles.

Despite this distinction, there are a number of similarities between Prahalad and Hamel and Stalk and his colleagues. First, both groups of authors make extensive use of Japanese companies as case studies of exemplary behavior. Secondly, they both observe that larger companies today are suffering from the 'tyranny' of the strategic business unit (SBU) and need to overcome it by developing corporatewide or organizational skills in moving competencies or capabilities from one business unit to another. Thirdly, they both believe that the process of identifying and building competencies or capabilities involves a top-down process, with the CEO and top management playing the key role. And finally, they both contend that competitive advantage should be found in resources and skills 'inside' the company, as opposed to the market environment 'outside' the company, as in the structural approach.

At first glance, these characteristics may give the impression that our theory of organizational knowledge creation resembles the resource-based view of strategy. Indeed, both are concerned with (1) how innovation takes place, (2) how Japanese companies have gained competitive advantage, (3) organizational skills rather than individual skills, (4) the role of top management as a key player, and (5) what takes place inside the company. But there are several fundamental differences between our theory and the resource-based approach to strategy.

First, while we are explicitly concerned with *knowledge*, Prahalad and Hamel and Stalk et al. treat knowledge only implicitly. Although several authors have recently incorporated the notion of knowledge into the resource-based approach, the focus is still blurred because of the lack of agreed-upon and well-defined definitions of terms. According to Teece et al. (1991): 'There remains a substantial level of ambiguity surrounding such terms as resources, capabilities, skills . . . and the conceptual framework is overdetermined in that there are too many competing explanations for the phenomena identified' (1991: 17–18).

Secondly, although Prahalad and Hamel and Stalk et al. make extensive use of Japanese case examples, these examples do not shed much light on how the companies actually went about *building* core competence or capabilities. In contrast, our primary research interest is in how Japanese companies go about creating knowledge organizationally. Our in-depth field research of selected Japanese companies provides a unique inside look at how Japanese companies actually go about the knowledge-creation process.

Thirdly, regarding middle managers, Stalk et al. (1992) argue as follows: 'Because capabilities are cross-functional, the change process [associated with building capabilities] can't be left to middle managers. It requires the hands-on guidance of the CEO and the active involvement of top line managers' (1992: 65). Prahalad and Hamel (1990) also assign the key role of identifying, developing, and managing competencies or capabilities to top management; the responsibilities of middle managers and front-line workers are not made clear in their approach. In contrast, middle managers play a key role in our theory, acting as 'knowledge engineers' within the company. They function as facilitators of knowledge creation, involving top management and front-line workers in a management process we call 'middle-up-down' management.

And finally, the resource-based approach has not yet reached the stage of being able to build a comprehensive theoretical framework. What is missing in the resource-based approach is a comprehensive framework that shows how various parts within the organization interact with each other over time to create something new and unique.

The Journey Ahead

Today, the Japanese economy is in trouble and Japanese companies appear considerably less invincible. Does this change of affairs invalidate our theory of knowledge creation?

We don't think so. Indeed, it is the skills of Japanese companies at creating systematic organizational knowledge that has allowed them again and again to innovate their way out of crisis. After all, the current situation is not the first time observers have noted the 'crisis' of the Japanese economy. During the Nixon shock of 1971 and the oil shock of the 1970s, similar concerns were raised about the sustainability of the Japanese miracle. But in both cases, Japanese companies used knowledge creation to turn economic crisis into competitive opportunity. We fully expect them to do so again.

As a case in point, just look at how Honda innovated itself out of a crisis with the development of the 1994 Accord. When Kawamoto took over as Honda's president in 1990, the year sales of autos in the Japanese market began to slide. American and European engineers and marketers were flown into Tokyo to help with early-stage planning for the new model, something that Honda had never done before. Similarly, for the first time ever, nearly 60 American production engineers and their families began moving to Japan for two- to three-year stints, working with development engineers at Honda's Sayama assembly plant and Wako engine plant. One of their key roles was to make sure that each part could be easily and cheaply manufactured at Honda's plants in Marysville, Ohio. Furthermore, Honda carried out a contest among Honda's design studios in Japan, the USA, and Europe to choose the 1994 Accord design – again, a company first. What Honda did was to create new knowledge on a global scale, with the American team making major contributions, to develop a jazzier looking and more affordable 1994 Accord. Looking at the brisk sales of the new Accord in the United States since its September 1993 introduction, this case may offer another example of how a Japanese company may emerge from a crisis stronger than ever before.

References

Argyris, C. and Schön, D.A. (1978) *Organizational Learning*. Reading, MA: Addison-Wesley.

Bateson, G. (1973) *Steps to an Ecology of Mind*. London: Paladin.

Cohen, M.D. and Sproull, L.S. (1991) 'Editor's introduction', *Organization Science*, 2 (1).

Dodgson, M. (1993) 'Organizational learning: a review of some literatures', *Organizational Studies*, 14: 375–94.

Drucker, P.F. (1993) *Post-Capitalist Society*. Oxford: Butterworth Heinemann.

Hedberg, B. (1981) 'How organizations learn and unlearn', in P. Nystrom and W. Starbuck (eds), *Handbook of Organizational Design* (Vol. 1). New York: Oxford University Press. pp. 3–27.

Levitt, T. (1991) *Marketing Imagination*. New York: The Free Press.

Penrose, E.T. (1959) *The Theory of the Growth of the Firm*. Oxford: Basil Blackwell.

Porter, M.E. (1980) *Competitive Strategy*. New York: Free Press.

Porter, M.E. (1985) *Competitive Advantage*. New York: Free Press.

Porter, M.E. (1990) *The Competitive Advantage of Nations*. New York: Free Press.

Prahalad, C.K. and Hamel, G. (1990) 'The core competence of the corporation', *Harvard Business Review*, May–June: 79–91.

Senge, P.M. (1990) *The Fifth Discipline: The Age and Practice of the Learning Organization*. London: Century Business.

Stalk, G., Evans, P. and Shulman, L.E. (1992) 'Competing on capabilities: the new rules of corporate strategy', *Harvard Business Review*, March–April: 57–69.

Takeuchi, H. and Nonaka, I. (1986) 'The new new product development game', *Harvard Business Review*, Jan.–Feb.: 137–46.

Teece, D.J., Pisano, G. and Shuen, A. (1991) 'Dynamic capabilities and strategic management'. Working paper, Center for Research in Management, University of California, Berkeley.

Toffler, A. (1990) *Powershift: Knowledge, Wealth and Violence at the Edge of the 21st Century*. New York: Bantam Books.

Weick, K.E. (1991) 'The nontraditional quality of organizational learning', *Organization Science*, 2 (1): 116–24.

Index